Currier's Price Guide to
Currier & Ives Prints

Current Average Retail Prices of Nearly 7000
Original Lithographs of the Currier & Ives Firm

THIRD EDITION

text written by Robert Kipp
prices edited by prominent dealers, nationally

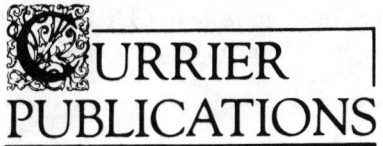

CURRIER
PUBLICATIONS

ISBN   0-935277-18-8 Softcover
Library of Congress
Catalog Card Number 94-70932

Printed in the United States of America

COVER PHOTO:

American Hunting Scenes. *"An Early Start"*, **Currier & Ives**, Hand Colored Lithograph, Large Folio, Courtesy of Sotheby's, Inc., NY, NY

Additional copies of this book may be obtained from bookstores and selected antique dealers. To order directly from the publisher, remit $18.95 per copy, plus $3.00 shipping(book rate) and handling, or $4.25(first class). Massachusetts addresses add 5% sales tax. For bulk order discounts (6 or more copies) please write, or call, for details to:

CURRIER PUBLICATIONS
241 Main Street
Stoneham, MA 02180
(800) 344-0760

[Make check or money order payable to CURRIER PUBLICATIONS]
(U.S. dollars only, please)

ACKNOWLEDGEMENTS

Many thanks for assistance with this third edition go out to:

Robert Kipp, for the many countless hours he spent initially writing the text, the thousands of titles and prices he reviewed, edited and averaged during the months prior to going to press.

Robert Wieland, John Rudisill, Robert Searjeant, and Bob Bascom for spending much of their valuable time assisting in editing the prices for this *Guide* and discussing changes needed.

Cynthia Tukis, for her expertise and valuable assistance in editing and proofreading everything I do.

Marshall R. Berkoff, president of The American Historical Print Collectors Society, for allowing us to publish the final selections for the *Best 50 - Revisited*.

My parents, Lillian and William, for their encouragement and support - as always.

My wife, Donna; her mother, Lorraine; my daughter, Danielle; and my son Christopher, for being so patient all these months. I thank you especially, with love.

William T. Currier

to all our valued customers

on this our tenth anniversary

About the Author and Contributors

Robert Kipp

The author, Robert Kipp, graduated from Olivet College, Olivet, Michigan with a degree in art and art history. While attending Olivet College, he published a limited edition book of his prints and staged several art shows for which he received an honorable mention. He later attended Alfred University, Alfred, New York for graduate studies in art.

Robert Kipp began collecting Currier & Ives prints twenty-five years ago, having been inspired by his parents who are avid antique collectors. In the mid 1970's he met and became closely associated with the late Ladd MacMillan. It was through their close friendship and common interest that Robert Kipp gained most of his valuable knowledge and appreciation of Currier & Ives prints. It was during this period that Robert Kipp began lecturing to appraisal and auctioneer associations on identifying original Currier & Ives prints. Also at this time he began professionally restoring original prints for clients and issuing catalogues featuring illustrations of Currier & Ives prints, acquired from auction sales, private collections, or consignments.

He has worked for the past fifteen years restoring prints for clients throughout the United States. Using a vacuum table to localize stain reduction, he is able to preserve most, if not all, of a print's original coloring. Other services which he offers include full conservation of paper documents, paper repairs and the demounting of old backings from original prints, watercolors and drawings. A brochure describing his conservation and restoration services and their estimated costs is available by calling him at: (508) 922-6852 or by writing to him at: 16 Wedgemere Road, Beverly, MA 01915

Robert Wieland

Robert Wieland was one of the four dealers, nationally, that provided assistance to Robert Kipp in editing most of the over 6,800 titles found in this *Guide*. His vast experience with Currier & Ives prints has made him well qualified for this task: He has been a dedicated collector of Currier & Ives prints for over 30 years, and a dealer for more than 25 years. His activity as a dealer has extended to forty-nine states, and a number of foreign countries among which are - England, France, Germany and Australia. His diversified list of clients includes collectors, dealers, museums, and corporations.

Mr. Wieland can be reached at 33 S. St. Andrews Drive, Ormond Beach, Florida 32174 (telephone: (904) 672-9972).

John Rudisill

John and Barbara Rudisill, of Rudisill's Alt Print Haus, have been antique enthusiasts most of their lives. John's father was a respected antique dealer in Pennsylvania for many years.

Twenty-odd years ago, they developed a particular interest in Currier & Ives prints. They began to collect and deal in the prints, and do so today with clientele throughout the United States and Canada. They have written articles on the history of Currier & Ives and on identifying reproductions. John and Barbara have also contributed material for a number of antique publications and are often cited as authorities on Currier & Ives prints.

The Rudisills are Charter members of the American Historical Print Collectors Society and can be reached by writing (or calling) to Post Office Box 199, Worton, MD 21678 (tel: 410-778-9290.)

Robert L. Searjeant

For over 40 years, Robert Searjeant has been an avid collector, and dealer, in Currier & Ives prints. He has exhibited portions of his own collection at prestigious galleries and museums all across the country. To his credit are numerous articles, published for the trade and general magazines, about the Currier & Ives firm and the joys of collecting.

He has assisted many publishers in assembling rare and accurate information with regards to the complete list of known Currier & Ives prints. In 1982, Crown Publishers asked Mr. Searjeant to write the forward to the updated edition of the *Currier & Ives Prints, An Illustrated Checklist*, by Frederic A. Conningham. And more recently, he assisted Gale Research in compiling the most comprehensive listing of Currier & Ives prints to date: *Currier & Ives - A Catalog Raisonne.* Truly, his breadth of experience, and contributions to collecting, are too numerous to cover here.

Always happy to help new collectors, Mr. Searjeant can be reached at Post Office Box 23942, Rochester, NY 14692 (telephone: (716) 424-2489).

Bob Bascom

A relative newcomer in interest in Currier & Ives prints, Bob Bascom, has been a collector and dealer now for seven years. He claims prior to that, Currier & Ives meant only Travellers Insurance Company calendars and Christmas cards to him. He warns everyone that having even a slight interest in "Curriers" can be fatal once the *Currier Bug*, that seems to lurk in old frames, bites you. Since that happened to Bob, it has been a near 24 hour a day passion as he travels the northeast and further, searching for the rare and desirable. He publishes a price list three times a year, and displays his prints at Middlebury Antique Center, Middlebury, Vermont. He can be reached by writing (or calling) to Box 4334, Burlington, VT 05406 (tel: 802-893-4082.)

TABLE OF CONTENTS

CHAPTER ONE
Introduction

CHAPTER TWO
Firm of Currier & Ives

CHAPTER THREE
Reproductions

CHAPTER FOUR
Popular Currier & Ives

CHAPTER FIVE
Standard Grading System

CHAPTER SIX
Conservation

CHAPTER SEVEN
Using This Guide

Currier & Ives Prints

Trade Cards

Appendix

PREFACE

The author, Robert Kipp, has provided for your use a newly revised *Guide* which will help you to quickly assess the average retail value of Currier & Ives prints which you are likely to encounter. For the past several months, leading up to press time, Mr. Kipp has spent countless hours adding editing titles and revising old prices. To assure accuracy in pricing, five prominent dealers, nationally - John Rudisill, Robert Wieland, Robert L. Searjeant, Bob Bascom, and Robert Kipp - have edited a master list of nearly 7,000 titles and prices. Each of the dealer's prices was averaged with the four others to give an accurate price for each title. At no time in the past, has this ever been done. The benefactors of such an effort will ultimately be the collectors who will now have the most accurate price guide available for prints produced by the Currier & Ives firm.

This *Guide* will be invaluable to: antique dealers, auctioneers, print collectors, estate lawyers, bank trust officers, art consultants, appraisers, and print dealers. *Currier's Price Guide to Currier & Ives Prints* may well be the most profitable investment that anyone, who has occasion to buy and sell Curreir & Ives prints, could ever make.

You will find that you have purchased the most accurate price guide to nearly 7,000 Currier & Ives titles available today. The compilation of data, here, will be useful to even the most seasoned Currier & Ives collector with accurate print titles, measurements, folio sizes, Conningham numbers, and average retail prices for prints in very good condition. Of special interest will be the publication of the newly selected *Best 50 - Revisted* (see details in Chapter Four).

There are many instances which can be sighted where this *Guide* will prove invaluable. Some examples follow.

Auctioneers can use the price ranges to help establish a starting bid on print titles with which they are unfamiliar, or help screen prints for possible consignment.

Collectors will find the *Guide* extremely interesting and especially helpful when hunting for titles which have values that they can afford. Many collectors will want to carry a copy with them as they frequent yard sales, flea markets, thrift shops, or country auctions.

Appraisers can use the *Guide* to quickly find an average retail price for a particular title. They can use this information as a starting point, then proceed to do a more accurate valuation based on the print's condition.

Because of information gleaned from our *Guide*, many estate executors may want to pursue a professional appraisal on certain Currier & Ives prints. It would not be unusual for someone running an estate "tag sale" to price a Currier & Ives print well below its true market value.

Antique dealers, who have occasion to buy and sell Currier & Ives prints, but who have very little knowledge of the market will find our *Guide* to be one of the most important reference books in their library. The *Guide* will help many dealers to avoid the problem of buying too high or selling too low. And help them to *quickly* assess the *potential* value of prints in many situations: house calls, estate sales, etc.

Add to the list, the many thrift shop owners, pickers, museum personnel, art framers, and yard sale and flea market fanatics who will find our *Guide* useful; and you can only agree that *Currier's Price Guide to Currier & Ives Prints* is the first place to look for values.

One final note: You are welcome and encouraged to comment, and feel free to suggest changes or additions which will improve this *Guide*. Please write or call:

CURRIER PUBLICATIONS
241 Main Street
Stoneham, MA 02180
(800) 344-0760

DISCLAIMER

Although every attempt, within reason, has been made to keep the prices herein as accurate as possible, there may be mistakes, both typographical and in content. Therefore, this guide should be used only as a general guide not as the final or ultimate source of the only prices which may be asked by dealers for any particular print. Besides condition, framing can drastically affect the pricing of a particular print. Always remember, prints in very poor condition may realize only a fraction of the price realized for a similar print in excellent condition.

The author and Currier Publications shall have neither liability nor responsibility to any person with respect to any loss or damage caused or alleged to be caused directly or indirectly by the information contained in this book.

CHAPTER ONE

Introduction

The partnership of Currier & Ives has virtually become a single word synonymous with a great American tradition. For more than fifty years, these men depicted the life of a young and growing nation with fidelity and imagination. They left us a panoramic record of America during her formative years. Their lithographs were well within the understanding and price range of the average American. They adorned many homes, businesses and institutions. It is no wonder that Currier & Ives is still called the "Printmaker to the American People."

The demand for Currier & Ives prints is immense, making it difficult for a buyer or seller to keep abreast of the escalating prices and current market values without help. Help is here in *Currier's Price Guide to Currier & Ives Prints*. You will find over six thousand different lithographs listed, including sizes, conningham numbers, and average retail values for prints in very good condition. In addition, a list of Currier & Ives trade cards will be provided with average retail values after the alphabetical listing of titles and prices.

Collectors' interest was so strong that in 1933 a list of the *Best 50* large and *Best 50* small folio prints were published, a bare twenty five years after the firm was dissolved and the last print was struck. Today, changing tastes and new discoveries have encouraged us to take a second look at the original large and small folio *Best 50* prints. This *Guide* includes a recently selected list of 50 large and 50 small folio prints (see pages ??-??) voted on by a select gathering of members of the American Historical Print Collectors Society. It is with the kind permission of the society's president, Marshall R. Berkoff, that we reproduce the list in this *Guide*.

Also, in our *Guide* is a brief history of Currier & Ives, advice on collecting, and ways of identifying original prints, restrikes and reproductions. In all, our *Guide* will provide you with current market values and solid background information. Enjoy it!

History of Currier & Ives

Born in 1813, in Roxbury, Massachusetts, a suburb of Boston, Nathaniel Currier was to become the premier lithographer of the era. At the age of fifteen Nathaniel Currier was apprenticed to the firm of William S. and John Pendleton. The firm, based in Boston, was the first successful lithography firm in the United States. Nathaniel Currier remained with the firm for five years, gaining the knowledge that was to become the cornerstone of his future success.

Nathaniel Currier then accepted a position with M.E.D. Brown, a Philadelphia based lithography firm. In 1834, a year later, Nathaniel Currier moved to New York City and purchased Pendleton's firm with a partner. The firm became Currier and Stodart, specializing in commercial work: bills, letterheads and sheet music. Currier and Stodart was dissolved in 1835 and N. Currier Press was established as a sole proprietorship.

Eventually Currier became involved in architectural and newsworthy prints, such as, *The Ruins of Planter's Hotel, New Orleans* and *Ruins of the Merchants Exchange, N.Y.* It was one such newsworthy print that catapulted him into fame and fortune as "Printmaker to the American People."

On January 13, 1840 the steamboat Lexington left New York City for Stonington, Connecticut burning coal rather than wood for the first time. She caught fire and over one hundred passengers and crew aboard perished. The news didn't reach New York City for two days. When it did, the *New York Sun*, a widely circulated newspaper, decided to publish a special edition covering the incident. They commissioned N. Currier Press to do a lithograph based on the survivors' accounts. N. Currier then commissioned artist W.K. Hewitt to sketch a pictorial account of the disaster. Three days later the first newspaper *Extra* was published. It was so popular that people all over the country clamored for it months later. Nathaniel Currier who had signed the print gained immediate popularity, nationwide. Work poured in and his firm quickly became a national company.

A man with ideas ahead of his time, Nathaniel Currier was more than capable of managing and promoting his company's growth. He instituted new marketing techniques whereby he sold his prints to peddlers, pushcart vendors and distributors throughout the country. Inexpensive pricing put his prints in reach of the average American. Small folio prints sold for twenty cents and large folio prints sold for up to four dollars. In a short time Currier's prints adorned many businesses, taverns, institutions and homes. Eventually the firm became involved in European distribution. Currier engaged a distributor in London, England, selling prints throughout France, Germany, and other European Nations.

Aware of increasing public demand, Currier introduced a constant flow of new subject matter. Along with newsworthy events, he produced portraits of famous people, cartoons, nautical, railroad, river, horse and numerous other genre prints. Never an artist himself, he hired both full-time and freelance artists to create the work that caught the public interest.

Charles Currier worked with his older brother as a commissioned agent throughout much of the firm's history. He is noted for his superior litho crayon which he manufactured independently of Currier & Ives. It was this crayon that was used exclusively by Currier & Ives in the production of their lithographs. Charles Currier also published from fifty to one hundred lithographs on his own.

Possibly his most valuable contribution to the firm was his brother-in-law, James Merrit Ives, who was hired as a bookkeeper in 1852 at Charles' recommendation. James Ives, like Nathaniel Currier, was a friendly man with a sharp business acumen and the ability to sense what would appeal to the public. An accomplished artist, James Ives proved so helpful that Nathaniel Currier made him a full partner in 1857, an arrangement that was mutually beneficial for nearly thirty years. The firm thus became Currier & Ives.

From the onset, the firm prospered and grew, eventually producing over 7,000 separate images. In 1880 Nathaniel Currier finally retired and was succeeded by his son Edward West Currier, who remained with the firm for 22 years. Nathaniel Currier died of a heart attack in 1888. James Ives worked until the time of his death in 1895, and was also succeeded by his son, Chauncy Ives.

From 1895 to 1902 the firm was being managed by the two sons of the original owners. At this time the firm was in a decline, chiefly due to advances in photography, new lithographic techniques and uninspired management. In 1902 Edwin Currier sold his interest to Chauncy Ives. In 1907 Chauncy Ives sold the firm to Daniel Logan, who planned to continue the business but was forced to close the doors late in 1907 due to ill health. Mr. Logan sold the lithographic stones by the pound, which closed the last chapter in the firm's activities and production.

Although times and taste's changed, Currier & Ives was not forgotten. A few years later, businessman and horse lover, Harry T. Peters came upon his first Currier & Ives print, *The Mare Lady Suffolk*, tacked up in a barn. This began a collection that eventually numbered over 3,000. It inspired Peter's definitive work: *Currier & Ives. Printmakers to the American People*. Peters became a moving force behind the collection of Currier & Ives prints. By the early 1930's with the publishing of the *Best 50* they were in the news again, rekindling interest in Currier and Ives prints.

Symbols of an America gone by, these prints have come to mean much more than the sentimental views they represent. Currier & Ives prints are a true record of our past. They are eminently collectible and always will be. They strike a chord of familiarity and touch us in a way that spans time.

The Currier Addresses

PUBLISHER	DATE	ADDRESS
Stodart & Currier	1834-1835	137 Broadway
N. Currier	1835	1 Wall
N. Currier	1836-1837	148 Nassau
N. Currier	1838-1856	152 Nassau & 2 Spruce
Currier & Ives	1857-1865	152 Nassau & 2 Spruce
Currier & Ives	1866-1872	152 Nassau & 33 Spruce
Currier & Ives	1872-1874	125 Nassau & 33 Spruce
Currier & Ives	1874-1877	123 Nassau & 33 Spruce
Currier & Ives	1877-1894	115 Nassau & 33 Spruce
Currier & Ives	1894-1896	108 Fulton & 33 Spruce
Currier & Ives	1896-1907	33 Spruce Street

The above information is helpful in determining approximately when undated prints were published by checking the addresses of the Currier firms.

CHAPTER TWO

Firm of Currier & Ives

History of lithography in America

Lithography was invented about 1798 by a Bavarian, Alois Senefelder, as a means to reproduce his plays. The new process involved drawing images on soft stone with a grease crayon, wetting the stone with acid to leave the grease marks in high relief, and inking those marks with oil-based ink that clung only to the image not to the whole stone. Lithography became a very popular means of printing both words and pictures.

Lithography came to America after 1819 when Alois Senefelder published a book, *Complete Course of Lithography*. It was this technical publication that was most instrumental in the development of lithography, worldwide.

In 1826 what was to become America's first major lithographic firm of the time was formed - Pendleton's of Boston. It was there that Nathaniel Currier apprenticed at the age of fifteen with William S. and John Pendleton. He stayed with them for five years, absorbing all they had to teach, knowledge that was the cornerstone of his future success. During the 1930's other lithographic firms were started, but none that would equal the successes of Currier & Ives. Among them were Bufford and Endicott of New York, M.E.D. Brown of Philadelphia and the Kelloggs of Hartford Connecticut.

The Artists of Currier & Ives

Frances (Fanny) Palmer (1810-1876)

Frances (Fanny) Palmer, who was born in England in 1810, came to America in 1844 with her husband and two sons. She was very versatile and was especially noted for her excellent rural and landscape views. She also helped the firm in doing the backgrounds and coloring of prints by other artists. Employed full time by the firm until her death, she was both a foremost lithographer and accomplished artist who is credited with over two hundred lithographs.

Her excellence as both lithographer and artist are exemplified by her railroad prints: *American Express Train* and *The Lightning Express' Trains*; river views: *A Midnight Race on the Mississippi* and *Wooding Up' on the Mississippi*; sporting scenes: *Woodcock Shooting* and *The Cares of a Family*; spectacular views: *View of San Francisco - California* and *Mount Washington*; and her still life and floral prints most typified in *Landscape, Fruit and Flowers*.

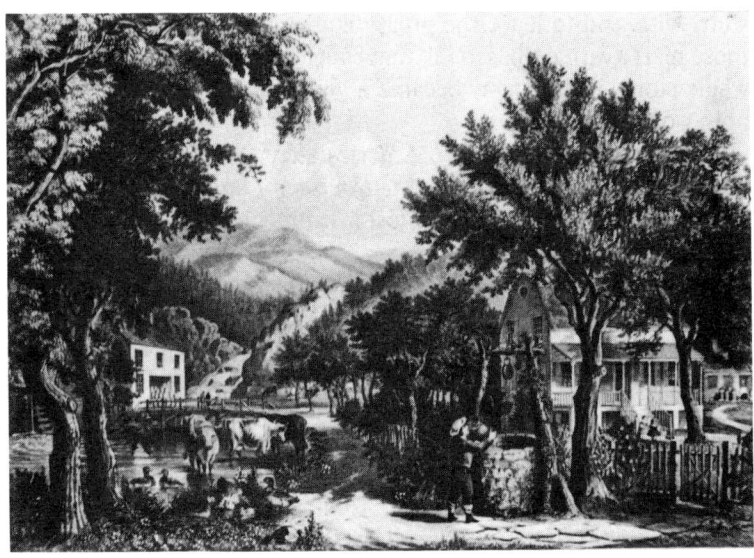

The Old Oaken Bucket
(Courtesy of Robert P. Kipp, Ipswich, MA)

Arthur Fitzwilliam Tait (1819-1905)

Arthur Fitzwilliam Tait, who came to America from England in 1850, painted western, sporting and hunting scenes with great precision and care. While he was not himself an employee of Currier & Ives, many of his fine paintings were used by the firm. His prints are in demand by collectors, and justly so, as ten of his large folio prints were selected for the original *Best 50* list.

Some of his notable work is portrayed in western prints: *Life on the Prairie- The ' Buffalo' Hunt* and *A Prairie Hunter- One Rubbed Out*; rural life: *American Forest Scene- Maple Sugaring, American Winter Sports- Fishing on Chateaugay Lake* and *Brook Trout Fishing - An Anxious Moment*. Others include camping scenes, such as, *Camping in the Woods. A Good Time Coming* and his *American Field Sports* series. Most notable are his prints of *Mink Trapping. Prime* and *The Life of a Hunter - A Tight Fix*, that has set a record price paid for a Currier & Ives print each time it was offered at auction.

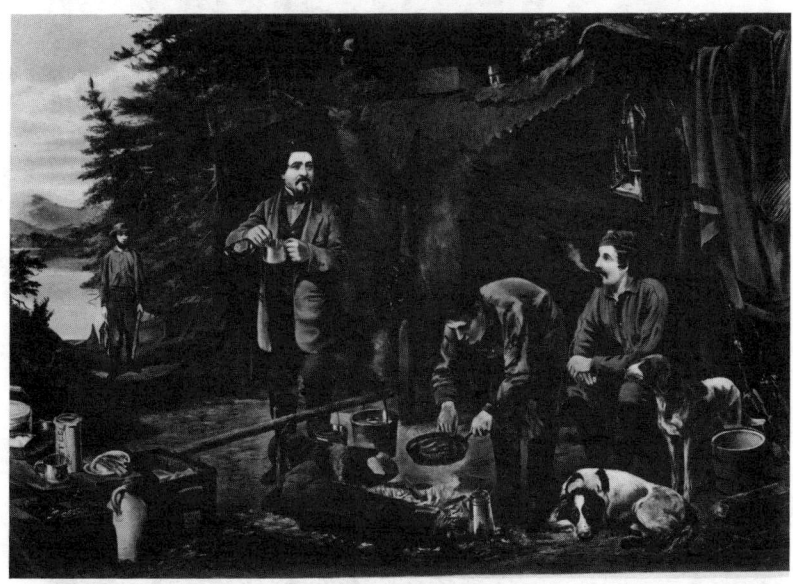

Camping in the Woods. "A good time coming"
(Courtesy of The Old Print Shop, Inc., Kenneth M. Newman)

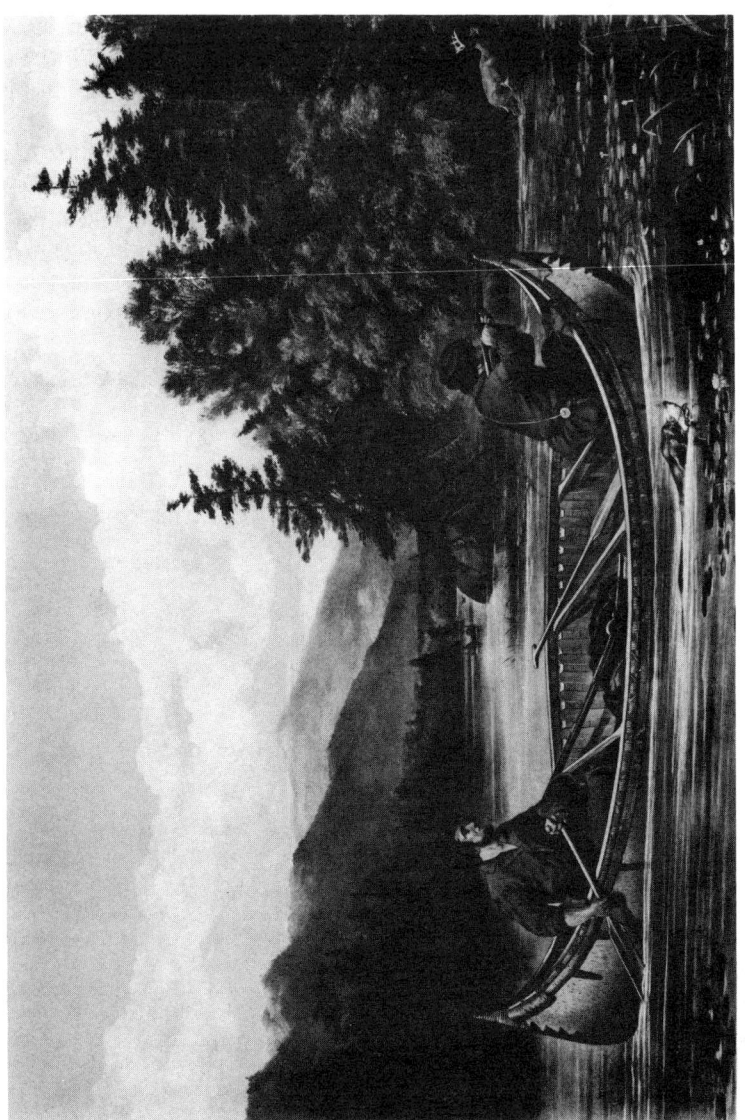

A Good Chance
(Courtesy of The Old Print Shop, Inc., Kenneth M. Newman)

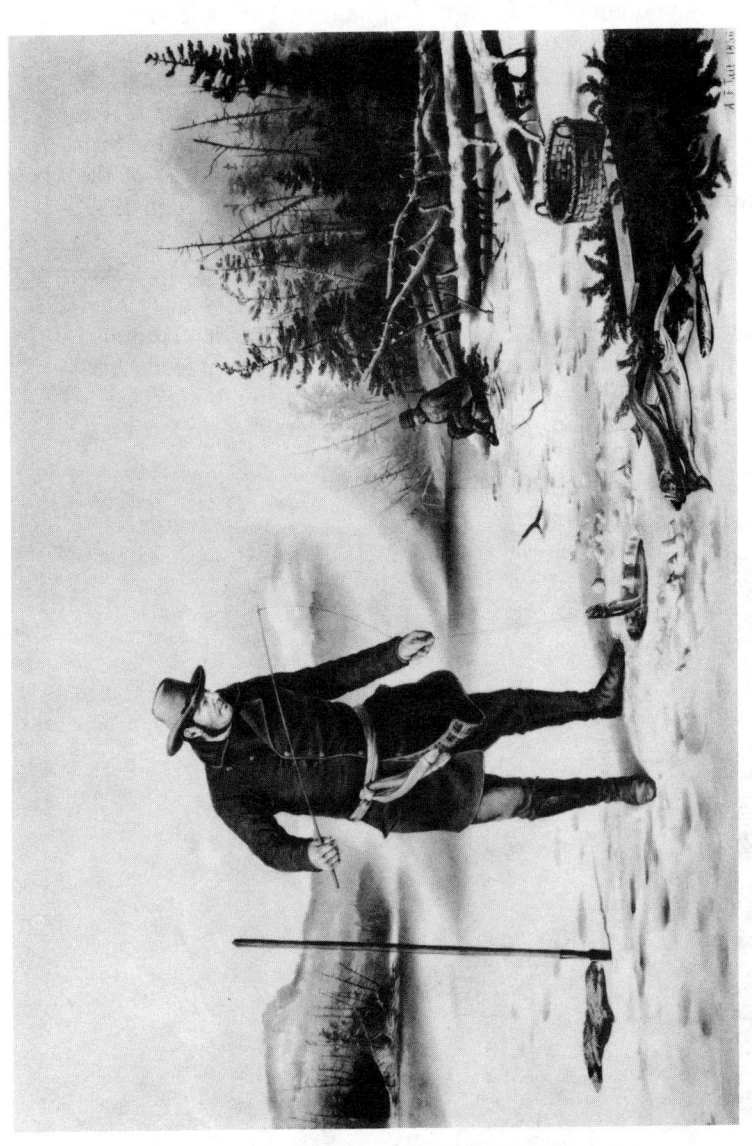

American Winter Sports. "Trout fishing on Chateaugay Lake"
(Courtesy of The Old Print Shop, Inc., Kenneth M. Newman)

Louis Maurer (1832-1932)

Louis Maurer was born in Germany in 1832 and came to America in 1850. He started working for a firm named Strong and within one year was employed by N. Currier Press. He worked actively for the firm for about ten years but was associated with Currier & Ives for fifty years. L. Maurer was the last person connected with the firm and it is through him that we owe much of our knowledge of the firm's actual operation. He lived to be ninety-nine and died in 1932. His wide range of talents made him invaluable to the firm.

Some of his most important work included the six large folio prints, *The Life of a Fireman* series, along with *The American Fireman- Always Ready* which is a portrait of Nathaniel Currier. He is also known for his fine horse racing prints, of which *Celebrated Horse Lexington* was one of his finest. A favorite is *Preparing for Market.* He is also credited with doing the first chromolithograph for Currier & Ives, *The Futurity Race, Sheepshead Bay 1888.*

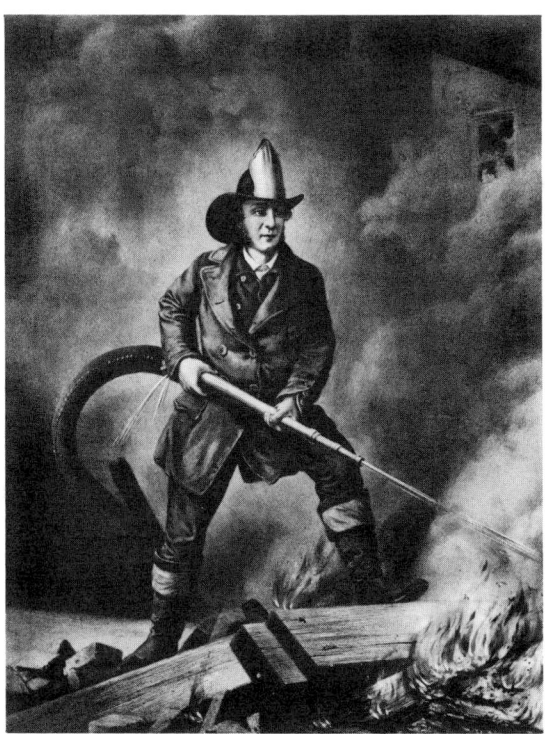

The American Fireman, "facing the enemy"
(Courtesy of The Old Print Shop, Inc., Kenneth M. Newman)

Thomas Worth (1834-1917)

Thomas Worth, a New York artist, took his first drawing at the age of twenty to Nathaniel Currier and was compensated five dollars. The print after some changes became *A Brush on the Road.* This was the beginning of a long line of work which T. Worth did for the firm.

He is most notably credited for his *Darktown Series* which was one of the firm's most prolific and profitable series. It is known that one print of the *Darktown Series* sold 73,000 copies. *Trotting Cracks at the Forge* and *Fashionable 'Turn- Outs' in Central Park* are fine examples of his horse prints. Another, *Trolling for Bluefish*, demonstrates his abilities as an artist and his love for fishing.

George H. Durrie (1820-1863)

George H. Durrie, born in New Haven Connecticut in 1820, was known for his New England scenes which truly captured the flavor of American country life. He is nicknamed the *snowman* for a group of winter scenes, such as, *The Old Homestead in Winter*, and *Winter in the Country - Getting Ice*. A popular and best known favorite print is his *Home to Thanksgiving*. A fine example of his artistic abilities in capturing New England life is depicted in *Autumn in New England - Cider Making.*

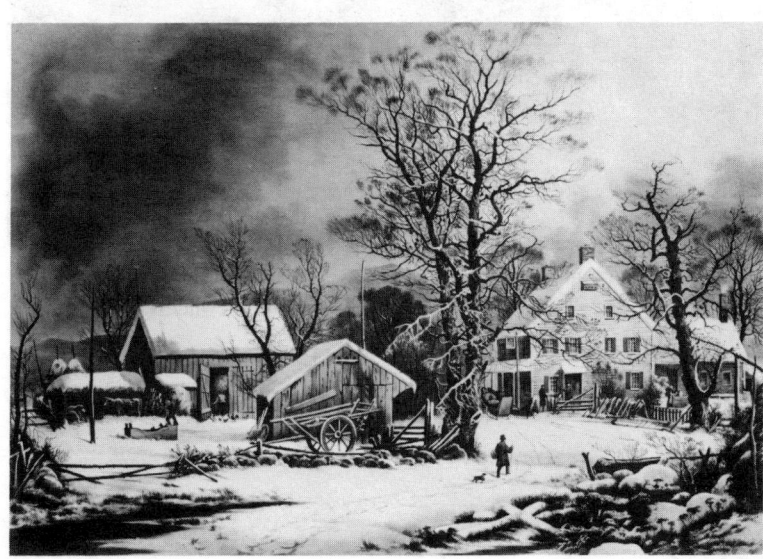

Winter in the Country. "A cold morning"
(Courtesy of The Old Print Shop, Inc., Kenneth M. Newman)

Charles Parsons (1821-1910)

Charles Parsons ranked among the finest of the firm's artists, producing extensive marine, river and steamboat prints. Some of Charles Parsons' most notable prints are: *Clipper Ship Comet of New York* and *Clipper Ship Nightingale*. Other views, other than marine, are: *Central Park, Winter, The Skating Pond* and *An American Railway Scene, at Hornellsville, Erie Railway*.

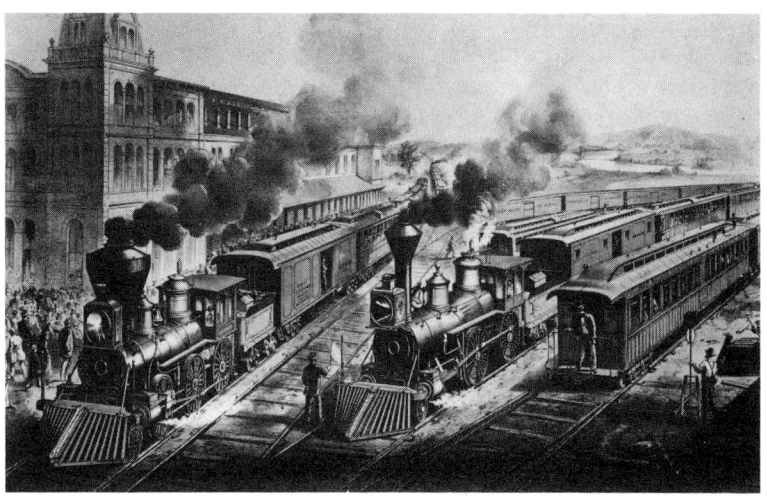

American Railroad Scene. "Lighting Express Train Leaving the Junction"
(Courtesy of The Old Print Shop, Inc., Kenneth M. Newman)

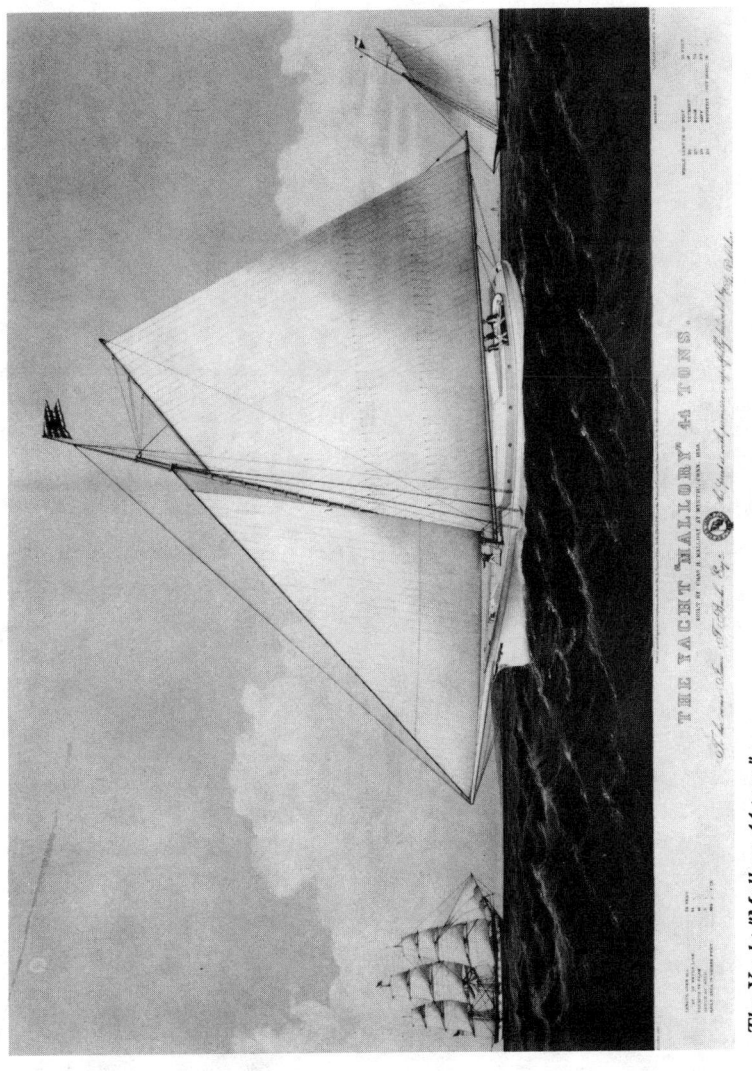

The Yacht "Mallory 44 tons"
(Courtesy of The Old Print Shop, Inc., Kenneth M. Newman)

James E. Butterworth (1817-1894)

James E. Butterworth was noted for his fine clipper ship prints which were frequently lithographed by C. Parsons. Some of his more famous prints include: *Clipper Ship Flying Cloud, Clipper Ship Great Republic* and *The Wreck of the Steam Ship - San Francisco.*

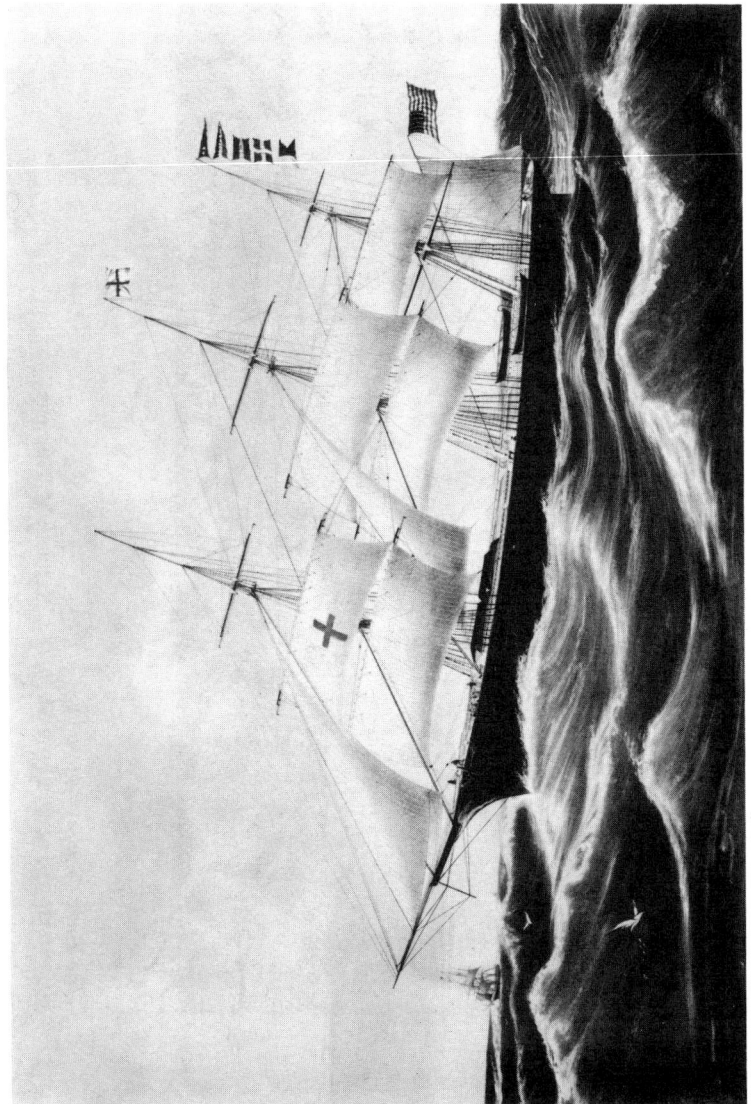

Clipper Ship "Dreadnought"
(Courtesy of The Old Print Shop, Inc., Kenneth M. Newman)

Eastman Johnson (1824-1906)

Eastman Johnson, a famous and accomplished painter of the period, had only one print published by Currier & Ives. This print, *Husking*, was so well received that it was judged the number one print on the original *Best 50* large folio list.

Otto Knirsch

Otto Knirsch worked independently and sold his finished stones to the Currier firm. His most notable print, *The Road - Winter*, is unusual in that his signature on the print is reversed. This print in 1989 brought the highest price paid for any Currier print sold at auction - $35,200.

C. Severin

C. Severin, who was considered a skillful craftsman, demonstrated this talent in his famous horse print of *Peytona and Fashion*. This was the first large sporting print of this type produced in America.

William Walker (1838-1921)

William Walker was known for his fine southern scenes. One print deservedly judged to be his best example is *The Levee. New Orleans*.

Napoleon Sarony

Napoleon Sarony, a master of lithography, produced works that were generally unsigned. Among his accomplishments, he helped design the famous horse print, *Lexington*. He had wide interests, one of which was photography, setting up a studio in 1868.

J. Schultz

J. Schultz, who did most of the lettering on the Currier & Ives prints, was also an accomplished artist. His print, *The Express Train*, was judged number one on the original *Best 50* small folio list.

Franz Venino

Franz Venino was the fastest, most prolific worker for the Currier & Ives firm. He was known to have completed a print from start to finish in the remarkable time of only one week.

John Cameron (1829-1862)

John Cameron, although he died at the early age of 33, contributed many great prints to the Currier & Ives firm. Scotish by birth, he emigrated to this country and while still a young adult, he was quickly recognized for his artistic talents. While employed by the Currier & Ives firm, he produced many popular prints. Among his most popular were *The Life of a Fireman - The Metropolitan System*, *Speeding on the Avenue*, *Celebrated Horse 'Dexter'*, and *Trotting Mare 'American Girl'*. Even today, over one hundred years after his death, many horse racing fans still refer to the invaluable racing records on his lithographs - the track, date, and times of the trotters.

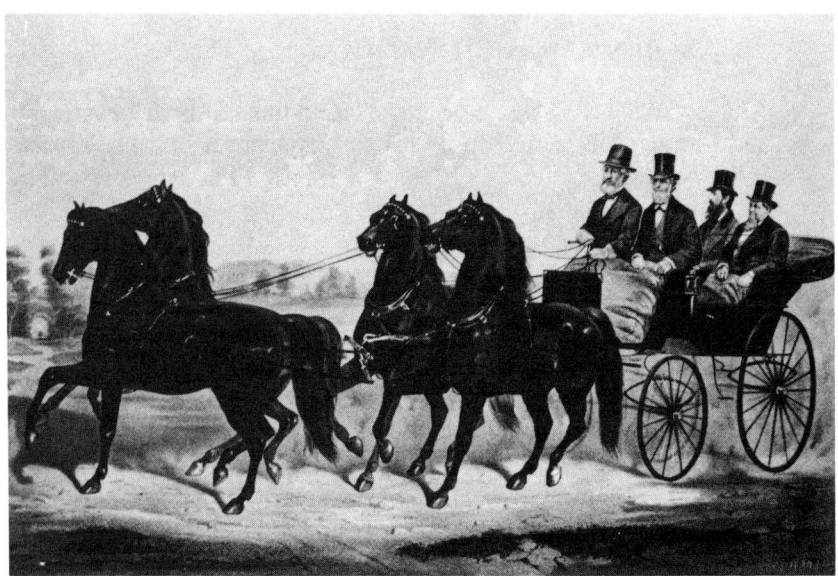

The Celebrated "Four in Hand" Stallion Team.
(Courtesy of Robert P. Kipp, Ipswich, MA)

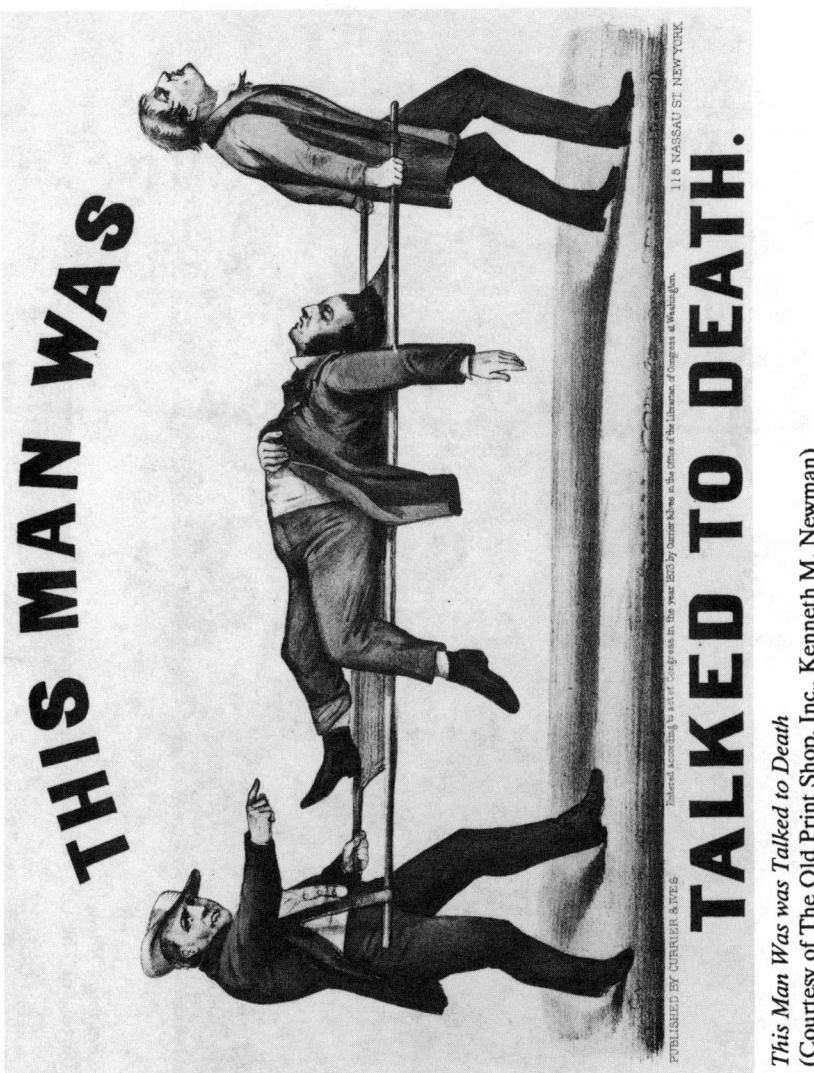

This Man Was was Talked to Death
(Courtesy of The Old Print Shop, Inc., Kenneth M. Newman)

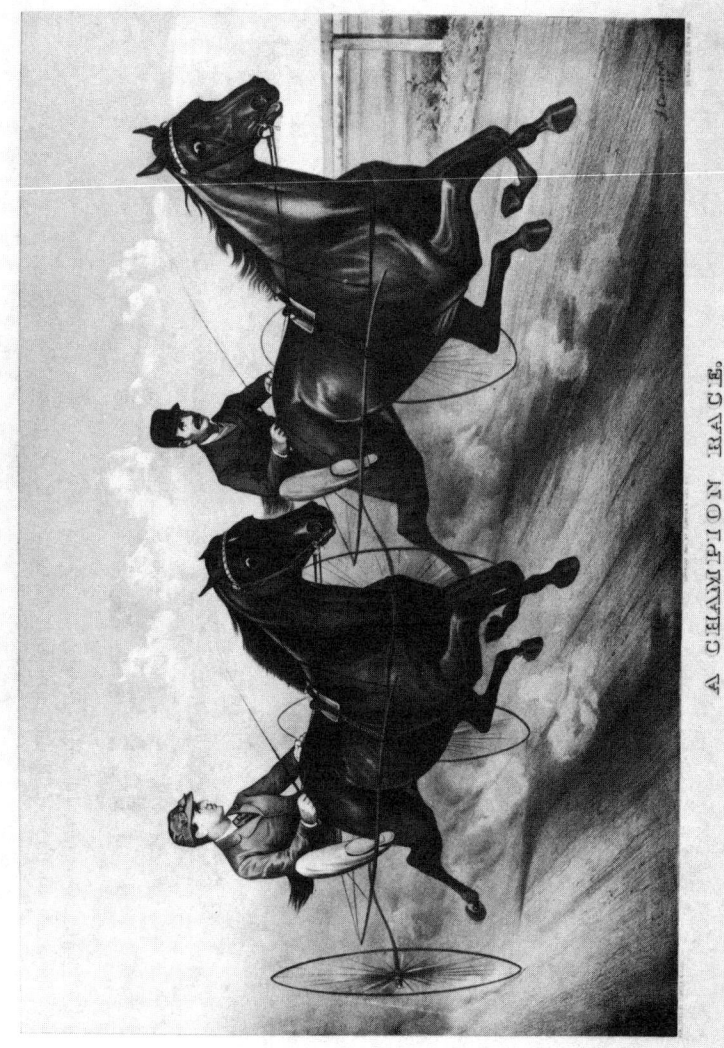

A Champion Race
(Courtesy of The Old Print Shop, Inc., Kenneth M. Newman)

It was these accomplished artists, along with the brilliant lithographic techniques that separated Currier & Ives from all of the other lithographic firms of this era. These artists did not always receive credit for their work, since the lithographer who finished the stone often appended his name to the prints. Several artists may have worked together on one print, but the lithographer's name usually appeared on most of the finished prints.

Coloring Currier & Ives prints

Once the black and white prints came off the lithographic presses, they were given to the firm's color specialists, Louis Maurer and Fanny Palmer. According to historical records, they produced the model coloring for each colorist to follow. The print was painted assembly line fashion by a staff of twelve women gathered around a large table. No one colorist completed a print but applied only one color, passing it along to the next colorist until the print was completed. A staff artist scrutinized the finished painting and made any required finishing touches. To avoid fading, Currier & Ives used the finest watercolors available. Stencils were used for large or rushed orders.

Large folio prints were usually shipped in lots of twelve with a model, for outside colorists to complete. They were usually struggling or unknown artists of the time, but recognized for their outstanding coloring ability.

A technique, which other lithographic firms of this era did not commonly use, was the applying of gum arabic. Gum arabic is a derivative of the acasia tree which, when applied to a particular area, gave a print a sheen of brilliance known as highlighting. This highlighting added an almost three dimensional effect to the important areas of a print.

Chromolithographs of Currier & Ives

Not to be confused with reproductions are chromolithographs, sometimes referred to as *chromos*. Chromolithographs are prints published by Currier & Ives but printed by outside firms equipped to handle this lengthy process. Chromolithographs were printed from multiple lithographic stones, each producing a separate color. This process, using up to twelve individual stones, gave the appearance of hand coloring but upon close examination, it is evident that the colors and tones are made up of irregular dot patterns, produced by the grain of the lithographic stones. Some of these chromolithographs had both the addition of hand coloring and gum arabic.

Characteristic of these prints are the *register marks* usually found mid-center on the edge of the print's image. These are pinholes that were used to align the print on the different stones being used. Chromolithographs will sometimes have the notation: *Printed in Colors by Currier & Ives* or *Printed in Oil Colors by Currier & Ives*. These original Currier & Ives prints were produced after 1888 and are typical of the prints produced by the firm in its later years of production.

Folio sizes of Currier & Ives prints

The size of a print is known as its folio size; the unprinted area outside of the print's image is known as its margins. The folio size of a print consists of the dimensions of the printed image, height by width, and does not include the title or publication lines printed in the margins, outside the image area.

Currier & Ives published prints in a variety of standard sizes but, because of their large output, could not honor requests for special or odd sized prints. The standard sizes of prints produced by Currier & Ives are as follows:

TC - Trade Cards:	about 3 1/4" x 5"
VS - Very small folio:	usually less than 7" x 9"
S - Small folio:	about 8" or 8 1/2" x 12 1/2"
M - Medium folio:	about 9" or 10" x 13" up to 19"
L - Large folio:	anything over 14" x 20"

A vignette is a borderless print whose background blends off into the edges of the print. A few examples of prints, produced as vignettes, were some of the small folio fruit and flower prints, sentimental prints whose titles sometimes begin with *Little*..... and busts of people. The folio size of a vignette is slightly less than the image sizes shown above, thus compensating for the absence of borders beyond the subject.

Large margins are sought after by collectors and make a print both more valuable and desirable. The minimum standard most collectors require for margin sizes are those stated for the grade of very good: 3/4 inch for small, 1 inch for medium and 1 1/2 inches for large folio prints. Some collectors are settling for slightly smaller margins in order to acquire a particularly rare or scarce print. This is usually done with the hope of upgrading this print, should the collector be fortunate enough to find a print in better condition.

States of Currier & Ives prints

An artist may make alterations to the original design of a print or may change publishers. Any such change or alteration made to a print from the previous edition represents a change of *state*. An example of different states is found in the Currier & Ives print, *American Winter Sports - Trout Fishing On Chateaugay Lake*. The first state, dated 1856, was printed for N. Currier by Endicott & Co. The second state, dated 1856, was printed by N. Currier, and the third state, also dated 1856, was printed by Currier & Ives. All three states had no image changes, only a change of publishers.

An example of a print with no changes of publisher but with image changes is *Preparing for Market*. All three states, dated 1856, were published by N. Currier. The image in the first state shows a child in the doorway having no toy, in the second state the child is holding a toy horse by a string and the third state shows the child holding a toy horse with another toy horse on the ground. These are a few examples of the different states found in Currier & Ives prints.

Restrikes of Currier & Ives prints

A restrike is a print which is later printed from the original stone by another publisher. In 1907, when the Currier & Ives firm was dissolved, some of the original lithographic stones were sold and prints were produced from them. The image measurements of these restrikes are identical to those listed in *Conningham's*. (Frederic A. Conningham's book, *Currier & Ives Prints - An illustrated check list*, is considered the standard reference - the "bible" - for checking the image size and the wording on original Currier & Ives prints.)

Some stones found their way to England and were subsequently published there by S. Lipshitz; others were purchased and published by Joseph Koehler. He placed his name on the stones and so the subsequent restrikes attributed to him are easily identified. Of the prints published from over twenty stones, the subjects were mostly comics and prints from the *Darktown Series*, plus one large folio, *Abraham Lincoln* and a small folio, *Washington as a Mason*.

Another group of restrikes was published by Max Williams around 1912. He purchased six large folio *Clipper Ship* stones and reissued these prints, making no changes in the publication name. One can identify these prints from those produced by Currier & Ives by their inferior quality of printing. The coloring was lightly applied making these restrikes seem a little pale. The paper used in producing these prints was thinner and not rag as used for originals. The titles and publication dates for these six restrikes are:

Clipper Ship - Dreadnought 'Off Sandy Hook'	1854
Clipper Ship - Dreadnought 'Off Tuskar Light'	1856
Clipper Ship - Flying Cloud	1852
Clipper Ship - Ocean Express 'Outward Bound'	1856
Clipper Ship - Sweepstakes	1853
Clipper Ship - Three Brothers	1875

Please note: The *Clipper Ship* restrikes do have market value. In today's market dealers may ask between $1200 and $1800 for these prints if they are in very good condition with 1 1/2" margins or larger. Additionally, these restrikes should have good original coloring.

CHAPTER THREE

Reproductions

Identifying reproductions

A reproduction is made by photographing an original print, etching a plate from the negative, and printing it on a modern press. This process is technically known as photomechanical offset lithography.

Reproductions possess certain distinct qualities which differ from those of original prints. For example, reproductions are usually dull in appearance and do not have the brilliance associated with hand-colored originals and chromolithographs.

To recognize a reproduction, there are some logical steps that can be taken. The best method for identifying a reproduction is by visual comparison. Placing an original print beside the print in question and examining the differences will, in most instances, immediately resolve any confusion. This, however, is usually not possible and additional means of identification become necessary. I will explain in detail the sometimes subtle differences between original prints and reproductions, and methods which will enable you to distinguish one from the other.

Comparing image size

Reproductions were often not printed in exactly the same dimensions as original Currier & Ives prints. Therefore, it is advisable to compare the size of a questionable print's image to a known image size. For an accurate listing of image sizes for Currier & Ives prints, I would recommend those listed in *Conningham's*, a proven source. You may deduct as much as 1/4 to 3/8 of an inch from the longest measurement which compensates for the shrinkage of old paper, a natural process occurring due to loss of the moisture content. If the print does not have the proper image measurements, it is safe to assume that it is a reproduction.

Titles of reproductions

The titles on reproduced Currier & Ives prints were sometimes changed. The titles must follow exactly those listed in *Conningham's*, including subtitles and the information below the title. The title may be close in wording but, to be an original, it must be exact in every word and sequence, including subtitles. Check to see if the publisher's credit says: *Republished from, Reprinted from, From the collection of,* or *Printed from* anywhere below the image. If any of the previous phrases appear on the print in question, it is a reproduction and further investigation is not necessary.

Printing original Currier & Ives

The Currier firm used the lithography process exclusively in the production of all their prints. There are no known exceptions. Therefore, any print not produced from a lithographic stone will be a reproduction.

The stones produced irregular, non-symmetrical black dots on the print. Even the finest line, like those produced on a ship's rigging, will be comprised of tiny non-geometric dots. These dots are produced by the grain of the stone from which they were printed, The use of a 10x loupe will enlarge an area for closer scrutiny. The irregular dots will be closer together and larger in size in areas of dark shading, further apart and smaller in size in areas of lighter shading.

Printing reproductions

Upon magnification, a reproduction's dots will form a symmetrical pattern throughout the entire print. Instead of being composed of irregular dots of black ink, as in an original print, the printed dots will appear as interwoven circles or portions of circles combined. A color on a reproduction is actually made by combining two or more separate colors together. For example, under magnification it can be seen that the color green will actually be made up of two small symmetrical patterns of blue and yellow. These symmetrical patterns are characteristic of a reproduced print. Remember, original Currier & Ives prints are comprised of *irregular* dots of ink.

Original hand coloring

As described earlier, large folio prints were sent out in lots of twelve to artists known for their outstanding coloring ability. Small and medium folio prints were given to an in-house team of colorists who hand colored each print.

Water colors were used for coloring and when washes were applied to large areas, some color did run over into an adjacent area. Original washes or hand coloring when examined with a loupe have no dot pattern. They are one solid color, only occasionally blending out to a lighter shade. Any dot pattern you see was produced by the litho stone from which it was printed.

Currier & Ives also used gum arabic to highlight important areas of a print's image. By holding a print at an angle to the light, the places where gum arabic has been applied will stand out and appear as a shiny area. These qualities identify a print as an original and enables the print to exude the characteristic feel of being done by hand.

Paper of originals

Currier & Ives used a medium to heavy weight of *rag* paper in the production of their prints , never a thin paper. All rag paper was made from cotton by beating up old cotton rags and adding a sizing agent to bond the fibers. After being formed the result is known today as all rag paper. All paper used in producing Currier & Ives prints was known as all rag paper until the late 1860's.

In 1867 the first commercial wood pulp mill in the United States was founded in Stockbridge, Massachusetts. After 1870 Currier & Ives switched from all rag to a rag paper, having some wood pulp added to it. Even though there is a slight difference in the two papers, all rag and rag are both commonly referred to as rag paper. Under magnification the cotton fibers can easily be seen in both types of rag papers, both appearing to be fluffy; the later addition of wood pulp can also be detected. The thickness of the paper changed for each folio size produced. The large folio prints were printed on paper which was thicker and had more sizing added for stiffness.

Paper of reproductions

Most reproductions of Currier & Ives prints have been produced on wood pulp paper and small wood fragments can be found. Some caution must be exercised when comparing original paper to that of reproductions. Do not confuse the few impurities present in rag paper with the wood fragments found in wood pulp paper of reproductions. The wood pulp paper of reproductions is always much thinner and lighter in weight. Feeling the paper between your fingers is a means of determining how thin the paper is. Typical paper used for reproductions is known as a hard finish paper, almost shiny.

Identifying a reproduction

I have in front of me, a large folio print sent to me by a customer in the hopes that it might be an original. The print, titled *The Road, - Winter* portrays a very dramatic winter scene depicting Nathaniel Currier. I will take you through the identification process of this print to show you how the above information can be used in determining if a print is an original or reproduction.

After checking the print's dimensions against the actual dimensions as stated in *Conningham's* it was determined that the size of this print was not consistent with the original, although the title was the same. Then, using a 10x loupe, I examined the print in question and found missing litho dots which were apparent in the lettering on the original. What I saw was very fine connecting lines between the dots, that looked to me like fine cobwebbing. Original prints have clear non-symmetrical dots.

I then noticed that some of the image's color was formed by dots, rather than a solid watercolor wash associated with an original. There was, however, some applied hand coloring and gum arabic, both associated with the original print. This was done by the publisher to make it look more like an original.

The paper was typical of a reproduction, wood pulp which felt much thinner than that of an original. On the reverse side of the print, its verso, there was a watermark within the paper. Watermarked paper was never used in the production of original Currier & Ives prints.

This print has some typical differences you may encounter when identifying a print as being a reproduction of a Currier & Ives print. The above print is an Andres' reproduction.

The Andres' reproductions

The Road - Winter is one of the twenty large folio prints produced by Andres', Inc. of New York in 1942. The prints they reproduced are difficult reproductions to identify, because at first you are fooled by the hand coloring and image size. They are the finest quality prints reproduced from Currier & Ives but they are still identifiable. These prints are old enough today to have some time toning and watermarks common on old prints. The untrimmed prints I measured which had a deckled edge were 22 3/4" x 32". All were printed on wood pulp paper; some had watermarks in the paper. They were sold in 1 1/2" molded wood frames by W. C. Omen, Inc. of Chicago Merchandise Mart and were trimmed to 21 1/2" x 30", which accommodated their stock frames. The titles as they appear on the reproductions are:

Across the Continent
American Express Train
The American National Game of Baseball
American Winter Scenes - Evening
American Winter Scenes - Morning
Central Park Winter - Skating Pond
Clipper Ship "Sweepstakes"
Clipper Ship "Red Jacket"
High Water on the Mississippi
Home to Thanksgiving
Hudson Highlands
Landscape Fruit and Flowers
The Lightning Express Trains
Low Water on the Mississippi
May Morning
New England Winter Scene
The Old Grist Mill
The Road, - Winter
Seasons of Life - Childhood
Seasons of Life - Middle Age

CHAPTER FOUR

Popular Currier & Ives

The original "Best 50"

Judging the most popular Currier & Ives prints in 1932 was no easy task. The project was spearheaded by the late Harry Shaw Newman of The Old Print Shop. Backing the project was Harry T. Peters, who assembled the largest collection of Currier & Ives prints and is a noted author on the history of Currier & Ives and their prints. Participants in the project also included Charles Messe's Stow, the antiques editor of the *New York Sun*. For fifty days running he printed the selected *Best 50* large folio prints picked by a jury of twelve qualified collectors. The selection process and publishing of these prints sparked a renewed interest in the collecting of Currier & Ives prints.

The project was so successful that the following year the jury was asked to select the *Best 50* small folio Currier & Ives prints, which included four medium folio size prints. [The original Best 50 - large and small folio prints - are listed beginning on page 47]. At this time The Old Print Shop in New York published two separate books illustrating and describing the prints selected. These books, today, form an important part of a serious collector's library.

New Best 50

In 1988 a new project was started by the American Historical Print Collectors Society (AHPCS) which was the undertaking of Marshall R. Berkoff, president of the society. Mr. Berkoff named this project *AHPCS Currier & Ives - The 'Best 50' - Revisited.* The purpose of this project was to provide a new selection process and to compare the original *Best 50* with the *Best 50* prints selected today, some fifty years later.

The AHPCS started this project by asking its membership to make recommendations of prints they wanted included for nomination - two hundred in total. A national panel, comprised of thirty collectors, dealers and institutions gathered in New York City on April 22, 1989 and viewed most of the nominated large and small folio prints. It is of special interest that the study and discussions of these prints took place at The Museum of the City of New York. This Museum houses the largest collection of Currier & Ives prints from the Harry T. Peters collection. This gave each panel member a fine opportunity of viewing the prints actually owned by Peters who was so involved in the first selections.

The final selection of the *New Best 50* was completed by June 1990, after the AHPCS membership voted on the *Best 50 - Revisited* prints from the 100 large and 100 small folio prints nominated by the national panel. On June 7, 1990, the Milwaukee Art Museum became the host institution for exhibiting the "New Best 50". You will find the "New Best 50" listed beginning on page 50.

These prints represent only a small number of the Currier & Ives prints worthy of collecting. They do, however, show us that certain prints have, for over fifty years, remained the most popular prints, when judged by competent collectors and dealers.

Beginning on page 53, the author, Robert Kipp, has combined both the "Old" list and the "New" list alphabetically, by title. Beside each title is its conningham number, and its ranking in the old and new list. If there are blank spot in the ranking that is an indication that that title was not selected for that particular old or new list.

ORIGINAL BEST 50: LARGE FOLIO

Con#	Rank	Title
3008	1	*HUSKING/ (Painted by E. Johnson) 1861*
157	2	*AMERICAN FOREST SCENE / "Maple Sugaring" 1856*
954	3	*CENTRAL PARK, WINTER / THE SKATING POND*
2882	4	*HOME TO THANKSGIVING/ 1867*
3522	5	*LIFE OF A HUNTER, THE / A Tight Fix, 1861*
3527	6	*LIFE ON THE PRAIRIE / The Buffalo Hunt, 1862*
3535	7	*LIGHTNING EXPRESS" TRAINS, THE / Leaving...*
4763	8	*PEYTONA" AND "FASHION*
5196	9	*ROCKY MOUNTAINS, THE - EMIGRANTS CROSSING...*
6158	10	*TROLLING FOR BLUE FISH/ 1866*
6627	11	*WHALE FISHERY, THE SPERM WHALE IN A FLURRY*
6738	12	*WINTER IN THE COUNTRY - THE OLD GRIST MILL*
136	13	*AMERICAN FARM SCENES / No.4 (Winter)*
180	14	*AMERICAN NATIONAL GAME OF BASEBALL, THE*
210	15	*AMERICAN WINTER SPORTS / Trout Fishing*
4139	16	*MINK TRAPPING/ "PRIME", 1862*
4870	17	*PREPARING FOR MARKET, 1856*
6737	18	*WINTER IN THE COUNTRY - GETTING ICE/ 1864*
33	19	*ACROSS THE CONTINENT / "Westward the Course...*
3528	20	*LIFE ON THE PRAIRIE / The Trapper's Defence*
4116	21	*MIDNIGHT RACE ON THE MISS. A/ Natchez-Eclipse*
5171	22	*ROAD - WINTER, THE/ 1853*
5876	23	*SUMMER SCENES IN NEW YORK HARBOR/ 1863*
6169	24	*TROTTING CRACKS" AT THE FORGE/ 1869*
6409	25	*VIEW OF SAN FRANCISCO, CALIFORNIA/ 1851*
5492	26	*SHIPS "ANTARCTIC" OF N.Y. AND "THREE BELLS"*
5961	27	*TAKING THE BACK TRACK - A DANGEROUS...*
149	28	*AMERICAN FIELD SPORTS / "Flush'd"/ 1857*
174	29	*AMERICAN HUNTING SCENES / "A Good Chance"*
208	30	*AMERICAN WINTER SCENES / "Morning" 1854*
322	31	*AUTUMN IN NEW ENGLAND / "Cider Making"*
845	32	*CATCHING A TROUT / "We Hab You Now, Sar!"*
1159	33	*CLIPPER SHIP "NIGHTINGALE", 1854*
3519	34	*LIFE OF A FIREMAN / The Night Alarm, 1854*
3848	35	*MAC AND ZACHERY TAYLOR, 1851*

4420	36	NEW ENGLAND WINTER SCENE, 1861
5054	37	RAIL SHOOTING ON THE DELAWARE, 1852
5581	38	SNOWED UP - RUFFED GROUSE IN WINTER, 1867
5907	39	SURRENDER OF GENL. BURGOYNE AT SARATOGA, N.Y.
5906	40	SURRENDER OF CORNWALLIS AT YORKTOWN, VA./ 1852
1165	41	CLIPPER SHIP "RED JACKET"/ 1855
209	42	AMERICAN WINTER SPORTS / "Deer Shooting"
371	43	BARK THEOXENA, THE
814	44	CARES OF A FAMILY, THE, 1856
887	45	CELEBRATED HORSE "LEXINGTON", 1855
2481	46	GRAND DRIVE CENTRAL PARK, NY, THE/ 1869
2615	47	GREAT FIRE AT CHICAGO/ 1871
3440	48	LANDSCAPE FRUIT AND FLOWERS/ 1862
3516	49	LIFE OF A FIREMAN / The Metropolitan System
5659	50	SPLENDID NAVAL TRIUMPH ON THE MISSISSIPPI

ORIGINAL BEST 50: SMALL FOLIO

Con#	Rank	Title
1790	1	EXPRESS TRAIN, THE/ (J. Schutz, del.)
187	2	AMERICAN RAILROAD SCENE / "Snowbound" 1871
445	3	BEACH SNIPE SHOOTING
3021	4	ICE-BOAT RACE ON THE HUDSON
953	5	CENTRAL PARK, WINTER / THE SKATING CARNIVAL
5701	6	STAR OF THE ROAD, THE/ 1849
2810	7	HIGH BRIDGE AT HARLEM, NY
3975	8	MAPLE SUGARING / EARLY SPRING IN THE N. WOODS
5475	9	SHAKERS NEAR LEBANON
6747	10	WINTER SPORTS - PICKEREL FISHING/ 1872
115	11	AMERICAN CLIPPER SHIP "WITCH OF THE WAVE"
2412	12	GOLD MINING IN CALIFORNIA/ 1871
2623	13	GREAT INTERNATIONAL BOAT RACE
6677	14	WILD TURKEY SHOOTING/ 1871
4754	15	PERRY'S VICTORY ON LAKE ERIE
6515	16	WASHINGTON AT MOUNT VERNON/ 1852
6626	17	WHALE FISHERY, THE "LAYING ON"

1020	18	CHATHAM SQUARE, NEW YORK
6567	19	WATER RAIL SHOOTING/ 1855
5554	20	SLEIGH RACE, THE/ #90/ 1848
2128	21	FRANKLIN'S EXPERIMENT/ 1876
6523	22	WASHINGTON CROSSING THE DELAWARE / #69
172	23	AMERICAN HOMESTEAD - WINTER/ 1868
6547	24	WASHINGTON TAKING LEAVE OF THE OFFICERS
5727	25	STEAMBOAT "KNICKERBOCKER"
3349	26	KISS ME QUICK/ #700
4607	27	ON THE MISSISSIPPI LOADING COTTON, 1870
627	28	BOUND DOWN THE RIVER
205	29	AMERICAN WHALERS CRUSHED IN ICE / "Burning..
1446	30	DARTMOUTH COLLEGE, 1834
5997	31	TERRIFIC COMBAT BETWEEN THE "MONITOR" 2 GUNS
2250	32	GENERAL FRANCIS MARION/ 1876
275	33	ART OF MAKING MONEY/ (Rebus)
2895	34	HON. ABRAHAM LINCOLN/ (Republican Candidate)
2261	35	GEN. GEORGE WASHINGTON / The Father of his..
543	36	BLACK BASS SPEARING / "On the Restigouche
1652	37	EARLY WINTER, 1869
6773	38	WOODCOCK SHOOTING / #175/ 1855
1640	39	"DUTCHMAN" AND "HIRAM WOODRUFF"/ (Vig.) 1871
2580	40	GREAT CONFLAGRATION AT PITTSBURGH, PA
446	41	BEAR HUNTING/ (Winter Scene)
1571	42	DESTRUCTION OF TEA AT BOSTON HARBOR, 1846
1258	43	CORNWALLIS IS TAKEN, 1876
3435	44	LANDING OF THE PILGRIMS AT PLYMOUTH MASS
2613	45	GREAT FIGHT FOR THE CHAMPIONSHIP BETWEEN...
499	46	BENJAMIN FRANKLIN / "The Statesman and Phil.
4494	47	NOAH'S ARK / #20/ (Sarony del.)
551	48	BLACK EYED SUSAN, 1848
573	49	BLOOMER COSTUME, THE
1176	50	CLIPPER YACHT "AMERICA", THE / Built by...

NEW BEST 50: LARGE FOLIO

Con#	Rank	Title
5171	1	ROAD - WINTER, THE/ 1853
4116	2	MIDNIGHT RACE ON THE MISS. A/ Natchez-Eclipse
3008	3	HUSKING/ (Painted by E. Johson) 1861
33	4	ACROSS THE CONTINENT / "Westward the Course...
6737	5	WINTER IN THE COUNTRY - GETTING ICE/ 1864
157	6	AMERICAN FOREST SCENE / "Maple Sugaring" 1856
954	7	CENTRAL PARK, WINTER / THE SKATING POND
136	8	AMERICAN FARM SCENES / No.4 (Winter)
180	9	AMERICAN NATIONAL GAME OF BASEBALL, THE
2882	10	HOME TO THANKSGIVING/ 1867
992	11	CHAMPIONS OF THE MISSISSIPPI / "A Race..
5196	12	ROCKY MOUNTAINS, THE - EMIGRANTS CROSSING...
3535	13	LIGHTNING EXPRESS" TRAINS, THE / Leaving...
130	14	AMERICAN EXPRESS TRAIN/ (Palmer) 1864
1165	15	CLIPPER SHIP "RED JACKET"/ 1855
3522	16	LIFE OF A HUNTER, THE / A Tight Fix, 1861
6158	17	TROLLING FOR BLUE FISH/ 1866
322	18	AUTUMN IN NEW ENGLAND / "Cider Making"
207	19	AMERICAN WINTER SCENES / "Evening" 1854
4420	20	NEW ENGLAND WINTER SCENE, 1861
6738	21	WINTER IN THE COUNTRY - THE OLD GRIST MILL
2615	22	GREAT FIRE AT CHICAGO/ 1871
6776	23	WOODING UP" ON THE MISSISSIPPI/ 1863
3528	24	LIFE ON THE PRAIRIE / The Trapper's Defence
208	25	AMERICAN WINTER SCENES / "Morning" 1854
4870	26	PREPARING FOR MARKET, 1856
6169	27	TROTTING CRACKS" AT THE FORGE/ 1869
265	28	ARGUING THE POINT 1855
3517	29	LIFE OF A FIREMAN / The New Era, 1861
3527	30	LIFE ON THE PRAIRIE / The Buffalo Hunt, 1862
3480	31	LEVEE - NEW ORLEANS, THE/ (19.15x29.14) 1884
6736	32	WINTER IN THE COUNTRY - A COLD MORNING
4160	33	MISSISSIPPI IN TIME OF PEACE, 1865
6623	34	WHALE FISHERY / ATTACKING A RIGHT WHALE
1890	35	FARMER'S HOME / Harvest, The/ 1864

294	36	*AT THE FAIR GROUNDS/ (High-wheeled sulkies)*
1892	37	*FARMER'S HOME / Winter, The/ 1863*
703	38	*BROOK TROUT FISHING / "An Anxious Moment"*
5581	39	*SNOWED UP - RUFFED GROUSE IN WINTER, 1867*
1271	40	*COTTON PLANTATION ON THE MISSISSIPPI, A*
173	41	*AMERICAN HUNTING SCENES / "An Early Start"*
210	42	*AMERICAN WINTER SPORTS / Trout Fishing*
3516	43	*LIFE OF A FIREMAN / The Metropolitan System*
185	44	*AMERICAN RAILROAD SCENE / Lightning Express*
3440	45	*LANDSCAPE FRUIT AND FLOWERS/ 1862*
6670	46	*WILD DUCK SHOOTING - A GOOD DAY'S SPORT/ 1854*
4474	47	*NIGHT ON THE HUDSON, A/ "Through at Daylight"*
4139	48	*MINK TRAPPING/ "PRIME", 1862*
845	49	*CATCHING A TROUT / "We Hab You Now, Sar!"*
6627	50	*WHALE FISHERY, THE SPERM WHALE IN A FLURRY*

NEW BEST 50: SMALL FOLIO

Con#	Rank	Title
187	1	*AMERICAN RAILROAD SCENE / "Snowbound" 1871*
3975	2	*MAPLE SUGARING / EARLY SPRING IN THE N. WOODS*
948	3	*CENTRAL PARK IN WINTER/ (Moonlight Scene)*
3021	4	*ICE-BOAT RACE ON THE HUDSON*
172	5	*AMERICAN HOMESTEAD - WINTER/ 1868*
4859	6	*PRAIRIE FIRES OF THE GREAT WEST, 1871*
205	7	*AMERICAN WHALERS CRUSHED IN ICE / "Burning..*
953	8	*CENTRAL PARK, WINTER / THE SKATING CARNIVAL*
4117	9	*MIDNIGHT RACE ON THE MISS., A/ Memphis-J Hwd.*
627	10	*BOUND DOWN THE RIVER*
2412	11	*GOLD MINING IN CALIFORNIA/ 1871*
6050	12	*THROUGH THE BAYOU BY TORCHLIGHT*
6734	13	*WINTER EVENING/ 1854*
6742	14	*WINTER MORNING IN THE COUNTRY/ 1873*
6051	15	*THROUGH TO THE PACIFIC/ 1870*
4607	16	*ON THE MISSISSIPPI LOADING COTTON, 1870*
2861	17	*HOME IN THE WILDERNESS, A/ 1870*
2155	18	*FROZEN UP/ (8.8x12.8) 1872*

5546	19	*SKATING SCENE / MOONLIGHT, 1868*
1571	20	*DESTRUCTION OF TEA AT BOSTON HARBOR, 1846*
1792	21	*EXPRESS TRAIN, THE, 1870*
2630	22	*GREAT MISSISSIPPI STEAM BOAT RACE*
1652	23	*EARLY WINTER, 1869*
5558	24	*SLEIGH RACE, THE / #90*
2876	25	*HOME ON THE MISSISSIPPI, A/ 1871*
5225	26	*ROUTE TO CALIFORNIA, THE/ 1871*
1790	27	*EXPRESS TRAIN, THE/ (J. Schutz, del.)*
6626	28	*WHALE FISHERY, THE "LAYING ON"*
6740	29	*WINTER MORNING/ 1861*
6747	30	*WINTER SPORTS - PICKEREL FISHING/ 1872*
2584	31	*GREAT EAST RIVER BRIDGE/ 1872*
6744	32	*WINTER PASTIME/ 1870*
578	33	*BLUE FISHING*
168	34	*AMERICAN HOMESTEAD - AUTUMN/ 1869*
2725	35	*HARBOR OF NEW YORK/ From The Brooklyn Bridge*
5475	36	*SHAKERS NEAR LEBANON*
376	37	*BASS FISHING*
2658	38	*GREAT WEST, THE/ (7.15x12.8) 1870*
171	39	*AMERICAN HOMESTEAD - SUMMER/ 1868*
5580	40	*SNOW STORM, THE*
446	41	*BEAR HUNTING/ (Winter Scene)*
3349	42	*KISS ME QUICK/ #700*
1822	43	*FALL OF RICHMOND, VIRGINIA, THE/ 1865*
4473	44	*NIGHT EXPRESS, THE/ "The Start"*
170	45	*AMERICAN HOMESTEAD - SPRING/ 1869*
206	46	*AMERICAN WINTER SCENE, AN/ (OVAL)*
327	47	*AWFUL CONFL. OF THE STEAM BOAT LEXINGTON*
6401	48	*VIEW OF NEW YORK*
543	49	*BLACK BASS SPEARING / "On the Restigouche*
2614	50	*GREAT FIRE AT BOSTON/ 1872*

"OLD" AND "NEW" BEST 50 COMBINED

The following list was compiled, by Robert Kipp, in the format you see, so that a collector could quickly look up a BEST 50 print by title, and then glance across to see what its ranking was on the "Old" and "New" list. Mr. Kipp and Currier Publications want to thank The American Historical Print Collectors Society for making their master list available for this purpose!

Con#	Old	New	Size	Title
33	19	4	L	*ACROSS THE CONTINENT / "Westward the Course...*
115	11		S	*AMERICAN CLIPPER SHIP "WITCH OF THE WAVE"*
130		14	L	*AMERICAN EXPRESS TRAIN/ (Palmer) 1864*
136	13	8	L	*AMERICAN FARM SCENES / No.4 (Winter)*
149	28		L	*AMERICAN FIELD SPORTS / "Flush'd"/ 1857*
157	2	6	L	*AMERICAN FOREST SCENE / "Maple Sugaring" 1856*
168		34	S	*AMERICAN HOMESTEAD - AUTUMN/ 1869*
170		45	S	*AMERICAN HOMESTEAD - SPRING/ 1869*
171		39	S	*AMERICAN HOMESTEAD - SUMMER/ 1868*
172	23	5	S	*AMERICAN HOMESTEAD - WINTER/ 1868*
173		41	L	*AMERICAN HUNTING SCENES / "An Early Start"*
174	29		L	*AMERICAN HUNTING SCENES / "A Good Chance"*
180	14	9	L	*AMERICAN NATIONAL GAME OF BASEBALL, THE*
185		44	L	*AMERICAN RAILROAD SCENE / Lightning Express*
187	2	1	S	*AMERICAN RAILROAD SCENE / "Snowbound" 1871*
205	29	7	S	*AMERICAN WHALERS CRUSHED IN ICE / "Burning..*
206		46	S	*AMERICAN WINTER SCENE, AN/ (OVAL)*
207		19	L	*AMERICAN WINTER SCENES / "Evening" 1854*
208	30	25	L	*AMERICAN WINTER SCENES / "Morning" 1854*
209	42		L	*AMERICAN WINTER SPORTS / "Deer Shooting"*
210	15	42	L	*AMERICAN WINTER SPORTS / Trout Fishing*
265		28	L	*ARGUING THE POINT 1855*
275	33	·	S	*ART OF MAKING MONEY/ (Rebus)*
294		36	L	*AT THE FAIR GROUNDS/ (High-wheeled sulkies)*
322	31	18	L	*AUTUMN IN NEW ENGLAND / "Cider Making"*
327		47	S	*AWFUL CONFL. OF THE STEAM BOAT LEXINGTON*
371	43		L	*BARK THEOXENA, THE*
376		37	S	*BASS FISHING*
445	3		M	*BEACH SNIPE SHOOTING*

446	41	41	S	BEAR HUNTING/ (Winter Scene)
499	46		S	BENJAMIN FRANKLIN / "The Statesman and Phil.
543	36	49	M	BLACK BASS SPEARING / "On the Restigouche
551	48		S	BLACK EYED SUSAN, 1848
573	49		S	BLOOMER COSTUME, THE
578		33	S	BLUE FISHING
627	28	10	S	BOUND DOWN THE RIVER
703		38	L	BROOK TROUT FISHING / "An Anxious Moment"
814	44		L	CARES OF A FAMILY, THE, 1856
845	32	49	L	CATCHING A TROUT / "We Hab You Now, Sar!"
887	45		L	CELEBRATED HORSE "LEXINGTON", 1855
948		3	S	CENTRAL PARK IN WINTER/ (Moonlight Scene)
953	5	8	S	CENTRAL PARK, WINTER / THE SKATING CARNIVAL
954	3	7	L	CENTRAL PARK, WINTER / THE SKATING POND
992		11	L	CHAMPIONS OF THE MISSISSIPPI / "A Race..
1020	18		S	CHATHAM SQUARE, NEW YORK
1159	33		L	CLIPPER SHIP "NIGHTINGALE", 1854
1165	41	15	L	CLIPPER SHIP "RED JACKET"/ 1855
1176	50		M	CLIPPER YACHT "AMERICA", THE / Built by...
1258	43		S	CORNWALLIS IS TAKEN, 1876
1271		40	L	COTTON PLANTATION ON THE MISSISSIPPI, A
1446	30		S	DARTMOUTH COLLEGE, 1834
1571	42	20	S	DESTRUCTION OF TEA AT BOSTON HARBOR, 1846
1640	39		S	"DUTCHMAN" AND "HIRAM WOODRUFF"/ (Vig.) 1871
1652	37	23	M	EARLY WINTER, 1869
1790	1	27	S	EXPRESS TRAIN, THE/ (J. Schutz, del.)
1792		21	S	EXPRESS TRAIN, THE, 1870
1822		43	S	FALL OF RICHMOND, VIRGINIA, THE/ 1865
1890		35	L	FARMER'S HOME / Harvest, The/ 1864
1892		37	L	FARMER'S HOME / Winter, The/ 1863
2128	21		S	FRANKLIN'S EXPERIMENT/ 1876
2155		18	S	FROZEN UP/ (8.8x12.8) 1872
2250	32		S	GENERAL FRANCIS MARION/ 1876
2261	35		S	GEN. GEORGE WASHINGTON / The Father of his..
2412	12	11	S	GOLD MINING IN CALIFORNIA/ 1871
2481	46		L	GRAND DRIVE CENTRAL PARK, NY, THE/ 1869
2580	40		S	GREAT CONFLAGRATION AT PITTSBURGH, PA
2584		31	S	GREAT EAST RIVER BRIDGE/ 1872
2613	45		S	GREAT FIGHT FOR THE CHAMPIONSHIP BETWEEN...

2614		50	S	*GREAT FIRE AT BOSTON/ 1872*
2615	47	22	L	*GREAT FIRE AT CHICAGO/ 1871*
2623	13		S	*GREAT INTERNATIONAL BOAT RACE*
2630		22	S	*GREAT MISSISSIPPI STEAM BOAT RACE*
2658		38	S	*GREAT WEST, THE/ (7.15x12.8) 1870*
2725		35	S	*HARBOR OF NEW YORK/ From The Brooklyn Bridge*
2810	7		S	*HIGH BRIDGE AT HARLEM, NY*
2861		17	S	*HOME IN THE WILDERNESS, A/ 1870*
2876		25	S	*HOME ON THE MISSISSIPPI, A/ 1871*
2882	4	10	L	*HOME TO THANKSGIVING/ 1867*
2895	34		S	*HON. ABRAHAM LINCOLN/ (Republican Candidate)*
3008	1	3	L	*HUSKING/ (Painted by E. Johnson) 1861*
3021	4	4	S	*ICE-BOAT RACE ON THE HUDSON*
3349	26	42	S	*KISS ME QUICK/ #700*
3435	44		S	*LANDING OF THE PILGRIMS AT PLYMOUTH MASS*
3440	48	45	L	*LANDSCAPE FRUIT AND FLOWERS/ 1862*
3480		31	L	*LEVEE - NEW ORLEANS, THE/ (19.15x29.14) 1884*
3516	49	43	L	*LIFE OF A FIREMAN / The Metropolitan System*
3517		29	L	*LIFE OF A FIREMAN / The New Era, 1861*
3519	34		L	*LIFE OF A FIREMAN / The Night Alarm, 1854*
3522	5	16	L	*LIFE OF A HUNTER, THE / A Tight Fix, 1861*
3527	6	30	L	*LIFE ON THE PRAIRIE / The Buffalo Hunt, 1862*
3528	20	24	L	*LIFE ON THE PRAIRIE / The Trapper's Defence*
3535	7	13	L	*LIGHTNING EXPRESS" TRAINS, THE / Leaving...*
3848	35		L	*MAC AND ZACHERY TAYLOR, 1851*
3975	8	2	S	*MAPLE SUGARING / EARLY SPRING IN THE N. WOODS*
4116	21	2	L	*MIDNIGHT RACE ON THE MISS. A/ Natchez-Eclipse*
4117		9	S	*MIDNIGHT RACE ON THE MISS., A/ Memphis-J Hwd.*
4139	16	48	L	*MINK TRAPPING/ "PRIME", 1862*
4160		33	L	*MISSISSIPPI IN TIME OF PEACE, 1865*
4420	36	20	L	*NEW ENGLAND WINTER SCENE, 1861*
4473		44	S	*NIGHT EXPRESS, THE/ "The Start"*
4474		47	L	*NIGHT ON THE HUDSON, A/ "Through at Daylight"*
4494	47		S	*NOAH'S ARK / #20/ (Sarony del.)*
4607	27	16	S	*ON THE MISSISSIPPI LOADING COTTON, 1870*
4754	15		S	*PERRY'S VICTORY ON LAKE ERIE*
4763	8		L	*PEYTONA" AND "FASHION*
4859		6	S	*PRAIRIE FIRES OF THE GREAT WEST, 1871*
4870	17	26	L	*PREPARING FOR MARKET, 1856*

5054	37		L	*RAIL SHOOTING ON THE DELAWARE, 1852*
5171	22	1	L	*ROAD - WINTER, THE/ 1853*
5196	9	12	L	*ROCKY MOUNTAINS, THE - EMIGRANTS CROSSING...*
5225		26	S	*ROUTE TO CALIFORNIA, THE/ 1871*
5475	9	36	S	*SHAKERS NEAR LEBANON*
5492	26		L	*SHIPS "ANTARCTIC" OF N.Y. AND "THREE BELLS"*
5546		19	S	*SKATING SCENE / MOONLIGHT, 1868*
5554	20		S	*SLEIGH RACE, THE/ #90/ 1848*
5558		24	S	*SLEIGH RACE, THE / #90*
5580		40	M	*SNOW STORM, THE*
5581	38	39	L	*SNOWED UP - RUFFED GROUSE IN WINTER, 1867*
5659	50		L	*SPLENDID NAVAL TRIUMPH ON THE MISSISSIPPI*
5701	6		S	*STAR OF THE ROAD, THE/ 1849*
5727	25		S	*STEAMBOAT "KNICKERBOCKER"*
5876	23		L	*SUMMER SCENES IN NEW YORK HARBOR/ 1863*
5906	40		L	*SURRENDER OF CORNWALLIS AT YORKTOWN, VA./ 1852*
5907	39		L	*SURRENDER OF GENL. BURGOYNE AT SARATOGA, N.Y.*
5961	27		L	*TAKING THE BACK TRACK - A DANGEROUS...*
5997	31		S	*TERRIFIC COMBAT BETWEEN THE "MONITOR" 2 GUNS*
6050		12	S	*THROUGH THE BAYOU BY TORCHLIGHT*
6051		15	S	*THROUGH TO THE PACIFIC/ 1870*
6158	10	17	L	*TROLLING FOR BLUE FISH/ 1866*
6169	24	27	L	*TROTTING CRACKS" AT THE FORGE/ 1869*
6401		48	S	*VIEW OF NEW YORK*
6409	25		L	*VIEW OF SAN FRANCISCO, CALIFORNIA/ 1851*
6515	16		S	*WASHINGTON AT MOUNT VERNON/ 1852*
6523	22		S	*WASHINGTON CROSSING THE DELAWARE / #69*
6547	24		S	*WASHINGTON TAKING LEAVE OF THE OFFICERS*
6567	19		S	*WATER RAIL SHOOTING/ 1855*
6623		34	L	*WHALE FISHERY / ATTACKING A RIGHT WHALE*
6626	17	28	S	*WHALE FISHERY, THE "LAYING ON"*
6627	11	50	L	*WHALE FISHERY, THE SPERM WHALE IN A FLURR*
6670		46	L	*WILD DUCK SHOOTING - A GOOD DAY'S SPORT/ 1854*
6677	14		S	*WILD TURKEY SHOOTING/ 1871*
6734		13	M	*WINTER EVENING/ 1854*
6736		32	L	*WINTER IN THE COUNTRY - A COLD MORNING*
6737	18	5	L	*WINTER IN THE COUNTRY - GETTING ICE/ 1864*
6738	12	21	L	*WINTER IN THE COUNTRY - THE OLD GRIST MILL*
6740		29	M	*WINTER MORNING/ 1861*

6742		14	S	*WINTER MORNING IN THE COUNTRY/ 1873*
6744		32	M	*WINTER PASTIME/ 1870*
6747	10	30	S	*WINTER SPORTS - PICKEREL FISHING/ 1872*
6773	38		S	*WOODCOCK SHOOTING / #175/ 1855*
6776		23	L	*WOODING UP" ON THE MISSISSIPPI/ 1863*

CHAPTER FIVE

Standard Grading System

To properly evaluate a print certain criteria must be applied. A standard grading system has been in place and used successfully by print collectors for years. Although the grading system is primarily based on the print's condition, the value is determined by a combination of condition, aesthetic appeal and rarity. A collector must have an understanding of the grading standards, so he can properly determine the value of a given piece.

Even the most advanced collector or dealer, at some point, may overlook a small flaw that could possibly drop the grade of a particular print. This becomes very important because a grade level drop will affect its value and may make the print unacceptable for a particular collection.

Caution must be exercised in evaluating a dealer's description of a particular print. I have seen prints described by dealers as being in fine condition despite a well repaired 2 inch tear. The dealer may be offering a visually spectacular print that lacks the requirement of no image damage, necessary for a rating of fine condition. It is for this reason that most dealers and galleries offer a five day return privilege. This allows you time to examine, first hand, the print offered and determine if the print meets the grading level stated. The five day return privilege also allows you time to obtain a second opinion from a reputable person, should you not feel comfortable with the stated grade level. In the final analysis, the dealer's grading of a print may be inaccurate, so a thorough investigation by the purchaser is advisable - although most galleries and dealers are reputable.

The details of a grading system will be discussed, so that a standard will be available for the rapidly expanding number of print collectors. Properly applying these standards to a print will make the use of this price *Guide* an invaluable reference in today's market.

Grading prints for condition

According to the Standard Grading System all prints can be classified into one of five separate categories, based on condition. The five categories, each followed by a numerical value, are: Pristine or Mint (10), Fine (9 or 8), Very Good (7 or 6), Good (5 or 4), Fair to Poor (3 to 1).

The grade assigned to a particular print is primarily a subjective opinion based upon its condition, that is, the extent of the deterioration or damage, if any, incurred over its history. These condition problems can be divided into three categories. Note that condition problems can include any of the following representative examples, but are not limited to these occurrences:

Acts of Nature   Water damage, bleaching from the sun, insect damage, etc.

Human Error   Trimmed margins to accommodate a frame, inappropriate restoration or conservation, incorrect framing or matting, improper storage or handling, etc.

Accidents   Damage caused by broken glass, scuffs, tears, folds, etc.

It is a combination of the various condition problems that will strongly affect the grade level. I have found that if the standards are rigidly adhered to, it is almost impossible to force a print into a higher grade. There will be some aspect of a print which you may question but, upon close examination, the final grade of the print will usually fall within the level required for that grade.

Evaluating condition

The five standard levels of condition are stated below, rating prints from pristine to poor. Following each grade heading, a numerical value (from 10 to 1) has been assigned to show how each grade interacts within the grading scale.

Pristine or Mint (10). Prints in pristine condition are the most sought after by collectors, but least available on the market today. They represent only about one half of one percent of the Currier & Ives prints available today and are quickly acquired by museums and knowledgeable collectors. A pristine print unaffected by time should be nearly perfect with full uncut margins, original brilliance of color and a quality patina. Prints of this grade do become available periodically, but a premium price is paid for these seldom offered, quality prints.

Fine (9 or 8). This is also a very sought after grade of print, representing a very small percentage of the Currier & Ives prints offered today. Bright fresh coloring and a sharp clear impression are characteristic of this grade print. Image defects, such as, stains and tears are unacceptable; however, allowable if present are the very lightest of time toning and margin discoloration. Margins should measure not less than 2" for large, 1 1/2" for medium and 1" for small folio prints.

Very Good (7 or 6). The grade of very good meets the condition requirements acceptable to most collectors. Image defects are unacceptable, including stains and tears; however, allowable if present are light time toning and a very small spot of discoloration that does not distract from the visual appeal of the print. Margins should measure not less than 1 1/2" for large, 1" for medium and 3/4" for small folio prints. A short repaired margin tear not entering the image is acceptable.

Good (5 or 4). This is a grade level collectors consider when higher quality prints are not available or when decorative prints are desirable. Collectors who are seeking scarce and rare prints may purchase these prints in anticipation of upgrading in the future. A print of this quality has good to bright coloring and a clear impression. One defect or a combination of two smaller, less significant flaws is acceptable and should be clearly stated. Allowable would be a short re-paired tear, some discoloration, foxing or an abrasion. Margins for this grade level should be no smaller than 3/4" for large, 1/2" for medium or 3/8" for small folio prints. Margins falling short of these minimums would reduce the value of the print, significantly.

Fair to Poor (3 to 1). This inferior grade of print generally has more than two major flaws or defects, such as, tears, stains, loss of original coloring or inferior paper quality. Since there are no mar-gin sizes required for this grade, a print could have narrow margins or may be trimmed to the image. Full restoration and conservation may make this print visually more attractive but the possibility of it becom-ing a collectable print is slight. Only a collector can determine if he is willing to purchase such prints for his collection. It is a gamble possi-bly worth taking should a print be rare or worthy of collecting for historical purposes.

As stated earlier, prints are generally graded according to a combination of image condition and minimum margin requirements. An exception to this system is that of grading by image condition alone; measurements of the margins are specified but do not enter into the grading of the print.

This grading system is often used by galleries when it is diffi-cult to measure margins, hidden under the mats of framed prints. Some dealers prefer to offer their inventory on lists, making it easier to state a print's grade with a letter or number code. Many use this grading system because a very rare or scarce print with spectacular image condition could be represented as being in fine condition - despite possibly not meeting the margin requirements for that partic-ular grade.

CHAPTER SIX

Conservation

Paper is exceedingly important to us as print collectors and yet, little is known or understood about fine paper. Paper is the essential ingredient used by artists in recording their creations, handed down as sketches, watercolors, pastels and prints. The prints of famous artists' have survived for centuries on fine paper, a tribute to the expertise of papermakers.

Once the basic properties of paper are understood, it will be surprising to you that paper has survived through time as well as it has. A collector's best defense in preserving any print is through understanding what paper is made of and how to avoid damage to it.

Unfortunately, some papers have inherent characteristics which, through some of the methods and materials used in making them, cause them to be weak or to slowly deteriorate. With man's move toward more modern and economical methods of papermaking, so came some disastrous consequences resulting in paper with a shorter life span. Today, collectors are cautioned to carefully examine all prints offered for sale. For further information on the history of papermaking please refer to the bibliography in the *Appendix*.

Prints, purchased from certain collections may have been restored years before a proper understanding of chemicals and their harmful affects on paper were known. Some unqualified framers and collectors have tried to remove surface dirt and stains, themselves, only to have actually set them deeper and more permanently into the paper fibers. A print which you purchased from a reputable dealer or auction house may look good but, in fact, could be a "time bomb" of problems, waiting to go off. Only with proper testing will these problems, if they exist, be known.

To counteract the years of neglect, physical damage to paper is best left to a professional restorer. Only he will have the knowledge and understanding of paper restoration to reverse the damaged condition. Proper restorations will result in satisfactory stain removal, properly mended tears, total paper deacidification and sizing, as required, and bring a print back to its original state.

Environmental affects on paper

Many of our prints come from an unfavorable environment, such as, attics, barns and basements. When purchased, they are usually framed flat against the glass, and often backed with old pine boards or cardboard. There are sometimes marks left in the print from these backings, along with water stains, foxing, mildew or holes from insects. The environment contributes to these conditions in different ways.

Humidity, in excess, encourages the growth of mold which shows up on paper as small areas of discoloration known as foxing. These areas, which look like small dots of rust on the paper's surface, are the result of spores growing on paper and feeding on the size of the paper.

Light can cause the paper to become brittle and fade fugitive colors on prints, a condition which causes a washed-out look and loss of the brilliance associated with a premium print. Prints which have been kept in average light possess a nice patina but those prints which have been subjected to direct sunlight are often dark and lack color intensity.

Heat will accelerate the destruction of paper and make it brittle which often causes it to crumble when handled. Do not hang prints over radiators or in direct sunlight.

Insects prefer a warm and damp environment, so if your print is located in such an atmosphere it is likely that insects will feed upon it. The worst problem with insects, especially silverfish, is that when they move in, rapid deterioration takes place in the form of holes.

Air pollution, such as, smoke and smog is ever increasing and today more frequently damages prints than ever before. These contaminants contain sulfur dioxide which converts to sulfuric acid. The acid penetrates the paper and causes it to discolor and become brittle.

This will occur especially on prints which have boards used for backing, where the space between the boards allows the pollutants to enter and become trapped. The damage manifests itself with dark lines across the print, known as board stains.

The best way of stopping deterioration of a print is with proper conservation and restoration. Proper storage will temporarily arrest or slow down the deterioration but the possibility later exists, that you may not have a salvageable print that can be conserved and restored, thus adversely affecting its value.

CHAPTER SEVEN

Using This Guide

Historical trends

Prior to the dissolving of the Currier & Ives firm in 1907, many people began collecting their prints. Among them was Frederic A. Conningham, who compiled the book, *Currier & Ives Prints - An Illustrated Check List*. Most notable was Fred Peters who assembled the largest collection of Currier & Ives prints in the world at that time.

The popularity of Currier & Ives prints was evident during the early 1920's, with Max Williams republishing the six *Clipper Ship* prints. In 1924 the first major Currier & Ives print auction was held, where an estimated 1,000 prints were offered by the Anderson Gallery. Auction sales for prints escalated - prices for many large folio prints broke the $100 mark, reaching a high of $220 for *Rocky Mountains - Emigrants Crossing the Plains*. In 1928 new records were set at auctions - $1,500 was paid for *American National Game of Baseball* and $3,000 for *Life of a Hunter - A Tight Fix*. During the 1940's to the 1960's prices grew steadily, with popular large folio prints being offered by dealers for $300 to $500, and some of the more popular prints like *Home to Thanksgiving* being offered for $3,700. The period of the 1970's showed growth in prices, as matched sets of the *American Homestead Series* were sold at auction for $1,000 and premium prints were being offered by dealers for over $5,000.

By the mid 1980's, record prices and sharp increases were

realized at auction approximately every six months. The following are some representative prices paid: *Across the Continent*, $18,700; *American Farm Scene #4*, $7,700; *American Forest Scene - Maple Sugaring*, $7,000; *American National Game of Baseball*, $44,000; *Autumn in New England - Cider Making*, $17,600; *Landscape, Fruit and Flowers*, $10,450; *Lightning Express Trains*, $19,800; *Mink Trapping - Prime*, $9,250; *The Rocky Mountains - Emigrants Crossing in the Plains*, $17,600; *Trolling for Blue Fish*, $8,800; and *Wooding Up on the Mississippi*, $16,500. As of April, 1994, the highest recorded price for any Currier print was $63,000 paid for *The Life of a Hunter - A Tight Fix* (private sale), I feel that strong price increases will be seen in years to come but caution should be exercised with regard to a print's condition and rarity.

Pricing prints for this guide

The prices stated in this *Guide* reflect the average retail prices of thousands of Currier & Ives prints in very good original condition being sold in today's market. In arriving at these prices, we took into consideration not only the subject matter of the print but also each particular print's rarity.

Every print and trade card price, for this third edition, was the average of the prices submitted by five prominent dealers, nationally: Robert Kipp, John Rudisill, Robert L. Searjeant, Bob Bascom, and Robert Wieland. Every print title, for the first time ever, had an average price established which involved the input of five dealers with more than 100 years combined experience in selling Currier & Ives prints.

The averaging of prices required more than 30,000 calculations, and every print was included - no exceptions! This method of averaging each dealers submitted prices was the only fair way to factor in each dealers opinion as to retail value for prints in very good condition. For consistency, odd price figures were rounded off to the next even increment (e.g., $256 would be rounded to $260).

Adjusting values for condition

As stated above, the prices set forth in this *Guide* apply only to prints in very good condition. Please consult the section on grading for an explanation of the condition requirements for a print in very good condition. Note that a value of 7 - 6 is given for this grade when judged on a scale of 10 to 1.

This *Guide* lists the print, *American Homestead - Autumn* at a retail value of $500. This is the price at which this print - in very good condition - may be valued in a 1994 market. Suppose you are considering purchasing the same print in fine condition, based upon our Standard Grading System, for $600. Is this a fair retail price? Certainly! If the print meets the criteria for a print in fine condition (grade 9-8) we can justify a 10% to 20% increase in value. Likewise, when we move down a grade to a print in good condition (grade 5-4) we can justify a 10% to 20% reduction in value.

Not quite as objective is the problem of figuring the price for prints in either pristine condition (grade 10) or poor condition (grade 3-1). Some dealers may argue that an increase in value for prints in pristine condition can be as much as 75% above one in very good condition. Likewise, they may argue that a print in poor condition - having no margins - may only be worth 10% of the value of same print in very good condition. It may also be worthy of mentioning that, if you are filling in your collection and require a premium or rare print, you may have to pay an inflated price for that print. However, in years to come the decision to purchase such a print could prove to be economically sound.

Prints requiring restoration

When considering purchasing a print requiring restoration, you should first calculate the total cost to you, by adding the cost of the restoration services to the price of the print in its present condition. Next, bear in mind that upon completion of the work the grade level of a print, in 99% of the cases, will advance only one grade level. To purchase a print in fair condition and expect that print to reach the grade level of a print in very good condition is in my opinion an impossibility. The reality is that, upon completion of the restoration work, you should have a print in good condition. This print may look 50 times better with the stains removed but the physical condition of the print usually will only advance that print one grade level.

Currier & Ives Prints

Con#	Title	Folio	Value
1	AARON CLARK/ Mayor of New York/ (Vig.) N. Currier	S	190
2	ABBEY, THE/ (5.8x7.8)	VS	95
3	ABBEY OF CLARE GALWAY, THE	S	90
4	ABBEY OF THE HOLY CROSS, THE	S	35
5	ABBOTTSFORD	M	125
6	ABIGAIL/ C. Currier	S	80
7	ABIGAIL/ N. Currier	S	80
8	ABIGAIL/ (Vig.)	S	80
9	ABIGAIL/ 1846, N. Currier	S	80
10	ABORIGINAL / Portfolio/ The/ C. Currier	S	135
11	ABRAHAM LINCOLN/ (Bearded portrait) 1862	L	310
12	ABRAHAM LINCOLN / Assassinated April 14th. 1865	M	195
13	ABRAHAM LINCOLN / Sixteenth President/ (Beardless) (11.8x12) 1860	S	325
14	ABRAHAM LINCOLN / Sixteenth President/ (Bust Port) (Vig.)	S	115
15	ABRAHAM LINCOLN / Sixteenth President/ (1/2 Port. To right) Und.	S	115
16	ABRAHAM LINCOLN / Sixteenth President/ (Bust portrait, Bearded)	S	115
17	ABRAHAM LINCOLN / Sixteenth President/ (Half length) (11.10x8.4)	S	115
18	ABRAHAM LINCOLN / Sixteenth President/ (Oval)	S	115
19	ABRAHAM LINCOLN / Sixteenth President/ (12.8x7.8)	S	115
20	ABRAHAM LINCOLN / Sixteenth President/ (Book in hand) (11.6x8.8) 1861	S	125
21	ABRAHAM LINCOLN / Sixteenth President/ (11.7x8.9) 1861	S	115
22	ABRAHAM LINCOLN / Sixteenth President/ (11.8x8.12)	S	115
23	ABRAHAM LINCOLN / The Martyr President/ 1860	L	280
24	ABRAHAM LINCOLN / The Martyr President/ (J. Koehler, Pub.) 1865	L	270
25	ABRAHAM LINCOLN / The Martyr President/ (Oval) (Vig.) 1865	M	175
26	ABRAHAM LINCOLN / The Nation's Martyr/ Und.	S	125
27	ABRAHAM LINCOLN / The Nation's Martyr/ (Golden & Sammons, Pub.)	S	125
28	ABRAHAM LINCOLN / The Nation's Martyr/ (To right, bearded)	L	160
29	ABRAHAM'S DREAM/ (Vig.) 1864	S	140
30	ACADEMY WALTZ/ (Vig.) N. Currier	S	75
31	ACCEPTED, THE/ (11.12x8.9) Und.	S	55
32	ACCOMMODATION TRAIN, THE / (Vig.) 1876	S	405

33	ACROSS THE CONTINENT / "Westward the Course of Empire takes its way"/ (17.14x27.6) 1868 [Old & New BEST 50]	L	16700
34	ACTRESS, THE/ (Vig.) N.Currier	S	85
35	ADA/ (Vig.) N.Currier	S	85
36	ADAM AND EVE DRIVEN OUT OF PARADISE/ (11.5x8.9)	S	120
37	ADAM AND EVE DRIVEN OUT OF PARADISE/ (12.8x8.2)	S	120
38	ADAM AND EVE IN THE GARDEN OF EDEN/ 1848, N. Currier	S	120
39	ADAM NAMING THE CREATURES/ 1847, N. Currier	S	155
40	ADAMS EXPRESS CO., THE/ (16.4x25.12) 1855, N. Currier	L	12800
41	ADELAIDE/ (Oval) 1846, N. Currier	S	80
42	ADELAIDE/ (Oval) 1847, N. Currier	S	80
43	ADELINE/ (3/4 length) (11.14x8.8) N. Currier	S	80
44	ADELINE/ (Vig.) N. Currier	S	80
45	ADELINE/ (Full length) (11.15x8.6) 1848, N. Currier	S	80
46	ADELINE/ (Left arm on fur piece) N. Currier	S	80
47	ADELINE/ (11.13x8.10) 1849, N. Currier	S	80
48	ADELINE/ (Seated at piano) (Vig.) N. Currier	S	80
49	ADIEU AT FONTAIN-BLEAU/ (Vig.) Und.	L	125
50	ADMIRAL FARRAGUT'S FLEET ENGAGING THE REBEL BATTERIES AT PORT HUDSON	S	360
51	ADMIRAL PORTER'S FLEET RUNNING THE REBEL BLOCKADE OF THE MISS./ 1863	S	360
52	AESTHETIC CRAZE/ (Vig.) 1882	S	180
53	AFFAIR OF HONOR, AN / "The Critical Moment"/ (Vig.)	S	185
54	AFFAIR OF HONOR, AN / "Stray Shot"/ (Vig.) 1884	S	185
55	AFRICA/ (Vig.) 1870	S	75
56	AFRICA/ Und. N. Currier	S	80
57	AFRICAN JUNGLE, THE/ (Puzzle Print) Und. N. Currier	S	325
58	AFTER MARRIAGE / "Experience"/ (Vig.) (Companion to #475) N. Currier	L	205
59	AFTER THE BATH/ (Vig.) Und. N. Currier	S	85
60	AGE OF BRASS, THE/ (Vig.) 1869	S	320
61	AGE OF IRON, THE / (Vig.) 1869	S	320
62	AGNES/ (3/4 length, Seated) N. Currier	S	80
62	AGNES/ (3/4 length, Standing) N. Currier	S	80
64	AGNES/ (J. Grevedon, del.) 1846, N. Currier	S	80
65	A. GOLDSMITH'S B.G. DRIVER BY VOLUNTEER/ (Vig.) 1879	S	285
66	AGRICULTURAL HALL/ (7.13x12.15) 1876	S	225
67	AGRICULTURAL SOCIETY, THE/ (Award Cert.) (14.15x19.10)	S	115
68	AHEAD OF THE WORLD / The Great Am. Four Track Railroad/ (Rarest Rail Road Print)	L	21000
69	AIN'T I SOME/ (Vig.) N. Currier	S	195

All prints are published by Currier & Ives unless otherwise stated.

70	AIN'T THEY CUNNING?/ (8.10x12.6)	S	120
71	ALABAMA STATE MARCH, THE/ (Vig.) N. Currier	S	90
72	ALARM, THE/ (10x14) 1868	S	455
73	ALEXANDER/ (Spirited White Horse)	S	200
74	ALICE/ 1844, N. Currier	S	80
75	ALICE/ (11x7.14) N. Currier	S	80
76	ALICE/ (Vig.)	S	80
77	ALL BROKE UP/ (Vig.) (Companion to #5899) 1884	S	235
78	ALL HAIL THE POWER OF CHRIST'S NAME	S	20
79	ALL NICE AND HOT/ (12.2x8.13) (Companion to #3006) N. Currier	S	190
80	ALL PRIMED	S	90
81	ALL RIGHT/ (12.5x8.14) (Companion to #84)	S	165
82	ALL SO TIRED	S	90
83	ALL THE WORLD IS SCHEMING/ (Vig.) (Companion to #81)	S	95
84	ALL WRONG/ (12.5x8.14) N. Currier	S	165
85	ALMIRA/ 1845, N. Currier	S	80
86	ALMIRA/ (Similar to #84) N. Currier	S	80
87	ALNWICK CASTLE, SCOTLAND	M	125
88	ALONZO AND CORA/ N. Currier	S	95
89	AMANDA/ (Letter in hand) N. Currier	S	80
90	AMANDA/ (11.12x8.11) 1846, N. Currier	S	80
91	AMANDA/ (3/4 Length) (Vig.) N. Currier	S	80
92	AMATEUR MUSCLE IN THE SHELL/ (11.2x15.11) 1876	M	395
93	AMATEUR MUSCLE IN THE SHELL/ 1879	S	320
94	AMATEUR MUSCLE IN THE SHELL/ 1880	TC	70
95	AMBUSCADE, THE/ (Winter Scene) (11.6x15.7)	M	1500
96	AMELIA/ 1845, N. Currier	S	80
97	AMELIA/ (Marine scene, through a window) N. Currier	S	80
98	AMELIA/ (Full Length Portrait) (12.3x8.10) 1845, N. Currier	S	80
99	AMELIA/ (Full Length) (12.2x8.10) 1845, N. Currier	S	80
100	AMELIA/ (Half Length) (Vig.) N. Currier	S	80
101	AMELIA/ (Bust Portrait) (Vig.)	S	80
102	AMERICA/ (Half Length, Scenery in background) N.Currier	S	80
103	AMERICA/ (Half Length, Girls Head, Indian Dress) N. Currier	S	80
104	AMERICA/ (3/4 View of archery bow) (Vig.) N. Currier	S	240
105	AMERICAN AUTUMN FRUITS/ (Vig.) 1875	S	145
106	AMERICAN AUTUMN FRUITS/ (20x27.14) 1865	L	1900
107	AMERICAN BEAUTY, THE/ (Vig.)	S	80
108	AMERICAN BROOK TROUT/ (8.7x12.7) 1872	S	335

109	AMERICAN BUFFALOES	S	855
110	AMERICAN CHAMPION YACHT "PURITAN", THE/ (9.12x14.1) 1885	S	415
111	AMERICAN CHOICE FRUITS/ (17x24) 1869	L	1325
112	AMERICAN CHOICE FRUITS/ Und.	L	1350
113	AMERICAN CLIPPER SHIP OFF SANDY HOOK LIGHT IN A SNOW-STORM/ (8.4x12.12) (Very rare)	S	1350
114	AMERICAN CLIPPER SHIP "BREWER"/ (Only one copy known)	S	2175
115	AMERICAN CLIPPER SHIP "WITCH OF THE WAVE"/ (8.14x12.14) [Old BEST 50]	S	1075
116	AMERICAN CLUB HUNT / "Halt On The Scent"/ 1884	S	230
117	AMERICAN CLUB HUNT / "Taking A Header"/ 1884	S	230
118	AMERICAN COAST SCENE / Desert Rock Light House, Maine	S	435
119	AMERICAN COAST SCENE / Desert Rock	L	3100
120	AMERICAN COTTAGE No. 1/ (8.2x5.5) N. Currier	S	175
121	AMERICAN COUNTRY LIFE / "May Morning"/ (16.14x23.15) 1855	L	2300
122	AMERICAN COUNTRY LIFE / "October Afternoon"/ (16.11x23.14) 1855	L	2300
123	AMERICAN COUNTRY LIFE / "Pleasures of Winter"/ (16.14x24) 1855	L	2375
124	AMERICAN COUNTRY LIFE / "Summer's Evening"/ (16.11x23.14) 1855	L	2350
125	AMERICAN DEAD GAME/ (19.11x27.11) 1866	L	650
126	AMERICAN ECLIPSE/ 1879	S	280
127	AMERICAN ECLIPSE / The Celebrated Racing Horse/ 1880	S	285
128	AMERICAN EXPRESS TRAIN/ 1853, N. Currier	S	1950
129	AMERICAN EXPRESS TRAIN/ (Parsons) (16.4x25.12) 1855	L	12400
130	AMERICAN EXPRESS TRAIN/ (Palmer) (18x31) 1864 [New BEST 50]	L	12500
131	AMERICAN FARM LIFE/ 1868	M	640
132	AMERICAN FARM SCENE, AN / "In The Olden Time"	S	295
133	AMERICAN FARM SCENES / No.3 (Autumn) (16.15x24.1)	L	3625
134	AMERICAN FARM SCENES / No.1 (Spring) (16.15x24.2)	L	3450
135	AMERICAN FARM SCENES / No.2 (Summer) (16.15x24.1)	L	3400
136	AMERICAN FARM SCENES / No.4 (Winter) (16.13x23.15) [Old & New BEST 50]	L	7100
137	AMERICAN FARM WINTER/ (One of views on sheet #3438) (2.11x4.3)	VS	365
138	AMERICAN FARMYARD - EVENING/ (16.13x23.14) 1857	L	2400
139	AMERICAN FARMYARD - MORNING/ (16.13x23.15) 1857	L	2400
140	AMERICAN FEATHERED GAME / MALLARD AND CANVAS BACKED DUCKS/ (First state) (Vig.) N. Currier	M	490
141	AMERICAN FEATHERED GAME / MALLARD AND CANVAS BACKED DUCKS/ (16.4x13.8) (Oval) N. Currier	M	490
142	AMERICAN FEATHERED GAME / PARTRIDGES/ (First state) Und. (Vig.) N. Currier	M	490
143	AMERICAN FEATHERED GAME / PARTRIDGES/ (16.5x13.8) (Oval) 1854, N. Currier	M	490

All prints are published by Currier & Ives unless otherwise stated.

144	AMERICAN FEATHERED GAME / WOOD DUCK AND GOLDEN EYE/ (First state) Und. (Vig.) N. Currier	M	490
145	AMERICAN FEATHERED GAME / WOOD DUCK AND GOLDEN EYE/ (16.4x13.7) (Oval) 1854, N. Currier	M	490
146	AMERICAN FEATHERED GAME / WOODCOCK AND SNIPE/ (First state) Und. (Vig.) N. Currier	M	490
147	AMERICAN FEATHERED GAME / WOODCOCK AND SNIPE/ (16.7x13.8) (Oval) 1854, N. Currier	M	490
148	AMERICAN FIELD SPORTS / "A Chance for Both Barrels"/ (18.10x26.12) 1857	L	3275
149	AMERICAN FIELD SPORTS / "Flush'd"/ (18.9x26.14) 1857 [Old BEST 50]	L	3575
150	AMERICAN FIELD SPORTS / "On A Point"/ (18.12x26.12) 1857	L	3275
151	AMERICAN FIELD SPORTS / "Retrieving"/ (18.9x26.12) 1857	L	3275
152	AMERICAN FIREMAN, THE / "Always Ready"/ 1858	M	1325
153	AMERICAN FIREMAN, THE / "Facing the Enemy"/ (17.2x13.7) 1858	M	1325
154	AMERICAN FIREMAN, THE / "Prompt to the Rescue"/ (17.5x13.12) 1858	M	1325
155	AMERICAN FIREMAN, THE / "Rushing to the Conflict"/ (17.7x13.6) 1858	M	1325
156	AMERICAN FOREST GAME / (19.11x27.14) 1866	L	895
157	AMERICAN FOREST SCENE / "Maple Sugaring"/ (18.11x27) 1856, N. Currier [Old & New BEST 50]	L	11200
158	AMERICAN FRONTIER LIFE / "The Hunter's Stratagem"/ (19x27.6) 1862	L	6000
159	AMERICAN FRONTIER LIFE / "On the Warpath"/ (18.9x27.6) 1863	L	6000
160	AMERICAN FRUIT PIECE/ (Fruit with watermelon) (8.7x12.7)	S	150
161	AMERICAN FRUIT PIECE/ (20.5x27.5) 1859	L	1950
162	AMERICAN FRUITS/ 1861	S	160
163	AMERICAN GAME/ (19.7x27.10) 1866	L	825
164	AMERICAN GAME FISH/ (19.10x27.12) 1866	L	1025
165	AMERICAN GIRL / By Amos' Cassius M. Clay Jr./ 1871	S	270
166	AMERICAN GIRL / RECORD 2:16 1/2/ 1871	S	270
167	AMERICAN GIRL AND LADY THORN / In Their Great Match for $2000/ 1869	L	1500
168	AMERICAN HOMESTEAD - AUTUMN/ (7.15x12.8) 1869 [New BEST 50]	S	500
169	AMERICAN HOMESTEAD - AUTUMN/ (Five trees shown, one copy known) Und.	S	2100
170	AMERICAN HOMESTEAD - SPRING/ (7.15x12.8) 1869 [New BEST 50]	S	400
171	AMERICAN HOMESTEAD - SUMMER/ (7.15x12.8) 1868 [New BEST 50]	S	400
172	AMERICAN HOMESTEAD - WINTER/ (8x12.8) 1868 [Old & New BEST 50]	S	775
173	AMERICAN HUNTING SCENES / "An Early Start"/ (18.15x27.11) 1863 [New BEST 50]	L	5900
174	AMERICAN HUNTING SCENES / "A Good Chance"/ (18.10x27.11) 1863 [Old BEST 50]	L	5800
175	AMERICAN JOCKEY CLUB RACES, JEROME PARK/ (16.6x26.4)	L	1500
176	AMERICAN LANDSCAPE / "Early Morning" (15.12x23.4)	L	1800

177	AMERICAN LANDSCAPE / SACANDAGA CREEK	VS	215
178	AMERICAN LANDSCAPES/ (Four prints on one page)	S	735
179	AMERICAN MOUNTAIN SCENERY/ (9.9x16.12) 1868	M	470
180	AMERICAN NATIONAL GAME OF BASEBALL, THE / "Grand Match For the Championship..."/ (19.14x29.14) 1862 [Old & New BEST 50]	L	31900
181	AMERICAN PATRIOT'S DREAM, THE/ 1861	M	205
182	AMERICAN PRIVATEER "GENERAL ARMSTRONG"/ (8.1x12.12)	S	560
183	AMERICAN PRIZE FRUIT/ 1862	L	1800
184	AMERICAN PRIZE FRUIT/ (Plate with knife and cut melon)	S	160
185A	AMERICAN RAILROAD SCENE/ 1872	S	1500
185A	AMERICAN RAILROAD SCENE/ 1874	S	1500
185	AMERICAN RAILROAD SCENE / Lightning Express Leaving the Junction/ (1st State) [New BEST 50]	L	14800
186	AMERICAN RAILROAD SCENE / Lightning Express Leaving the Junction/ (2nd State)	L	13500
187	AMERICAN RAILROAD SCENE / "Snowbound"/ (8.8x12.7) 1871 [Old & New BEST 50]	S	3425
188	AMERICAN RAILROAD SCENE / "Snowbound"/ (8.8x12.7) 1872	S	3425
189	AMERICAN RAILWAY SCENE AT HORNELLSVILLE/ (19x29) 1874	L	12600
190	AMERICAN RIVER SCENERY / "View on the Androscoggin, Maine"/ (9.10x16.14)	M	580
191	AMERICAN SCENERY, PALENVILLE, N.Y./ (8.1x12.5)	S	225
192	AMERICAN SHIP RESCUING THE OFFICERS AND CREW OF A BRITISH/ (11.9x16.6) 1863	M	660
193	AMERICAN SLOOP YACHT MAYFLOWER/ 1886	L	1825
194	AMERICAN SLOOP YACHT VOLUNTEER/ (19.8x28) 1888	L	1825
195	AMERICAN SPECKLED BROOK TROUT/ (16x22) 1864	L	1275
196	AMERICAN STEAMBOATS ON THE HUDSON/ (19.5x33.2) 1874	L	2750
197	AMERICAN SUMMER FRUITS/ (Vig.) 1875	S	160
198	AMERICAN TAR, THE / "Don't Give Up the Ship"/ (11.14x8.8) 1845, N. Currier	S	340
199	AMERICAN THOROUGHBREDS/ (7.14x12.5)	S	365
200	AMERICAN TROTTING STUD, ETHAN ALLEN, POCAHONTAS/ (16.13x26.2) 1866	L	2650
201	AMERICAN TROTTING STUD, MAMBRINO PILOT, FLORA TEMPLE/ (16.12x25.11) 1866	L	2650
202	AMERICAN TROTTING STUD, THE / Widow McChree-Hambletonian/ 1867	L	2650
203	AMERICAN VIEWS/ (Four views on one sheet)	S	680
204	AMERICAN WHALER/ (8.9x12.13) N. Currier	S	1400
205	AMERICAN WHALERS CRUSHED IN ICE / "Burning the Wrecks to..."/ (8.8x12.8) [Old & New BEST 50]	S	1700
206	AMERICAN WINTER SCENE, AN/ (5.8x7.8) (Very rare) (Oval) [New BEST 50]	VS	1800

207	AMERICAN WINTER SCENES / "Evening"/ (16.12x24.2) 1854 [New BEST 50]	L	6300
208	AMERICAN WINTER SCENES / "Morning"/ (16.8x24.1) 1854 [Old & New BEST 50]	L	6200
209	AMERICAN WINTER SPORTS / "Deer Shooting "On Shattagee"/ (17.14x25.14) 1855 N.Currier [Old BEST 50]	L	6900
210	AMERICAN WINTER SPORTS / Trout Fishing "On Chateaugay Lake"/ (First State) (Prtd. Endicott) 1856 N.Currier [Old & New BEST 50]	L	7100
211	AMERICAN WINTER SPORTS / Trout Fishing "On Chateaugay Lake"/ (Second state) 1856, N. Currier	L	7100
212	AMERICAN WINTER SPORTS / Trout Fishing "On Chateaugay Lake"/ (Third state) 1856, Currier & Ives	L	6900
213	AMONG THE HILLS	S	265
214	AMONG THE PINES / "A First Settlement"/ (8.8x12.8)	S	360
215	ANCIENT CROSS OF CLONMACNOISE	S	20
216	ANDREW JACKSON / Seventh President of the U.S./ (11.8x9.2) N. Currier	S	145
217	ANDREW JACKSON, THE / The Union "It Must and shall be Preserved	M	215
218	ANDREW JOHNSON / Seventeenth President of the U.S.	M	240
219	ANGEL FOOTSTEPS/ (Vig.) 1878	S	230
220	ANGEL GABRIEL, THE	S	20
221	ANGEL OF PRAYER, THE/ (12x9.4) (Oval)	S	20
222	ANGEL OF PRAYER, THE/ (12x9.4) 1875	S	20
223	ANGEL OF THE BATTLEFIELD/ 1865	S	90
224	ANGEL OF THE COVENANT/ (12.2x9.5) (Oval)	S	20
225	ANGEL VOICES SWEETLY CALLING / (Man pushing cart) (9.12x12.12)	S	150
226	ANGELINE/ (Half length, flowers under bonnet) N. Currier	S	80
227	ANGELINE/ (11.12x8.10) 1846, N. Currier	S	80
228	ANGELS OF THE BATTLEFIELD, THE/ (14.10x17.6)	M	180
229	ANIMAL CREATION/ (8.10x12.3) 1875	S	180
230	ANN/ (12x8.3) 1848, N. Currier	S	85
231	ANN/ (To Right) (11.11x8.4) N. Currier	S	85
232	ANN/ (To Left) N. Currier	S	85
233	ANN/ (11.8x8) N. Currier	S	85
234	ANN MARIA/ (3/4 Length) 1846, N. Currier	S	80
235	ANN MARIA/ (Half Length) (Vig.) N. Currier	S	80
236	ANN MARIA/ (3/4 Length) 1849, N. Currier	S	80
237	ANN MARIA/ (Half Length) (Vig.) N. Currier	S	80
238	ANNIE/ (11x9) (Vig.)	S	80
239	ANNUNCIATION, THE/ 1844, N. Currier	S	20
240	ANTELOPE SHOOTING / "Fatal Curiosity"/ (12.14x18.4)	M	1400
241	ANXIOUS MOMENT / "A Three Pounder Sure"/ (14x18.8) 1874	M	2650

242	ANXIOUS MOTHER, THE/ (8.8x12.8)	S	125
243	ANXIOUS NURSE, THE	S	120
244	ANY PORT IN A STORM	S	105
245	ANY PORT IN A STORM/ (Vig.) 1884	S	130
246	APOLLO / Sired by Seneca Chief, by Rysdyk's/ 1884	S	275
247	APOLLO / Sired by Seneca Chief, by Rysdyk's/ (Vig.) 1885	M	440
248	APPLES / (Painted by W.M. Brown) 1868	S	170
249	APPLES AND PLUMS / First Premium/ 1870	S	160
250	APRIL SHOWERS, THE/ (L. Maurer, del.)	M	265
251	AQUARIUM, THE	S	120
252	ARABIAN/ 1846, N. Currier	S	120
253	ARABS BRIDE, THE/ (12x8.15) N. Currier	S	70
254	ARABY'S DAUGHTER/ (12.6x8.10) N. Currier	S	75
255	ARABY'S DAUGHTER/ (Full Length)	S	75
256	ARCHED BRIDGE, THE/ (2.8x4.11)	VS	175
257	ARCHITECTURAL DESIGNS / Plan of Capitol of Indiana/ N. Currier	S	395
258	ARCHITECTURAL DESIGNS / Temple of Thesus/ N. Currier	S	210
259	ARCHITECTURAL DESIGNS Pyonstyle Doric/ N. Currier	S	210
260	ARCHITECTURAL DESIGNS OF DORIC/ N. Currier	S	210
261	ARCHITECTURAL DESIGNS OF DORIC CAPITALS/ N. Currier	S	210
262	ARCHITECTURAL PLAN / ASTOR'S HOTEL/ (Davis, arch't.) Stodart and Currier	S	455
263	ARCHITECTURAL PLAN / ASTOR'S HOTEL/ 1832 Stodart and Currier	S	455
264	ARCTIC EXPLORING YACHT JEANNETTE/ 1881	L	1825
265	ARGUING THE POINT/ (18.5x23.14) 1855, N. Currier [New BEST 50]	L	4400
266	ARION, By Electioneer/ (Vig.) 1892	S	275
267	ARISTOCRACY OF COLOR/ N. Currier	S	85
268	ARISTOTLE/ (Low wheel sulky) 1893	M	465
269	ARISTOTLE BYARIOSTOS / As A Producer and Stock Horse/ 1893	M	475
270	ARKANSAS TRAVELLER, THE / (7.14x12.8) (Companion to #6248) 1870	S	280
271	ARMOURED STEEL CRUISER "BROOKLYN"/ 1893	M	260
272	ARMOURED STEEL CRUISER "BROOKLYN"/ Und.	M	260
273	ARMOURED STEEL CRUISER "NEW YORK"/ 1893	M	260
274	ART GALLERY/ (7.12x12.12)	S	265
275	ART OF MAKING MONEY/ (Rebus) [Old BEST 50]	S	585
276	ARTHUR CHAMBERS / Lightweight Champion	M	315
277	ARTIST IN HAIR/ (12.11x8.1) 1872	S	165
278	ARTISTS' CREEK / North Conway	M	930
279	AS HE WAS / A Young Man of Fashion	S	185

280	AS KIND AS A KITTEN/ (Vig.) 1879	S	225
281	AS KIND AS A KITTEN/ (Man on Horse) (Vig.)	S	225
282	ASCENSION, THE/ (11.14x8.11) 1844, N. Currier	S	20
283	ASCENSION, THE / La ascencion/ N. Currier	S	20
284	ASCENSION OF CHRIST	S	20
285	ASCENSION OF THE VIRGIN/ (12.13x8.10) 1848, N. Currier	S	20
286	ASIA/ (Oriental type girl) (Upright) (Vig.) 1870	S	75
287	ASIA/ (Not Upright) (Vig.)	S	75
288	ASIA/ (Half Length) (Vig.) (Companion to #2364) N. Currier	S	75
289	ASKING A HAND/ (Comic) (Vig.) (Companion to #2364) 1887	S	220
290	ASLEEP/ (8.10x12.13) (Companion to #326) 1848, N. Currier	S	90
291	ASSASSINATION OF PRESIDENT LINCOLN, THE/ (7.15x12.5) 1865	S	170
292	ASSUMPTION OF THE HOLY VIRGIN	S	20
293	ASTORIA INSTITUTE/ N. Currier	S	215
294	AT THE FAIR GROUNDS/ (High-wheeled sulkies) (19.2x28.4) 1890 [New BEST 50]	L	2000
295	AT THE FAIR GROUNDS/ (Low-wheeled sulkies) (19.2x28.4) 1894	L	1550
296	AT THE FOOT OF THE CROSS	S	20
297	ATALIBA RECEIVING THE LAST EMBRACES OF HIS FAMILY/ N. Currier	S	55
298	ATLANTIC MISSISSIPPI AND OHIO Railroad/ (17.12x27.12) 1864	L	12500
299	ATTACK AND MASSACRE OF CREW OF SHIP "TONQUIN"/ (7.7x3.7)	VS	235
300	ATTACK OF THE GUNBOATS UPON THE CITY AND CASTLE OF SAN JUAN DE ULLOA/ N. Currier	S	210
301	ATTACK OF THE LION/ (11.11x8.8) N. Currier	S	110
302	ATTACK ON THE CASTLE OF CHAPULTEPEC/ (7.10x12.4) 1848, N. Currier	S	125
303	ATTACK ON THE HOME GUARD/ (22x18) (Companion to #1598) 1864	L	600
304	ATTACK ON THE WIDOW M'CORMACK'S HOUSE/ (8.3x12.5) 1848, N. Currier	S	90
305	ATTACKING THE BADGER/ (8.6x12.11) N. Currier	S	195
306	AUBURN HORSE, THE/ (16.11x25.15) 1866	L	1450
307	AUGUSTA/ (12.1x8.2) 1848, N. Currier	S	75
308	AUGUSTA/ (3/4 length, seated) N. Currier	S	75
309	AUGUSTA / In The Roll of Bayadere/ 1837, N. Currier	S	75
310	AUTHOR, THE/ (Frontispiece)	VS	110
311	AUTUMN/ (From an English Print) (8x12.8) N.Currier	S	135
312	AUTUMN/ (Girl's Head) (Vig.) 1871, Currier & Ives	S	75
313	AUTUMN/ (3/4 Length) (Vig.)	S	80
314	AUTUMN/ (Girl with grapes) (Vig.)	M	125
315	AUTUMN CROSS, THE/ (Vig.)	S	25

316	AUTUMN FOLIAGE	S	155
317	AUTUMN FRUITS/ (12.8x17.10) 1861	M	405
318	AUTUMN FRUITS	S	160
319	AUTUMN FRUITS/ (5.8x7.8) Oval	S	160
320	AUTUMN FLOWERS/ (5.8x7.8) Oval	S	155
321	AUTUMN GIFT, THE/ (7.15x18.8) 1870	S	165
322	AUTUMN IN NEW ENGLAND / "Cider Making"/ (14.13x25.4) 1866 [Old & New BEST 50]	L	12600
323	AUTUMN IN THE ADIRONDACKS / Lake Harrison/ (7.15x12.7)	S	305
324	AUTUMN ON LAKE GEORGE/ (8.7x12.8)	S	250
325	AVAILABLE CANDIDATE, AN / "The One Qualification For A Whig President"/ (Vig.)	S	155
326	AWAKE/ (8.10x12.13) (Companion to #290) 1848, N. Currier	S	90
327	AWFUL CONFLAGRATION OF THE STEAM BOAT LEXINGTON/ (8.7x12) (First State) [New BEST 50]	S	4050
328	AWFUL CONFLAGRATION OF THE STEAM BOAT LEXINGTON/ (8.7x12)	S	3625
329	AWFUL EXPLOSION OF THE "PEACEMAKER"/ (8x12.13) 1844, N. Currier	S	260
330	AWFUL WRECK OF THE MAGNIFICENT STEAMER "ATLANTIC"/ (7.14x12.13) 1846, N. Currier	S	295
331	AXTELL / Record 2:12	S	270
332	AXTELL / Record 2:12/ (J. Cameron, del.) 1890	L	1400
333	AZTEC CHILDREN, THE/ (Vig.)	S	120

B

Con#	Title	Folio	Value
334	BABES IN THE WOODS / "Young Partridges"/ 1868	S	465
335	BABY'S FIRST VISIT/ (8.4x12.12)	S	80
336	BACKED TO WIN/ (Vig.) 1880	S	185
337	BAD BREAK/ (Vig.) 1879	S	305
338	BAD BREAK, A / Going It Like Bricks/ (Vig.)	S	305
339	BAD CASE OF HEAVES, A/ 1875	S	290
340	BAD DREAM, A/ N. Currier	S	175
341	BAD EGG, A/ (12.5x8.8) N. Currier	S	175
342	BAD EGG, A / "Fuss and Feathers" N. Currier	S	205
343	BAD HUSBAND, THE	S	140
344	BAD MAN AT THE HOUR OF DEATH, THE/ (11.8x8.10)	S	85
345	BAD POINT ON A GOOD POINTER, A/ (Vig.) 1879	S	195

All prints are published by Currier & Ives unless otherwise stated.

346	BAD POINT ON A GOOD POINTER, A/ 1879	TC	65
347	BAD STREAK, A/ 1879	S	125
348	BALK ON A SWEEPSTAKE/ (Vig.) 1881	S	285
349	BALL PLAY DANCE/ (Catlin, del.)	M	1525
350	BALLS ARE ROLLING / Clear The Track	S	215
351	BALLYNAHINCH/ (Ireland)	S	75
352	BALTIMORE BAKERY/ (17.8x11.1)	M	345
353	BALTIMORE CLIPPER/ (8.9x12.15) (Rare)	S	1700
354	BALTIMORE IN 1880/ 1880	S	480
355	BALTIMORE ORIOLE/ (7.14X4.14)	VS	170
356	BANKS OF DOON, THE/ (14.15x20.4)	M	115
357	BAPTISM OF CHRIST / #150/ (11.14x8.10)	S	20
358	BAPTISM OF JESUS CHRIST/ (11.12x8.7)	S	20
359	BAPTISM OF JESUS CHRIST	S	20
360	BAPTISM OF JESUS CHRIST/ (24.2x18.2) 1893	L	50
361	BAPTISM OF POCAHONTAS, THE	S	160
362	BAPTISMAL CERTIFICATE	S	50
363	BARBER, THE/ (12x8.10)	S	190
364	BARD, THE/ (Vig.) 1887	S	235
365	BARE CHANCE, A/ (Vig.) 1879	S	260
366	BARE CHANCE, A/ 1879	TC	80
367	BAREFACED CHEEK/ 1881	S	245
368	BAREFOOT BOY, THE/ (Stone signed FFP) (11.14x8.6) 1872	S	210
369	BAREFOOT BOY, THE/ (11.9x8) 1873	S	190
370	BAREFOOT GIRL, THE/ (11.9x8.1)	S	180
371	BARK THEOXENA, THE/ (17x24.6) (Rare) [Old BEST 50]	L	7900
372	BARON'S CASTLE, THE/ (7.15x12.5)	S	85
373	BARSQUALDO'S STATUE/ (Only authorized edition)	S	245
374	BASE HIT, A/ (Vig.) 1882	S	315
375	BASS FISHING / at Macomb's Dam/ (12.8x20.2) 1852	L	2850
376	BASS FISHING/ (7.15x12.7) Und. N. Currier [New BEST 50]	S	1000
377	BATTERY NEW YORK, THE / By Moonlight/ (8.1x12.4) N. Currier	S	600
378	BATTLE AT BUNKER'S HILL/ (7.15x12.3) N. Currier	S	265
379	BATTLE AT BUNKER'S HILL	S	260
380	BATTLE AT CEDAR MOUNTAIN, THE/ (9x11.3)	S	205
381	BATTLE AT CEDAR MOUNTAIN, THE/ (8.1x12.10)	S	205
382	BATTLE AT FIVE FORKS, VA, THE/ (8.3x12.9)	S	205
383	BATTLE AT MISSIONARY RIDGE, GA	S	205
384	BATTLE OF ANTIETAM, MD, THE/ (7.15x12.7)	S	210

385	BATTLE OF BATON ROUGE, LA/ (8x12.8)	S	215
386	BATTLE OF BENTONVILLE, NORTH CAROLINA	S	205
387	BATTLE OF BOONVILLE / OR THE GREAT MISSOURI "LYON" HUNT	S	215
388	BATTLE OF BUNKER'S HILL	S	260
389	BATTLE OF BUENA VISTA/ (8.4x12.10) 1847, N. Currier	S	130
390	BATTLE OF BUENA VISTA/ (8.3x12.13) 1847, N. Currier	S	135
391	BATTLE OF BULL RUN, VA/ (7.13x12.5)	S	220
392	BATTLE OF CEDAR CREEK, VA/ (7.13x12.10)	S	205
393	BATTLE OF CERRO GORDO/ (8.4x12.11) 1847, N. Currier	S	130
394	BATTLE OF CHAMPION HILLS, MISS	S	205
395	BATTLE OF CHANCELLORSVILLE, VA	S	200
396	BATTLE OF CHATTANOOGA, TENN/ (7.15x12.7)	S	205
397	BATTLE OF CHICKAMAUGA, GA/ (8.2x12.10)	S	205
398	BATTLE OF CHURUBUSCO/ (7.14x12.11) 1847, N. Currier	S	130
399	BATTLE OF CLONTARF/ (Ireland) N. Currier	S	70
400	BATTLE OF COAL HARBOR, VA	S	200
401	BATTLE OF CORINTH, MISS/ (8.3x12.11)	S	200
402	BATTLE OF FAIR OAKS, VA/ (8.1x12.8) 1862	S	225
403	BATTLE OF FAIR OAKS, VA/ (15.7x21.15) 1862	L	1000
404	BATTLE OF FORT DOUGLAS	S	190
405	BATTLE OF FREDERICKSBURG, VA/ (7.15x12.13) 1862	S	210
406	BATTLE OF GETTYSBURG, PA, THE/ (15.10x22.7) 1863	L	1425
407	BATTLE OF GETTYSBURG, PA, THE/ (8x12.8)	S	255
408	BATTLE OF JONESBORO, GA/ 1864	S	210
409	BATTLE OF LEXINGTON, THE	S	220
410	BATTLE OF MALVERN HILL, VA	S	205
411	BATTLE OF MEXICO, THE/ (8.4x13) 1847, N. Currier	S	125
412	BATTLE OF MILL SPRING, KY	S	205
413	BATTLE OF MILL SPRING, KY/ (8.2x12.9)	S	205
414	BATTLE OF MONTEREY/ (8.7x12.11) 1846, N. Currier	S	125
415	BATTLE OF MURFREESBORO, TENN/ 1862	L	1050
416	BATTLE OF NEW ORLEANS, THE/ (Demolished Cannon) 1842, N. Currier	S	210
417	BATTLE OF NEW ORLEANS, THE/ (8.10x12.11) N. Currier	S	190
418	BATTLE OF NEW ORLEANS, THE/ (Cannon facing left)	S	190
419	BATTLE OF NEWBURN, NC, THE/ (8.2x12.6) 1862	S	200
420	BATTLE OF PEA RIDGE, ARK/ 1862	S	230
421	BATTLE OF PEA RIDGE, THE	L	835
422	BATTLE OF PETERSBURG, VA/ (8.2x12.8)	S	205
423	BATTLE OF PITTSBURGH, TENN, THE/ 1862	S	200

424	BATTLE OF PITTSBURGH, TENN, THE	S	200
425	BATTLE OF PITTSBURGH, TENN, THE	L	920
426	BATTLE OF RESACA DE LA PALMA/ (7.14x12.12) 1846, N. Currier	S	125
427	BATTLE OF SACREMENTO/ 1847, N. Currier	S	130
428	BATTLE OF SACREMENTO, THE	S	130
429	BATTLE OF SHARPSBURG, THE	S	200
430	BATTLE OF SPOTTSYLVANIA	S	205
431	BATTLE OF BOYNE	S	60
432	BATTLE OF THE GIANTS / "Buffalo Bulls on the American Prairies"/ (8.14x12.8)	S	1475
433	BATTLE OF THE KINGS, THE/ 1884	L	1525
434	BATTLE OF THE KINGS, THE	L	1525
435	BATTLE OF THE WILDERNESS, VA, THE	L	1075
336	BATTLE OF THE WILDERNESS, VA, THE	S	205
437	BATTLE OF WATERLOO/ N. Currier	S	150
438	BATTLE OF WILLIAMSBURG, VA	S	205
439	BATTLE OF WILLIAMSBURG, VA/ (16x22.14) 1862	L	1075
440	BAY GELDING "ALLEY"/ By Volunteer / Record 2:19/ (Vig.) 1879	S	285
441	BAY GELDING FRANK BY PATHFINDER/ 1877	S	285
442	BAY OF ANNAPOLIS, NOVA SCOTIA, THE/ (8.8x12.8)	S	260
443	BAY STALLION "HAMBRINO"/ Record 2:21.75/ (Vig.)	S	285
444	BE NOT WISE IN THINE OWN EYES/ (12.8x8.7) 1872	S	370
445	BEACH SNIPE SHOOTING/ (11.14x15) 1869 [Old BEST 50]	M	2875
446	BEAR HUNTING/ (Winter Scene) (8.6x12.4) [Old & New BEST 50]	S	1800
447	BEAR HUNTING / "Close Quarters"/ (8.8x12.10)	S	720
448	BEATRICE CENCI/ (Vig.)	S	55
449	BEAU AWAKE/ (8.2x12.7)	S	60
450	BEAUTIES OF BILLIARDS / "A Carom On the Dark Red"/ (16.6x24.14) (Companion to #995) 1869	L	2125
451	BEAUTIES OF THE BALLET/ N. Currier	S	120
452	BEAUTIFUL BLONDE/ (12x15)	M	90
453	BEAUTIFUL BRUNETTE/ (Vig.)	S	75
454	BEAUTIFUL DREAMER, THE	S	65
455	BEAUTIFUL EMPRESS, THE/ (Eugenie, Empress of France) (Oval)	S	55
456	BEAUTIFUL PAIR/ (Comic) (12.10x8) 1872	S	170
457	BEAUTIFUL PERSIAN, THE / #112/ (Oval)	S	75
458	BEAUTIFUL PERSIAN, THE/ (9x11) (Oval)	S	75
459	BEAUTIFUL QUADROON, THE	S	75
460	BEAUTY ASLEEP/ (8.4x12.7)	S	65
461	BEAUTY AWAKE/ (8x12.4)	S	65

462	BEAUTY OF NEW ENGLAND	S	65
463	BEAUTY OF THE ATLANTIC/ (Head) (Vig.)	S	65
464	BEAUTY OF THE ATLANTIC/ (Port. of Jennie Cramer) (Vig.)	S	75
465	BEAUTY OF THE MISSISSIPPI/ (Vig.)	S	65
466	BEAUTY OF THE NORTH, THE/ (Oval)	S	65
467	BEAUTY OF THE NORTHWEST/ (11x15)	M	100
468	BEAUTY OF THE PACIFIC, THE/ (Vig.)	S	65
469	BEAUTY OF THE RHINE	S	60
470	BEAUTY OF THE SOUTH/ (Vig.)	S	70
471	BEAUTY OF THE SOUTH/ (Oval)	L	120
472	BEAUTY OF THE SOUTHWEST, THE	S	65
473	BEAUTY OF VIRGINIA/ (Vig.)	S	65
474	BED TIME	S	65
475	BEFORE MARRIAGE / "Anticipation"/ (Companion to #58)	L	225
476	BEG SIR/ (Child and Dog) (8.4x11.8)	S	130
477	BEGGING A BITE/ (Girl and Dog) (8.11x11.10)	S	125
478	BEGGING A CRUST	M	135
479	BEHOLD! HOW BRIGHTLY BREAKS THE MORNING/ (Sheet Music)	S	80
480	BELGIAN ROYAL & U.S. MAIL STEAMER "Westernland"	S	240
481	BELGIAN ROYAL & U.S. MAIL STEAMER "Noordland"	S	240
482	BELIEVER'S VISION, THE/ (Round Top, Upright)	M	75
483	BELIEVER'S VISION, THE/ (11.8x10)	S	20
484	BELL RINGERS, THE	S	60
485	BELLA/ (8.6x14.15) 1876	S	280
486	BELLE HAMLIN/ (Vig.) 1889	S	270
487	BELLE HAMLIN AND JUSTINA/ 1877	S	275
488	BELLE OF CHICAGO/ (Vig.)	S	65
489	BELLE OF NEW YORK/ (Upright) (Vig.)	S	65
490	BELLE OF NEW YORK/ (3/4 Length) (Not a Vig.)	S	65
490A	BELLE OF SARATOGA, THE	M	80
491	BELLE OF THE EAST/ (8.6x12) 1846, N. Currier	S	65
492	BELLE OF THE EAST	M	85
493	BELLE OF THE SEA, THE/ N. Currier	S	65
494	BELLE OF THE WEST, THE/ (8.6x12.1) 1846, N. Currier	S	65
495	BELLE OF THE WINTER, THE/ (Vig.)	M	445
496	BELL-Y PUNCH, THE/ (8.9x12.9) 1876	S	320
497	BELTED WILL'S TOWER, NAWORTH, IRELAND	S	75
498	BENDING HER BEAU/ (Vig.) 1880	S	185
499	BENJAMIN FRANKLIN / "The Statesman and Philosopher"/ 1847, N. Currier [Old BEST 50]	S	440

500	BENJA. FRANKLIN/ (Bust Portrait)	S	195
501	BESSIE/ (Vig.) 1872	S	75
502	BEST HORSE, THE	S	135
503	BEST IN THE MARKET, THE/ 1879	S	145
504	BEST IN THE MARKET, THE/ (Vig.) 1880	S	145
505	BEST LIKENESS, THE/ 1858	M	185
506	BEST SCHOLAR, THE/ (Vig.)	S	155
507	BEST TIME ON RECORD,THREE HEATS/ GOLDSMITH MAID AND JUDGE FULLERTON/ (Vig.)	S	290
508	BETHESDA FOUNTAIN, CENTRAL PARK, NY/ (8.8x12.5)	S	295
509	BETROTHED, THE/ (Girl) N. Currier	S	85
510	BETROTHED, THE/ (Two Portraits) N. Currier	S	85
511	BETWEEN TWO FIRES/ (Vig.) 1879	S	220
512	BETWEEN TWO FIRES/ 1879	TC	70
513	BEWILDERED HUNTER, THE / "Puzzle Picture"/ (8.7x12.8) 1877	S	355
514	BEWILDERED HUNTER, THE / "Puzzle Picture"/ (8.7x12.8) 1872	S	355
515	B.F. PROCTOR/ (Vig.)	S	45
516	B.F. PROCTOR/ (Oval) (Vig.)	S	45
517	BIBLE AND TEMPERANCE, THE / #409/ (8.3x12.7) N. Currier	S	110
518	BIBLE AND TEMPERANCE, THE / #410/ (8.4x12.6) N. Currier	S	110
519	BIBLE AND TEMPERANCE, THE / #411/ (8.4x12.6) N. Currier	S	110
520	BIBLE AND TEMPERANCE, THE / #412/ (8.4x12.6) N. Currier	S	110
521	BIG THING ON ICE, A/ 1862	M	700
522	BILLIARDS- DOUBLE CAROM/ (8.6x12.13) 1874	S	320
523	BILLIARDS- FROZE TOGETHER/ (8.6x12.14) 1874	S	320
524	BILLIARDS- PLAYED OUT/ (8.6x12.4) 1874	S	320
525	BILLY EDWARDS / "Lightweight Champion of the World"/ (14.13x12.4)	M	355
526	BIRD TO BET ON, THE/ (Vig.) 1872	S	130
527	BIRDIE AND PET/ (7x5.7)	VS	160
528	BIRDS EYE VIEW OF MOUNT VERNON/ (13.2x17.15) C.Currier	M	425
529	BIRDS EYE VIEW OF PHILADELPHIA	S	385
530	BIRDS EYE VIEW OF THE CENTENNIAL EXHIBITION BUILDINGS	S	245
530A	BIRDS EYE VIEW OF THE GREAT SUSPENSION BRIDGE/ 1883	L	2325
531	BIRDS EYE VIEW OF THE CITY OF NEW YORK/ (4x6.14)	VS	330
532	BIRDS EYE VIEW OF THE PAUPER LUNATIC ASYLUM, BLACKWELL'S ISLAND, NEW YORK	S	250
533	BIRD'S NEST, THE	S	115
534	BIRTH OF OUR SAVIOR/ (12.11x8.3) 1867	S	20
535	BIRTH OF OUR SAVIOR	S	20
536	BIRTHPLACE OF GENERAL FRANK PIERCE, THE/ (7.9x12.11) 1852, N. Currier	S	185

537	BIRTHPLACE OF HENRY CLAY, THE/ N. Currier	S	185
538	BIRTHPLACE OF SHAKESPEARE, THE/ N. Currier	M	145
539	BIRTHPLACE OF WASHINGTON, THE/ (8.8x12.8)	S	255
540	BITE ALL AROUND, A/ 1879	S	105
541	BITE ALL AROUND, A/ 1880	TC	70
542	BITING LIVELY/ (Vig.) 1882	S	295
543	BLACK BASS SPEARING / "On the Restigouche, New Brunswick"/ (11.6x15.14) [Old & New BEST 50]	M	2250
544	BISHOP ALLEN OF THE AFRICAN CHURCH	S	20
545	BLACK BLOND, THE/ 1882	S	75
546	BLACK CLOUD" / Record 2:17.25/ (Vig.) 1882	S	285
547	BLACK DUCK SHOOTING/ (Vig.) 1879	S	325
548	BLACK DUCK SHOOTING/ 1879	TC	70
549	BLACK EYED BEAUTY, THE	S	65
550	BLACK EYED SUSAN/ (3/4 Length) N. Currier	S	175
551	BLACK EYED SUSAN/ (11.11x8.13) 1848, N. Currier [Old BEST 50]	S	280
552	BLACK EYED SUSAN/ (Head & Shoulders) N. Currier	S	145
553	BLACK EYED SUSAN	S	140
554	BLACK GELDING FRANK, BY PATHFINDER 2ND, THE	S	290
555	BLACK HAWK"/ (12.14x20.13) 1850, N. Currier	M	1100
556	BLACK HAWK" AND "JENNY LIND"/ (18.1x26.11) 1850, N. Currier	L	2075
557	BLACK ROCK CASTLE	S	80
558	BLACK PERSIAN, THE	S	70
559	BLACK SQUALL, A/ (Vig.) (Companion to #3804) 1879	S	225
560	BLACKBERRY DELL/ (11.6x15.14)	M	305
561	BLACKFISH NIBBLE, A. / Hush! I Feel Him!/ 1880	S	290
562	BLACKWELLS ISLAND, EAST RIVER FROM 82nd STREET, NY/ (11.1x15.11) 1860	M	1050
563	BLACKWOOD, JR."/ (Vig.)	S	290
564	BLARNEY CASTLE	S	65
565	BLESSED SHEPHERDESS, THE / Divini Rergere	S	20
566	BLESSED SHEPHERDESS, THE / La Pastora Bendita/ (11.15x8.8)	S	20
567	BLESSED VIRGIN MARY	S	20
568	BLESSING OF A WIFE/ (Companion to #4151)	S	155
569	BLESSING OF LIBERTY, THE/ N. Currier	S	75
570	BLOCKADE ON THE "CONNECTICUT PLAN"/ (Vig.)	S	185
571	BLOOD WILL TELL/ (Vig.) 1879	S	195
572	BLOOD WILL TELL/ 1879	TC	70
573	BLOOMER COSTUME, THE/ (11.10x8.5) [Old BEST 50] 1851, N. Currier	S	420
574	BLOOMER COSTUME, THE/ Und. N. Currier	S	300

575	BLOWER / The King of the Road	S	290
576	BLUE EYED BEAUTY	S	70
577	BLUE EYED MARY/ (11.12x8.10)	S	70
578	BLUE FISHING/ (8x12.8) [New BEST 50]	S	955
579	BLUE MONDAY/ (8.3x12.8) (Companion to #6374)	S	170
580	BOATSWAIN, THE/ (11.15x8.8) N. Currier	S	205
581	BODINE / "Trotting Whirlwind of the West"/ (Vig.) 1876	S	290
582	BODY OF GENERAL ROBERT E. LEE LYING IN STATE, THE	S	150
583	BODY OF HIS HOLINESS POPE PIUS IX LYING IN STATE	S	20
584	BODY OF THE MARTYR PRESIDENT, ABRAHAM LINCOLN/ (12x8.4) 1865	S	85
585	BODY OF THE MOST REV. ARCHBISHOP HUGHES LYING IN STATE/ (7.14x12.5) 1864	S	20
586	BODY OF THE MOST REVEREND ARCHBISHOP HUGHES LYING IN STATE/ 1864	S	20
587	BOLTED!/ (T. Worth, del.) (Companion to #6278)	S	285
588	BOLTED!/	TC	65
589	BOMBARDMENT AND CAPTURE OF FORT FISHER/ (7.15x12.7) N.Currier	S	385
590	BOMBARDMENT AND CAPTURE OF FORT HENRY, TENN./ (7.10x12.3)	S	385
591	BOMBARDMENT AND CAPTURE OF FORT HINDMAN, ARK./ (8.1x12.8)	S	405
592	BOMBARDMENT AND CAPTURE OF FREDERICKSBURG/ (7.15x12.15)	S	215
593	BOMBARDMENT AND CAPTURE OF ISLAND "NUMBER TEN" ON THE MISSISSIPPI RIVER/ (15.10x22.2) 1862	L	1200
594	BOMBARDMENT AND CAPTURE OF THE FORTS AT HATTERAS INLET	S	350
595	BOMBARDMENT OF FORT PULASKI COCKSPUR ISLAND, GEO./ (7.14x11.14)	S	280
596	BOMBARDMENT OF FORT SUMTER/ (7.14x11.13)	S	295
597	BOMBARDMENT OF FORT SUMTER, CHARLESTON HARBOR, FROM FORT MOULTRIE/ (8x12)	S	300
598	BOMBARDMENT OF ISLAND "NUMBER TEN" IN THE MISSISSIPPI RIVER/ (7.10x12.4) 1862	TC	320
599	BOMBARDMENT OF SEBASTOPOL	S	200
600	BOMBARDMENT OF TRIPOLI/ (7.12x12.15) 1846, N. Currier	S	215
601	BOMBARDMENT OF VERA CRUZ / #458/ (8.5x12.12) 1847, N. Currier	S	140
602	BOMBARDMENT OF VERA CRUZ / #467/ (8.6x12.13) 1847, N. Currier	S	140
603	BONEFACED CHEEK	S	65
604	BONESETTER"/ 1881	S	290
605	BONESETTER RECORD 2:19/ 1881	TC	85
606	BONNIE" YOUNG CHIEFTAIN, THE/ (14.7x10.13) N. Currier	M	120
607	BONNINGTON LINN/ (5.6x7.6) (Oval)	VS	125

608	BOOMERANG, A/ (Vig.) (Companion to #5502) 1880	S	150
609	BOQUET OF FRUIT, A	S	155
610	BOQUET, THE	S	135
611	BOQUET OF ROSES	S	115
612	BOSS HORSE. THE / Driven by the King Pin/ (Vig.)	S	285
613	BOSS OF THE MARKET, THE/ (Vig.) 1880	S	220
614	BOSS OF THE RING, THE/ (Vig.)	S	215
615	BOSS OF THE ROAD, THE/ (8x12.6)	S	220
616	BOSS OF THE ROAD, THE/ 1880	TC	80
617	BOSS OF THE ROAD/ 1883	S	215
618	BOSS OF THE ROAD, THE/ (16.4x24) 1884	L	700
619	BOSS OF THE TRACK, THE/ (Vig.) 1881	S	215
620	BOSS ROOSTER, DE/ (Companion to #1249)	S	230
621	BOSS STATE CARRIER, THE	S	240
622	BOSS TEAM, THE	S	250
622A	BOSTON & BANGOR STEAMSHIP CO./ 1883	TC	95
623	BOSTON HARBOR	S	415
624	BOTHWELL CASTLE ON THE CLYDE/ (11.9x17)	M	115
625	BOTHWELL CASTLE ON THE CLYDE/ (11.10x16.15)	M	115
626	BOTHWELL CASTLE ON THE CLYDE/ (5.8x7.8)	VS	75
627	BOUND DOWN THE RIVER/ (7.14x12.7) 1870 [Old & New BEST 50]	S	980
628	BOUND TO HEAR BEECHER/ 1881	S	185
629	BOUND TO HEAR BEECHER/ (5.8x7.8)	VS	95
629A	BOUND TO HEAR BEECHER	TC	75
630	BOUND TO SHINE!!/ (Companion to #633) 1870	S	260
631	BOUND TO SHINE/ 1880	S	265
632	BOUND TO SHINE/ 1880	TC	70
633	BOUND TO SMASH/ (8.15x13.8) (Companion to #630) 1877	S	255
634	BOUQUET, THE/ 1846, N. Currier	S	115
635	BOUQUET OF FRUIT/ 1875	S	150
636	BOUQUET OF ROSES/ 1862	S	110
637	BOUQUET OF THE VASE, THE/ 1875	S	115
638	BOWER OF BEAUTY	S	65
639	BOWER OF ROSES, THE	L	300
640	BOY AND DOG	S	165
641	BOY OF THE PERIOD, THE/ (Vig.)	S	145
642	BOYNE WATER, THE	S	85
643	BOZ/ (Charles Dickens) N. Currier	S	85
644	BRACE OF MEADOW LARKS/ (Vig.) 1879	S	180

645	BRACK DOG WINS, DE/ (Vig.) (Companion to #6641) 1889	S	190
646	BRANCH AND THE VINE, THE	S	130
647	BRANCH CANNOT BEAR FRUIT, THE/ (8.7x12.7) 1872	S	125
648	BRANDING SLAVES/ (11.15x8.8) 1845, N. Currier	S	450
649	BRANDY SMASH/ (Vig.) 1884	S	190
650	BRAVE BOY OF THE WAXHAWS, THE/ (8.8x12.4) 1876	S	280
651	BRAVE WIFE, THE/ (11.12x8.10)	S	100
652	BREAKING IN / "A Black Imposition"/ (Vig.) 1881	S	185
653	BREAKING OUT / "A Lively Scrimmage"/ (Vig.) 1881	S	185
654	BREAKING THAT "BACKBONE"	S	215
655	BRER THULDY'S STATUE / "Liberty Frightenin De World"/ (Vig.) 1884	S	225
656	BRIAN BORUE / At the Battle of Clontarf/ N. Currier	S	50
657	BRIC-A-BRAC MANIA/ (Vig.) 1882	S	140
658	BRIDAL BOUQUET, THE	S	110
659	BRIDAL VEIL" FALL / Yo-semite Valley, California/ (8.8x12.8)	S	510
660	BRIDAL WREATH, THE/ (Vig.)	S	110
661	BRIDE, THE / #125/ (12.1x8.6) 1847, N. Currier	S	100
662	BRIDE, THE/ (Vig.) N. Currier	S	100
663	BRIDE, THE/ N. Currier	S	100
664	BRIDE & BRIDEGROOM, THE	S	100
665	BRIDE OF LAMMERMOOR, THE/ (12x8.14) N. Currier	S	45
666	BRIDE OF THE WHITE HOUSE, THE/ (Mrs. Grover Cleveland) (Vig.) 1886	S	165
667	BRIDESMAID, THE/ 1857	S	80
668	BRIDESMAID, THE/ 1857	L	150
669	BRIDGE, THE/ (5x7)	VS	155
670	BRIDGE AT THE OUTLET, LAKE MEMPHREMAGOG/ (7.14x12.8)	S	195
671	BRIDGET/ (3/4 Length) 1845, N. Currier	S	80
672	BRIDGET/ (Full Length) N. Currier	S	80
673	BRIG/ N. Currier	S	405
674	BRIG. GEN. FRANZ SIGEL/ (Vig.) 1861	S	105
675	BRIG. GEN. IRWIN McDOWELL	S	105
676	BRIG. GEN. LOUIS BLENKER/ (Vig.)	S	105
677	BRIG. GENERAL NATHL. LYON/ (Vig.) 1861	S	105
678	BRIG. GENERAL W.T. SHERMAN, U.S.A./ (Vig.) 1861	S	105
679	BRIG. GENL. AMBROSE E. BURNSIDE	S	105
680	BRIG. GENL. MICHAEL CORCORAN/ (Upright)	S	105
681	BRIG. GENL. MICHAEL CORCORAN/ (3/4 Vig.)	S	105
682	BRIG. GENL. NATHTL. LYON, UNITED STATES ARMY	S	105
683	BRIG. GENL. ROBERT ANDERSON / "The Hero of Fort Sumter"/ (Vig.)	S	105

684	BRIG. GENL. THOMAS FRANCIS MEAGHER	S	105
685	BRIG. GENL. WM. SPRAGUE, U.S.A.	S	105
686	BRIG. GENL. W.S. ROSECRANS, U.S.ARMY/ (Vig.)	S	103
687	BRIG VISION, CAPT. DONOVAN	S	150
688	BRIGAND, THE	S	125
689	BRIGHAM YOUNG	M	115
690	BRILLIANT CHARGE OF CAPTAIN MAY/ (8.8x12.12) 1846, N. Currier	S	115
691	BRILLIANT CHARGE OF CAPTAIN MAY/ (8.8x12.12) 1846, N. Currier	S	115
692	BRILLIANT NAVAL VICTORY/ (7.14x12.8) 1862	S	330
693	BRING UP YOUR HORSES/ (18.2x27.3) 1886	L	1625
694	BROADWAY BELLE, A/ (Vig.)	S	70
695	BROADWAY FASHIONS, NEW YORK/ 1865, C. Currier	L	730
696	BROADWAY FASHIONS, NEW YORK/ 1866, C. Currier	L	730
697	BROADWAY, NEW YORK, FROM THE WESTERN UNION TELEGRAPH BUILDING, LOOKING NORTH/ (16.6x24) 1875	L	3250
698	BROADWAY, NEW YORK, SOUTH FROM THE PARK/ (8.1x12.13) N. Currier	S	505
699	BROADWAY, NEW YORK, SOUTH FROM THE PARK/ Currier & Ives	S	505
700	BRONZE STATUE OF ANDREW JACKSON, WASHINGTON D.C.	S	175
701	BROOK, THE	S	195
702	BROOK, SUMMER, THE/ (12x9)	S	190
703	BROOK TROUT FISHING / "An Anxious Moment"/ (18.10x27.2) 1862 [New BEST 50]	L	6100
704	BROOK TROUT FISHING/ (8.8x12.7) 1872	S	840
705	BROOK TROUT - JUST CAUGHT/ (11x16.14) 1858, N. Currier	M	635
706	BROTHER AND SISTER/ (11.13x8.10)	S	90
707	BROTHER AND SISTER/ (Oval) N. Currier	S	90
708	BROTHER AND SISTER / #169/ N. Currier	S	90
709	BROTHER AND SISTER/ (11.13x8.13) N. Currier	S	90
710	BRUSH FOR THE LEAD, A/ (19.8x29.8) 1867	L	2575
711	BRUSH ON THE HOMESTRETCH, THE/ (17.3x27.2) 1869	L	1600
712	BRUSH ON THE ROAD, A / Best 2 in 3/ (7.8x13) (Vig.) 1872, N. Currier	S	290
713	BRUSH ON THE ROAD, A / Mile Heats, Best 2 in 3/ (Vig.) 1853, N. Currier	M	515
714	BRUSH ON THE ROAD, A / Mile Heats, Best 2 in 3/ (Vig.) 1855, N. Currier	S	290
715	BRUSH ON THE ROAD, A / Mile Heats, Best 2 in 3/ 1855, Currier & Ives	S	290
716	BRUSH ON THE SNOW/ 1871	M	2300
717	BRUSH WITH WEBSTER CARTS, A/ 1884	L	1600
718	BUCK" TAKING THE "POT"/ (Vig.)	S	175
719	BUDD" OF THE DRIVING PARK/ 1876	M	630
720	BUDS OF PROMISE/ (12.1x8.10) N. Currier	S	80

721	BUFFALO AND CHICAGO STEAM PACKET "EMPIRE STATE"/ (8.2x13.2) N. Currier	S	375
722	BUFFALO BULL / CHASING BACK / Turn About Is Fair Play	M	1625
723	BUFFALO CHASE, THE / "Singling Out"	M	1625
724	BUFFALO DANCE / TO MAKE THE BUFFALOES COME/ (12.2x17.14)	M	1650
725	BUFFALO HUNT ON SNOW SHOES / "Winter on the Northern Prairies"/ (12.12x17.14)	M	1975
726	BUFFALO HUNT / "Surrounding the Herd"/ (12.13x18.8)	M	1600
727	BUFFALO HUNT ON THE BANKS OF UPPER MISSOURI	M	1600
728	BUFFALO HUNT UNDER THE WHITE WOLF SKIN/ (12.2x17.14)	M	1600
729	BULL DOZED!!/ 1875	S	200
730	BULL DOZED!!/ 1877	TC	70
731	BULL DOZED/ 1875	S	200
732	BULLY TEAM, THE / Scalding and Early Nose/ (Vig.) 1882	S	245
733	BURIAL OF CHRIST, THE/ (9.6x7.2) N. Currier	S	20
734	BURIAL OF CHRIST, THE/ (9.6x7.2) N. Currier	S	20
735	BURIAL OF DESOTO/ (8.13x12.13) 1876	S	45
736	BURIAL OF THE BIRD, THE	S	80
737	BURNING GLASS, THE/ (16.14x13.11) 1860	M	180
738	BURNING OF CHICAGO, THE/ (8x12.10) 1871	S	450
739	BURNING OF THE CITY HALL, N.Y./ (8.1x12.4)	S	545
740	BURNING OF THE CLIPPER SHIP "GOLDEN LIGHT"	S	460
741	BURNING OF THE "HENRY CLAY", NEAR YONKERS/ (7.9x13.8) 1852, N. Currier	S	400
742	BURNING OF THE INMAN LINE STEAMSHIP "CITY OF MONTREAL"/ (9x13.12) 1887	S	345
743	BURNING OF THE NEW YORK CRYSTAL PALACE/ (16.12x25.4)	L	3200
744	BURNING OF THE NEW YORK CRYSTAL PALACE/ (8x12.10)	S	440
745	BURNING OF THE "OCEAN MONARCH" OF BOSTON/ (8.3x12.9) 1848, N. Currier	S	300
746	BURNING OF THE PALACE STEAMER "ROBERT E. LEE"/ (8.8x13.9) 1882	S	290
747	BURNING OF THE PALACE STEAMSHIP "ERIE" OFF SILVER CREEK, LAKE ERIE/ (8.4x12.8) N. Currier	S	410
748	BURNING OF THE STEAMSHIP "AUSTRIA"/ (8.2x12.6)	S	265
749	BURNING OF THE STEAMSHIP "GOLDEN GATE"/ (8.2x12.6)	S	445
750	BURNING OF THE STEAMSHIP "GOLDEN GATE"/ (8.3x12.9)	S	445
751	BURNING OF THE STEAMSHIP "NARRAGANSETT"	S	355
752	BURNING OF THE THRONE, PARIS/ (8x12.9) 1848, N. Currier	S	95
753	BURNING OF THE U.S. SHIP OF THE LINE "PENNSYLVANIA"/ (8.8x12.10) 1861	S	425
754	BURNING OF WARWICK CASTLE, Dec. 3, 1871/ (8.7x12.8)	S	75

755	BUSTIN' A PICNIC/ (Companion to #5898) 1881	S	195
756	BUSTING THE POOL/ (Companion to #1129) 1889	S	195
757	BUSTIN THE RECORD/ (Vig.) 1883	S	290
758	BUTT OF THE JOKERS, THE/ (Vig.) (Companion to #4814) 1879	S	195
758A	BUTT OF THE JOKERS, THE/ 1879	TC	75
759	BUTTERMILK FALLS/ (Oval) (5.7x7.7)	VS	210
760	BY THE SEASHORE/ 1868	M	350
761	BYRON AND MARIANNA/ N. Currier	S	65
762	BYRON IN THE HIGHLANDS/ (11.9x8)	S	60
763	BYRON'S FIRST LOVE/ N. Currier	S	60

C

Con#	Title	Folio	Value
764	CAIRN'S QUICK STEP/ N. Currier	S	105
765	CAKE WALK, DE/ (Vig.) 1883	S	125
766	CALIFORNIA BEAUTY, THE	S	70
767	CALIFORNIA GOLD/ N. Currier	S	885
768	CALIFORNIA SCENERY / "Seal Rocks - Point Lobos"/ (8x12.8)	S	450
769	CALIFORNIA WONDER "OCCIDENT" OWNED BY GOV. L. STANFORD, THE/ (Vig.) 1873	S	290
770	CALIFORNIA WONDER "OCCIDENT" (Formerly "Wonder") (Vig.) 1873	S	290
771	CALIFORNIA WONDER HINDA ROSE, THE/ Record 2:19.50/ (Vig.) 1883	S	290
772	CALIFORNIA SEEKING THE ELEPHANT/ N. Currier	S	290
773	CAMPING IN THE WOODS / "A Good Time Coming"/ (18.12x27.8) 1863	L	4100
774	CAMPING IN THE WOODS / "Laying Off"/ (18.12x27.9) 1863	L	4150
775	CAMPING OUT / "A Life In The Woods For Me"/ (Vig.)	S	395
776	CAMPING OUT / "Life in the Woods"/ 1879	M	830
777	CAMPING OUT / "Some of the Right Sort"/ (19x27.6) 1856, N. Currier	L	3225
778	CAN YOU KEEP A SECRET?/ (Vig.) 1872	S	95
779	CANADIAN VOYAGEURS WALKING A CANOE UP THE RAPID/ (7.15x12.8)	S	265
780	CANADIAN WINTER SCENE/ (9.15x16.12)	M	1750
781	CANAL SCENE / MOONLIGHT/ (Erie Canal) (8.7x12.10)	S	315
782	CANARY BIRD, THE	S	85
783	CANDIDATE ON THE STUMP / The Secesh Democratic Pirate Sunk by the U.S. Gun Boat/ (Vig.)	M	185
784	CAN'T BE BEAT!/ (Vig.) 1880	S	175

785	CAN'T PLAY/ (Companion to #1599) N. Currier	S	150
786	CAN'T PLAY/ (11.9x8.3) N. Currier	S	145
787	CAN'T YOU TALK?/ (Child and Animal) (12.8x9)	S	135
788	CANVAS-BACKS/ (8.8x12.8)	S	330
789	CAPABILITY AND AVAILABILITY/ N. Currier	M	235
790	CAPITAL CIGAR, A	TC	70
791	CAPITAL JOKE, A	S	135
792	CAPITOL AT WASHINGTON/ N. Currier	S	285
793	CAPITOL AT WASHINGTON/ (3/4 Front View) N. Currier	S	285
794	CAPITOL AT WASHINGTON/ (Almost Direct Front View) C. Currier	S	285
795	CAPITOL, INDIANA. PLAN OF PRINCIPAL FLOOR.../ (Vig.) N. Currier	S	360
796	CAPITOL OF THE STATE OF INDIANA/ (Vig.) N. Currier	S	360
797	CAPITULATION AT VERA CRUZ/ (7.12x12.9) 1847, N. Currier	S	125
798	CAPT. CHARLES WILKES, U.S.N./ (Vig.)	S	90
799	CAPT. THOMAS FRANCIS MEAGHER	S	75
800	CAPTIVE KNIGHT, THE	S	95
801	CAPT. JOHN T. CAIRNS/ N. Currier	VS	90
802	CAPTURE AND FALL OF CHARLESTON, S.C.	S	260
803	CAPTURE OF AN UNPROTECTED FEMALE, or CLOSE OF THE REBELLION	M	195
804	CAPTURE OF ANDRE, 1780/ (8x11.12) 1845, N. Currier	S	215
805	CAPTURE OF ANDRE, 1780/ 8.12x12.11) 1876	S	215
806	CAPTURE OF ANDRE, 1780	S	215
807	CAPTURE OF ATLANTA, GA./ N. Currier	S	235
808	CAPTURE OF GENERAL LA VEGA/ (8.8x12.10) 1846	S	125
809	CAPTURE OF JEFF DAVIS, THE	M	225
810	CAPTURE OF ROANOKE ISLAND/ (8.2x12.4)	S	250
811	CAPTURING A WILD HORSE/ (12.2x17.14)	M	1500
812	CAPTURING THE WHALE/ N. Currier	S	1500
813	CARDINAL JAMES GIBBONS	S	20
814	CARES OF A FAMILY, THE/ (18.6x22.12) 1856, N. Currier [Old BEST 50]	L	3100
815	CARES OF A FAMILY, THE/ (Companion to "Infant Brood") (8.12x12.8)	S	500
816	CARES OF A FAMILY, THE/ (8.12x12.8) (Oval) (Companion to #3100)	S	680
817	CARES OF A FAMILY/ (Child Feeding Nest of Birds)	S	155
818	CARLO'S ABC's	S	75
819	CARLO'S FIRST LESSON/ (14.11x10.8)	M	135
820	CAROLINE/ (Seated at table) N. Currier	S	80
821	CAROLINE/ (Half Length) N. Currier	S	80
822	CAROLINE/ (Two trees) N. Currier	S	80

823	CAROLINE/ (Hair ornaments) N. Currier	S	80
824	CAROLINE/ (11.14x8.7) N. Currier	S	80
825	CAROLINE/ (Full Length) 1844, N. Currier	S	80
826	CAROLINE/ 1846, N. Currier	S	80
827	CAROLINE/ (11.15x8.6) 1847, N. Currier	S	80
828	CAROLINE/ (11.15x8.2) 1848, N. Currier	S	80
829	CAROLINE/ (Half Length) (Vig.) N. Currier	S	80
830	CARRIE/ (Vig.)	S	80
831	CARRIER DOVE, THE / The Departure/ N. Currier	S	50
832	CARRIER DOVE, THE / The Departure/ (Vig.) N. Currier	S	50
833	CARRIER DOVE, THE / The Return/ N. Currier	S	50
834	CARRIER DOVE, THE / The Return/ (Vig.) N. Currier	S	50
835	CARRY ME BACK TO OLD VIRGINNY	S	105
836	CASH ON DELIVERY/ (8.14x12) 1868	S	365
837	CASH SYSTEM/ (12.12x8.3) 1877	S	355
838	CASSIUS M. CLAY OF KENTUCKY/ (11.8x8.10) 1846, N. Currier	S	95
839	CASTLE, BLARNEY, IRELAND, THE	S	85
840	CASTLE GARDEN NEW YORK, FROM THE BATTERY/ (8.1x12.9) 1848, N. Currier	S	500
841	CASTLE HOWARD	M	115
842	CASTLE OF CHILLON, LAKE OF GENEVA	S	95
843	CASTLE OF CHILLON, LAKE OF GENEVA	M	135
844	CAT-ASTROPHE/ N. Currier	S	135
845	CATCHING A TROUT / "We Hab You Now, Sar!"/ (18.5x25.12) 1854, N. Currier [Old & New BEST 50]	L	4800
846	CATHERINE/ (Half Length, Holding Fan) N. Currier	S	80
847	CATHERINE/ (3/4 Length, Holding Fan) N. Currier	S	80
848	CATHERINE/ (3/4 Length, Holding Bird) N. Currier	S	80
849	CATHERINE/ (11.13x8.4) 1845, N. Currier	S	80
850	CATHERINE/ (11.13x8.4) 1845, N. Currier	S	80
851	CATHERINE/ (Red dress) (11.15x8.5) 1848, N. Currier	S	80
852	CATHERINE HAYES / The Swan of Erin/ N. Currier	S	80
853	CATHOLIC MEMORY/ N. Currier	S	20
854	CAT NAP, A/ 1859	M	255
855	CAT NAP, A/ 1858	L	365
856	CAT'S PAW, THE/ (11.12x8.14)	S	155
857	CATTERSKILL FALL, THE/ (8.7x12.11)	S	235
858	CATTERSKILL FALLS/ (7.15x12.8)	S	235
859	CATTSKILL CREEK/ (5x7) (Vig.)	VS	175
860	CATSKILL MOUNTAINS/ (14.14x20) 1860	L	2500

All prints are published by Currier & Ives unless otherwise stated.

861	CAUGHT IN THE ACT/ (Vig.)	S	115
862	CAUGHT NAPPING/ (Vig.) 1879	S	225
863	CAUGHT NAPPING/ 1879	TC	80
864	CAUGHT ON THE FLY/ (Vig.) (Companion to #3426) 1879	S	280
865	CAUGHT ON THE FLY/ 1880	TC	75
866	CAUSE AND EFFECT / "Natural Result"/ (Vig.) 1887	S	220
867	CAUSE AND EFFECT / "Timely Warning"/ (Vig.) 1887	S	220
868	CAVALRY TACTICS BY THE HORSE GUARDS/ (Vig.) (Companion to #3111) 1887	S	250
869	CAVED IN - THE BUSTED SCULLER/ (11x15.3) 1876	M	345
870	CAVING IN, OR, A REBEL "DEEPLY HUMILIATED"	M	255
871	CECELIA/ 1844, N. Currier	S	75
872	CEDARS OF LEBANON, THE	S	40
873	CELA WINDER/ 1883	S	45
874	CELEBRATED BOSTON TEAM "MILL BOY" AND "BLONDINE"/ (20.8x33) 1882	L	1475
875	CELEBRATED CLIPPER BARK "GRAPESHOT"/ N. Currier	S	635
876	CELEBRATED CLIPPER SHIP "DREADNOUGHT"	S	615
877	CELEBRATED CLIPPER SHIP "DREADNOUGHT" OFF TUSKAR LIGHT/ (Vig.)	S	635
878	CELEBRATED ETHIOPIAN MELODIES/ N. Currier	S	20
879	CELEBRATED FIGHTING PIG "PAPE"/ N. Currier	M	480
880	CELEBRATED "FOUR IN HAND" STALLION TEAM / Superb and His Three Sons/ (18.2x28) 1875	L	2100
881	CELEBRATED "FOUR IN HAND" STALLION TEAM / ...Ethan Allen/ (18.2x28) 1875	L	2000
882	CELEBRATED HORSE "BLOWER" KING OF THE ROAD, THE	S	290
883	CELEBRATED HORSE "DEXTER" / "The King of the Turf"/ (16.14x26.10) 1865	L	1675
884	CELEBRATED HORSE "DEXTER" / "The King of the World"/ (17.2x26.13) 1867	L	1675
885	CELEBRATED HORSE "GEORGE M. PATCHEN" / "The Champion of the Turf"/ (17.2x26.14) 1860	L	1725
886	CELEBRATED HORSE "JOHN STEWART"/ (16.8x25.8) 1869	L	1550
887	CELEBRATED HORSE "LEXINGTON"/ (18.13x26.6) 1855, N. Currier [Old BEST 50]	L	2550
888	CELEBRATED HORSE "LEXINGTON"	L	2500
889	CELEBRATED KOOK FAMILY/ (13.11x10.4)	S	155
890	CELEBRATED MARE "FLORA TEMPLE" / "The Queen of the Turf"/ 1853, N. Currier	L	1775
891	CELEBRATED MARE "FLORA TEMPLE" / "The Queen of the Turf"/ Und. Currier & Ives	L	1750
892	CELEBRATED MARE "FLORA TEMPLE" / "The Queen of the Turf"/ (17.4x27.3) 1860, N. Currier	L	1675

893	CELEBRATED PACING MARE "POCAHONTAS"/ 1855, N. Currier	L	1700
894	CELEBRATED PLOUGH HORSE "CAPTAIN LEWIS"/ (Vig.) 1862	S	290
895	CELEBRATED / SPRING-FLOWER POLKA, THE	S	85
896	CELEBRATED STALLION TRIO, A	M	615
897	CELEBRATED STALLIONS "GEORGE WILKES" AND "COMMODORE VANDERBILT"/ (17x26.8) 1866	L	1625
898	CELEBRATED TERRIER DOG "MAJOR", Performing His Wonderful Feat of Killing 100 Rats/ (14.2x20.6) N. Currier	L	1200
899	CELEBRATED TROTTER JAY EYE SEE DRIVEN BY E.D. BITHER/ 1883	L	1350
900	CELEBRATED TROTTER "MOOSE" / Record 2:19.50/ (Vig.) 1881	S	290
901	CELEBRATED TROTTING HORSE "CAMORS"/ (Vig.) 1874	S	290
902	CELEBRATED TROTTING HORSE "GLOSTER"/ 1874	S	290
903	CELEBRATED TROTTING HORSE "HENRY"/ (Vig.) 1872	S	290
904	CELEBRATED TROTTING HORSE "HENRY"/ (Vig.) 1874	S	290
905	CELEBRATED TROTTING HORSE "HOPEFUL" / Record 2:14.75/ 1881	L	1525
906	CELEBRATED TROTTING HORSE "HOPEFUL." / Record 2:14.75/ (18.6x28) 1881	L	1525
907	CELEBRATED TROTTING HORSE "JOHN STEWART"/ 1868	L	1475
908	CELEBRATED TROTTING HORSE "JOHN STEWART"/ 1869	L	1450
909	CELEBRATED TROTTING HORSE "JUDGE FULLERTON"/ (16.10x26.1) 1874	L	1450
910	CELEBRATED TROTTING HORSE "PROSPERO"/ (Vig.) 1877	S	290
911	CELEBRATED TROTTING HORSE "TRUSTEE"/ (18.6x27) 1848	L	1500
912	CELEBRATED TROTTING MARE "DAISY DALE" / Record 2:19.75/ (Vig.) 1881	S	290
913	CELEBRATED TROTTING MARE "FLORA TEMPLE"/ (Vig.) 1872	S	290
914	CELEBRATED TROTTING MARE GOLDSMITH MAID 2:19 3/4.../ 1871	S	290
915	CELEBRATED TROTTING MARE GOLDSMITH MAID 2:20 1/2.../ 1871	S	290
916	CELEBRATED TROTTING MARE "HATTIE WOODWARD"/ (18.6x27.12) 1881	L	1425
917	CELEBRATED TROTTING MARE "HUNTRESS"/ (Vig.) 1873	S	290
918	CELEBRATED TROTTING MARE "LADY THORN"/ 1866	L	1475
919	CELEBRATED TROTTING MARE "LADY THORN"/ (With Pedigrees) 1866	L	1475
920	CELEBRATED TROTTING MARE "LUCILLE GOLDDUST" / Record 2:16.25/ (Vig.) 1877	S	290
921	CELEBRATED TROTTING MARE "LUCY" Passing the Judges Stand/ (16.12x26.8) 1872	L	1525
922	CELEBRATED TROTTING MARE "LULA"/ (Vig.) 1874	S	290
923	CELEBRATED TROTTING MARE "LULA"/ (Vig.) 1877	S	290
924	CELEBRATED TROTTING MARE "WIDOW McCHREE"... 1867	L	1450
925	CELEBRATED TROTTING MARES "MAUD S." AND "ALDINE"/ (20.12x33.1) 1883	L	1475

926	CELEBRATED TROTTING STALLION "ALEXANDER" / Record 2:19/ 1882	L	1450
926A	CELEBRATED TROTTING STALLION COL. UPTON, WILL, THE/ 1881	L	1450
927	CELEBRATED TROTTING STALLION "ETHAN ALLEN"/ (Vig.) 1872	S	290
928	CELEBRATED TROTTING STALLION "FRANCE'S ALEXANDER"/ 1882	S	290
929	CELEBRATED TROTTING STALLION "FRANCE'S ALEXANDER", THE/ 1882	L	1450
930	CELEBRATED TROTTING STALLION "GEORGE WILKES" BY RYSDYK'S HAMBLETONIAN / (Vig.) 1885	M	575
931	CELEBRATED TROTTING STALLION "GEORGE WILKES" BY RYSDYK'S HAMBLETONIAN/ 1885	S	290
932	CELEBRATED TROTTING STALLION "GEORGE WILKES", Formerly "Robert Fillingham"/ 1866	L	1475
933	CELEBRATED TROTTING STALLION "JAY GOULD"/ (Vig.) 1877	S	290
934	CELEBRATED TROTTING STALLION PATRON BY PANCOAST/ 1887	S	290
935	CELEBRATED TROTTING STALLION SMUGGLER.../ 1875	L	1475
936	CELEBRATED TROTTING STALLION SMUGGLER.../ 1876	L	1475
937	CELEBRATED TROTTING STALLION "WOODFORD MAMBRINO"/ (8.15x12.7) 1878	S	290
938	CELEBRATED TROTTING STALLIONS E. ALLEN & G. PATCHEN/ 1858	L	1750
939	CELEBRATED TROTTING STALLIONS "YOUNG WOFUL" AND "ABDALLAH CHIEF"/ (16.13x25.13) 1866	L	1675
940	CELEBRATED TROTTING TEAM "EDWARD" AND "SWIVELLER"/ (20x34.2) 1882	L	1450
941	CELEBRATED WINNING HORSES AND JOCKEYS OF THE AMERICAN TURF/ 1888	L	1250
942	CELEBRATED WINNING HORSES AND JOCKEYS OF THE AMERICAN TURF/ (20.4x34.2) 1889	L	1250
943	CELEBRATED WINNING HORSES AND JOCKEYS OF THE AMERICAN TURF/ 1891	L	1250
944	CELEBRATED YACHT "AMERICA"/ (9.6x13.7)	S	650
945	CELEBRATED YACHTS, THE/ (9.8x13.14)	M	850
946	CENTENNIAL BOCK BIER/ 1876	M	345
947	CENTENNIAL EXHIBITION BUILDINGS, PHIL./ 1875	S	220
948	CENTRAL PARK IN WINTER/ (Moonlight Scene) (8.8x12.7) [Old & New BEST 50]	S	1725
949	CENTRAL PARK / THE BRIDGE/ (8x12.9)	S	370
950	CENTRAL PARK, N.Y. / THE BRIDGE/ (8.2x12.10)	S	265
951	CENTRAL PARK / THE DRIVE/ (11.2x15.8) 1862	M	2025
952	CENTRAL PARK / THE LAKE/ (11.2x15.7) 1862	M	1500
953	CENTRAL PARK, WINTER / THE SKATING CARNIVAL/ (8.1x12.9) [New BEST 50]	S	2150
954	CENTRAL PARK, WINTER / THE SKATING POND/ (18.6x26.12) 1862 [Old & New BEST 50]	L	18200

955	CENTER HARBOR, LAKE WINNIPISEOGEE, NH/ (11.11x20.7)	L	2650
956	CENTERVILLE" AND "BLACK DOUGLAS"/ (17.3x26.14) 1853	L	1600
957	CERITO IN THE SYLPHIDE/ (8.1x11.12) 1846, N. Currier	S	80
958	CERTIFICATE OF BAPTISM	S	20
959	CERTIFICATE OF BAPTISM/ (German) (8.13x12.13) N. Currier	S	20
960	CERTIFICATE OF HONOR/ (8.14x12.7) 1863	S	50
961	CERTIFICATE OF MARRIAGE	S	65
962	CH. MAURICE DE TALLYRAND	VS	35
963	CHAMPION IN DANGER, THE / Golly!/ (Vig.) 1882	S	220
964	CHAMPION IN LUCK, THE / "Dar-I know'd sumfin 'ud happen"/ (Vig.) 1882	S	220
965	CHAMPION IRISH SETTER, "ROVER"/ (8.14x12.12)	S	230
966	CHAMPION PACER DIRECT, BY DIRECTOR/ 1891	S	290
967	CHAMPION PACER DIRECT, BY DIRECTOR/ 1891	L	1400
968	CHAMPION PACER "JOHNSTON"/ Record 2:10/ (18.4x27) 1884	L	1450
969	CHAMPION PACER "MASCOT"/ Record 2:04/ (Vig.) 1892	S	280
970	CHAMPION PACER "MASCOT"/ Record 2:04	L	1325
971	CHAMPION RACE, A/ 1887	L	1450
972	CHAMPION RACE, A/ (18.4x27.15) 1894	L	1450
973	CHAMPION ROWIST, THE / PRIDE OF THE CLUB/ (10.12x15.7) 1876	M	460
974	CHAMPION SLUGGER - KNOCKING 'EM OUT, THE/ (Vig.) 1883	S	265
975	CHAMPION STALLION "DIRECTUM" / Record 2:05 1/4/ (Vig.) 1893	S	290
976	CHAMPION STALLION "GEORGE WILKES"/ (18.5x28) 1888	L	1475
977	CHAMPION STALLION "MAXY COBB" / Record 2:13.25/ (17.9x26.8) 1885	L	1450
978	CHAMPION STEER OF THE WORLD/ 1877	M	300
979	CHAMPION TROTTING QUEEN "ALIX"/ (Vig.) 1893	S	290
980	CHAMPION TROTTING QUEEN "ALIX" / Record 2:03.75/ (18.10x27.2) 1894	L	1450
981	CHAMPION TROTTING STALLION "NELSON" 2:10 3/4.../ (19.10x27) 1891	L	1475
982	CHAMPION TROTTING STALLION "NELSON" 2:09.../ (19.10x27) 1891	L	1475
983	CHAMPION TROTTING STALLION "SMUGGLER"/ (16.12x26.4) 1875	L	1475
984	CHAMPION TROTTING STALLION "SMUGGLER" OWNED BY../ 1876	L	1475
985	CHAMPIONS AT CLOSE QUARTERS/ (High Wheeled) 1892	L	1500
986	CHAMPIONS AT CLOSE QUARTERS/ (Small Rubber Tires) 1894	L	1250
987	CHAMPIONS OF BALL RACKET / "At the Close of the Season"/ (Vig.) 1885	S	285
988	CHAMPIONS OF BALL RACKET / "On the Diamond Field"/ (Vig.) 1886	S	285
989	CHAMPIONS OF THE BARN/ (9.3x13.2) 1876	S	190
990	CHAMPIONS OF THE BARN YARD	S	190
991	CHAMPIONS OF THE FIELD, THE/ Steady On A Point	S	500
992	CHAMPIONS OF THE MISSISSIPPI / "A Race for the Buckhorns"/ (18.4x27.14) 1866 [New BEST 50]	L	7700

993	CHAMPIONS OF THE UNION, THE/ 1861	M	415
994	CHANCE FOR BOTH BARRELS, A/ (Same Stone As Am. Field Sports) 1857	L	3350
995	CHANCES OF BILLIARDS, THE/ "A Scratch All Around"/ (16.6x24.14) (Companion to #450) 1869	L	2050
996	CHANG" AND "ENG" / The World Renowned Siamese Twins/ (12x9) 1860	S	180
997	CHANGE OF BASE, A/ (Vig.) (Companion to #5901) 1883	S	275
998	CHANGE OF DRIVERS UNDER THE RULE, A/ (Above Title) 1876	M	560
999	CHANGED MAN / This Man by his wife's advice/ 1880	S	160
1000	CHAPPAQUA FARM / West Chester County, NY/ (8.8x12.8) 1872	S	230
1001	CHARLES/ 1845, N. Currier	S	155
1002	CHARLES/ (Black Background) N. Currier	L	170
1003	CHARLES F. ADAMS/ (11.7x8.15) 1848, N. Currier	S	120
1004	CHARLES GAVAN DUFFY	S	75
1005	CHARLES O. SCOTT / The Prize Baby.../ 1855, N. Currier	VS	85
1006	CHARLES ROWELL / "The Celebrated Pedestrian"/ (12.13x9.2) 1879	S	175
1007	CHARLES STEWART PARNELL, M.P.	S	80
1008	CHARLES STEWART PARNELL, M.P./ (13.1x9.6) 1881	S	80
1009	CHARLES SUMNER	S	90
1010	CHARLES WESLEY, A.M./ N. Currier	S	70
1011	CHARLEY FORD/ (Vig.) 1880	S	215
1012	CHARLEY / THE PRIZE BABY BOY/ 1857	S	80
1013	CHARLIE IS MY DARLING/ (11.15x8) 1872	S	80
1014	CHARLOTTE/ N. Currier	S	80
1015	CHARLOTTE / #118/ N. Currier	S	80
1016	CHARLOTTE / #118/ 1845, N. Currier	S	80
1017	CHARLOTTE / #118/ (12.3X8.13) N. Currier	S	80
1018	CHARTER OAK! CHARTER OAK! / ANCIENT AND FAIR/ (Vig.)	S	80
1019	CHASE - IN THE OLDEN TIME/ N. Currier	S	85
1020	CHATHAM SQUARE, NEW YORK/ (8.1x12.10) N. Currier [Old BEST 50]	S	585
1021	CHECK, A / "Keep Your Distance"/ N. Currier	L	3150
1022	CHEPSTOW RUINS / SOUTH WALES	VS	80
1023	CHERRY TIME/ 1866	M	465
1024	CHESTER A. ARTHUR	S	80
1025	CHESTNUT HILL/ (Vig.) 1879	S	290
1026	CHICAGO AS IT WAS/ (8.6x12.14)	S	590
1027	CHICAGO IN FLAMES/ (8.8x12.8)	S	560
1028	CHICAGO PLATFORM AND CANDIDATE, THE	M	250
1029	CHICKY'S DINNER/ (8.8x11.8)	S	130
1030	CHIEF COOK AND BOTTLE WASHER/ (8.6x13) (Companion to #4858) N. Currier	S	145

1031	CHILD JESUS, THE	S	20
1032	CHILDHOOD'S HAPPY DAYS/ (11.5x15.12) 1863	M	280
1033	CHILDREN IN THE WOODS, THE/ (11.14x8.8)	S	145
1034	CHILDREN IN THE WOODS, THE/ 1867	S	145
1035	CHILDREN'S PIC-NIC, THE/ (12.6x9.3)	S	155
1036	CHINCHA ISLANDS, THE/ (7.13x13.14) 1860	S	125
1037	CHINESE JUNK KEYING, THE/ (7.14x13.1) 1847, N. Currier	S	365
1038	CHIP OFF THE OLD BLOCK, A/ N. Currier	L	385
1039	CHOICE APPLES/ (Vig.)	S	160
1040	CHOICE BOUQUET/ (8.7x12.8) 1872	S	125
1041	CHOICE BOUQUET/ (Vig.) 1874	S	125
1042	CHOICE FRUIT/ 1865	L	900
1043	CHOICE FRUITS	VS	150
1044	CHOICE SEGARS AND FINE TOBACCO/ (Tobacco ad.)	S	200
1045	CHRIST AND THE ANGELS/ (11.11x8.6)	S	20
1046	CHRIST AND THE WOMAN OF SAMARIA AT JACOB'S WELL/ (12.6x8.12) N. Currier	S	20
1047	CHRIST AND THE WOMAN OF SAMARIA AT JACOB'S WELL/ (12.6x8.13)	S	20
1048	CHRIST AT THE WELL/ (11.14x8.10) 1846, N. Currier	S	20
1049	CHRIST AT THE WELL / "WHOSOEVER SHALL DRINK..."	S	20
1050	CHRIST AT THE WELL	S	20
1051	CHRIST BEARING HIS CROSS / #196/ (10.2x7.15) N. Currier	S	20
1052	CHRIST BEARING HIS CROSS/ (12.11x8.12) N. Currier	S	20
1053	CHRIST BEFORE PILATE / #195/ (12.11x8.15) 1847, N. Currier	S	20
1054	CHRIST BEFORE PILATE	S	20
1055	CHRIST BEFORE PILATE / "He delivers them up to be crucified"/ (12.11x8.15) 1847, N. Currier	S	20
1056	CHRIST BLESSING LITTLE CHILDREN/ (11.11x8.5)	S	20
1057	CHRIST BLESSING LITTLE CHILDREN/ #266	S	20
1058	CHRIST BLESSING LITTLE CHILDREN/ (11.15x8.9)	S	20
1059	CHRIST BLESSING THE CHILDREN	S	20
1060	CHRIST HEALING THE SICK/ (12.11x8.3)	S	20
1061	CHRIST IN THE GARDEN	S	20
1062	CHRIST IN THE GARDEN OF OLIVES	S	20
1063	CHRIST IS OUR LIGHT- OUR STAR OF REDEMPTION/ (12.11x9.4) 1849	S	20
1064	CHRIST IS OUR LIGHT- OUR STAR OF REDEMPTION/ 1866	S	20
1065	CHRIST RESTORETH THE BLIND / El Senor da Vista a un Ciego/ 1846, N. Currier	S	20
1066	CHRIST RESTORETH THE BLIND	S	20
1067	CHRIST RESTORETH THE BLIND/ 1846, N. Currier	S	20

All prints are published by Currier & Ives unless otherwise stated.

1068	CHRIST STILLING THE TEMPEST/ (7.13x12.7) 1871	S	20
1069	CHRIST THE CONSOLER/ (8.12x11.18)	S	20
1070	CHRIST WALKING ON THE SEA/ N. Currier	S	20
1071	CHRIST WALKING ON THE SEA/ (7.14x12.9)	S	20
1072	CHRIST WASHING HIS DISCIPLES' FEET	S	20
1073	CHRIST WEEPING OVER JERUSALEM/ (7.15x12.7)	S	20
1074	CHRIST WEEPING OVER JERUSALEM/ 1847	S	20
1075	CHRIST'S ENTRY INTO JERUSALEM/ (7.14x12.6)	S	20
1076	CHRIST'S SERMON ON THE MOUNT / "The Parable of the Lily"/ 1866	M	25
1077	CHRIST'S SERMON ON THE MOUNT / "The Parable of the Lily"/ 1866	S	20
1078	CHRISTENING, THE	S	60
1079	CHRISTIAN'S HOPE/ (Vig.) 1874	S	20
1080	CHRISTIAN'S REFUGE, THE/ 1868	M	25
1081	CHRISTMAS SNOW/ (7.15x4.15) (Companion to #5140)	VS	770
1082	CHRISTOPHER COLUMBUS/ 1892	L	265
1083	CHRISTUS CONSOLATOR/ (8.6x12.6)	S	20
1084	CHRISTUS CONSOLATUS	S	20
1084A	CIRCULAR PLEASURE RAILWAY/ In Hoboken, N.J./ N. Currier	S	1325
1085	CITY HALL AND COUNTY COURT HOUSE, NEWARK, NJ/ (7.4x11.8)	S	430
1086	CITY HALL, NEW YORK/ (8x12.6) N. Currier	S	470
1087	CITY HALL, NEW YORK/ (8.4x12.8) N. Currier	S	470
1088	CITY HALL AND VICINITY, NEW YORK CITY/ (8.6x12.7)	S	470
1089	CITY HOTEL, BROADWAY, NY/ N. Currier	L	2900
1090	CITY OF BALTIMORE, THE/ 1880	L	3200
1091	CITY OF BOSTON, THE / 1873	L	3200
1092	CITY OF BROOKLYN/ 1879	L	3200
1093	CITY OF BROOKLYN/ (Fireman's Certificate)	S	210
1094	CITY OF CHICAGO, THE/ 1892	L	3300
1095	CITY OF CHICAGO, THE/ 1874	L	3225
1096	CITY OF CHICAGO/ (Steamship) 1892	L	1200
1097	CITY OF JUNGO/ 1840, N. Currier	S	115
1098	CITY OF MEXICO / Vista de Mexico	S	115
1099	CITY OF NEW ORLEANS, THE/ (21.4x35.4) 1885	L	3200
1100	CITY OF NEW ORLEANS	S	740
1101	CITY OF NEW YORK/ 1844, N. Currier	S	580
1102	CITY OF NEW YORK/ (20.14x29) 1855, N. Currier	L	3100
1103	CITY OF NEW YORK/ 1856, N. Currier	L	3100
1104	CITY OF NEW YORK, THE/ (20.6x32.13) 1870, N. Currier	L	3100
1105	CITY OF NEW YORK, THE/ (20.5x32.13) 1870, N. Currier	L	3100

1106	CITY OF NEW YORK, THE/ (Birds Eye View) 1884, N. Currier	L	3100
1107	CITY OF NEW YORK, THE/ (Birds Eye View From South) 1876, N. Currier	L	3100
1108	CITY OF NEW YORK, THE/ 1886, N. Currier	L	3100
1109	CITY OF NEW YORK, THE/ 1889, N. Currier	L	3100
1110	CITY OF NEW YORK, THE/ 1892, N. Currier	L	3100
1111	CITY OF NEW YORK AND ENVIRONS/ (8.9x13.2) 1875	S	690
1112	CITY OF NEW YORK FROM JERSEY CITY/ (8.2x12.10) 1849, N. Currier	S	600
1113	CITY OF NEW YORK, THE/ (Equitable Life) (Bldg.) 1876	L	1550
1114	CITY OF NEW YORK, THE/ (Equitable Life) (Birds-eye view) 1876	L	1575
1115	CITY OF PEKING" / Pacific Mail Steamship Co.	S	275
1116	CITY OF PHILADELPHIA, THE / 1876	L	3200
1117	CITY OF ST. LOUIS, THE/ (20.8x32.10) 1874	L	3200
1118	CITY OF SAN FRANCISCO/ (Bird's Eye View from the Bay) 1877	S	2000
1119	CITY OF SAN FRANCISCO, THE/ 1889	L	4200
1120	CITY OF SAN FRANCISCO SKETCHED AND DRAWN BY C.R. PARSONS/ 1878	L	4300
1121	CITY OF VERA CRUZ / Vista de Vera Cruz	S	90
1122	CITY OF WASHINGTON, THE/ 1880	L	3150
1123	CITY OF WASHINGTON, THE/ 1892	L	3150
1124	CLAM BOY ON HIS MUSCLE	S	175
1125	CLARA/ N. Currier	S	75
1126	CLARA/ (12.4x8.11) 1849, N. Currier	S	75
1127	CLARA	S	75
1128	CLARISSA/ N. Currier	S	75
1129	CLEAN SWEEP, A/ (Vig.) (Companion to #756) 1889	S	190
1130	CLEAR GRIT/ (Dog and Rat)	S	110
1131	CLEARING, A / "On the American Frontier"/ (8.7x12.7)	S	335
1132	CLEARING, THE	S	280
1133	CLEVELAND FAMILY, THE/ 1893	S	95
1134	CLEVELAND FAMILY, THE/ 1893	L	140
1135	CLEVELAND SMILE, THE/ (Vig.)	S	85
1136	CLIFTON HALL, BRISTOL COLLEGE, PA/ (10.2x13.10) 1835, N. Currier	S	185
1137	CLINGSTONE / Record 2:12/ 1882	TC	85
1138	CLINGSTONE / By Rysdyk's Dam Gretchen.../ 1882	S	290
1139	CLIPPER SHIP "ADELAIDE" / 'Hove to for a Pilot'/ (16x24.8) 1856	L	5600
1140	CLIPPER SHIP "COMET" OF NY/ (16.2x23.10) 1855, N. Currier	L	3475
1141	CLIPPER SHIP "CONTEST"/ (16x23.2) 1853, N. Currier	L	3400
1142	CLIPPER SHIP "COSMOS," THE	M	1325
1143	CLIPPER SHIP "DREADNOUGHT"/ (16.8x24.4) 1854, N. Currier	L	3025

1144	CLIPPER SHIP "DREADNOUGHT" OFF TUSKAR LIGHT/ (16.2x24.10) 1856, N. Currier	L	3050
1145	CLIPPER SHIP "FLYING CLOUD"/ (16.8x23.15) 1852, N. Currier	L	3600
1146	CLIPPER SHIP "GREAT REPUBLIC"/ (16x23.6) 1853, N. Currier	L	2625
1147	CLIPPER SHIP "GREAT REPUBLIC"/ (16.4x24) 1855, N. Currier	L	2625
1148	CLIPPER SHIP "GREAT REPUBLIC"/ N. Currier	S	415
1149	CLIPPER SHIP "GREAT REPUBLIC"/ (8.15x12.7)	S	415
1150	CLIPPER SHIP "GREAT REPUBLIC" / #347/ (Vig.)	S	405
1151	CLIPPER SHIP "GREAT REPUBLIC"/ (Sailing to right) (Vig.)	S	405
1152	CLIPPER SHIP "GREAT REPUBLIC" (Ship in distance) (Vig.)	S	405
1153	CLIPPER SHIP "HURRICANE"/ (14.8x21.12) 1852, N. Currier	L	6000
1154	CLIPPER SHIP IN A HURRICANE, A	M	1950
1155	CLIPPER SHIP IN A HURRICANE, A/ (Second State)	S	630
1156	CLIPPER SHIP IN A HURRICANE, A/ (Lifeboat removed)	S	600
1157	CLIPPER SHIP IN A SNOW SQUALL, A/ (8.8x12.8)	S	705
1158	CLIPPER SHIP "LIGHTNING"/ 1854, N. Currier	L	5200
1159	CLIPPER SHIP "NIGHTINGALE"/ (16.5x24) 1854, N. Currier [Old BEST 50]	L	5100
1160	CLIPPER SHIP "OCEAN EXPRESS"/ (16.3x24.4) 1856, N. Currier	L	3000
1161	CLIPPER SHIP OFF CAPE HORN, A	S	630
1162	CLIPPER SHIP OFF THE PORT	S	665
1163	CLIPPER SHIP "QUEEN OF CLIPPERS"/ N. Currier	S	610
1164	CLIPPER SHIP "RACER"/ (16.4x24.2) 1854, N. Currier	L	5000
1165	CLIPPER SHIP "RED JACKET"/ 1855 [Old & New BEST 50]	L	5900
1166	CLIPPER SHIP "RED JACKET"/ (Vig.)	S	835
1167	CLIPPER SHIP "SOVEREIGN OF THE SEAS"/ (15.12x23.12) 1852, N. Currier	L	5300
1168	CLIPPER SHIP "SWEEPSTAKES"/ (16.5x23.10) 1853, N. Currier	L	4700
1169	CLIPPER SHIP "THREE BROTHERS"/ 1875	L	2400
1170	CLIPPER SHIP "THREE BROTHERS"	S	460
1171	CLIPPER SHIP "YOUNG AMERICA"/ (16x23.4) 1853, N. Currier	L	4400
1172	CLIPPER SHIPS HOMEWARD BOUND (8x12.6)	S	735
1173	CLIPPER YACHT "AMERICA", THE / Built by George Steers of New York/ N. Currier [Old BEST 50]	M	1150
1174	CLIPPER YACHT "AMERICA", THE / Review of the Royal Yacht/ (Sailing to Left) N.Currier	M	1050
1175	CLIPPER YACHT "AMERICA", THE / Winner of the Royal Yacht Squadron Cup, 1851/ N. Currier	M	1050
1176	CLIPPER YACHT "AMERICA" OF NY/ N. Currier	S	620
1177	CLOSE CALCULATION, A / "Don't You Wish You May Get It?"/ (8.7x12.14) N. Currier	S	135
1178	CLOSE FINISH, A/ (Vig.) 1874	S	285

1179	CLOSE HEAT, A/ (16.12x26) 1873	L	1575
1180	CLOSE LAP ON THE RUN IN, A/ (18x27.9) 1886	L	1550
1181	CLOSE QUARTERS/ (25x19.12) 1866	L	1175
1182	COACHING- FOUR IN HAND/ 1876	M	690
1183	COCK-A-DOODLE-DO/ (Rooster)	S	155
1184	COCK OF THE WALK/ (Vig.) 1879	S	195
1185	COD FISHING OFF NEWFOUNDLAND/ (8.7x12.7) 1872	S	1250
1186	COL. E.L. SNOW/ (Vig.) C. Currier	S	75
1187	COL. EDWARD D. BAKER	S	75
1188	COL. ELMER E. ELLSWORTH / 1st Regt. New York Fire Zouaves	S	95
1189	COL. ELMER E. ELLSWORTH / 1st Regt. New York Fire Zouaves/ (Vig.)	S	95
1190	COL. ELMER E. ELLSWORTH / 1st Regt. New York Fire Zouaves / He Who...	S	95
1191	COL. FRANK P. BLAIR/ "First Regiment Missouri Volunteers"/ (Vig.) 1861	S	85
1192	COL. FREMONT'S LAST GRAND EXPLORING EXPEDITION IN 1856/ (Political Cartoon) (Vig.)	S	140
1193	COL. H.S. RUSSELL'S "SMUGGLER"/ (Vig.) 1876	S	290
1194	COL. HARNEY AT THE DRAGOON FIGHT AT MEDELIN, NEAR VERA CRUZ/ (8.6x12.8) 1847, N. Currier	S	130
1195	COL. JOHN E. WOOL/ 1847, N. Currier	S	80
1196	COL. JOHN O'MAHONEY/ (Vig.)	S	75
1197	COL. JAMES A. MULLIGAN	S	80
1198	COL. MAX WEBER/ (Vig.)	S	80
1199	COL. MICHAEL CORCORAN AT THE BATTLE OF BULL RUN, VA/ (8.2x12.8)	S	215
1200	COL. MICHAEL CORCORAN/ (Vig.)	S	80
1201	COL. RICHARD M. JOHNSON/ 1846, N. Currier	S	75
1202	COL. THEODORE ROOSEVELT U.S.V.	S	80
1203	COLORED BEAUTY/ (Vig.) 1872	S	75
1204	COLORED BEAUTY/ (Vig.) 1877	S	75
1205	COLORED BELLE, THE	S	75
1206	COLORED ENGRAVINGS / FOR THE PEOPLE/ N. Currier	M	760
1207	COLORED VOLUNTEER, THE	M	230
1208	COLORED VOLUNTEER MARCHING INTO DIXIE, THE / (12.4x8.3)	S	175
1209	COLORING HIS MEERSCHAUM/ 1879	VS	180
1209A	COLORING HIS MEERSCHAUM/ 1879	TC	75
1210	COLORING HIS MEERSCHAUM/ 1880	S	160
1211	COLORING HIS MEERSCHAUM	S	145
1212	COLUMBIA/ (Girl's Head)	S	75
1213	COM. ANDREW H. FOOTE/ (Vig.)	S	80
1214	COM. FARRAGUT'S FLEET PASSING THE FORTS ON THE MISSISSIPPI/ (7.14x12.9) 1862	S	395

All prints are published by Currier & Ives unless otherwise stated.

1215	COMBAT AT THE MILITARY STATION OF CHATEAU d'EAU/ (8x12.10) 1848, N. Currier	S	135
1216	COME GANG AWA'WI'ME/ N. Currier	S	80
1217	COME INTO THE GARDEN, MAUD	S	105
1218	COME TAKE A DRINK/ (Vig.) 1868	S	205
1219	COMING FROM THE TROT/ (18.10x28.10) 1869	L	2050
1220	COMING HOME WITH A FAMILY	S	165
1221	COMING IN "ON HIS EAR"/ (Vig.) 1875	S	195
1222	COMING MATCH/ 1881	S	165
1223	COMING THE PUTTY/ (8.3x12.6) (Companion to #4168) 1853 N. Currier	S	310
1224	COMING UP SMILING/ (Vig.) (Companion to #3636) 1884	S	205
1225	COMMANDER IN CHIEF, THE/ 1863	S	130
1226	COMMODORE NUTT, THE/ (Midget) N. Currier	S	130
1227	COMMODORE NUTT, THE/ $30,000 NUT/ Smallest Man Alive	S	130
1228	COMMON LOT, THE/ (Vig.) N. Currier	S	75
1229	COMPAGNE GENERALE TRANSATLANTIQUE STEAMER "LA BOURGOGNE"	S	270
1230	COMPAGNE GENERALE TRANSATLANTIQUE STEAMER "LA BRETAGNE"	S	270
1231	COMPAGNE GENERALE TRANSATLANTIQUE STEAMER "LA CHAMPAGNE"	S	270
1232	COMPAGNE GENERALE TRANSATLANTIQUE STEAMER "LA GASCOGNE"	S	270
1233	COMPAGNE GENERALE TRANSATLANTIQUE STEAMER "L'AQUTAINE"	S	270
1234	COMPAGNE GENERALE TRANSATLANTIQUE STEAMER "LA LORRAINE"	S	270
1235	COMPAGNE GENERALE TRANSATLANTIQUE STEAMER "LA TOURAINE"	S	270
1236	CONFEDERACY- THE SECESSION MOVEMENT	S	280
1237	CONGRESSIONAL SCALES- A TRUE BALANCE/ 1850, N. Currier	M	180
1238	CONSTANCE	L	145
1239	CONSTITUTION AND GUERRIERE, THE/ (Broadside View) 1846, N. Currier	S	525
1240	CONSTITUTION AND GUERRIERE, THE/ N. Currier	S	525
1241	CONSTITUTION AND JAVA/ 1845, N. Currier	S	525
1242	CONSTITUTION AND JAVA/ 1846, N. Currier	S	525
1243	CONSTITUTION AND JAVA/ (7.14x13) 1846	S	525
1244	CONSTITUTION AND JAVA/ (7.12x12.14) 1846, N. Currier	S	525
1245	CONTESTED SEAT, A/ (Political Cartoon) N. Currier	S	180
1246	COOLING STREAM, THE/ (11.3x15.14)	M	440
1247	COON CLUB HUNT, THE / "Hot On The Scent"/ (Vig.) 1885	S	235

1248	COON CLUB HUNT, THE / "Taking A Header"/ (Vig.) 1885	S	235
1249	COPPED AT A COCK FIGHT/ (Vig.) (Companion to #620) 1884	S	230
1250	CORDELIA HOWARD AS "EVA" IN "UNCLE TOM'S CABIN"/ 1852, C. Currier	VS	195
1251	CORINTHIAN RACE, A / "A High Toned Start"/ (Vig.) 1883	S	220
1252	CORINTHIAN RACE, A / "A Low Toned Finish"/ (Vig.) 1883	S	220
1253	CORK CASTLE AND BLACK ROCK CASTLE, THE	S	85
1254	CORK RIVER, THE	S	70
1255	CORNED BEEF	S	190
1256	CORNELIA/ (11.11x8.8) 1846, N. Currier	S	75
1257	CORNELIA/ 1847, N. Currier	S	75
1258	CORNWALLIS IS TAKEN/ (8.12x12.11) 1876 [Old BEST 50]	S	445
1259	CORRECT LIKENESS OF MR. H. ROCKWELL'S HORSE ALEXANDER/ N. Currier	M	430
1260	CORRECT LIKENESS OF MR. H. ROCKWELL'S HORSE ALEXANDER/ N. Currier	S	285
1261	CORSAIRS ISLE, THE	M	300
1262	CORTELYOU MANSION-OLD MANSION HOUSE/ N. Currier	S	180
1263	COTTAGE BY THE CLIFF, THE/ (8.7x12.7)	S	190
1264	COTTAGE BY THE WAYSIDE, THE/ (8.8x12.6)	S	210
1265	COTTAGE DOORYARD-EVENING, THE/ (10.7x14.15) 1855, N. Currier	M	390
1266	COTTAGE LIFE-SPRING/ (10.10x15) 1856	M	400
1267	COTTAGE LIFE-SUMMER	S	235
1268	COTTAGE LIFE-SUMMER/ (10.6x15) 1856	M	405
1269	COTTAGES, THE/ (Vig.)	VS	165
1270	COTTER'S SATURDAY NIGHT	S	135
1271	COTTON PLANTATION ON THE MISSISSIPPI, A/ (20x30.1) 1884 [New BEST 50]	L	4600
1272	COURAGEOUS CONDUCT OF A YOUNG GIRL/ 1848, N. Currier	S	125
1273	COURSE OF TRUE LOVE, THE/ (11.6x8.8) 1875	S	75
1274	COURTSHIP/ N. Currier	S	85
1275	COUSINS, THE/ N. Currier	S	75
1276	COVE OF CORK, THE/ (8x12.8)	S	75
1277	COZZEN'S DOCK, WEST POINT, HUDSON RIVER/ (10.13x15.4)	M	780
1278	CRACK SHOT/ 1879	S	140
1279	CRACK SHOT/ 1880	TC	70
1280	CRACK SHOTS IN POSITION/ 1875	S	140
1281	CRACK" SLOOP IN A RACE TO THE WINDWARD, A/ (Yacht "Gracie") (19x28.1) 1882	L	1750
1282	CRACK TEAM" AT A SMASHING GAIT, A/ (16.7x24.14) 1869	L	1550
1283	CRACK TROTTER, A/ "Coming Around"/ (Vig.) 1880	S	290

1284	CRACK TROTTER, A/ "A Little Off"/ (Vig.) 1880	S	290
1285	CRACK TROTTER BETWEEN THE HEATS/ 1880	TC	75
1286	CRACK TROTTER BETWEEN THE HEATS/ (Vig.) 1875	M	495
1287	CRACK TROTTER IN THE HARNESS OF THE PERIOD/ 1880	TC	75
1288	CRACK TROTTER IN THE HARNESS OF THE PERIOD/ (Vig.) 1875	M	495
1289	CRACOVIENNE, THE/ (Village background) N. Currier	S	90
1290	CRACOVIENNE, THE/ (Rustic background) N. Currier	S	90
1291	CRADLE OF LIBERTY, THE / (11.15x8.14) 1876	S	175
1292	CRAPS- A BUSTED GAME/ "Sebben and Lebben Scoops de Crowd"/ (Vig.) 1890	S	240
1293	CRAPS- A CLOSE CALL/ (Vig.) 1890	S	240
1294	CRAYON STUDIES / #464/ N. Currier	S	225
1295	CRAYON STUDIES / #472/ N. Currier	S	225
1296	CRAYON STUDIES / #473/ N. Currier	S	225
1297	CRAYON STUDIES / OLD MANSION HOUSE/ N. Currier	S	225
1298	CRAYON STUDIES / SUMMER NOON/ N. Currier	S	225
1299	CRAYON STUDIES / VIEW ON FULTON AVENUE, BROOKLYN/ N. Currier	S	225
1300	CREAM OF LOVE/ (Vig.) 1879	S	180
1301	CREATING A SENSATION/ "The Bully Boy on a Bicycle"/ (Vig.) 1881	S	260
1302	CROMWELL'S BRIDGE, GLENGARIFF, IRELAND (8x12.8)	S	85
1303	CROSS AND ANCHOR OF ROSES	S	75
1304	CROSS AND CROWN OF FLOWERS	S	75
1305	CROSS AND CROWN/ 1870	M	95
1306	CROSS" MATCHED RACE/ (12.2x18.13) 1891	M	560
1307	CROSS MATCHED TEAM, A/ (Vig.) 1878	S	290
1308	CROSSED BY A MILK TRAIN/ (Vig.) 1884	S	265
1309	CROSSED BY A MILK TRAIN/ (Vig.) 1885	S	265
1310	CROW QUADRILLES, THE/ (Vig.) 1837, N. Currier	S	95
1311	CROWD" THAT "SCOOPED" THE POOLS, THE/ 1878	TC	75
1312	CROWD" THAT "SCOOPED" THE POOLS, THE/ (Vig.) (Companion to #5668) 1878	S	255
1313	CROWING MATCH	TC	70
1314	CROWN OF THORNS, THE/ (10.13x8.11)	S	20
1315	CROW'S NEST, NORTH RIVER/ N. Currier	S	335
1316	CROXIE"/ Record 2:19.25/ (Vig.)	S	290
1317	CRUCIFIXION, THE / #31/ 1847, N. Currier	S	20
1318	CRUCIFIXION, THE/ 1894, N. Currier	S	20
1319	CRUCIFIXION, THE/ (11.14x8.8) N. Currier	S	20
1320	CRUCIFIXION, THE/ (12.4x8.13) N. Currier	S	20

1321	CRUCIFIXION, THE	M	20
1322	CRUCIFIXION, THE	S	20
1323	CRUCIFIXION, THE / LA CRUCIFIXION/ 1849	M	20
1324	CRUISER "NEW YORK", THE	S	360
1325	CRYSTAL PALACE, THE / (8x12.11) N. Currier	S	310
1326	CRYSTAL PALACE, THE MAGNIFICENT BUILDING FOR THE WORLD'S FAIR OF 1851, HYDE PARK, LONDON/ (8x12.8)	S	310
1327	CUMBERLAND VALLEY/ (15.13x20.8) 1865	L	1600
1328	CUP THAT CHEERS, THE/ (Vig.) 1884	S	170
1329	CUNARD STEAMSHIP "SERVIA"	S	285
1330	CUPID'S OWN/ 1879	S	125
1331	CUPID'S OWN/ (Cigar advertising card) 1880	TC	70
1332	CURFEW BELL, THE	S	125
1333	CUSTER'S LAST CHARGE/ (Vig.) 1876	S	340
1334	CUSTOM HOUSE, NEW YORK/ (8.5x12.10) N. Currier	S	560
1335	CUSTOM HOUSE, NEW YORK/ N. Currier	M	760
1336	CUTTER YACHT "BIANCA"	L	1200
1337	CUTTER YACHT "GALATEA"	S	385
1338	CUTTER "GENESTA"/ (15.4x21) 1885	L	1200
1339	CUTTER "GENESTA"/ (9.11x13.14)	S	385
1340	CUTTER "MADGE"	S	385
1341	CUTTER YACHT "MARIA" / In her trial of speed/ 1852, N. Currier	L	1200
1342	CUTTER YACHT "MARIA" / Modelled by R. E. Stevens/ 1852, N. Currier	M	740
1343	CUTTER YACHT "SCUD" OF PHILADELPHIA/ 1855, N. Currier	L	1875
1344	CUTTER YACHT "THISTLE"/ (10x13.10) 1887	S	385

D

Con#	Title	Folio	Value
1345	DAIRY FARM, THE	S	190
1346	DAISY AND HER PETS/ (11.12x9.6) 1876	S	95
1347	DAN RICE"/ (16.12x26) 1868	L	1450
1348	DAN RICE"/ (16.14x26.4) 1866	L	1450
1349	DANCING LESSON, THE (11.12x8.12)	S	120
1350	DANGER SIGNAL, THE/ (1st state) (17.2x28.15) 1884	L	6075
1351	DANGER SIGNAL, THE/ (2nd state) 1884	L	5750
1352	DANL. D. TOMPKINS	VS	45
1353	DANIEL T. TOMPKINS" AND "BLANC NEGRE"/ 1851, N. Currier	L	2150

1354	DANIEL IN THE LIONS DEN/ (12.6x9.4) N. Currier	S	70
1355	DANIEL IN THE LIONS DEN/ (11.14x8.7)	S	70
1356	DANIEL O'CONNELL / The Champion of Freedom / #164/ N. Currier	S	70
1357	DANIEL O'CONNELL / The Champion of Freedom/ (11.14x8.15) N. Currier	S	70
1358	DANIEL O'CONNELL / The Champion of Freedom / #724	S	70
1359	DANIEL O'CONNELL / The Champion of Freedom/ (11.13x8.9)	S	70
1360	DANIEL O'CONNELL / The Champion of Freedom/ N. Currier	S	70
1361	DANIEL O'CONNELL / The Great Irish "Liberator"/ (11.12x8.10)	S	70
1362	DANIEL WEBSTER/ N. Currier	L	220
1363	DANIEL WEBSTER / "Defender of the Constitution"/ (11.1x8.12) 1851, N. Currier	S	190
1364	DANIEL WEBSTER / "New England's Choice for Twelfth President/ #130/ (11.10x8.15) 1847, N. Currier	S	190
1365	DANIEL WEBSTER / "New England's Choice for Twelfth President/ (11.10x8.15) 1847, N. Currier	S	190
1366	DANIEL WEBSTER / "Secretary of State"/ N. Currier	S	190
1367	DARGLE GLEN, IRELAND	M	95
1368	DARK EYED BEAUTY, THE	S	75
1369	DARK FORESHADING ON A FLASH PICTURE/ (Vig.) (Companion to #4852) 1890	S	255
1370	DARKTOWN ATHLETICS QUARTER-MILE DASH/ (Vig.) 1893	S	240
1371	DARKTOWN ATHLETICS RUNNING HIGH JUMP/ (Vig.) 1893	S	240
1372	DARKTOWN BANJO CLASS / All in tune/ (Vig.) 1886	S	240
1373	DARKTOWN BANJO CLASS / Off the key/ (Vig.) 1886	S	240
1374	DARKTOWN BICYCLE CLUB KNOCKED OUT/ (Vig.) 1892	S	240
1375	DARKTOWN BICYCLE CLUB ON PARADE/ (Vig.) 1892	S	240
1376	DARKTOWN BICYCLE RACE - A SUDDEN HALT/ (Vig.) 1895	S	240
1377	DARKTOWN BICYCLE RACE - THE START/ (Vig.) 1895	S	240
1378	DARKTOWN BICYCLING - A TENDER PAIR/ (Vig.) 1897	S	240
1379	DARKTOWN BICYCLING - SCOOPED DE PEAR/ (Vig.) 1897	S	240
1380	DARKTOWN BOWLING CLUB, THE / Bowled out/ (Vig.) 1888	S	240
1381	DARKTOWN BOWLING CLUB, THE / Watching for a strike/ (Vig.) 1888	S	240
1382	DARKTOWN DONATION PARTY, A / A Doubtful Acquisition	S	240
1383	DARKTOWN DONATION PARTY, A / An Object Lesson/ (Vig.) 1893	S	240
1384	DARKTOWN ELOPEMENT, THE / Skip softly lub/ (Vig.) 1885	S	240
1385	DARKTOWN ELOPEMENT, THE / Hurry/ (Vig.) 1885	S	240
1386	DARKTOWN FIRE BRIGADE, THE / "A Prize Squirt"/ (Vig.)	S	255
1387	DARKTOWN FIRE BRIGADE, THE / All on their Mettle/ (Vig.) 1889	S	255
1388	DARKTOWN FIRE BRIGADE, THE / Hook and Ladder Gymnastics/ (Vig.)	S	255
1388A	DARKTOWN FIRE BRIGADE, THE / Hook and Ladder Gymnastics/ 1888	TC	75
1389	DARKTOWN FIRE BRIGADE, THE / Investigating a Smoke/ (Vig.) 1894	S	255

1390	DARKTOWN FIRE BRIGADE, THE / Taking a Rest/ (Vig.)	S	255
1391	DARKTOWN FIRE BRIGADE, THE / Saved/ (Vig.) 1884	S	255
1392	DARKTOWN FIRE BRIGADE, THE / Slightly Demoralized/ (Vig.) 1889	S	255
1393	DARKTOWN FIRE BRIGADE / The Chief on Duty/ (Vig.) 1885	S	255
1394	DARKTOWN FIRE BRIGADE / The Foreman on Parade/ (Vig.) 1885	S	255
1395	DARKTOWN FIRE BRIGADE / The Last shake/ (Vig.) 1885	S	255
1396	DARKTOWN FIRE BRIGADE / To the Rescue, The/ (Vig.) 1884	S	255
1397	DARKTOWN FIRE BRIGADE / Under Full Steam, The/ (Vig.) 1887	S	255
1397A	DARKTOWN FIRE BRIGADE / Under Full Steam, The/ 1888	TC	75
1398	DARKTOWN FOOTBALL MATCH / The Kick Off, The/ (Vig.)	S	145
1399	DARKTOWN FOOTBALL MATCH / The Scrimmage, The/ (Vig.)	S	245
1400	DARKTOWN GLIDE, THE/ (Vig.) 1884	S	245
1401	DARKTOWN HOOK AND LADDER CORPS / Going to the Front/ (Vig.) 1884	S	255
1402	DARKTOWN HOOK AND LADDER CORPS / Going to the Front/ 1891	L	590
1403	DARKTOWN HOOK AND LADDER CORPS, THE / In Action/ (Vig.) 1884	S	255
1404	DARKTOWN FIRE BRIGADE / Saved, The/ (Vig.) 1891	L	590
1405	DARKTOWN HUNT / Presenting the Brush, The/ (Vig.) 1892	S	240
1406	DARKTOWN HUNT / The Meet , The/ (Vig.) 1892	S	240
1407	DARKTOWN LAW SUIT / Cheerful Milker/ (Vig.) 1886	S	245
1408	DARKTOWN LAW SUIT / Part Two/ (Vig.) 1887	S	245
1409	DARKTOWN LAWN PARTY, A / A Bully Time/ (Vig.) 1888	S	240
1410	DARKTOWN LAWN PARTY, A / Music in the Air (Vig.)	S	240
1411	DARKTOWN OPERA / The Lovers Leap/ (Vig.) 1886	S	240
1412	DARKTOWN OPERA / The Serenade/ (Vig.) 1886	S	240
1413	DARKTOWN OTHELLO/ (Vig.) 1886	S	240
1414	DARKTOWN RACE / Facing the Flag, A/ (Vig.) 1892	S	240
1415	DARKTOWN RACE / Won by a Neck, A/ (Vig.) 1892	S	240
1416	DARKTOWN RIDING CLASS / Gallop/ (Vig.) 1890	S	240
1417	DARKTOWN RIDING CLASS / Trot/ (Vig.) 1890	S	240
1418	DARKTOWN SLIDE, THE / "Golly! am dere an Erfquake?"/ (Vig.) 1884	S	240
1419	DARKTOWN SLIDE, THE / "Golly! Wot's Busted?"/(Vig.) 1844	S	240
1420	DARKTOWN SOCIABLES / A "Fancy Dress" Hoodoo/ (Vig.) 1890	S	240
1421	DARKTOWN SOCIABLES / A "Fancy Dress" Surprise/ (Vig.) 1890	S	240
1422	DARKTOWN SOCIETY / On their Feed/ (Vig.) 1890	S	240
1423	DARKTOWN SOCIETY / On their Manners/ (Vig.) 1890	S	240
1424	DARKTOWN SPORTS / A Grand Spurt/ (Vig.) 1885	S	240
1425	DARKTOWN SPORTS / Winning Easy/ (Vig.) 1885	S	240
1426	DARKTOWN TALLY-HO / Straightened out/ (Vig.) 1889	S	240

1427	DARKTOWN TALLY-HO / Tangled up/ 1889	S	240
1428	DARKTOWN TOURISTS / Coming back on their Dig/ (Vig.) 1886	S	240
1429	DARKTOWN TOURISTS / Going off on their Blubber/ (Vig.) 1886	S	240
1430	DARKTOWN TOURNAMENT / Close quarters/ (Vig.) 1890	S	240
1431	DARKTOWN TOURNAMENT / First Tilt/ (Vig.) 1890	S	240
1432	DARKTOWN TRIAL / The Judge's Charge/ (Vig.) 1887	S	240
1433	DARKTOWN TRIAL / The Verdict/ (Vig.) 1887	S	240
1434	DARKTOWN TROLLEY / "Clar de track/ (Vig.) 1896	S	240
1435	DARKTOWN TROLLEY / Through car in danger/ (Vig.) 1896	S	240
1436	DARKTOWN TROTTER / Ready for the World, A/ (Vig.) 1892	S	240
1437	DARKTOWN WEDDING / The Parting Salute, A/ (Vig.) 1892	S	240
1438	DARKTOWN WEDDING / The Send Off, A/ (Vig.) 1892	S	240
1439	DARKTOWN YACHT CLUB / Hard up for a Breeze/ (Vig.)	S	240
1440	DARKTOWN YACHT CLUB / "Ladies Day" / "In cose I will, honey"/ (Vig.) 1896	S	240
1441	DARKTOWN YACHT CLUB/ "Ladies Day" / "You'll just ballast"/ (Vig.) 1896	S	240
1442	DARKTOWN YACHT CLUB, THE / On the Winning Tack/ (Vig.) 1885	S	240
1443	DARLING, I AM GROWING OLD"/ (Vig.)	S	130
1444	DARLING ROSY/ (Vig.)	S	80
1445	DARRYMANE ABBEY, IRELAND	M	120
1446	DARTMOUTH COLLEGE/ (8.5x12.13) 1834, N. Currier (Rare) [Old BEST 50]	S	3050
1446A	DARTMOUTH COLLEGE/ (8.5x12.13) (Tyler Name Removed) Und. N. Currier (Rare)	S	3050
1447	DARTMOUTH COLLEGE/ (8.5x12.13) (Stodart & Tyler Names Removed) Und. N. Currier (Rare)	S	3050
1448	DASH FOR THE POLE, A	L	1325
1449	DAUGHTER OF ERIN, THE/ N. Currier	S	75
1450	DAUGHTER OF THE NORTH WEST, THE	S	75
1451	DAUGHTER OF THE REGIMENT, THE/ (11.7x8.10) 1849, N. Currier	S	175
1452	DAUGHTER OF THE SOUTH, A	S	75
1453	DAUGHTERS OF TEMPERANCE/ (11.11x8.8) N. Currier	S	90
1454	DAVENPORT BROTHERS/ 1864	S	75
1455	DAVID AND GOLIATH	S	70
1456	DAWN OF LOVE	TC	70
1457	DAWN OF LOVE, THE/ (11.6x8.10) N. Currier	S	75
1458	DAWN OF LOVE, THE/ (11.12x8.3) N. Currier	S	90
1459	DAY BEFORE MARRIAGE, THE / #113/ (11.13x8.5) 1847, N. Currier	S	110
1460	DAY BEFORE MARRIAGE, THE/ (8x10) 1847, N. Currier	S	110
1461	DAY BEFORE MARRIAGE - THE BRIDE'S JEWELS/ (11.8x8.8)	S	110
1462	DAY BEFORE THE WEDDING/ N. Currier	S	105

1463	DAY OF REST, THE/ (9.10x16.13) 1869	M	195
1464	DEACON'S MARE, THE/ 1880	TC	75
1465	DEACON'S MARE GETTING THE WORD GO.../ (Vig.) 1879	S	330
1466	DEAD BEAT, A	S	180
1467	DEAD BROKE/ (11.12x8.15) 1873	S	275
1468	DEAD GAME - QUAIL/ (12.6x8.12) 1872	S	200
1469	DEAD GAME - WOODCOCK AND PARTRIDGE/ (12.7x8.14) 1872	S	200
1470	DEAREST SPOT ON EARTH TO ME/ (9x12.10) 1878	S	285
1471	DEATH BED OF THE MARTYR PRESIDENT, ABRAHAM LINCOLN/ (11.1x16.4) 1865	M	145
1472	DEATH OF ANDREW JOHNSON/ (8.5x12.7) 1875	S	90
1473	DEATH OF CALVIN/ (8.4x12.6) 1846, N. Currier	S	75
1474	DEATH OF CHARLES SUMNER/ (8.5x12.7) 1874	S	75
1475	DEATH OF COL. EDWARD D. BAKER/ (8.6x12.8) 1861	S	90
1476	DEATH OF COL. ELLSWORTH/ (Vig.) 1861	S	100
1477	DEATH OF COL. JOHN J. HARDIN/ (8.5x12.9) 1847, N. Currier	S	75
1478	DEATH OF COL. PIERCE M. BUTLER / At the battle of Churubusco/ (8.3x12.13) 1847, N. Currier	S	75
1479	DEATH OF DANIEL O'CONNELL/ (8.4x12.8) 1847, N. Currier	S	65
1480	DEATH OF GENL. ANDREW JACKSON/ (8.9x11.13) 1845, N. Currier	S	90
1481	DEATH OF GENERAL GRANT/ (8.15x13.7) 1885	S	90
1482	DEATH OF GEN. JAMES A. GARFIELD/ (8.13x13.5) 1881	S	85
1483	DEATH OF GENERAL LYON/ (8.6x12.10) 1861	S	135
1484	DEATH OF GEN. ROBERT E. LEE/ (7.10x12.3) 1870	S	140
1485	DEATH OF GEN. ZACHARY TAYLOR/ (8.4x12) 1850, N. Currier	S	90
1486	DEATH OF HARRISON/ (8.7x12.15) 1841, N. Currier	S	85
1487	DEATH OF HARRISON/ (8.8x12.14) 1841, N. Currier	S	85
1488	DEATH OF HON. HENRY CLAY JR./ (8 keys) 1852	S	95
1489	DEATH OF HON. HENRY CLAY JR./ (no keys) (8.10x11.14) 1852	S	95
1490	DEATH OF JOHN QUINCY ADAMS/ (8.4x12.13) 1848, N. Currier	S	95
1491	DEATH OF LIEUT. COL. HENRY CLAY JR./ (8.4x12.8)	S	110
1492	DEATH OF LIEUT. COL. HENRY CLAY JR./ (8.4x12.7)	S	110
1493	DEATH OF MAJOR GEN JAMES B. M'PHERSON	S	85
1494	DEATH OF MAJOR RINGGOLD/ (8.8x12.10) 1846, N. Currier	S	110
1495	DEATH OF MAJOR RINGGOLD/ (8.9x12.12) 1846, N. Currier	S	110
1496	DEATH OF MINNEHAHA, THE/ (14.10x20.14) 1867	L	305
1497	DEATH OF MONTGOMERY/(11.15x8.12) N. Currier	S	130
1498	DEATH OF NAPOLEON/ (8.5x12.10) N. Currier	S	80
1499	DEATH OF POPE PIUS IX/ (7.15x12.5) 1878	S	20
1500	DEATH OF PRESIDENT LINCOLN/ (8.10x12.15) 1865	S	100

1501	DEATH OF PRESIDENT LINCOLN/ (8.7x12.14) 1865	S	100
1502	DEATH OF PRESIDENT LINCOLN/ (13x15.8) 1865	M	175
1503	DEATH OF ST. JOSEPH/ (8.3x11.12)	S	20
1504	DEATH OF ST. JOSEPH/ C. Currier	S	20
1505	DEATH OF ST. PATRICK/ (8.8x12) 1872	S	20
1506	DEATH OF "STONEWALL" JACKSON/ (7.13x12.5) 1872	S	125
1507	DEATH OF TECUMSEH/ (11.8x9.1) 1841, N. Currier	S	105
1508	DEATH OF TECUMSEH/ (12x8.14) 1841, N. Currier	S	105
1509	DEATH OF TECUMSEH/ 1842, N. Currier	S	105
1510	DEATH OF TECUMSEH/ 1845, N. Currier	S	105
1511	DEATH OF TECUMSEH/ (8.4x12.5) 1846, N. Currier	S	105
1512	DEATH OF THE BLESSED VIRGIN	S	20
1513	DEATH OF THE JUST, THE/ (8.4x12.10)	S	20
1514	DEATH OF THE SINNER, THE/ (8.3x12.11)	S	20
1515	DEATH OF WARREN AT THE BATTLE OF BUNKER HILL/ (11.10x8.6) N. Currier	S	135
1516	DEATH OF WASHINGTON/ (8.9x12.15) 1841, N. Currier	S	90
1517	DEATH OF WASHINGTON/ (5 keys) N. Currier	S	90
1518	DEATH OF WASHINGTON/ (Head to left) N. Currier	S	90
1519	DEATH OF WASHINGTON/ (8.4x12.13) N. Currier	S	90
1520	DEATH OF WASHINGTON/ (8.8x13) N. Currier	S	90
1521	DEATH OF WASHINGTON/ 1846, N. Currier	S	90
1522	DEATH OF WASHINGTON/ N. Currier	M	135
1523	DEATH SHOT, THE/ (8.7x12.8)	S	200
1524	DECLARATION, THE/ #107/ (11.15x8.6) 1846, N. Currier	S	95
1525	DECLARATION, THE/ #107/ (11.14x8.5)	S	95
1526	DECLARATION, THE/ C. Currier	S	95
1527	DECLARATION, THE/ #107/ (11.14x8.7) N. Currier	S	95
1528	DECLARATION, THE/ N. Currier	S	95
1529	DECLARATION, THE/ (8.14x7.2) N. Currier	S	95
1530	DECLARATION COMMITTEE, THE/ 1876	S	300
1531	DECLARATION OF INDEPENDENCE, THE/ #385/ (8.2x12.7) N. Currier	S	215
1532	DECLARATION OF INDEPENDENCE, THE/ (8.2x12.7) N. Currier	S	215
1533	DECLARATION OF INDEPENDENCE, THE/ C. Currier	S	225
1534	DECORATION OF THE CASKET OF GEN. LEE	S	105
1535	DEER AND FAWN/ (8.6x12.6)	S	250
1536	DEER HUNTING BY TORCHLIGHT/ (10.6x15.3)	M	880
1537	DEER HUNTING ON THE SUSQUEHANNA/ (10.4x14.12)	M	880
1538	DEER IN THE WOODS/ (8.8x12.8)	S	250

1539	DEER SHOOTING IN THE NORTHERN WOODS/ (8.8x12.8)	S	605
1540	DEFENSE OF THE FLAG	S	200
1541	DEFIANCE!/ (Stag and Deer) (8.6x12.6)	S	225
1542	DELAYING A START/ (Vig.) 1881	S	220
1543	DELIA/ N. Currier	S	80
1544	DELICIOUS COFFEE/ (Vig.) 1881	S	350
1545	DELICIOUS FRUIT/ 1865	VS	160
1546	DELICIOUS FRUIT/ (Vig.) 1875	S	150
1547	DELICIOUS FRUIT/ (Oval) (Vig.) 1865	M	325
1548	DELICIOUS FRUIT/ (Circle) (Vig.) 1865	M	325
1549	DELICIOUS ICE CREAM	S	490
1550	DEMOCRACY IN SEARCH OF A CANDIDATE/ 1868	M	160
1551	DEMOCRATIC PLATFORM, THE/ N. Currier	M	195
1552	DEMOCRATIC REFORMERS/ (Vig.) 1876	S	160
1553	DEPARTED WORTH/ N. Currier	S	75
1554	DEPTHS OF DESPAIR, THE/ (11.7x8.4) (Companion to #5881)	S	85
1555	DER HUGERN VON VATERLAND/ N. Currier	S	40
1556	DESCENT FROM THE CROSS, THE/ (12.10x8.14)	S	20
1557	DESCENT FROM THE CROSS, THE / #207/ (12.10x8.14) 1847, N. Currier	S	20
1558	DESCENT FROM THE CROSS, THE / #290/ (12.2x8.9)	S	20
1559	DESCENT FROM THE CROSS, THE/ (9.13x7.14) N. Currier	S	20
1560	DESIGN FOR A MODEL SCHOOL HOUSE/ N. Currier	S	180
1561	DESIGN FOR ASTOR'S HOTEL..../ N. Currier	S	290
1562	DESIGN FOR ASTOR'S HOTEL, N.Y./ N. Currier	S	290
1563	DESIGN FOR PADDLE WHEEL STEAMER..../ N. Currier	M	450
1564	DESIGN MADE FOR ASTOR'S HOTEL/ N. Currier	S	250
1565	DESPERATE FINISH/ 1885	S	290
1566	DESPERATE FINISH/ 1895	L	1500
1567	DESPERATE PEACE MAN	S	180
1568	DESSERT OF FRUIT, A/ (Vig.)	S	155
1569	DESSERT OF FRUIT, A/ 1869	L	900
1570	DESTRUCTION OF JERUSALEM BY THE ROMANS/ (19.7x29) 1853, N. Currier	L	150
1571	DESTRUCTION OF TEA AT BOSTON HARBOR/ 1846, N. Currier [Old & New BEST 50]	S	1000
1572	DESTRUCTION OF THE REBEL MONSTER "MERRIMAC"/ (8.2x12.2)	S	520
1573	DESTRUCTION OF THE REBEL RAM "ARKANSAS"/ (8.2x12.10)	S	480
1574	DEVIL'S GLEN KILLARNEY, THE	S	85
1575	DEWDROP"/ (Horse) (Vig.) 1886	S	290
1576	DE WITT CLINTON	VS	80

1577	DEXTER	S	290
1578	DEXTER*, "ETHAN ALLEN" AND "MATE" / (Passing Judges Stand) (Vig.) 1874	S	290
1578A	DEXTER*, "ETHAN ALLEN" AND "MATE" / (Judges Stand Removed) (Vig.) 1874	S	290
1579	DEXTEROUS WHIP, A/ 1876	S	285
1580	DICK SWIVELLER/ (Vig.) 1878	S	290
1581	DIE FAMILIE DES KAISER'S VAN DEUTSCHLAND	S	60
1582	DIRECT, DRIVEN BY GEO. STARR	S	290
1583	DIRECTOR/ (Horse) 1882	TC	85
1584	DISCHARGING THE PILOT/ (16.4x24.4) 1856, N. Currier	L	3000
1585	DISCOVERY OF THE MISSISSIPPI, THE/ (8.15x12.15) 1876	S	250
1586	DISLOYAL BRITISH "SUBJECT", A/ (Vig.)	S	155
1587	DISPUTED HEAT / Claiming A Foul/ (17.13x26.15) 1878	L	1800
1588	DISPUTED PRIZE, THE/ (Sparrows)	S	180
1589	DISTANCED!!/ (Vig.) 1878	S	220
1590	DISTANT RELATIONS (8.7x11.6)	S	180
1591	DISTINGUISHED MILITIA GEN. DURING AN ACTION, A	S	180
1592	DIS-UNITED STATES, THE / Or, The Southern Confederacy/ (Vig.)	S	220
1593	DO YOU LOVE BUTTER?/ (11.12x9.1) 1878	S	135
1594	DODGE THAT WON'T WORK, A/ (Political) (Vig.)	S	175
1595	DODGER / Carter H. Harrison Against the Boodlers, The	S	150
1596	DOLLY VARDEN/ 1872	S	90
1597	DOMESTIC BLISS	S	85
1598	DOMESTIC BLOCKADE, THE/ (22.13x18.8) (Companion to #303)	L	700
1599	DOMINO/ (Companion to #785) N. Currier	S	190
1600	DON JUAN / Plate 1/ (8.7x13.1) N. Currier	S	85
1601	DON JUAN / Plate 2/ (8.8x13.2) N. Currier	S	85
1602	DON JUAN AND LAMBRO / Plate 3/ N. Currier	S	85
1603	DON JUAN SEPARATED FROM HAIDEE / Plate 4/ N. Currier	S	85
1604	DONE GONE BUSTED!/ (Vig.) (Companion to #6246) 1883	S	195
1605	DON'T HURT MY BABY/ (11.8x8.10) 1872	S	160
1606	DON'T SAY NAY/ 1846, N. Currier	S	95
1607	DON'T YOU WANT ANOTHER BABY?	S	110
1608	DON'T YOU WISH YOU MAY GET IT?/ (12.7x8.5) N. Currier	S	105
1609	DOREMUS, SUYDAMS AND NIXON/ (9.12x15.4) N. Currier	S	220
1610	DOTTY DIMPLE/ (12x8.8)	S	85
1611	DOUBLE-BARRELED BREECH LOADER/ (Vig.) 1880	S	205
1612	DOVE, THE/ (Girls and Dove) (12.1x8.13) N. Currier	S	85
1613	DOVE'S REFUGE, THE	S	95

1614	DOWN CHARGE (8.12x12.13)	S	340
1615	DR. FRIEDR. HECKER/ N. Currier	S	75
1616	DR. WILLIAM VALENTINE/ (12.12x18.6) N. Currier	M	160
1617	DRAW POKER / Getting 'em Lively/ (Vig.) 1886	S	260
1617A	DRAW POKER / Getting 'em Lively/ 1888	TC	70
1618	DRAW POKER / Getting 'em Lively/ 1886	M	320
1619	DRAW POKER / Laying for 'em Sharp/ (Vig.) 1886	S	260
1619A	DRAW POKER / Laying for 'em Sharp/ 1888	TC	70
1620	DRAWING CARDS FOR BEGINNERS/ (6 views)	S	240
1621	DRAWING CARDS FOR BEGINNERS/ (8 views)	S	240
1622	DRAWING STUDIES/ (4 views) (Vig.)	S	250
1623	DRAWING STUDIES/ (4 rural scenes on sheet) (Vig.)	S	240
1624	DREADFUL WRECK OF THE MEXICO ON HEMPSTEAD BEACH/ (6.13x10.4)	S	2400
1625	DREAMS OF YOUTH/ (9.10x16.13)	M	300
1626	DREW" AND "ST. JOHN", THE/ 1878	L	2050
1627	DRIVE THROUGH THE HIGHLANDS, THE/ (10.4x14.12)	M	720
1628	DRIVING FINISH, A/ (Three Horse Heads) 1891	L	880
1629	DRUNKARD'S PROGRESS, THE/ (8.7x12.12) 1846, N. Currier	S	435
1630	DRYBURGH ABBEY, SCOTLAND	S	95
1631	DUBLIN BAY, IRELAND/ (2 People)	S	85
1632	DUBLIN BAY, IRELAND/ (4 People)	S	85
1633	DUCHESS OF ORLEANS/ N. Currier	S	80
1634	DUDE BELLE, A/ (Vig.) 1883	S	225
1635	DUDE SWELL/ (Vig.) 1883	S	225
1636	DUKE AND DUCHESS OF EDINBURGH, THE	S	75
1637	DUSTED AND DISGUSTED/ (Comic) (Vig.) 1878	S	290
1638	DUTCHESS" OF ONEIDA	S	135
1639	DUTCHMAN"/ 1850, N. Currier	L	1925
1640	DUTCHMAN" AND "HIRAM WOODRUFF"/ (Vig.) 1871 [Old BEST 50]	S	660
1641	DUTCHMAN	S	290
1642	DWIGHT L. MOODY/ (Vig.)	S	70
1643	DYING BUFFALO BULL/ (12.2x17.13)	M	870

E

Con#	Title	Folio	Value
1644	E. FORREST AS METAMORA/ #180/ (12.5x8.14) N. Currier	S	185
1645	E. FORREST AS METAMORA/ (12.5x8.14) N. Currier	S	185
1646	E PLURIBUS UNUM/ 1875	S	290
1647	EAGER FOR THE RACE/ 1893	L	1650
1648	EARLY AUTUMN IN THE CATSKILLS	M	885
1649	EARLY AUTUMN, SALMON BROOK, GRANBY, CONN./ 1869	S	570
1650	EARLY PIETY/ (8.11x12.2) 1846, N. Currier	S	20
1651	EARLY SPRING	M	620
1652	EARLY WINTER/ (9.10x16.15) 1869 [Old & New BEST 50]	M	3700
1653	EASTER CROSS, THE	S	20
1654	EASTER CROSS, THE/ (Vig.) 1869	L	45
1655	EASTER FLOWERS/ 1869	S	25
1656	EASTER FLOWERS/ 1874	S	25
1657	EASTER FLOWERS	S	25
1658	EASTER MORNING/ (11.8x8.4)	S	20
1659	EASTER OFFERING, AN/ (12.2x8.8) 1871	S	20
1660	EASTER OFFERING, AN/ (Vig.)	S	20
1661	EASTERN BEAUTY, THE/ (Vig.)	S	60
1662	EATING CROW ON A WAGER / De fust brace/ (Comic) (Vig.) 1883	S	255
1663	EATING CROW ON A WAGER / De last lap/ (Comic) (Vig.) 1883	S	255
1664	ECHO LAKE, WHITE MOUNTAINS/ (11.3x14.9) (Oval)	M	860
1665	ECHO LAKE, WHITE MOUNTAINS/ (8.7x12)	S	470
1666	ECLIPSE AND SIR HENRY	L	1525
1667	EDITH/ (Vig.)	S	80
1668	EDWARD/ (Boy) 1879	S	80
1669	EDWARD/ Record 2:19/ (Vig.)	S	290
1670	EDWARD" AND "SWIVELLER"/ 1882	S	290
1671	EDWIN FORREST/ 1860	S	80
1672	EDWIN FORREST (Vig.)	M	125
1673	EDWIN FORREST/ N. Currier	S	80
1674	EDWIN FORREST AS METAMORA/ (12.5x8.14) N. Currier	S	80
1675	EDWIN FORREST/ N. Currier	S	275
1676	EDWIN FORREST / Record 2:11.75/ (Vig.) 1878	S	290
1677	EDWIN THORNE / Record 2:17.50/ (Vig.) 1882	S	290
1677A	EDWIN THORNE / Record 2:16 1/2/ 1882	TC	85
1678	EGYPTIAN BEAUTY, THE/ (Vig.)	M	85
1679	EGYPTIAN BEAUTY, THE/ (Vig.)	S	70
1680	(EIGHTEEN SEVENTY-SIX) 1876 - On Guard	S	275

1681	EL CAPITAN / From Mariposa Trail/ (8.8x12.8)	S	620
1682	EL DORADO PAIN ABSTRACTOR, THE/ 1846, N. Currier	S	275
1683	EL NINO CANTIVO	S	20
1684	EL SANTO NINO DE ATOCHA	S	20
1685	ELECTRIC LIGHT, THE/ 1880	S	285
1686	ELECTRIC LIGHT- TOBACCO	S	270
1687	ELEPHANT AND HIS KEEPERS, THE	M	340
1688	ELIZA/ #49/ Und. N. Currier	S	75
1689	ELIZA/ Und. N. Currier	S	75
1690	ELIZA/ 1844, N. Currier	S	75
1691	ELIZA/ #49/ Currier & Ives	S	75
1692	ELIZA/ #78/ 1844, N. Currier	S	75
1693	ELIZA/ (11.15x8.2) 1848, N. Currier	S	75
1694	ELIZA/ (1/2 Length) Currier & Ives	S	80
1695	ELIZA/ Und. N. Currier	S	75
1696	ELIZA JANE/ (11.9x8.8) 1847, N. Currier	S	75
1697	ELIZABETH/ N. Currier	S	80
1698	ELIZABETH/ (12.2x8.7) 1846, N. Currier	S	80
1699	ELIZABETH/ #69/ 1848, N. Currier	S	80
1700	ELIZABETH/ #45/ Currier & Ives	S	80
1701	ELIZABETH/ Currier & Ives	S	80
1702	ELIZABETH/ N. Currier	S	80
1703	ELIZABETH/ #15/ N. Currier	S	80
1704	ELIZABETH/ #15/ (3/4 Length) N. Currier	S	85
1705	ELLA (Vig.)	S	80
1706	ELLEN/ #51/ Und. N. Currier	S	80
1707	ELLEN/ 1844, N. Currier	S	80
1708	ELLEN/ 1848, N. Currier	S	80
1709	ELLEN/ #76/ 1848, N. Currier	S	80
1710	ELLEN/ #51/ 1846, N. Currier	S	80
1711	ELLEN/ #51/ 1845, N. Currier	S	80
1712	ELLEN/ #51/ Und. N. Currier	S	80
1713	ELLEN TREE / "...Wrecker's Daughter"/ (Vig.) 1837, N. Currier	S	95
1714	ELLEN TREE AS HERO IN "WOMAN'S WIT"/ 1838, N. Currier	S	95
1715	ELLEN TREE AS ION/ N. Currier	S	95
1716	ELOPEMENT, THE/ (12.10x8.4) (Companion to #4975) N. Currier	S	100
1717	EMBLEM OF HOPE/ (Vig.)	S	95
1718	EMBLEM OF SALVATION/ (Vig.) 1874	S	20
1719	EMBRACING AN OPPORTUNITY	S	95

1720	EMELINE/ N. Currier	S	75
1721	EMELINE/ #87/ (11.15x8.4) 1848, N. Currier	S	75
1722	EMELINE/ #253/ (Vig.) N. Currier	S	80
1723	EMILY/ (In window) N. Currier	S	85
1724	EMILY/ (At table) N. Currier	S	85
1725	EMILY/ #52/ 1846, N. Currier	S	75
1726	EMMA/ #258	S	75
1727	EMMA/ 1849, N. Currier	S	75
1728	EMMA/ (Dog under arms) N. Currier	S	80
1729	EMMA/ (Standing) N. Currier	S	80
1730	EMMA/ (Vig.)	S	80
1731	EMMET'S BETROTHED	S	70
1732	EMPEROR, THE/ N. Currier	S	70
1733	EMPEROR OF NORFOLK/ (Vig.) 1888	S	225
1734	EMPRESS, THE	S	75
1735	EMPRESS EUGENIE/ N. Currier	S	70
1736	EMPRESS EUGENIE AND QUEEN VICTORIA/ (Vig.)	S	70
1737	EMPRESS JOSEPHINE/ (Vig.)	S	70
1738	EMPTY CRADLE/ N. Currier	S	20
1739	ENCHANTED CAVE, THE/ 1867	L	235
1740	ENCHANTED ISLES, THE / (7.15x12.8) 1869	S	90
1741	END OF THE LONG BRANCH, THE/ (Political Cartoon) (Vig.)	S	195
1742	ENGLISH BEAUTY, THE/ (Vig.)	S	75
1743	ENGLISH SNIPE/ N. Currier	S	365
1744	ENGLISH SNIPE/ (8.8x12.8) 1871, Currier & Ives	S	375
1745	ENGLISH WINTER SCENE, AN/ (8.8x12.8)	S	470
1746	ENGLISH YACHT OFF SANDY HOOK, AN/ (9x12.8)	S	360
1747	ENOCH ARDEN - THE HOUR OF TRIAL/ 1869, N. Currier	L	220
1748	ENOCH ARDEN - THE HOUR OF TRIAL/ N. Currier	S	105
1749	ENOCH ARDEN - THE LONELY ISLE/ (14.13x22.14) 1869	L	310
1750	ENOS T. THROOP	VS	50
1751	ENTRANCE TO THE HIGHLANDS, THE/ 1864	L	1950
1752	ENTRANCE TO THE HOLY SEPULCHRE, JERUSALEM/ (8.6x12) 1849, N. Currier	S	20
1753	ERIN GO BRAGH/ (Rifle Match) (11.3x15.15) 1875	M	320
1754	ESCAPE OF SERGEANT CHAMPE, THE/ (8.10x12.6) 1876	S	185
1755	ESTHER/ #276/ N. Currier	S	75
1756	ESTHER/ N. Currier	S	75
1757	ETHAN ALLEN" AND "MATE" AND "DEXTER"/ (17.6x27.6) 1867	L	1550

1758	ETHAN ALLEN" AND "MATE" AND "LANTERN" AND "MATE" / Crossing the.../ (17.6x27.12) 1859	L	1600
1759	ETHAN ALLEN" AND "MATE" AND "LANTERN" AND "MATE"/ In their.../ 1859	L	1600
1760	ETHAN ALLEN & MATE TO WAGON/ 1874	S	290
1761	ETTA	S	70
1762	EUCHERED"/ (Vig.) (Companion to #2204) 1884	S	120
1763	EUGENIE/ (Vig.)	S	75
1764	EUROPA/ (Steamship)	M	430
1765	EUROPE/ (Head) (Vig.) 1870	S	70
1766	EUROPE/ (Vig.)	S	85
1767	EUROPEAN BOWLING ALLEY, THE/ 1870	S	190
1768	EUROPEAN WAR DANCE/ (12.3x17.2) 1877	M	295
1769	EVACUATION OF RICHMOND, VA, THE/ 1865	S	255
1770	EVANGELINE	S	75
1771	EVANGELINE	L	195
1772	EVENING OF LOVE, THE (11.8x8.4)	S	65
1773	EVENING PRAYER, THE/ (9.14x7.14) (Companion to #4206) N. Currier	S	25
1774	EVENING PRAYER, THE/ #8/ (11.12x8.6) N. Currier	S	25
1775	EVENING PRAYER, THE/ Und.	S	25
1776	EVENING STAR, THE/ (Girl) N. Currier	S	70
1777	EVENING STAR, THE/ #500/ (Girl)	S	70
1778	EVENING STAR, THE/ (Girl) (Vig.)	S	70
1779	EVENING STAR, THE/ 1846, N. Currier	S	70
1780	EVENTIDE - OCTOBER/ "The Village Inn"/ (14.9x25) 1867	L	2375
1781	EVENTIDE - THE CURFEW	S	180
1782	EVERYBODY'S FRIEND/ (Vig.) 1876	M	280
1783	EVERYTHING COMING DOWN/ (Vig.) 1870	S	285
1784	EVERYTHING LOVELY/ (Vig.) 1880	S	180
1785	EXCITING FINISH/ 1895	S	290
1786	EXCITING FINISH/ (18.12x27.12) 1884	L	1400
1787	EXPRESS STEAMSHIP "AUGUSTA VICTORIA"	S	320
1788	EXPRESS STEAMSHIP "COLUMBIA"	S	320
1789	EXPRESS STEAMSHIP "FURST BISMARK", THE/ (8.15x14.14)	S	320
1790	EXPRESS TRAIN, THE/ (J. Schutz, del.) (7.12x12.14) N. Currier [Old & New BEST 50]	S	3050
1791	EXPRESS TRAIN, THE/ (C. Parsons, del.) (17.8x26.8) 1859, N. Currier	L	11800
1792	EXPRESS TRAIN, THE/ (8x12.8) 1870, N. Currier [New BEST 50]	S	1900
1793	EXPRESS TRAIN, THE/ (8x12.7) 1870, N. Currier	S	1900
1794	EXPRESS TRAIN, THE/ #127/ (Vig.)	S	2425

1795	EXPULSION OF ADAM AND EVE/ N. Currier	S	100
1796	EXQUISITE, THE/ The "Pet of the Ladies"/ (Oval)	M	165
1797	EXTRA COOL LAGER BEER/ (Store card)	S	350
1798	EXTRAORDINARY EXPRESS ACROSS THE ATLANTIC/ Pilot boat.../ (8.4x12.11) 1846, N. Currier	S	380

F

Con#	Title	Folio	Value
1799	FAIR BEAUTEOUS QUEEN/ (Port. of Queen Victoria) (10.7x8.7) N. Currier	S	70
1800	FAIR EQUESTRIAN/ 1857	L	620
1801	FAIR EQUESTRIAN, THE/ N. Currier	S	140
1802	FAIR FIELD AND NO FAVOR, A/ (18x28.2) 1891	L	1325
1803	FAIR MOON TO THEE I SING/ (Vig.) 1879	S	150
1804	FAIR MOON TO THEE I SING/ 1880	TC	75
1805	FAIR PATRICIAN, THE/ (Vig.)	S	90
1806	FAIR PATRICIAN, THE/ (Tinted background) (Vig.)	M	170
1807	FAIR PURITAN, THE/ (Vig.)	S	85
1808	FAIR START, A/ (Companion to #5120) 1884	S	275
1808A	FAIR START, A/ 1884	M	480
1809	FAIREST FLOWER SO PALELY DROOPING/ 1847, C. Currier	S	75
1810	FAIREST OF THE FAIR, THE/ (Vig.)	S	75
1811	FAIRIES HOME, THE/ (14.13x20.7)	L	380
1812	FAIRIES HOME, THE/ 1868	M	225
1813	FAIRMOUNT WATER WORKS/ (11x15.6)	M	480
1814	FAIRY GROTTO, THE/ (14.12x20.8) 1867	L	385
1815	FAIRY GROTTO, THE/ 1867	S	110
1816	FAIRY ISLE, THE	S	95
1817	FAIRY TALES	S	65
1818	FAITH, HOPE, AND CHARITY/ 1874	S	60
1819	FALL AND WINTER FASHIONS FOR 1837 & 8	L	1025
1820	FALL FROM GRACE, A/ (Vig.) (Companion to #4979) 1883	S	280
1821	FALL OF RICHMOND, VIRGINIA, THE/ (16x22.4) 1865	L	1800
1822	FALL OF RICHMOND, VIRGINIA, THE/ 1865 [New BEST 50]	S	270
1823	FALL OF RICHMOND, VIRGINIA, THE/ (Similar to preceding but with changes) 1865	S	270
1824	FALLING SPRINGS, VA/ 1868	S	295
1825	FALL OF SEBASTOPOL, THE/ N. Currier	S	75

1826	FALLS "DES CHATS" / OTTAWA RIVER, CANADA/ (8x12.8)	S	255
1827	FALLS OF NIAGARA / FROM CLIFTON HOUSE/ N. Currier	S	235
1828	FALLS OF NIAGARA / FROM THE CANADA SIDE/ (18.4x27.13)	L	1625
1829	FALLS OF NIAGARA / FROM THE CANADA SIDE/ (18.2x28.2)	L	1625
1830	FALLS OF THE OTTAWA RIVER, CANADA (7.15x12.7)	S	270
1831	FALLS OF TIVOLI, ITALY	S	105
1832	FALSETTO/ (Vig.) 1879	S	260
1832A	FALSETTO/ 1881	TC	85
1833	FAMILIEN REGISTER/ 1846	S	50
1834	FAMILIEN REGISTER/ 1869	S	50
1836	FAMILY DEVOTION/ "Reading the Scriptures"/ N. Currier	S	30
1835	FAMILY DEVOTION/ (7.14x12.5) 1871	S	30
1837	FAMILY GARLAND/ (Vig.) 1874	S	85
1838	FAMILY GARLAND	S	55
1839	FAMILY OF LOUIS KOSSUTH/ 1851, N. Currier	S	45
1840	FAMILY PETS, THE/ N. Currier	S	115
1841	FAMILY PHOTOGRAPH REGISTER, THE	S	105
1842	FAMILY PHOTOGRAPH REGISTER, THE	M	140
1843	FAMILY PHOTOGRAPH TREE/ (8.8x12) 1871	S	135
1844	FAMILY RECORD	S	50
1845	FAMILY REGISTER/ C. Currier	S	50
1846	FAMILY REGISTER/ 1845, N. Currier	S	50
1847	FAMILY REGISTER/ 1850, N. Currier	S	50
1848	FAMILY REGISTER/ 1846, N. Currier	S	50
1849	FAMILY REGISTER/ 1852	S	50
1850	FAMILY REGISTER/ 1853, N. Currier	S	50
1851	FAMILY REGISTER/ N. Currier	S	50
1852	FAMILY REGISTER/ 1864	S	65
1853	FAMILY REGISTER/ #74/ 1862	S	70
1854	FAMILY REGISTER/ 1869	S	60
1855	FAMILY REGISTER/ 1873	S	60
1856	FAMILY REGISTER/ [A]/ 1874	S	50
1857	FAMILY REGISTER/ [C]/ 1874	S	50
1858	FAMILY REGISTER/ FOR COLORED PEOPLE/ 1873	S	60
1859	FAMILY REGISTER/ 1864	M	90
1860	FAMOUS DOUBLE TROTTING TEAM "SIR MOHAWK" AND "NELLIE SONTAG"/ (19.3x30) 1889	L	1425
1861	FAMOUS TROTTER MAJOLICA, THE/ (19.1x27.10) 1884	L	1425
1862	FAMOUS TROTTER POLICE GAZETTE, FORMERLY EMMA B.	L	1425

1863	FAMOUS TROTTING GELDING GUY BY KENTUCKY PRINCE	S	290
1864	FAMOUS TROTTING MARE "GOLDSMITH MAID" / Record 2:14/ 1871	S	290
1865	FANCIED SECURITY, OR, THE RATS ON A BENDER/ (Vig.)	S	140
1866	FANNIE/ (Vig.)	S	80
1867	FANNIE	S	75
1868	FANNY / #132/ (Bouquet in hand) N. Currier	S	80
1869	FANNY / #132/ (Rose in hand) N. Currier	S	80
1870	FANNY/ N. Currier	S	75
1871	FANNY/ (Vig.) N. Currier	S	80
1872	FANNY ELSSLER / " In the Shadow Dance"/ (8.2x11.13) 1846, N. Currier	S	150
1873	FANNY ELSSLER / " In the Favorite Dance La Cachucha"/ (12.2x9.6) N. Currier	S	150
1874	FAREWELL, THE/ (Companion to #5125)	S	90
1875	FAREWELL, THE/ (Oval)	M	115
1876	FAREWELL A'WHILE MY NATIVE ISLE/ N. Currier	S	75
1877	FARM AND FIRESIDE/ 1878	M	300
1878	FARM LIFE IN SUMMER / The Cooling Stream/ 1867	L	1325
1879	FARM YARD, THE / No. 1, THE/ (9.9x13.10) N. Currier	S	195
1880	FARM YARD, THE / #717/ N. Currier	S	675
1881	FARM YARD IN WINTER, THE/ (16.4x23.9) 1861	L	4500
1882	FARM YARD PETS	S	175
1883	FARM YARD PETS	S	175
1884	FARM YARD / Winter	S	590
1885	FARMER GARFIELD/ (Vig.) 1880	S	130
1886	FARMER'S DAUGHTER, THE/ (12x8.10) (Companion to #1895)	S	110
1887	FARMER'S FRIENDS, THE/ (12.12x8.14) N. Currier	S	200
1888	FARMER'S FRIENDS, THE/ (8x12.8)	S	200
1889	FARMER'S HOME / Autumn, The/ (16.1x23.6) 1864	L	2000
1890	FARMER'S HOME / Harvest, The/ (16x23.6) 1864 [New BEST 50]	L	2175
1891	FARMER'S HOME / Summer, The/ (16x23.6) 1864	L	2100
1892	FARMER'S HOME / Winter, The/ (16.3x23.13) 1863 [New BEST 50]	L	4700
1893	FARMER'S HOUSE / Plans for Building/ (8.2x5.14) N. Currier	S	165
1894	FARMER'S PRIDE, THE/ 1852, N. Currier	S	90
1895	FARMER'S SON, THE (12.4x8.8) (Companion to #1886)	S	95
1896	FASHIONABLE TURNOUTS IN CENTRAL PARK/ (18.10x28.14) 1869	L	4650
1897	FASHIONS / For Fall & Winter/ 1854 & 5	L	1525
1898	FAST HEAT, A/ (18.4x27.5) 1887	L	1425
1899	FAST HEAT, A/ 1894	L	1350
1900	FAST TEAM OUT ON THE LOOSE, A/ (Vig.)	S	290

1901	FAST TEAM OUT ON THE LOOSE, A/ (10.7x15.1) (Companion to #1904)	M	530
1902	FAST TEAM OUT ON THE LOOSE, A/ (8.3x12.8)	S	290
1903	FAST TEAM / TAKING A SMASH, A	S	290
1904	FAST TEAM / TAKING A SMASH, A/ (Companion to #1901)	M	490
1905	FAST TEAM / #307	S	290
1906	FAST TROTTERS ON A FAST TRACK/ (17.3x27.15) 1889	L	1550
1907	FAST TROTTERS ON HARLEM LANE, NY/ (18.10x28.11) 1870	L	3600
1908	FAST TROTTING IN THE WEST/ (16.11x25.14) 1871	L	1625
1909	FAST TROTTING TO FAST WHEELS/ (18.5x28.2) 1893	L	1450
1910	FATE OF THE RADICAL PARTY	S	190
1911	FATHER AND CHILD/ (12.2x8.1) 1849, N. Currier	S	95
1912	FATHER, INTO THY HANDS I COMMEND MY SPIRIT/ N. Currier	S	20
1913	FATHER MATHEW/ 1848, N. Currier	S	45
1914	FATHER MATHEW/ N. Currier	S	45
1915	FATHER'S PET/ 1851, N. Currier	S	90
1916	FATHER'S PET	S	85
1917	FATHER'S PRIDE/ 1846, N. Currier	S	85
1918	FATHER'S PRIDE/ (Vig.) 1859	S	85
1919	FATHER'S PRIDE / #400/ 1859, N. Currier	S	90
1920	FATHER'S PRIDE/ (oval)	S	95
1921	FAVORITE CAT, THE/ (12.3x8) N. Currier	S	640
1922	FAVORITE HORSE, THE/ N. Currier	S	280
1923	FAVORITE HORSE, THE/ (similar to preceding, but with changes in composition) N. Currier	S	280
1924	FAVORITE HORSE, THE/ (8.12x12.7)	S	280
1925	FAVORITE HORSE, THE/ (8.7x12.11)	S	280
1926	FAVORITE* IN THE POOLS/ 1876	M	565
1927	FAVORITE JERSEYS	M	265
1928	FAVORITE JERSEYS (12.12x9.14)	S	205
1929	FAVORITE PONY, A/ (13.3x8.13) N. Currier	S	235
1930	FAVORITE SET OF QUADRILLES FOR THE PIANO, A/ N. Currier	S	115
1931	FAVORITES, THE/ N. Currier	S	95
1932	FAWN'S LEAP, CATSKILLS/ (2.9x4) (Oval) (Companion to #5275)	VS	325
1933	FAWN'S LEAP, CATSKILLS/ (5.7x7.7)	VS	295
1934	FEAST OF FRUITS, A/ (Oval)	S	165
1935	FEAST OF ROSES/ (Vig.) 1873	S	105
1936	FEAST OF STRAWBERRIES, A	S	175
1937	FEATHERWEIGHT MOUNTING A SCALPER, A/ (Vig.) 1881	S	265
1938	FEDERAL PAP!/ (16.12x10.8) N. Currier	M	250

1939	FEEDING THE SWANS/ (7.14x12.5)	S	245
1940	FENIAN VOLUNTEER, THE/ 1866	S	75
1941	FERNS/ (Vig.)	S	100
1942	FERRY BOAT, THE/ (10.9x15) N. Currier	M	680
1943	FIDO'S LESSON/ (11.7x8.5)	S	125
1944	FIDELE/ N. Currier	S	115
1945	FIEND OF THE ROAD, THE/ (15.13x24) 1881	L	1350
1946	FIFTH AVENUE BELLE, A/ (Vig.)	S	95
1947	FINEST IN THE WORLD/ 1885	L	1475
1948	FINEST IN THE WORLD/ ("R.B. Crouch" on reins) 1885	L	1475
1949	FINISH IN THE GREAT MATCH RACE FOR $5000 A SIDE	S	290
1950	FIRE DEPARTMENT CERTIFICATE/ 1877	S	210
1951	FIRE DEPARTMENT CERTIFICATE/ 1889	M	385
1952	FIRE DEPARTMENT CERTIFICATE	S	210
1953	FIRE DEPARTMENT CERTIFICATE/ 1877	M	385
1954	FIRE ENGINE No. ....../ N. Currier	S	250
1955	FIRE ENGINE CO. "PACIFIC", BROOKLYN	S	270
1956	FIREMEN'S CERTIFICATE/ 1889	M	370
1957	FIRST APPEARANCE OF JENNY LIND IN AMERICA/ (9.3x14.1) 1850, N. Currier	S	280
1958	FIRST AT THE RENDEZVOUS/ N. Currier	S	135
1959	FIRST BIRD OF THE SEASON, THE/ 1879	S	295
1960	FIRST BIRD OF THE SEASON, THE/ 1880	TC	75
1961	FIRST BLOOD	S	65
1962	FIRST CARE, THE/ "The Young Mother"/ (Oval)	S	120
1963	FIRST CARE, THE/ "The Young Mother"/ (11x8.15) (Oval)	S	120
1964	FIRST CHRISTMAS MORN, THE	S	60
1965	FIRST COLORED SENATOR AND REPRESENTATIVES IN THE 41st, 42nd CONGRESS/ (Vig.) 1872	S	205
1966	FIRST COMPANY, GOVERNMENT FOOT GUARDS OF CONN..	S	145
1967	FIRST DUTCHESS OF ONEIDA	S	85
1968	FIRST EASTER DAWN, THE	S	65
1969	FIRST FIGHT BETWEEN IRON CLAD SHIPS OF WAR, THE/ (7.13x12.12) 1862	S	545
1970	FIRST FLIRTATION, THE/ (11.2x8.4)	S	110
1971	FIRST GAME/ (Companion to #5133) N. Currier	S	125
1972	FIRST LANDING OF COLUMBUS, THE/ (18.1x28) 1892	L	500
1973	FIRST LESSON, THE/ N. Currier	L	440
1974	FIRST LOVE #2/ N. Currier	S	80
1975	FIRST MEETING OF WASHINGTON AND LAFAYETTE/ (8.12x12.12) 1876	S	210

1976	FIRST PANTS	M	205
1977	FIRST PARTING, THE	S	80
1978	FIRST PARTY, THE/ (10x8.3)	S	95
1979	FIRST PLAYMATE, THE	S	80
1980	FIRST PRAYER/ (Oval) 1870	S	35
1981	FIRST PRAYER/ (Oval) 1870	M	45
1982	FIRST PREMIUM GRAPES/ (17.15x14.13) 1865	M	285
1983	FIRST PREMIUM MUSCAT GRAPES/ 1861	M	280
1984	FIRST PREMIUM POULTRY	S	155
1985	FIRST PRESIDENT OF THE MORMONS/ 1879	S	80
1986	FIRST PRESIDENTS / OF THE / CHURCH / OF / JESUS CHRIST / OF / THE LATTER DAY SAINTS/ (14.6x10) 1879	S	90
1987	FIRST RIDE, THE/ (12.8x9) 1849, N. Currier	S	130
1988	FIRST RIDE, THE/ (12.1x8.12) 1849	S	130
1989	FIRST SCHOLAR, THE	S	130
1990	FIRST SMOKE / All Right/ (Vig.) 1870	S	205
1991	FIRST SMOKE, THE / All Wrong/ (Vig.)	S	205
1992	FIRST SNOW, THE	S	565
1993	FIRST STEP, THE/ (10.13x8.13) (Oval)	S	95
1994	FIRST STEP, THE/ (10.15x8.15)	S	100
1995	FIRST STEP, THE "Come to Mama"/ 1859	S	95
1996	FIRST STEP, THE "Come to Mama"/ 1859	M	165
1997	FIRST TOILET/ (11.8x8.3) 1873	S	100
1998	FIRST TROT OF THE SEASON/ (18.8x28.14) 1870	L	1800
1999	FIRST VIOLET, THE	S	85
2000	FIRST UNDER THE WIRE/ (Vig.) 1878	S	290
2001	FISH OUT OF WATER/ N. Currier	M	185
2002	FISHERMAN'S COT, THE	VS	220
2003	FISHERMAN'S DOG, THE/ N. Currier	M	265
2003A	$5 CUT RATE TO CHICAGO/ 1881	TC	100
2004	FLAG OF OUR UNION, THE	M	285
2005	FLEETY GOLDDUST"/ (Vig.) 1874	S	290
2006	FLEETY GOLDDUST, RECORD 2:10 1/2	S	290
2007	FLIGHT INTO EGYPT/ N. Currier	S	55
2008	FLIGHT OF ELIZA, THE	S	60
2009	FLIGHT OF THE MEXICAN ARMY AT THE BATTLE OF BUENA VISTA/ (8.5x12.8) 1847, N. Currier	S	115
2010	FLIGHT OF THE MEXICAN ARMY AT THE BATTLE OF BUENA VISTA/ (8.6x12.9) 1847, N. Currier	S	115
2011	FLIGHT OF THE STAKEHOLDER/ (Vig.)	S	140

2012	FLOATING DOWN TO MARKET/ (7.15x12.7) 1870	S	650
2013	FLORA/ 1846, N. Currier	S	80
2014	FLORA	VS	85
2015	FLORA TEMPLE*/ 1853, N. Currier	L	1750
2016	FLORA TEMPLE* AND *HIGHLAND MAID*/ (17.6x26.13) 1853, N. Currier	L	1750
2017	FLORA TEMPLE* AND *LANCET*/ N. Currier	L	1750
2018	FLORA TEMPLE* AND *LANCET*/ (16.12x25.14) N. Currier	L	1750
2019	FLORA TEMPLE* AND *PRINCESS*/ (17.8x26.13) 1859	L	1675
2020	FLORA TEMPLE* AND *PRINCESS/ (17.7x26.15) 1859	L	1675
2021	FLORAL BEAUTIES/ (Vig.)	S	175
2022	FLORAL BOUQUET	S	125
2023	FLORAL CROSS	S	90
2024	FLORAL GEMS/ (Vig.)	S	115
2025	FLORAL GIFT	S	110
2026	FLORAL GIFT	VS	195
2027	FLORAL GROUP	S	110
2028	FLORAL OFFERING/ (Vig.)	S	110
2029	FLORAL TREASURE	VS	195
2030	FLORAL TRIBUTE/ (Vig.)	S	110
2031	FLORA'S BOUQUET/ (Vig.)	S	110
2032	FLORA'S GIFT/ (Vig.)	VS	165
2033	FLORA'S TREASURE/ (Vig.)	VS	165
2034	FLORA'S TREASURES/ (Vig.)	S	100
2035	FLORENCE	S	80
2036	FLORIDA/ (19.2x27.2)	L	1600
2037	FLORIDA COAST/ (8.8x12.7)	S	225
2038	FLOWER BASKET/ (12.8x8.8) 1872	S	140
2039	FLOWER BASKET, A/ (Vig.)	S	140
2040	FLOWER BASKET, THE	S	140
2041	FLOWER DANCE, THE/ (8.5x12) (Companion to #2743) 1846, N. Currier	S	135
2042	FLOWER GIRL, THE/ (11.15x8.11) 1845, N. Currier	S	85
2043	FLOWER OF THE HAREM, THE/ (11.12x8.10) N. Currier	S	90
2044	FLOWER PIECE	S	115
2045	FLOWER STAND, THE	S	115
2046	FLOWER STREWN GRAVE/ 1867	S	35
2047	FLOWER VASE, THE/ #249/ (Vig.) 1848, N. Currier	S	135
2048	FLOWER VASE, THE/ N. Currier	S	135
2049	FLOWER VASE, THE/ 1859	S	125
2050	FLOWER VASE, THE/ (Vig.) 1870	S	125

2051	FLOWER VASE, THE/ (Vig.) 1875	S	125
2052	FLOWER VASE, THE/ 1859	M	265
2053	FLOWER VASE, THE/ (Vig.)	L	455
2054	FLOWER VASE, THE	S	125
2055	FLOWER VASE, THE/ #249	S	130
2056	FLOWERS/ N. Currier	S	125
2057	FLOWERS	S	120
2058	FLOWERS/ (3 roses 10 buds) N. Currier	S	105
2059	FLOWERS/ (4 roses 6 buds) N. Currier	M	205
2060	FLOWERS/ (3 roses 7 buds, Sweet Peas, Daisies, Orchid)	S	115
2061	FLOWERS No. 1/ #565/ N. Currier	S	115
2062	FLOWERS No. 1/ N. Currier	S	115
2063	FLOWERS No. 1/ #656/ 1848, N. Currier	S	120
2064	FLOWERS No. 1/ #569/ N. Currier	S	115
2065	FLOWERS No. 2/ N. Currier	S	115
2066	FLOWERS No. 2/ 1848, N. Currier	S	120
2067	FLOWERS / Roses and Bluebells/ 1870	S	125
2068	FLOWERS / Roses and Bluebells	M	155
2069	FLOWERS / Roses and Buds	S	115
2070	FLOWERS / Roses and Buds	S	115
2071	FLUSHING A WOODCOCK/ (8x12.8)	S	380
2072	FLY FISHING/ (Vig.) 1879	S	275
2073	FLYING DUTCHMAN C. MARLOW AND VOLTIGEUR/ N. Currier	L	1550
2074	FOLIAGE	VS	170
2075	FOLIAGE	VS	170
2076	FOLIAGE	VS	170
2077	FOLIAGE	VS	170
2078	FOLLY OF SECESSION/ 1861	S	120
2079	FONT AT EASTER, THE	S	40
2080	FONT AT EASTER, THE/ 1869	S	50
2081	FORDING THE RIVER/ (10.6x14.15) N. Currier	M	500
2082	FORDING THE RIVER	S	290
2083	FORDS OF THE JORDAN	S	85
2084	FOREST SCENE ON THE LEHIGH/ (14.15x20.3)	L	690
2085	FOREST SCENE, SUMMER	S	230
2086	FOREST SCENE, SUMMER/ (7.15x12.8)	S	230
2087	FORK OVER WHAT YOU OWE/ (12.15x8.14) 1868	S	330
2088	FORT PICKENS/ Pensacola Harbor, Florida/ (7.15x12.5)	S	275
2089	FORT SUMTER / Charleston Harbor, S.C./ (7.13x12.7)	S	270

2090	FOUL TIP, A/ 1882	S	265
2091	FOUR-IN-HAND*/ (17.9x27.14) 1861	L	2125
2092	FOUR-IN-HAND*/ (Used as an ad) 1861	L	2125
2093	FOUR-IN-HAND*/ 1887	L	2100
2094	FOUR MASTED STEAMSHIP "EGYPT" OF THE NATIONAL LINE/ N. Currier	S	395
2095	FOUR OARED SHELL RACE, A/ (18.8x28.1) 1884	L	3550
2096	FOUR SEASONS OF LIFE, CHILDHOOD, THE/ (15.13x23.12) 1868	L	1425
2097	FOUR SEASONS OF LIFE, MIDDLE AGE, THE/ (15.14x23.14) 1868	L	1150
2098	FOUR SEASONS OF LIFE, MIDDLE AGE/ (15.6x23.10) 1868	L	1150
2099	FOUR SEASONS OF LIFE. OLD AGE, THE/ (15.10x23.10) 1868	L	1250
2100	FOUR SEASONS OF LIFE. YOUTH, THE/ (15.13x23.14) 1868	L	1475
2101	FOURTH OF JULY/ 1867	S	495
2102	FOURTH OF JULY / Young America Celebrating (Vig.)	L	1025
2103	FOX CHASE / Gone Away/ (8.8x12.11) N. Currier	S	370
2104	FOX CHASE / In Full Cry/ (8.8x12.10) 1846, N. Currier	S	370
2105	FOX CHASE / The Death/ (8.8x12.11) 1846, N. Currier	S	370
2106	FOX CHASE / Throwing Off/ (8.8x12.10) 1846, N. Currier	S	370
2107	FOX HOUNDS/ N. Currier	S	380
2108	FOX-HUNTER, THE/ (8.4x12.12) N. Currier	S	370
2109	FOX-HUNTER, THE/ (At the death) (8.4x12.12) N. Currier	S	245
2110	FOX-HUNTING / Full Cry/ (11.7x15.14)	M	670
2111	FOX-HUNTING / The Death/ (11.7x12.12)	M	670
2112	FOX-HUNTING / The Find/ (11.7x15.15)	M	670
2113	FOX-HUNTING / The Meet/ (11.6x15.15)	M	670
2114	FOX WITHOUT A TAIL / Or the Southern Confederacy/ 1861	S	155
2115	FOXHALL*/ 1882	L	1400
2116	FOXHALL	S	290
2117	FOXHALL*/ 1882	TC	85
2118	FOX'S OLD BOWERY THEATRE / The last scene in G.I. Fox's pantomine/ C. Currier	M	770
2119	FRAGRANT AND FAIR/ (Vig.)	S	150
2120	FRAGRANT CUP/ (Vig.) 1884	M	270
2121	FRANCES/ N.Currier	S	80
2122	FRANCIS R. SHUNK / Gov. of PENN/ (11.9x8.11) 1844, N. Currier	S	80
2123	FRANKIE AND TIP	S	80
2124	FRANKLIN/ (Vig.)	S	185
2125	FRANKILN/ (Vig.)	M	255
2126	FRANKLIN PIERCE / * Democratic Candidate for 14th President of the U.S./ N. Currier	S	170

2127	FRANKLIN PIERCE / "Fourteenth President of the U.S./ 1852, N. Currier	S	155
2128	FRANKLIN'S EXPERIMENT/ (8.7x12.7) 1876 [Old BEST 50]	S	780
2129	FRAUD AGAINST TRUTH/ 1872	S	105
2130	FREDERICK DOUGLASS / Colored Champion of Freedom/ (Vig.)	S	125
2131	FREE FOR ALL/ 1875	M	570
2132	FREE LUNCH/ 1872	M	230
2133	FREE SOIL BANNER/ 1848, N. Currier	S	205
2134	FREE TRADE AND PROTECTION/ 1888	M	215
2135	FREEDMEN'S BUREAU, THE/ (11.15x8.12) 1868	S	240
2136	FREEDOM TO IRELAND/ (Vig.) 1866	M	115
2137	FREEDOM TO THE SLAVES/ (11.13x8.11)	S	400
2138	FREELAND/ (Vig.) 1885	S	290
2139	FRENCH REVOLUTION, THE/ (8.5x12.11) 1848, N. Currier	S	125
2140	FRENCH REVOLUTION, THE / "Scene in the Throne-Room of the Tuileries"/ (8.5x12.10) 1848, N. Currier	S	125
2141	FRESH BOUQUET, A/ (Vig.)	S	125
2142	FRESH COOL	S	315
2143	FRIEND CLEVELAND/ 1881	S	105
2144	FRIEND IN NEED, A/ (8x12.8)	S	105
2145	FRIENDS OF FLOWERS / #359	S	105
2146	FRIENDSHIP, LOVE, AND TRUTH/ (13x9.1) 1874	S	200
2147	FRIGHTENED BROOD, THE	S	165
2148	FRIGHTENED BROOD, THE (8.2x11.12)	S	160
2149	FROLICSOME KITS/ (8.3x11.3) N. Currier	S	140
2150	FROLICKSOME KITS/ 1880	TC	75
2151	FROLICSOME PETS/ (12.3x8.3)	S	145
2152	FROM SHORE TO SHORE	S	105
2153	FRONTIER LAKE, THE/ (8x12.8)	S	255
2154	FRONTIER SETTLEMENT, A/ (11.2x16.12)	M	600
2155	FROZEN UP/ (8.8x12.8) 1872 [New BEST 50]	S	1950
2156	FRUIT/ 1861	M	295
2157	FRUIT/ (Peaches, Grapes and Butterflies) (Vig.)	S	155
2158	FRUIT/ (Apples, Plums, Grapes and Butterflies) (Vig.)	S	155
2159	FRUIT No. 1, THE/ (12.1x8.8) 1848, N. Currier	S	155
2160	FRUIT AND FLOWER PIECE/ (11.2x15.8) 1863	M	405
2161	FRUIT AND FLOWER PIECE	S	145
2162	FRUIT AND FLOWER PIECE/ 1870	S	155
2163	FRUIT AND FLOWERS/ 1848, N. Currier	S	155
2164	FRUIT AND FLOWERS. No. 1/ 1848, N. Currier	S	155

2165	FRUIT AND FLOWERS. No. 2/ 1848, N. Currier	S	155
2166	FRUIT AND FLOWERS/ 1870	S	145
2167	FRUIT AND FLOWERS	S	145
2168	FRUIT AND FLOWERS/ (Vase of bleeding hearts) 1870	S	145
2169	FRUIT AND FLOWERS/ (12x8.12)	S	145
2170	FRUIT AND FLOWERS IN SUMMER	S	145
2171	FRUIT AND FLOWERS OF AUTUMN	M	370
2172	FRUIT AND FLOWERS OF AUTUMN/ (Companion to #2191) 1865	M	370
2173	FRUIT GIRL, THE/ (11.12x8.7) 1845, N. Currier	S	105
2174	FRUIT GIRL, THE/ 1847, N. Currier	S	105
2175	FRUIT GIRL, THE/ 1845, N. Currier	S	100
2176	FRUIT PIECE, THE/ 1845, N. Currier	S	155
2177	FRUIT PIECE, THE/ 1859	M	370
2178	FRUIT PIECE, THE/ 1867	M	370
2179	FRUIT PIECE/ 1870	S	155
2180	FRUIT PIECE / #607	S	155
2181	FRUIT PIECE	VS	205
2182	FRUIT PIECE / Summer Gift	S	155
2183	FRUIT PIECE / Autumn Gift	S	155
2184	FRUIT VASE / #451 (Vig.) 1847, N. Currier	S	155
2185	FRUIT VASE/ 1847, N. Currier	S	155
2186	FRUIT VASE/ 1870	S	155
2187	FRUIT VASE, THE/ #451 (Vig.)	S	155
2188	FRUITS AND FLOWERS/ (11.14x8.12)	S	155
2189	FRUITS, AUTUMN VARIETIES/ (8.7x12.7) 1871	S	155
2190	FRUITS, SUMMER VARIETIES/ 1871	S	155
2191	FRUITS AND FLOWERS OF SUMMER/ (Companion to #2172) 1865	M	370
2192	FRUITS OF INTEMPERANCE, THE/ 1848, N. Currier	S	200
2193	FRUITS OF INTEMPERANCE, THE/ (8x12.6) 1870	S	200
2194	FRUITS OF TEMPERANCE, THE/ (8.3x12.13) 1848, N. Currier	S	200
2195	FRUITS OF TEMPERANCE, THE/ 1870	S	200
2196	FRUITS OF THE GARDEN	S	155
2197	FRUITS OF THE GOLDEN LAND/ (8.8x12.8) 1871	S	240
2198	FRUITS OF THE SEASON/ (7.14x12.7) 1870	S	155
2199	FRUITS OF THE SEASON/ #569	S	155
2200	FRUITS OF THE SEASON - Autumn	S	155
2201	FRUITS OF THE SEASON/ 1872	S	155
2202	FRUITS OF THE SEASON/ #569/ (8.4x12.3)	S	155
2203	FRUITS OF THE TROPICS/ (8.7x12.7) 1871	S	165

2204	FULL HAND, A*/ (Vig.) (Companion to #1762) 1884	S	125
2205	FUNERAL OF DANIEL O'CONNELL, THE/(7.15x12.12) N. Currier	S	55
2206	FUNERAL OF PRESIDENT LINCOLN/ (8.3x13) 1865	S	265
2207	FUST BLOOD, DE/ (Companion to #2208) (Vig.) 1882	S	245
2208	FUST KNOCK-DOWN, DE/ (Vig.) 1882	S	245
2209	FUTURITY RACE AT SHEEPSHEAD BAY/ 1889	L	1500

G

Con#	Title	Folio	Value
2210	GALLANT CHARGE OF THE 54th, MASSACHUSETTS REGIMENT/ (8.4x12.8) 1865	S	325
2211	GALLANT CHARGE OF THE KENTUCKY CAVALRY UNDER COL. MARSHALL/ 1847, N. Currier	S	165
2212	GALLANT CHARGE OF THE KENTUCKIANS/ 1847	S	165
2213	GALLANT CHARGE OF THE "69th"	S	205
2214	GAME COCK, THE/ (Vig.) N. Currier	S	190
2215	GAME COCK, THE - TRIMMED/ (Vig.) N. Currier	S	190
2216	GAME COCK, THE	S	200
2217	GAME DOG, A/ (Vig.) 1879	S	190
2218	GAME OF THE ARROW (12.2x17.14)	M	1550
2219	GAP OF DUNLOE, THE	S	70
2220	GARDEN OF GETHSEMANE, THE/ (8.6x12.4) 1846, N. Currier	S	20
2221	GARDEN ORCHARD AND VINE/ (15x20.5) 1867	M	760
2222	GARFIELD FAMILY, THE (8.9x12.11)	S	90
2223	GARNET POOL, THE (10.7x14.15)	M	600
2224	GARRETT DAVIS/ (18.12x36.4) 1854, N. Currier	L	1525
2225	GATE OF BELEN/ (Title in Spanish) N. Currier	S	65
2226	GAY DECEIVER, THE/ (Dogs in courtroom) 1872	M	240
2227	GEBURTS UND TAUFSCHEIN	S	25
2228	GEM OF THE ATLANTIC, THE/ (8.12x12.15) 1849, N. Currier	S	640
2229	GEM OF THE PACIFIC, THE/ (8.13x12.15) 1849, N. Currier	S	640
2230	GEMS OF AMERICAN SCENERY	S	375
2231	GENERAL AMPUDIA TREATING FOR THE CAPITULATION OF MONTEREY, WITH GEN. TAYLOR/ N. Currier	S	135
2232	GENERAL AND MRS. WASHINGTON/ 1876	S	90
2233	GENERAL ANDREW JACKSON / "The Hero" (12.2x8.9)	S	105
2234	GENERAL ANDREW JACKSON / "The Hero" (12.2x8.7)	S	105

2235	GEN. ANDREW JACKSON / "The Hero of New Orleans"	S	110
2236	GEN. ANDREW JACKSON / "The Hero of New Orleans" (Vig.)	S	110
2237	GEN. ANDREW JACKSON / "The Hero of New Orleans"	S	110
2238	GENERAL ANDREW JACKSON AT NEW ORLEANS (11.15x8.7)	S	110
2239	GENERAL ANDREW JACKSON / BORN 15TH MARCH, 1767...	S	105
2240	GENL. ANDREW JACKSON/ "The Union Must And Shall Be Preserved" (Vig.)	S	105
2241	GEN. BEM,/ "The Hungarian Hero"/ N. Currier	S	60
2242	GEN. BENJAMIN F. BUTLER	S	70
2243	GENERAL BUTLER" AND "DEXTER"/ (16.10x26.12) 1866	L	1625
2244	GENERAL BUTLER" AND "DEXTER"/ (Vig.)	S	290
2245	GEN. CHESTER A. ARTHUR/ (Vig.) 1880	M	110
2246	GEN. CHESTER A. ARTHUR - 21ST PRESIDENT/ (Vig.) 1880	M	155
2247	GEN. D.E. TWIGGS AT THE STORMING OF THE FORTRESS OF CHAPULETEPEC/ (11.8x8.8) N. Currier	S	115
2248	GENL. DEMBINSKY/ (Vig.) 1849, N. Currier	S	60
2249	GENL. E. CAVAIGNAC/ (12x8.15)	S	60
2250	GENERAL FRANCIS MARION/ (8.8x12.8) 1876 [Old BEST 50]	S	470
2251	GENL. FRANK P. BLAIR, JR.	S	80
2252	GENL. FRANKLIN PIERCE/ 1852, N. Currier	L	220
2253	GENL. FRANKLIN PIERCE/ N. Currier	S	80
2254	GENL. FRANZ SIGEL/ (Vig.) 1862	S	90
2255	GENL. FRANZ SIGEL AT THE BATTLE OF PEA RIDGE, ARK./ (11.10x8.13)	S	95
2256	GENL. G.T. BEAUREGARD	S	95
2257	GENERAL GARIBALDI / " The Hero of Italy"/ #17/ (11.13x8.12)	S	60
2258	GENERAL GARIBALDI / " The Hero of Italy" (12x8.15)	S	60
2259	GENL. GEO. B. McCLELLAN AND STAFF/ (At Williamsburg) 1862	S	95
2260	GENL. GEO. B. McCLELLAN AND STAFF BEFORE YORKTOWN, VA/ (11.14x9.1)	S	120
2261	GEN. GEORGE WASHINGTON / The Father of his Country/ (Equestrian) N. Currier [Old BEST 50]	S	175
2262	GEN. GEORGE WASHINGTON / The Father of his Country/ (Vig.)	S	110
2263	GEN. GEORGE WASHINGTON / The Father of his Country/ #60/ (11.2x9) (Vig.)	S	110
2264	GENERAL GEORGE WASHINGTON / The Father of his Country/ (11.2x8.12)	S	110
2265	GENL. GEORGE WASHINGTON / The Father of his Country/ (L.M. on stone)	M	215
2266	GENL. GEORGE WASHINGTON / The Father of his Country/ (11.1x6.10)	S	110
2267	GENL. GEORGE WASHINGTON MORRISON NUTT / 16 years old 29 inches in height	S	125

2268	GENL. GORGEY / "The Hungarian Patriot" (Vig.)	S	55
2269	GENERAL GRANT/ 1884	S	90
2270	GENERAL GRANT/ (Military uniform) 1885	L	240
2271	GENERAL GRANT, U.S.	L	240
2272	GENERAL GRANT / In His Library, Writing His Memoirs	L	270
2273	GENERAL GRANT AND FAMILY/ (8.2x12.5) 1867	S	80
2274	GENERAL GRANT AT THE TOMB OF A. LINCOLN/ (8x12.8) 1868	S	105
2275	GENERAL HELMUTH VON MOLTKE VON PREUSSEN (11x10)	S	50
2276	GENERAL ISRAEL PUTNAM/ C. Currier	S	115
2277	GENL. ISRAEL PUTNAM/ #367/ N. Currier	S	115
2278	GENL. ISRAEL PUTNAM/ (11.12x8.9) N. Currier	S	115
2279	GENERAL ISRAEL PUTNAM/ Currier & Ives	S	115
2280	GEN. JAMES A. GARFIELD/ 1880	S	80
2281	GENERAL JAMES A. GARFIELD / 20th PRESIDENT	M	165
2282	GENL. JAMES IRVIN/ (11.6x8.10) 1847, N. Currier	S	90
2283	GEN. JOHN C. BRECKINRIDGE	S	90
2284	GENL. JOHN B. WOOL AT THE BATTLE OF BUENA VISTA/ (Vig.) N. Currier	S	90
2285	GEN. JOSEPH E. JOHNSTON/ 1861	S	95
2286	GENERAL LAFAYETTE/ N. Currier	S	100
2287	GENERAL LAFAYETTE/ (12x8.9) N. Currier	S	100
2288	GENL. LEWIS CASS/ (11.10x8.11) 1846, N. Currier	S	80
2289	GENL. MEAGHER AT THE BATTLE OF FAIR OAKS, VA/ (7.15x12.7) 1862	S	155
2290	GENERAL PHILIP KEARNEY	S	115
2291	GENERAL ROBERT E. LEE	S	160
2292	GEN. ROBERT E. LEE AT THE GRAVE OF "STONEWALL" JACKSON	S	175
2293	GENERAL SCOTT'S VICTORIOUS ENTRY INTO THE CITY OF MEXICO/ (12.11x8.5) 1847, N. Currier	S	110
2294	GENERAL SHIELDS AT THE BATTLE OF WINCHESTER, VA/ (7.15x12.8) 1862	S	195
2295	GENERAL STONEMAN'S GREAT CAVALRY RAID/ (8x12.14)	S	215
2296	GENERAL TAYLOR AND STAFF/ (12.2x8.8) 1847, N. Currier	S	95
2297	GENL. TAYLOR AT THE BATTLE OF PALO ALTO/ (8.8x12.8) 1846, N. Currier	S	125
2298	GENL. TAYLOR AT THE BATTLE OF PALO ALTO/ 1846, N. Currier	S	125
2299	GENL. TAYLOR AT THE BATTLE OF RESACA DE LA PALMA/ (8.7x12.11) 1846, N. Currier	S	125
2300	GENL. TAYLOR AT THE BATTLE OF RESACA DE LA PALMA/ (8.9x12.11) 1846, N. Currier	S	125
2301	GENL. THOMAS FRANCIS MEAGHER AT... FREDERICKSBURG	S	125
2302	GENERAL TOM THUMB/ (11.13x8.10) N. Currier	S	145

2303	GENERAL TOM THUMB- Barnum's Gallery of Wonders, No. 1/ (12.4x8.8) 1849, N. Currier	S	145
2304	GENERAL TOM THUMB- "Born in 1832, is 28 in. high, Etc.	S	145
2305	GENERAL TOM THUMB / THE SMALLEST MAN ALIVE	S	145
2306	GENL. TOM THUMB / STANDING BY...	S	145
2307	GENL. TOM THUMB & WIFE, COM. NUTT & MINNIE WARREN- "The Greatest Wonders in the World"/ 1863	S	145
2308	GENL. TOM THUMB AS HOP O' MY THUMB	S	145
2309	GENL. TOM THUMB'S MARRIAGE/ 1863	S	145
2310	GENERAL TRANSATLANTIC COMPANY'S STEAMER "NORMANDIE"	S	280
2311	GENERAL TROCHU	S	60
2312	GEN. U.S. GRANT/ 1884	S	90
2313	GEN. U.S. GRANT/ (9.9x12.4) 1885	S	90
2314	GEN. U.S. GRANT/ (8.1x6.13) 1885	S	90
2315	GENERAL U.S. GRANT/ GENERAL IN CHIEF...	S	90
2316	GEN. U.S. GRANT/ THE NATION'S CHOICE...	S	90
2317	GENERAL U.S. GRANT/ PRESIDENT OF THE U.S.	S	105
2318	GENERAL U.S. GRANT/ Und.	S	90
2319	GENERAL VIEW OF THE CITY OF TORONTO, NC (11.14x17.14)	M	560
2320	GENL. VON STEINMETZ VON PREUSSEN (Vig.)	S	50
2321	GENL. WILLIAM F PACKER/ "Gov. of Penna." (11.6x8.10)	S	80
2322	GENERAL WILLIAM H. HARRISON / HERO OF TIPPECANOE/ (12x8.15)	S	85
2323	GENERAL WILLIAM H. HARRISON / HERO OF TIPPECANOE/ (12x10.1)	S	85
2324	GEN. WILLIAM H. HARRISON AT THE BATTLE OF TIPPECANOE/ #57/ (11.10x9.11) N. Currier	S	140
2325	GENERAL WILLIAM H. HARRISON AT THE BATTLE OF TIPPECANOE/ (11.2x8.11) N. Currier	S	150
2326	GENL. WILLIAM J. WORTH/ (Vig.) 1847, N. Currier	S	75
2327	GENL. WILLIAM T. SHERMAN	S	110
2328	GEN. WINFIELD S. HANCOCK (Vig.)	S	75
2329	GEN. Z. TAYLOR/ " The Hero of the Rio Grande"/ (Vig.) 1846, N. Currier	S	105
2330	GEN. Z. TAYLOR/ "Rough and Ready"/ (12.3x8.13) 1846	S	105
2331	GENERAL Z. TAYLOR/ "Rough and Ready"/ (11.15x8.8) 1847	S	105
2332	GENTEEL STEPPER, A	TC	65
2333	GENTEEL STEPPER, A/ (Used as an ad)	TC	65
2334	GENUINE HAVANA, A	S	110
2335	GEORGE	S	125
2336	GEORGE AND LUCY	S	95
2337	GEORGE AND MARTHA WASHINGTON/ (Pair on same sheet.) (Vig.)	S	100

2338	GEORGE B. McCLELLAN	M	140
2339	GEORGE CLINTON	VS	70
2340	GEORGE M. DALLAS/ 1846, N. Currier	S	85
2341	GEORGE M. DALLAS/ "The People"s Candidate"/ N. Currier	S	95
2342	GEORGE M. DALLAS/ "The People"s Candidate"/ N. Currier	S	95
2343	GEORGE M. DALLAS/ "Vice President of the U.S."/ (11.10x8.11) 1844, N. Currier	S	120
2344	GEORGE M. PATCHEN", "BROWN DICK" AND "MILLER'S DAMSEL"/ (17.8x27.8) 1859	L	1825
2345	GEORGE W. WILLIAMS	S	75
2346	GEORGE WASHINGTON/ (Head and shoulders)	M	160
2347	GEORGE WASHINGTON/ (Bust to right, lace jabot) (Vig.)	M	160
2348	GEORGE WASHINGTON/ (Bust to right, plain jabot)	M	160
2349	GEORGE WASHINGTON/ (Vig.)	S	95
2350	GEORGE WASHINGTON/ (Facsimile signature)	S	95
2351	GEORGE WASHINGTON/ (Full length, uniform)	S	95
2352	GEORGE WASHINGTON/ (11.6x9) (Right arm on table)	S	95
2353	GEORGE WASHINGTON / FIRST PRESIDENT OF THE U.S./ (Right arm on table, sword resting in left arm)	S	155
2354	GEORGE WASHINGTON / FIRST PRESIDENT OF THE U.S./ (Sword resting in left arm)	S	155
2355	GEORGE WASHINGTON / FIRST PRESIDENT OF THE U.S.	S	155
2356	GEORGE WASHINGTON AND HIS FAMILY	L	380
2357	GEORGIANA/ (11.9x8.7) 1846, N. Currier	S	80
2358	GEORGIANA/ (10.14x8.10) (Oval) Currier & Ives	S	85
2359	GEORGIE/ "Quite Tired"/ (Vig.)	S	80
2360	GEORGIE/ "Quite Tired"/ (Half length) (Vig.) N. Currier	S	80
2361	GERMAN BEAUTY, THE/ (Vig.)	S	75
2362	GERTRUDE/ (11.12x8.4) 1846, N. Currier	S	75
2363	GETTING A BOOST/ (Vig.) (Companion to #4600) 1882	S	250
2364	GETTING A FOOT/ (Companion to #289) 1887	S	245
2365	GETTING A HOIST/ A Bad Case of the Heaves/ (Vig.) 1875	S	250
2366	GETTING A HOIST/ 1879	TC	75
2367	GETTING DOWN/ (Comic) (Companion to #2370) N. Currier	S	250
2368	GETTING IN/ N. Currier	S	250
2369	GETTING OUT/ N. Currier	S	250
2370	GETTING UP/ (Comic) (Companion to #2367) N. Currier	S	250
2371	GHOST, THE/ (Cartoon) (Vig.)	S	210
2372	GIANT'S CAUSEWAY, THE, Ireland (8.8x12.9)	S	75
2373	GIFT OF AUTUMN, A/ (Vig.) 1875	S	150
2374	GIPSIE'S CAMP THE	M	225

2375	GIRARD AVENUE BRIDGE, FAIRMOUNT PARK, PHILA. (8.8x12.8)	S	265
2376	GIRL I LOVE, THE/ (Vig.) 1870	S	75
2377	GIRL OF MY HEART (Vig.)	S	75
2378	GIRL OF THE PERIOD, THE (Vig.)	S	175
2379	GIVE ME LIBERTY, OR GIVE ME DEATH!"/ (8.13x12.11) 1876	S	290
2380	GIVE US THIS DAY OUR DAILY BREAD/ (Scroll with bread & wheat) (Vig.) 1872	S	160
2381	GIVE US THIS DAY OUR DAILY BREAD/ 1878	S	70
2382	GIVING HIM TAFFY/ 1881	S	95
2382A	GIVING HIM TAFFY/ 1881	TC	70
2383	GLEN AT NEWPORT, THE (8.8x12.8)	S	245
2384	GLENGARIFF INN, IRELAND (8x12.12)	S	85
2385	GLIMPSE OF THE HOMESTEAD, A/ 1863	M	580
2386	GLIMPSE OF THE HOMESTEAD, A/ 1865	M	580
2387	GLIMPSE OF THE HOMESTEAD, A/ (11.2x15.8) 1859	M	580
2388	GLORIOUS CHARGE OF HANCOCK'S DIVISION (8.1x12.9)	S	225
2389	GO AS YOU PLEASE	S	80
2390	GO IN AND WIN/ 1880	S	235
2391	GOD BLESS FATHER AND MOTHER/ (Vig.) 1876	S	115
2392	GOD BLESS OUR HOME/ (Vig.)	S	190
2393	GOD BLESS OUR SCHOOL/ 1874	S	300
2394	GOD BLESS THEE AND KEEP THEE	S	205
2395	GOD IS LOVE"/ (Vig.)	S	115
2396	GOD SAVE MY FATHER'S LIFE/ (Vig.) N. Currier	S	30
2397	GOD SPAKE ALL THESE WORDS/ (Vig.) 1876	S	20
2398	GOING AGAINST THE STREAM/ (Companion to #2410) N. Currier	M	255
2399	GOING FOR A SHINE/ (Vig.) (Companion to #4818) 1888	S	240
2400	GOING FOR HIM/ (8.4x12.3) (Companion to #6648) 1868	S	235
2401	GOING FOR THE MONEY/ (18x28) 1891	L	1575
2402	GOING IT BLIND/ N. Currier	S	240
2403	GOING TO PASTURE - EARLY MORNING	S	185
2404	GOING TO THE FRONT! (Vig.) 1878	S	195
2405	GOING TO THE FRONT	S	195
2406	GOING TO THE FRONT/ 1880	TC	70
2407	GOING TO THE MILL/ N. Currier	S	195
2408	GOING TO THE MILL/ 1859	M	395
2409	GOING TO THE TROT - A GOOD DAY AND A GOOD TRACK/ (18.13x28.12) 1869	L	1800
2410	GOING WITH THE STREAM/ (Companion to #2398) N. Currier	M	235
2411	GOLD DUST/ (Vig.) 1875	S	290

2412	GOLD MINING IN CALIFORNIA/ (8.8x12.8) 1871 [Old & New BEST 50]	S	1575
2413	GOLD SEEKERS, THE/ 1851, N. Currier	S	980
2414	GOLDEN FRUITS OF CALIFORNIA/ (14.15x20.7) 1869	L	1175
2415	GOLDEN MORNING, A/ N. Currier	M	360
2416	GOLDEN MORNING, THE	M	360
2417	GOLDEN MORNING, THE/ (12.8x8.8)	S	300
2418	GOLDSMITH MAID/ Record 2:14/ (2.12x4.12) 1881	S	290
2418A	GOLDSMITH MAID/ Record 2:14/ 1881	TC	85
2419	GOLDSMITH MAID/ Record 2:14/ 1871	S	290
2420	GOLDSMITH MAID" AND "AMERICAN GIRL"/ (17.11x27.11) 1868	L	1625
2421	GOLDSMITH MAID" AND "JUDGE FULLERTON"/ (8x13.4) 1874	S	290
2422	GOLDSMITH MAID" AND "LUCY"/ 1874	S	290
2423	Was a duplicate of # 65. (A. Goldsmith...)	S	290
2424	GOOD CHANCE, A/ (19.4x28.4) 1863	L	4100
2425	GOOD DAY'S SPORT, A - HOMEWARD BOUND/ (18x25.12) 1869	L	3775
2426	GOOD ENOUGH/ (Vig.)	S	70
2427	GOOD EVENING/ (Dog and Child)	S	80
2428	GOOD FIDO AND NAUGHTY KITTY (8.8x12.3)	S	130
2429	GOOD FOR A COLD	S	95
2430	GOOD FOR NOTHING (15.14x12.14)	M	190
2431	GOOD FRIENDS, THE	S	75
2432	GOOD HUSBAND, THE/ (7.14x12.10) 1870	S	190
2433	GOOD LITTLE BROTHER/ (11.11x8.11) 1872	S	80
2434	GOOD LITTLE GIRL/ (Vig.) 1871	S	80
2435	GOOD LITTLE SISTERS, THE/ (11.9x8.8)	S	105
2436	GOOD LUCK TO YE/ (Women holding horseshoe)	TC	70
2437	GOOD MAN AT THE HOUR OF DEATH, THE/ N. Currier	S	55
2438	GOOD MORNING/ (Dog and Child)	S	95
2439	GOOD MORNING LITTLE FAVORITE/ (12.7x8.12)	S	105
2440	GOOD NATURED MAN, THE/ N. Currier	S	75
2441	GOOD NIGHT, LITTLE PLAYFELLOW/ (12.8x8.11)	S	90
2442	GOOD OLD DOGGIE	M	225
2443	GOOD OLD ROVER AND KITTIE	S	130
2444	GOOD RACE, WELL WON, A/ (18.1x27.1) 1887	L	1375
2445	GOOD SAMARITAN, THE/ #677/ 1849, N. Currier	S	20
2446	GOOD SAMARITAN, THE/ 1849	S	20
2447	GOOD SEND OFF, A - GO!/ 1888	L	1400
2448	GOOD SEND OFF - GO!, A/ (17.3x26.7) 1872	L	1400
2449	GOOD SHEPHERD, THE	S	25

2450	GOOD SHEPHERDESS/ (11.14x8.8) 1846, N. Currier	S	25
2451	GOOD TIMES ON THE OLD PLANTATION/ (8.9x12.9)	S	705
2452	GOSPEL ORDINANCE, THE/ 1846, N. Currier	S	20
2453	GOT 'EM BOTH/ 1882	S	280
2453A	GOT 'EM BOTH/ (Comic billiards) 1882	TC	75
2454	GOT 'EM BOTH/ (23x36) 1892	L	480
2455	GOT THE DROP ON HIM/ (Vig.) 1881	S	255
2456	GOVERNMENT GUARDS - CONNECTICUT 1st COMPANY	S	160
2457A	GOV. BENJ. GRATZ BROWN OF MISSOURI LIBERAL REPUBLICAN CANDIDATE FOR V.P. OF U.S.	S	95
2457	GOV. GROVER CLEVELAND	M	140
2458	GOVERNMENT HOUSE	L	585
2459	GOVERNOR RUTHERFORD B. HAYES	S	85
2460	GOVERNOR SAMUEL J. TILDEN	S	90
2461	GOVERNOR SPRAGUE - BLACK TROTTING STALLION	S	290
2462	GOVERNOR THOMAS A. HENDRICKS/ (Vig.)	S	80
2463	GOVERNOR WADE HAMPTON/ (Vig.)	S	80
2464	GRACE DARLING/ (Shipwreck) N. Currier	S	265
2465	GRACE, MERCY AND PEACE	S	160
2466	GRACES OF THE BICYCLE, THE/ (Vig.) 1880	S	435
2467	GRACES OF THE BICYCLE, THE/ 1880	TC	85
2468	GRACIE/ (Vig.)	S	80
2469	GRAF VON BISMARK/ (Vig.)	S	40
2470	GRAND BANNER OF THE RADICAL DEMOCRACY / FOR 1864/ (11.14x8.13)	S	225
2471	GRAND BIRD'S EYE VIEW OF / THE EAST RIVER SUSPENSION BRIDGE	L	1725
2472	GRAND BIRD'S EYE VIEW OF THE GREAT COLUMBIAN EXHIBITION	L	1700
2473	GRAND CALIFORNIA FILLY "SUNOL", Record 2:10.50/ (Vig.) 1889	S	290
2474	GRAND CALIFORNIA FILLY "WILDFLOWER"/ (Vig.) 1883	S	305
2475	GRAND CALIFORNIA TROTTING MARE "SUNOL"/ (18.6x28.3) 1890	L	1475
2476	GRAND CENTENNIAL SMOKE/ 1876	M	305
2477	GRAND CENTENNIAL WEDDING/ 1876	M	305
2478	GRAND DEMOCRATIC FREE SOIL BANNER/ (12.3x9.1) 1848	S	210
2479	GRAND DISPLAY OF FIREWORKS AND ILLUMINATIONS	S	620
2480	GRAND DISPLAY OF FIREWORKS AND ILLUMINATIONS/ (12x17.9)	M	895
2481	GRAND DRIVE CENTRAL PARK, NY, THE/ (17.7x27.15) 1869 [Old BEST 50]	L	3400
2482	GRAND FIGHT FOR THE CHAMPION'S BELT - BETWEEN GRANITE PIERCE AND OLD CHAPULTEPEC	S	275
2483	GRAND FOOTBALL MATCH / Darktown against Blackville/ "A Kick Off"/ 1881	S	260

2484	GRAND FOOTBALL MATCH / Darktown against Blackville/ "A Scrimmage"/ (Vig.) 1888	S	260
2485	GRAND FUNERAL PROCESSION IN MEMORY OF GENERAL JACKSON/ (8.12x12.8) N. Currier	S	80
2486	GRAND FUNERAL PROCESSION OF THE VICTIMS OF THE REVOLUTION/ (8.6x12.13) 1848, N. Currier	S	75
2487	GRAND HORSE "ST. JULIEN", "THE KING OF THE TROTTERS"/ (Vig.) 1880	S	290
2488	GRAND HORSE "ST. JULIEN", "THE KING OF THE TROTTERS"/ (Vig.) 1881	S	290
2489	GRAND NATIONAL AMERICAN BANNER/ (11.13x8.5) 1856, N. Currier	S	255
2490	GRAND NATIONAL DEMOCRATIC BANNER, POLK AND DALLAS/ (11.12x8.5) 1844, N. Currier	S	205
2491	GRAND NATIONAL DEMOCRATIC BANNER, POLK AND DALLAS/ (11.12x8.5) 1844, N. Currier	S	205
2492	GRAND NATIONAL DEMOCRATIC BANNER, CASS AND BUTLER/ (11.10x8.3) 1848, N. Currier	S	215
2493	GRAND NATIONAL DEMOCRATIC BANNER, PIERCE AND KING/ 1852, N. Currier	S	215
2494	GRAND NATIONAL DEMOCRATIC BANNER, PRESS ONWARD	S	210
2495	GRAND NATIONAL DEMOCRATIC BANNER, BUCHANAN AND BRECKINRIDGE/ 1856, N. Currier	S	210
2496	GRAND NATIONAL DEMOCRATIC BANNER FOR 1860/ BRECKINRIDGE AND LANE/ 1860	S	220
2497	GRAND NATIONAL DEMOCRATIC BANNER / PEACE! UNION! AND VICTORY!	S	215
2498	GRAND NATIONAL DEMOCRATIC BANNER/ 1876	S	210
2499	GRAND NATIONAL DEMOCRATIC BANNER/ 1880	L	360
2500	GRAND NATIONAL DEMOCRATIC BANNER/ 1880	S	215
2501	GRAND NATIONAL LIBERAL REPUBLICAN BANNER FOR 1872	S	205
2502	GRAND NATIONAL REPUBLICAN BANNER, FREE LABOR...	S	225
2503	GRAND NATIONAL REPUBLICAN BANNER FOR 1872, GRANT AND GREELEY/ 1872	S	210
2504	GRAND NATIONAL REPUBLICAN BANNER, LIBERTY & UNION	S	215
2505	GRAND NATIONAL REPUBLICAN BANNER/ (Garfield & Arthur) 1880	S	225
2506	GRAND NATIONAL REPUBLICAN BANNER/ 1880	L	365
2507	GRAND NATIONAL TEMPERANCE BANNER/ (11.14x8.10) N. Currier	S	200
2508	GRAND NATIONAL TEMPERANCE BANNER/ Currier & Ives	S	195
2509	GRAND NATIONAL UNION BANNER FOR 1860/ (12.4x8.10)	S	210
2510	GRAND NATIONAL UNION BANNER FOR 1864/ (12x8.13)	S	250
2511	GRAND NATIONAL WHIG BANNER/ 1844	S	205
2512	GRAND NATIONAL WHIG BANNER/ (11.11x8.3) 1844	S	205
2513	GRAND NATIONAL WHIG BANNER / ZACHARY TAYLOR...	S	205
2514	GRAND NATIONAL WHIG BANNER / PRESS ONWARD	S	205

All prints are published by Currier & Ives unless otherwise stated.

2515	GRAND, NATIONAL, WHIG BANNER	S	205
2516	GRAND NEW STEAMBOAT "PILGRIM", THE LARGEST IN THE WORLD/ (20.12x35) 1883	L	1525
2517	GRAND PACER "FLYING JIB", Record 2:04/ (Vig.) 1892	S	290
2518	GRAND PACER "MASCOT", BY DECEIVER	L	1425
2519	GRAND PACER "RICHBALL", Record 2:12.50/ (Vig.)	S	290
2520	GRAND PATENT INDIA - RUBBER AIRLINE RAILWAY TO CALIFORNIA/ (Cartoon) (10.12x17.7)	M	700
2520A	GRAND TROTTER "CLINGSTONE" DRIVEN BY G.H. SAUNDERS/ Record 2:14/ 1883	L	1500
2521	GRAND RACER "KINGSTON"/ (19.15x27.2) 1891	L	1500
2522	GRAND RECEPTION OF KOSSUTH/ (8.2x12.2) 1851, N. Currier	S	105
2523	GRAND SALOON OF THE PALACE STEAMER "DREW"/ 1878	L	1375
2524	GRAND STALLION "ALLERTON"	S	290
2525	GRAND STALLION "MAXY COBB"/ Record 2:13.25/ (Vig.)	S	290
2526	GRAND STALLION "MAXY COBB"/ Record 2:13.25/ (Vig.)	S	290
2527	GRAND THROUGH ROUTE BETWEEN NORTH AND SOUTH/ 1878	S	500
2528	GRAND TROTTER "CLINGSTONE"/ Record 2:14/ (17.13x26.9) 1883	L	1450
2529	GRAND TROTTER "CLINGSTONE"/ Record 2:14/ 1882	S	290
2530	GRAND TROTTER "EDWIN THORNE"	L	1425
2531	GRAND TROTTING "QUEEN NANCY HANKS"	L	1425
2532	GRAND TROTTING STALLION "AXTELL"	L	1425
2533	GRAND TROTTING STALLION "BONESETTER"	S	290
2534	GRAND TROTTING STALLION "BONESETTER"	S	290
2535	GRAND TROTTING STALLION "ST. JULIEN"	L	1425
2536	GRAND UNITES ORDER OF ODD FELLOWS CHART/ (13.6x10) 1881	S	105
2537	GRAND UNITED STATES CENTENNIAL EXHIBITION 1876	S	235
2538	GRAND YOUNG TROTTER "JAY EYE SEE"/ Record 2:10 (Vig.)	S	290
2539	GRAND YOUNG TROTTING MARE "NANCY HANKS"/ (Vig.) 1890	S	290
2540	GRAND YOUNG TROTTING STALLION "AXTELL"/ (Vig.) 1889	S	290
2541	GRANDEST PALACE DRAWING ROOM STEAMERS IN THE WORLD, "DREW" AND "ST. JOHN"/ (21x34.11) 1878	L	1675
2542	GRANDFATHER'S ADVICE	S	95
2543	GRANDMA'S "SPECS"	S	100
2544	GRANDMA'S "SPECS"/ #272	S	100
2545	GRANDMA'S TREASURES	S	100
2546	GRANDMOTHER'S PRESENT, THE/ (9.12x7.10) N. Currier	S	90
2547	GRANDPA'S SPECS"/ (Little girl)	S	100
2548	GRANDPA'S SPECS"/ (12x9.7)	S	100
2549	GRANDPA'S CANE	M	180
2550	GRANDPAPA'S CANE	S	105

2551	GRANDPAPA'S RIDE/ N. Currier	S	160
2552	GRANDPAPA'S RIDE	M	265
2553	GRANT AND HIS GENERALS/ (Vig.) 1865	M	235
2554	GRANT AND LEE MEETING NEAR APPOMATTOX COURTHOUSE, VA/ 1868	S	270
2555	GRANT AT HOME/ 1869	S	95
2556	GRANT AT HOME/ (E. Blinner, del.) 1869	L	240
2557	GRANT IN PEACE	S	95
2558	GRASS HOPPER STRUT, THE	S	125
2559	GRAVE OF STONEWALL JACKSON, LEXINGTON, VA/ (8x12.8) 1870	S	120
2560	GRAY EAGLE	L	1650
2561	GRAY GELDING "JACK" BY PILOT MEDIUM/ Record 2:19 3/4 (Vig.) 1888	S	290
2562	GRAY'S ELEGY - IN A COUNTRY CHURCHYARD/ (16x23.2) 1864	L	780
2563	GRAZING FARM, THE/ (16.12x24.14) 1867	L	1275
2564	GREAT AMERICAN BUCK HUNT OF 1856, THE	M	280
2565	GREAT AMERICAN TANNER/ (Cartoon) (Vig.)	S	190
2566	GREAT BARTHOLDI STATUE, THE / (Daylight scene) (3x5.12) 1884	TC	100
2567	GREAT BARTHOLDI STATUE, THE / (Moonlight scene) (2.15x5.9) 1884	TC	100
2568	GREAT BARTHOLDI STATUE, THE / Liberty Enlightening the World	TC	100
2569	GREAT BARTHOLDI STATUE, THE / Liberty Enlightening the World/ (6 adtl. lines)	S	355
2570	GREAT BARTHOLDI STATUE, THE / Liberty Enlightening the World/ The Gift of France/ 1882	L	1200
2571	GREAT BARTHOLDI STATUE, THE / Liberty Enlightening the World/ The Gift of France/ 1884	L	1200
2572	GREAT BARTHOLDI STATUE, THE / Liberty Enlightening the World/ The Gift of France/ 1883	L	1200
2573	GREAT BARTHOLDI STATUE, THE / Liberty Enlightening the World/ The Gift of France/ 1885	M	640
2574	GREAT BARTHOLDI STATUE, THE / Liberty Enlightening the World/ The Gift of France/ 1885	M	810
2574A	GREAT BARTHOLDI STATUE, THE / The Liberty Enlightening the World/ The Gift of France/ 1885	L	1200
2575	GREAT BARTHOLDI STATUE, THE / Liberty Enlightening the World/ The Gift of France/ 1886	L	1150
2576	GREAT BARTHOLDI STATUE, THE / Liberty Enlightening the World/ With the world renowned and beautiful/ 1885	M	640
2577	GREAT BATTLE OF MURFREESBORO, TENN/ 1863	S	210
2578	GREAT BLACK SEA LION, THE MONARCH OF THE ARTIC SEAS/ (Vig.)	S	340
2579	GREAT COMMAND, THE/ 1866	M	25
2580	GREAT CONFLAGRATION AT PITTSBURGH, PA/ (8.3x12.8) N. Currier	S	695
2581	GREAT CONFLAGRATION AT PITTSBURGH, PA/ (8.3x12.8) N. Currier [Old BEST 50]	S	655

All prints are published by Currier & Ives unless otherwise stated.

2582	GREAT DOUBLE TEAM TROT/ (17.7x28.2) 1891	L	1525
2583	GREAT DOUBLE TEAM TROT/ (16.13x27.5) 1870	L	1525
2584	GREAT EAST RIVER BRIDGE/ (8.7x12.6) 1872 [New BEST 50]	S	350
2585	GREAT EAST RIVER BRIDGE/ 1882	S	350
2586	GREAT EAST RIVER BRIDGE, No. 1/ (Postcard) 1883	TC	90
2587	GREAT EAST RIVER BRIDGE, No. 2/ (Postcard) 1883	TC	90
2588	GREAT EAST RIVER BRIDGE, No. 3/ (Postcard) 1883	TC	90
2589	GREAT EAST RIVER SUSPENSION BRIDGE/ 1883	VS	235
2590	GREAT EAST RIVER SUSPENSION BRIDGE/ (View from Brooklyn) 1883	VS	235
2591	GREAT EAST RIVER SUSPENSION BRIDGE/ (View from N.Y.) 1883	VS	235
2592	GREAT EAST RIVER SUSPENSION BRIDGE/ 1874	L	1600
2593	GREAT EAST RIVER SUSPENSION BRIDGE/ 1877	L	1600
2594	GREAT EAST RIVER SUSPENSION BRIDGE/ 1881	S	350
2595	GREAT EAST RIVER SUSPENSION BRIDGE/ 1881	S	360
2596	GREAT EAST RIVER SUSPENSION BRIDGE/ 1883	L	1600
2597	GREAT EAST RIVER SUSPENSION BRIDGE/ 1883	L	1600
2598	GREAT EAST RIVER SUSPENSION BRIDGE/ 1883	VS	220
2599	GREAT EAST RIVER SUSPENSION BRIDGE/ 1885	L	1500
2600	GREAT EAST RIVER SUSPENSION BRIDGE/ 1886	L	1500
2601	GREAT EAST RIVER SUSPENSION BRIDGE/ 1890	L	1500
2602	GREAT EAST RIVER SUSPENSION BRIDGE/ 1892	L	1500
2603	GREAT EASTERN / THE MAMMOTH TROTTING GELDING	S	290
2604	GREAT EASTERN," THE / 22,500 TONS	M	485
2605	GREAT EASTERN," THE / 22,500 TONS	S	290
2606	GREAT EASTERN" / THE IRON STEAMSHIP "LEVIATHAN	L	1075
2607	GREAT EXHIBITION OF 1851/ (9.14x16.14) N. Currier	M	375
2608	GREAT EXHIBITION OF 1860	M	345
2609	GREAT FAIR ON A GRAND SCALE, A/ 1894	M	1000
2610	GREAT FIELD IN A GRAND RUSH, A/ 1888	L	1275
2611	GREAT FIGHT AT CHARLESTON, SC/ (8.1x12.9) 1863	S	405
2612	GREAT FIGHT BETWEEN THE "MERRIMAC" AND " MONITOR"/ (8.3x12.10) 1862	S	660
2613	GREAT FIGHT FOR THE CHAMPIONSHIP BETWEEN JOHN C. HEENAN "THE BENICIA BOY" AND TOM SAYERS [Old BEST 50]	S	405
2614	GREAT FIRE AT BOSTON/ (8x12.11) 1872 [New BEST 50]	S	335
2615	GREAT FIRE AT CHICAGO/ (16.14x24.8) 1871 [Old & New BEST 50]	L	6350
2616	GREAT FIRE AT ST. JOHN, NB/ (8.1x12.11) 1877	S	380
2617	GREAT FIRE AT ST. LOUIS, MO/ (8.3x12.13) 1849, N. Currier	S	705
2618	GREAT FIRE OF 1835	L	2550
2619	GREAT FIRE OF 1835/ "The Ruins"	L	2550

2620	GREAT FIVE MILE ROWING MATCH FOR $4,000/ 1867	L	4350
2621	GREAT FOOTRACE FOR THE PRESIDENTIAL PURSE	M	245
2622	GREAT HORSES IN A GREAT RACE "SALVATOR" AND "TENNY"/ (18.1x28) 1891	L	1450
2623	GREAT INTERNATIONAL BOAT RACE (8x12.7) [Old BEST 50]	S	1625
2624	GREAT INTERNATIONAL UNIVERSITY BOAT RACE, THE	L	3900
2625	GREAT INTERNATIONAL YACHT RACE, AUGUST 8,/ (17.12x27.12) 1870	L	2225
2626	GREAT INTERNATIONAL YACHT RACE OF/ (8.3x12.10) 1870	S	385
2627	GREAT MATCH AT BALTIMORE, THE/ (Political Cartoon)	M	315
2628	GREAT MATCH RACE/ " A Dead Heat"	M	585
2629	GREAT MISSISSIPPI STEAM BOAT RACE/ (8x12.8) 1870	S	685
2630	GREAT MISSISSIPPI STEAM BOAT RACE/ (8x12.7) [New BEST 50]	S	725
2631	GREAT MISSISSIPPI STEAM BOAT RACE	S	650
2632	GREAT NAVAL BLOCKADE OF ROUND ISLAND, THE	M	565
2633	GREAT NAVAL VICTORY IN MOBILE BAY/ (8x12.9)	S	420
2634	GREAT OCEAN YACHT RACE/ 1867	L	2175
2635	GREAT OYSTER EATING MATCH/ "The Start"/ (Vig.) 1886	S	295
2636	GREAT OYSTER EATING MATCH/ "The Finish"/ (Vig.) 1886	S	295
2637	GREAT PACER JOHNSTON/ Record 2:10/ (Vig.) 1883	S	290
2638	GREAT PACER "SORREL DAN"/ Record 2:14/ (Vig.) 1880	S	290
2639	GREAT POLE MARES, "BELLE HAMLIN" AND "JUSTINA"/ 1890	S	290
2640	GREAT PONTOON DRAWBRIDGE, THE	S	460
2641	GREAT PRESIDENTIAL SWEEPSTAKES OF 1856/ (Vig.)	M	310
2642	GREAT RACE AT BALTIMORE/ (Vig.) 1877	S	335
2643	GREAT RACE FOR THE WESTERN STAKES/ (Vig.) 1870	S	275
2644A	GREAT RACE ON THE MISSISSIPPI, THE / From New Orleans.../ (Daylight scene) 1870	L	4850
2644	GREAT RACE ON THE MISSISSIPPI, THE / From New Orleans.../ (Night scene) 1870	L	4850
2645	GREAT RACING CRACK HINDOO/ (Vig.) 1881	S	280
2646	GREAT REPUBLICAN REFORM PARTY/ (Vig.)	S	180
2647	GREAT RIOT AT THE ASTOR PLACE OPERA HOUSE, NY/ (8.4x12.11) 1849	S	520
2648	GREAT ST. LOUIS BRIDGE ACROSS THE MISSISSIPPI/ (Vig.)	S	600
2649	GREAT SALT LAKE, UTAH/ (8.8x12.8)	S	390
2650	GREAT "SCULLERS RACE" ON THE ST. LAWRENCE, THE	S	1325
2651	GREAT SIRE OF TROTTERS "ELECTIONEER"/ (Vig.) 1891	S	290
2652	GREAT THROUGH ROUTE BETWEEN THE / NORTH AND SOUTH	L	1675
2653	GREAT VICTORY IN THE SHENANDOAH VALLEY, VA/ (7.12x12.8)	S	205
2654	GREAT WALK- "Come In As You Can"/ (Vig.) 1879	S	185
2655	GREAT WALK- "Go As You Please"/ (Vig.) 1879	S	185

All prints are published by Currier & Ives unless otherwise stated.

2656	GREAT WALK- "Come In As You Can, The"/ 1879	TC	75
2657	GREAT WALK- "Go As You Please, The"/ 1879	TC	75
2658	GREAT WEST, THE/ (7.15x12.8) 1870 [New BEST 50]	S	1125
2659	GRECIAN BEND, THE/ "Fifth Avenue Style"/ (Vig.) 1868	S	210
2660	GREY EAGLE/ 1850, N. Currier	L	1900
2661	GREY EDDY/ (16.15x26.6) 1855, N. Currier	L	1700
2662	GREY MARE "EMMA B"/ Record 2:22.50/ (Vig.)	S	290
2663	GREY MARE "LUCY" - THE PACING QUEEN/ (Vig.) 1879	S	290
2664	GREY MARE "POLICE GAZETTE"/ (Vig.) 1879	S	290
2665	GREY TROTTING WONDER "HOPEFUL"/ Record 2:14.75/ (Vig.)	S	290
2666	GROTTOES OF THE SEA	S	95
2667	GROTTOES OF THE SEA	S	95
2668	GROUP OF FRUIT/ (Vig.) 1875	S	160
2669	GROUP OF FLOWERS	S	125
2670	GROUP OF LILIES	S	120
2671	GROUP OF LILIES/ (Vig.)	S	120
2672	GROUP OF LILIES/ (Vig.)	S	120
2673	GROVER CLEVELAND - PRESIDENT OF THE U. S.	S	90
2674	GROWLING MATCH, A	S	110
2675	GUARDIAN ANGEL, THE/ (11.12x8.4)	S	25
2676	GUARDIAN ANGEL, THE/ #328/ (11.12x8.4)	S	25
2677	GUARDIAN ANGEL, THE/ #358/ (11.7x8)	S	25
2678	GUARDIAN ANGEL, THE/ (Title repeated in French and Spanish) (11.12x8.15)	S	25
2679	GUION LINE STEAMSHIP "ARIZONA"	S	310
2680	GULICK GUARD, THE/ 1838, N. Currier	M	185
2681	GUNBOAT CANDIDATE, THE	S	165
2682	GUNBOAT CANDIDATE, THE/ (Vig.)	S	165
2683	GUSTAV STRUVE/ (11.12x8.10) 1848, N. Currier	S	50
2684	GUY / By Kentucky Prince	S	290

H

Con#	Title	Folio	Value
2685	HADLEY FALLS	M	420
2686	HAGUE STREET EXPLOSION	S	405
2687	HAIDEE/ #425	S	55
2688	HAIDEE	S	55
2689	HAIL MARY, MOTHER OF GOD	S	20
2690	HAIR TONIC EXPLOSION/ (9x13.12) 1884	S	170
2691	HALLS OF JUSTICE, NEW YORK/ (3/4 View) (7.8x11.12) N. Currier	S	200
2692	HALLS OF JUSTICE, NEW YORK/ (7.8x11.12) N. Currier	S	200
2693	HALLS OF JUSTICE, NEW YORK/ (View in front, no pedestrians) N. Currier	S	210
2694	HALT BY THE WAYSIDE, A/ (8x12.7)	S	300
2695	HAMBLETONIAN/ 1871	S	290
2696	HAMBRINO/ 1879	S	290
2697	HAMBURG - AMERICAN LINE MAIL STEAMER / FRISIA/ (8x13.11)	S	335
2698	HANDSOME MAN, THE	S	100
2699	HAND-WRITING ON THE WALL, THE/ (Vig.)	S	110
2700	HANNAH/ (8.6x11.13) 1846, N. Currier	S	75
2701	HANNAH/ (3/4 View) N. Currier	S	80
2702	HANNAH/ (Half Length) N. Currier	S	80
2703	HANNIS/ 1879	S	290
2704	HANNIS/ 1881	S	290
2705	HANOVER/ (Vig.) 1887	S	290
2706	HAPPY FACES	S	80
2707	HAPPY FAMILY, A/ (Family Group) N. Currier	S	100
2708	HAPPY FAMILY, A/ (3 Puppies) N. Currier	S	130
2709	HAPPY FAMILY, THE/ (Farm Scene) 1869	S	150
2710	HAPPY FAMILY, THE/ (More Animals than 2709) 1874	S	150
2711	HAPPY FAMILY, THE	S	145
2712	HAPPY FAMILY, THE - RUFFED GROUSE AND YOUNG/ (19.13x27.13) 1866	L	4800
2713	HAPPY HOME, THE/ (11.14x8.8) N. Currier	S	100
2714	HAPPY HOUR, THE/ N. Currier	S	85
2715	HAPPY LAND, THE/ (10.12x8.15) (Oval)	S	105
2716	HAPPY LITTLE CHICKS/ (9.14x13.15) 1866	M	270
2717	HAPPY LITTLE PUPS/ (10x8)	S	130
2718	HAPPY MOTHER, THE/ (11.14x8.12)	S	95
2719	HAPPY MOTHER/ (11.13x15)	M	150
2720	HAPPY MOTHER, THE/ (Doe and fawn)	S	315
2721	HAPPY NEW YEAR/ (Companion to #4109) N. Currier	S	355

All prints are published by Currier & Ives unless otherwise stated.

2722	HAPPY NEW YEAR, A/ 1876	S	665
2723	HAPPY NEW YEAR, A/ Und.	S	645
2724	HARBOR FOR THE NIGHT, A/ (8.9x12.8)	S	280
2725	HARBOR OF NEW YORK/ From The Brooklyn Bridge Tower/ (9x12.15) [New BEST 50]	S	645
2726	HARBOR OF NEW YORK/ (No Statue of Liberty)	S	635
2727	HARD ROAD TO TRAVEL, A/ (8.4x12.14) 1862	S	200
2728	HARD ROAD TO TRAVEL/ (8.4x12.10)	S	200
2729	HARRIET/ (Half Length) N. Currier	S	80
2730	HARRIET/ #116/ (White Shawl) (Vig.)	S	80
2731	HARRIET/ (Head, facing right)	S	75
2732	HARRIET/ (Book in hand) 1845, N. Currier	S	80
2733	HARRISBURG AND THE SUSQUEHANNA/ 1865	M	745
2734	HARRY BASSETT/ 1871	S	290
2735	HARRY BASSETT AND LONGFELLOW/ (Vig.) 1872	L	1425
2736	HARRY BASSETT AND LONGFELLOW / AT SARATOGA	S	290
2737	HARRY BLUFF	S	90
2738	HARRY WILKES/ (18.2x27.2) 1885	L	1500
2739	HARRY WILKES/ Record 2:13 1/2/ (2.12x4.12) 1886	TC	85
2740	HARVARD COLLEGE, CAMBRIDGE, MA/ N. Currier	S	980
2741	HARVEST/ (8.5x12.11) (Companion to #5671) 1849, N. Currier	S	255
2742	HARVEST/ Currier & Ives	S	255
2743	HARVEST DANCE, THE/ (8.5x11.14) (Companion to #2041) 1846, N. Currier	S	125
2744	HARVEST DANCE, THE/ 1847, N. Currier	S	125
2745	HARVEST FIELD, THE/ (11.6x15) (Oval) N. Currier	M	485
2746	HARVEST MOON, THE/ (11.11x16.3)	M	485
2747	HARVEST QUEEN, THE/ (Vig.)	S	75
2748	HARVESTER, THE	M	285
2749	HARVESTING (8.8x12.5)	S	250
2750	HARVESTING - THE LAST LOAD (8.7x12.8)	S	320
2751	HAT THAT MAKES THE MAN/ 1869	S	140
2752	HAT THAT MAKES THE MAN, THE/ 1880	S	165
2753	HAT THAT MAKES THE MAN, THE/ 1880	TC	75
2754	HATTIE/ (Vig.)	S	80
2755	HATTIE WOODWARD/ 1881	TC	85
2756	HAUNTED CASTLE, THE/ (7.14x12.6)	S	85
2757	HAUNTS OF THE WILD SWAN, THE/ (8.7x12.8) 1872	S	445
2758	HAVANA	S	90
2759	HAVE A PEACH	S	140

2760	HAYING-TIME/ "The First Load"/ (15.14x23.14) 1868	L	3800
2761	HAYING-TIME/ "The Last Load"/ (15.15x23.15) 1868	L	3800
2762	HE IS SAVED/ (8.14x12.7)	S	75
2763	HE LOVES ME/ (9.7x12.4)	S	90
2764	HEAD AND HEAD FINISH AT THE WINNING POST	L	1425
2765	HEAD AND HEAD FINISH, A	M	565
2766	HEAD AND HEAD FINISH, A/ (Poster) (30x42)	L	875
2767	HEAD AND HEAD FINISH, A/ (Poster with no advertising) (18x28)	L	1125
2768	HEADS OF THE DEMOCRACY	S	180
2769	HEALTH TO THE KING AND BISMARCK/ (Vig.) 1870	S	75
2770	HEART OF DIVINE LOVE	S	25
2771	HEART OF JESUS/ (Vig.) 1876	S	20
2772	HEART OF THE WILDERNESS, THE/ (11.7x16.8)	M	495
2773	HEATHEN CHINEE/ (7.15x12.7) 1871	S	260
2774	HEBE	VS	80
2775	HEIGHT OF IMPUDENCE, THE	S	145
2776	HEIR TO THE THRONE/ 1860	M	220
2777	HELEN/ #439/ (Vig.) 1855, N. Currier	S	75
2778	HELEN/ (Vig.)	S	80
2779	HENRIETTA/ N. Currier	S	75
2780	HENRY/ 1845, N. Currier	S	120
2781	HENRY/ Record 2:20.50 (Vig.)	S	290
2782	HENRY BIBB/ (Slave)	S	235
2783	HENRY CLAY/ 1853, N. Currier	L	220
2784	HENRY CLAY / JUSTICE TO HARRY OF THE WEST	S	100
2785	HENRY CLAY / NOMINATED FOR 11TH PRES./ N. Currier	S	100
2786	HENRY CLAY / OF KENTUCKY/ (12.4x8.15) 1842, N. Currier	S	100
2787	HENRY CLAY / OF KENTUCKY/ (12.2x8.13) 1844, N. Currier	S	100
2788	HENRY CLAY / OF KENTUCKY/ (11.11x8.8) 1844, N. Currier	S	100
2789	HENRY CLAY / OF KENTUCKY/ #189, N. Currier	S	100
2790	HENRY CLAY / OF KENTUCKY/ (Seated, 1/2 Length) N. Currier	S	100
2791	HENRY CLAY / OF KENTUCKY/ J.L. McGee, del. N. Currier	S	100
2792	HENRY CLAY / OF KENTUCKY/ (12.1x8.10) N. Currier	S	100
2793	HENRY CLAY / OF KENTUCKY/ (11.8x8.13) 1848, N. Currier	S	100
2794	HENRY CLAY / PAINTED AND ENGRAVED BY A.H. RITCHIE	S	100
2795	HENRY CLAY/ "THE FARMER OF ASHLAND"/ N. Currier	S	105
2796	HENRY CLAY / THE NATION'S CHOICE FOR ELEVENTH PRESIDENT/ (To Left)	S	105
2797	HENRY CLAY / THE NATION'S CHOICE FOR ELEVENTH PRESIDENT/ (To Right)	S	105

All prints are published by Currier & Ives unless otherwise stated.

2798	HENRY WILKES	S	290
2799	HERCULES OF THE NATION SLAYING THE GREAT DRAGON OF SECESSION/ (Pol. Cartoon)	S	185
2800	HERO AND FLORA TEMPLE/ (17.2x26.2) 1856, N. Currier	L	1900
2801	HEROES OF "76" MARCHING TO THE FIGHT	S	295
2802	HEROINE OF MONMOUTH/ (Molly Pitcher) (8.9x12) 1876	S	295
2803	HEROINE OF THE LIGHTHOUSE, THE	S	185
2804	HEWITT'S QUICK STEP	S	90
2805	HIAWATHA'S DEPARTURE/ 1868	L	500
2806	HIAWATHA'S WEDDING (8.8x12.8)	S	215
2807	HIAWATHA'S WEDDING/ 1858	L	500
2808	HIAWATHA'S WOOING/ N. Currier	S	215
2809	HIAWATHA'S WOOING/ (14.14x20.14) 1860	L	500
2810	HIGH BRIDGE AT HARLEM, NY/ (Horse & Buggy) N. Currier [Old BEST 50]	S	480
2811	HIGH BRIDGE AT HARLEM, NY/ (Rowboat, 2 figures) N. Currier	S	430
2812	HIGH OLD SMOKE - GO IN FELLERS/ (Vig.) 1881	S	265
2813	HIGH PRESSURE STEAMBOAT "MAYFLOWER"/ (16.4x28.2) 1855, N. Currier	L	2700
2814	HIGH-SPEED STEAM YACHT "STILETTO"	S	405
2815	HIGH TONED/ (2.15x4.12) 1880	TC	75
2816	HIGH TONED/ (3.7x4.9) 1880	TC	75
2817	HIGH TONED/ (4.7x7.3) 1880	VS	135
2818	HIGH TONED/ (Vig.) 1880	S	170
2819	HIGH WATER IN THE MISSISSIPPI/ (18.1x28) (Companion to #3824) 1868	L	4650
2820	HIGHLAND BEAUTY, THE/ (Vig.)	S	75
2821	HIGHLAND BOY, THE/ Currier & Ives	S	75
2822	HIGHLAND GIRL, THE/ N. Currier	S	75
2823	HIGHLAND FLING/ (Oval) 1846, N. Currier	S	80
2824	HIGHLAND FLING/ (11.4x16) 1876	M	220
2825	HIGHLAND LOVERS, THE/ 1846, N. Currier	S	75
2826	HIGHLAND MARY/ 1876	S	75
2827	HIGHLAND WATERFALL/ (Oval)	VS	180
2828	HIGHLANDER/ (19.1x26.5) 1854, N. Currier	L	1150
2829	HIGHLANDER'S RETURN, THE/ (14.6x11.4)	M	135
2830	HILLSIDE PASTURE - CATTLE/ (10.12x14.4)	M	265
2831	HILLSIDE PASTURE - SHEEP	M	265
2832	HILLSIDE, THE	VS	210
2833	HINDOO, WINNER OF THE KENTUCKY DERBY/ 1881	TC	85
2834	HIS EMINENCE / CARDINAL McCLOSKEY	M	30

2835	HIS MOTHER-IN-LAW/ (Vig.) 1877	S	120
2836	HOLD THE FORT/ (8.10x12.8) 1875	S	65
2837	HOLD YOUR HORSE, BOSSY/ (8.7x12.2) 1877	S	195
2838	HOLIDAYS IN THE COUNTRY	L	1825
2839	HOLY BIBLE, THE	S	20
2840	HOLY CATHOLIC FAITH, THE	S	20
2841	HOLY COMMUNION/ (11.12x8.9) 1873	S	20
2842	HOLY CROSS, THE/ (Vig.)	S	20
2843	HOLY CROSS ABBEY ON THE SUIR	S	20
2844	HOLY EUCHARIST, THE/ (11.14x8.7) 1848, N. Currier	S	20
2845	HOLY EUCHARIST, THE/ Currier & Ives	S	20
2846	HOLY FACE, THE	S	20
2847	HOLY FAMILY/ #77	S	20
2848	HOLY FAMILY/ C. Currier	S	20
2849	HOLY FAMILY/ #227/ (11.13x8.3) N. Currier	S	20
2850	HOLY FAMILY, THE	S	20
2851	HOLY SACRAMENT OF THE ALTAR	S	20
2852	HOLY SEPULCHRE, THE/ (12.4x8.8)	S	20
2853	HOLY VIRGIN PRAY FOR US/ (Vig.) 1876	S	20
2854	HOLY WELL, THE/ (Ireland) (12.8x8.7)	S	20
2855	HOME AND FRIENDS	S	125
2856	HOME FROM THE BROOK - THE LUCKY FISHERMEN/ (16.12x24.14) 1867	L	2300
2857	HOME FROM THE WAR/ 1862	S	115
2858	HOME FROM THE WAR/ THE SOLDIER'S RETURN/ (Companion to #4539) 1861	S	125
2859	HOME FROM THE WOODS - THE SUCCESSFUL SPORTSMEN/ (16.13x24.15) 1867	L	2250
2860	HOME IN THE COUNTRY, A/ (12.9x17.5)	M	600
2861	HOME IN THE WILDERNESS, A/ (8x12.8) 1870 [New BEST 50]	S	590
2862	HOME IN THE WOODS, A	S	335
2863	HOME OF EVANGELINE, THE/ (16.1x23.6) 1864	L	1125
2864	HOME OF FLORENCE NIGHTINGALE, THE/ (11.4x15.7)	M	280
2865	HOME OF THE DEER - MORNING IN THE ADIRONDACKS/ (18.7x23.13) 1862	L	3950
2866	HOME OF THE DEER, THE/ (10x15.6) 1870	M	490
2867	HOME OF THE DEER, THE/ (9.15x15.7)	M	500
2868	HOME OF THE SEAL, THE	S	225
2869	HOME OF THE SOUL, THE/ (8.9x12) 1876	S	65
2870	HOME OF WASHINGTON, MT. VERNON/ 1852, C. Currier	M	335
2871	HOME OF WASHINGTON, MT. VERNON/ (8.9x12.8)	S	205

All prints are published by Currier & Ives unless otherwise stated.

2872	HOME OF WASHINGTON, MT. VERNON/ (Rounded Top Corners)	M	325
2873	HOME OF WASHINGTON, MT. VERNON	L	595
2874	HOME OF WASHINGTON, MT. VERNON/ (11.8x15.3)	M	325
2875	HOME "ON SICK LEAVE"	S	75
2876	HOME ON THE MISSISSIPPI, A/ (8.7x12.7) 1871 [New BEST 50]	S	565
2877	HOME SWEET HOME	L	1800
2878	HOME, SWEET HOME/ (Motto) (Vig.) 1874	S	210
2879	HOME SWEET HOME/ (Cattle in brook) (8.8x12.9)	S	200
2880	HOME SWEET HOME	M	330
2881	HOME SWEET HOME/ (Motto)	S	225
2882	HOME TO THANKSGIVING/ (Painted by G.H. Durrie) (14.12x25.1) 1867 [Old & New BEST 50]	L	15000
2883	HOME TREASURES/ (Vig.)	S	90
2884	HOMEWARD BOUND/ #378/ N. Currier	S	770
2885	HOMEWARD BOUND/ #378/ 1845, N. Currier	S	765
2886	HOMEWARD BOUND/ (Vig.) (Companion to #4666)	S	765
2887	HONEST ABE TAKING THEM ON THE HALF SHELL	M	320
2888	HONOR THE LORD/ (Fruit Piece)	S	35
2889	HONOR THE LORD WITH THY SUBSTANCE/ (Vig.) 1872	S	20
2890	HON. ABRAHAM LINCOLN/ OF ILLINOIS, 1860	L	430
2891	HON. ABRAHAM LINCOLN/ OUR NEXT PRESIDENT, 1860	S	160
2892	HON. ABRAHAM LINCOLN/ OUR NEXT PRESIDENT/ (Vest shows 4 buttons)	S	160
2893	HON. ABRAHAM LINCOLN/ OUR NEXT PRESIDENT/ (Full face) (Vig.)	S	155
2894	HON. ABRAHAM LINCOLN/ (Republican Candidate) (Vig.) 1860	M	360
2895	HON. ABRAHAM LINCOLN/ (Republican Candidate) (12.4x9) (Oval) 1860 [Old BEST 50]	S	265
2896	HON. ABRAHAM LINCOLN - 16TH PRESIDENT/ (Vig.) 1860	M	290
2897	HON. CHARLES GAVAN DUFFY/ 1849, N. Currier	S	60
2898	HON. DANIEL WEBSTER/ N. Currier	S	85
2899	HON. EDWARD EVERETT/ (14.10x12.4)	M	140
2900	HON. HANNIBAL HAMLIN - OUR NEXT VICE PRESIDENT/ 1860	S	125
2901	HON. HANNIBAL HAMLIN - REPUBLICAN CANDIDATE FOR VICE PRESIDENT/ (Oval)	S	125
2902	HON. HANNIBAL HAMLIN - REPUBLICAN CANDIDATE FOR VICE PRESIDENT	M	190
2903	HON. HERSCHEL V. JOHNSON/ 1860	S	90
2903A	HON. HENRY WILSON, NATIONAL REPUBLICAN AND WORKINGMAN'S CANDIDATE FOR V.P./ 1872	S	125
2904	HON. HORACE GREELEY/ (Vig.) 1872	S	95
2905	HON. HORATIO SEYMOUR/ (Vig.)	S	95

2906	HON. HORATIO SEYMOUR/ (Vig.)	M	110
2907	HON. JAMES G. BLAINE/ (Vig.)	L	135
2908	HON. JAMES G. BLAINE/ (Vig.)	S	95
2909	HON. JEFFERSON DAVIS/ (12x8.8)	S	150
2910	HON. JOHN A. LOGAN/ (Vig.)	S	95
2911	HON. JOHN BELL OF TENNESSEE/ (Vig.) 1860	M	110
2912	HON. JOHN BELL OF TENNESSEE/ (Vig.) 1860	L	135
2913	HON. JOHN BELL / OUR NEXT PRESIDENT	S	95
2914	HON. JOHN C. BRECKINRIDGE/ (Vig.) 1860	S	95
2915	HON. JOHN C. BRECKINRIDGE/ (Vig.) 1860	M	110
2916	HON. JOHN C. BRECKINRIDGE / OF KENTUCKY	L	130
2917	HON. JOHN CILLEY	L	120
2918	HON. JOSEPH LANE/ (Vig.) 1860	S	95
2919	HON. SCHUYLER COLFAX/ (10.8x9)	S	95
2920	HON. STEPHEN A. DOUGLAS-DEMOCRATIC CANDIDATE	S	95
2921	HON. STEPHEN A. DOUGLAS/ 1860	L	125
2922	HON. STEPHEN A. DOUGLAS OF ILLINOIS/ 1860	S	95
2923	HON. STEPHEN A. DOUGLAS OF ILLINOIS/ (Vig) 1860	L	120
2924	HON. STEPHEN A. DOUGLAS SENATOR/ (Vig.)	S	95
2925	HON. WM. A. WHEELER OF NEW YORK	S	95
2926	HON. WILLIAM H. ENGLISH	M	110
2927	HONOUR!/ (7.7x11.15) N. Currier	S	135
2928	HOOKED!/ (8.8x12.8) (Companion to #5981) 1874	S	500
2929	HOPEFUL/ GREY GELDING BY GODFREY'S PATCHEN/ (Dam Unknown)	S	305
2930	HOPEFUL/ GREY GELDING BY GODFREY'S PATCHEN/ 1876	L	1450
2931	HOPEFUL/ GREY GELDING, (3/4 View to left) 1877	S	290
2932	HOPEFUL/ GREY GELDING/ (Broadside to left)	S	290
2933	HOPEFUL/ BY GODFREY'S PATCHEN/ 1879	L	1425
2934	HOPEFUL/ RECORD 2:16 1/2 TO WAGON/ 1881	TC	85
2935	HOPEFUL DRIVER, A - YOU CAN BET YOUR LIFE ON ME	S	270
2936	HORACE GREELEY	M	150
2937	HORACE GREELEY / OUR NEXT PRESIDENT/ 1872	M	140
2938	HORSE CAR SPORTS - GOING TO A CHICKEN SHOW/ (Vig.) 1886	S	220
2939	HORSE CAR SPORTS - ON THE BACK TRACK/ (Vig.) 1886	S	220
2940	HORSE FAIR, THE/ (7.14x12.2)	S	330
2941	HORSE FOR THE MONEY, THE/ (Vig.)	S	275
2942	HORSE SHED STAKES/ 1877	S	240
2943	HORSE SHED STAKES/ 1880	TC	75

2944	HORSE THAT DIED ON THE MAN'S HANDS, THE/ (9.2x13.1) 1878	S	220
2945	HORSE THAT TOOK THE POLE, THE/ 1875	M	405
2946	HORSEMAN OF THE PERIOD/ 1876	M	620
2947	HORSEMAN OF THE PERIOD/ 1877	M	660
2948	HORSES AT THE FORD/ 1867	L	1325
2949	HORSES IN A THUNDERSTORM	S	335
2950	HORTICULTURAL HALL/ (7.14x13)	S	235
2951	HOT RACE FROM THE START, A/ 1893	L	1525
2952	HOT RACE TO THE WIRE, A/ 1876	S	290
2953	HOT RACE TO THE WIRE, A/ 1887	S	290
2954	HOUR OF VICTORY, THE/ (Vig.) 1861	M	305
2955	HOUSE IN ROXBURY, MASS, THE/ (Vig.) N. Currier	S	185
2956	HOUSE, KENNEL AND FIELD	L	540
2957	HOUSEHOLD PETS/ 1845, N. Currier	S	105
2958	HOUSEHOLD PETS / #493/ (Round Top)	S	105
2959	HOUSEHOLD PETS / #334/ 1857, N. Currier	S	105
2960	HOUSEHOLD TREASURES / #493	S	95
2961	HOUSEHOLD TREASURES/ 1874	S	95
2962	HOVE TO FOR A PILOT"/ (16.11x25) 1856, N. Currier	L	3725
2963	HOW PRETTY!	S	90
2964	HOW SWEET!/ (Vig.)	S	90
2965	HOWLING SWELL - ON THE WAR PATH/ (Vig.) 1890	S	225
2966	HOWLING SWELL - WITH HIS SCALP IN DANGER/ (Vig.) 1890	S	225
2967	HOWTH CASTLE/ (Ireland)	S	75
2968	H-OXFORD'S, YOU KNOW	S	110
2969	H R H ALBERT / PRINCE OF WALES	S	65
2970	H R H PRINCESS LOUISE	S	65
2971	HUDSON AT PEEKSKIL, THE/ (8.1x12.10)	S	285
2972	HUDSON FROM WEST POINT, THE/ (11.3x15.11) 1862	M	1050
2973	HUDSON HIGHLANDS, THE/ FROM THE PEEKSKILL/ 1857	L	1450
2974	HUDSON HIGHLANDS, THE/ FROM THE PEEKSKILL/ 1867	L	1500
2975	HUDSON HIGHLANDS, THE/ 1871	S	420
2976	HUDSON HIGHLANDS NEAR NEWBURG, NY	S	275
2977	HUDSON NEAR COLDSPRING, THE/ (7.15x12.8)	S	260
2978	HUDSON RIVER - CROW'S NEST/ (8x12.7)	S	265
2979	HUDSON RIVER - CROW'S NEST	S	265
2980	HUDSON RIVER STEAMBOAT "BRISTOL"	S	300
2981	HUDSON RIVER STEAMBOAT "ST. JOHN"/ 1864	L	1575
2982	HUES OF AUTUMN, THE/ "On Racquet River"/ (8.7x12.8)	S	300

2983	HUG ME CLOSER, GEORGE/ (Bear) (Vig.) 1886	S	430
2984	HUMMING TROT, A/ 1893	M	400
2985	HUNDRED LEAF ROSE/ (J. Schutz, del.) N. Currier	S	110
2986	HUNDRED LEAF ROSE/ Currier & Ives	S	105
2987	HUNDRED LEAF ROSE/ #564/ N. Currier	S	105
2988	HUNDRED LEAF ROSE/ 1870, Currier & Ives	S	105
2989	HUNG UP - WITH THE STARCH OUT/ (Vig.) 1878	S	225
2990	HUNG UP - WITH THE STARCH OUT/ 1878	TC	70
2991	HUNGRY LITTLE KITTIES	S	140
2992	HUNTER'S DOG, THE/ (8x12.4) N. Currier	S	300
2993	HUNTER'S SHANTY, THE - IN THE ADIRONDACKS/ (14.10x20.12) 1861	L	2000
2994	HUNTER'S SHANTY, THE	VS	275
2995	HUNTING CASUALTIES, No.575 - A TURN OF SPEED OVER THE FLATS/ N. Currier	S	425
2996	HUNTING CASUALTIES, No.576 - A STRANGE COUNTRY/ N. Currier	S	425
2997	HUNTING CASUALTIES, No.577 - DISPATCHED TO HEADQUARTERS/ N. Currier	S	425
2998	HUNTING CASUALTIES, No.578 - UP TO SIXTEEN STONE/(8.3x12.7) N. Currier	S	425
2999	HUNTING CASUALTIES, No.579 - A RARE SORT FOR THE DOWNS/ N. Currier	S	425
3000	HUNTING CASUALTIES, No.580 - A MUTUAL DETERMINATION/ N. Currier	S	425
3001	HUNTING, FISHING AND FOREST SCENES - GOOD LUCK ALL AROUND/ (16.13x25) 1867	L	2000
3002	HUNTING, FISHING AND FOREST SCENES - SHANTYING ON THE LAKE SHORE/ 1867	L	2000
3003	HUNTING IN THE NORTHERN WOODS/ (8.8x12.7)	S	450
3004	HUNTING ON THE PLAINS/ (8.7x12.7) 1871	S	760
3005	HUNTING ON THE SUSQUEHANNA (10.5x14.11)	M	600
3006	HURRY UP THE CAKES/ (Companion to #79) N. Currier	S	135
3007	HUSH! I'VE A NIBBLE/ (8.8x12.8)	S	275
3008	HUSKING/ (Painted by E. Johson) (21.1x27.6) 1861 [Old & New BEST 50]	L	9900
3009	H.W. BEECHER	M	100
3010	HYDE PARK - ON THE HUDSON RIVER/ #260/ (8.4x11.10) N. Currier	S	305
3011	HYDE PARK - ON THE HUDSON RIVER/ #232	S	295
3012	HYDROGRAPHIC MAP/ (Showing Counties of N.Y.)	M	375
3013	HYDROGRAPHIC MAP SHOWING THE DISTRIBUTION OF RAIN/ C. Currier	L	585

I

Con#	Title	Folio	Value
3014	I AM AS DRY AS A FISH/ (12.15x8.15)	S	270
3015	I CANNA BID HIM GANG, MITHER	S	75
3016	I SEE YOU/ (12.11x8.7) N. Currier	S	80
3017	I TOLD YOU SO"/ 1860	S	195
3018	I TOLD YOU SO"/ 1860	M	300
3019	I WILL NOT ASK TO PRESS THAT CHEEK/ (Vig.) 1875	S	150
3020	I WILL NOT ASK TO PRESS THAT CHEEK/ 1880	TC	70
3021	ICE-BOAT RACE ON THE HUDSON [Old & New BEST 50]	S	3000
3022	ICE COLD SODA WATER/ (Vig.) 1879	S	225
3023	ICE CREAM RACKET, AN - FREEZING IN/ (Vig.) 1889	S	195
3024	ICE CREAM RACKET, AN - THAWING OUT/ (Vig.) 1889	S	195
3025	ICED LEMONADE/ 1879	M	340
3026	IDLEWILD - ON THE HUDSON/ "The Glen"	S	260
3027A	IL GRANDE PONTE SOSPESO DEL! / "East River" Suspension Bridge/ 1886	L	325
3027	ILLUMINATED CARDS / FOR SCHOOLS	S	145
3028	ILLUMINATED CARDS / FOR SCHOOLS	S	145
3029	IMMACULATE CONCEPTION	S	20
3030	IMPEACHMENT OF DAME BUTLER, FESSENDEN, BUTLER, BEN WADE	S	65
3031	IMPENDING CATASTROPHE, AN	S	140
3032	IMPENDING CATASTROPHE, AN/ 1868	S	140
3033	IMPENDING CRISIS, THE	M	240
3034	IMPERIAL BEAUTY, THE/ (Vig.)	S	75
3035	IMPERIAL GERMAN MAIL STEAMER "ALLER"	S	280
3036	IMPERIAL GERMAN MAIL STEAMER "ELBE", OF THE NORTH GERMAN LLOYD LINE	S	280
3037	IMPERIAL GERMAN MAIL STEAMER "FULDA", OF THE NORTH GERMAN LLOYD LINE	S	280
3038	IMPERIAL GERMAN MAIL STEAMER "HAVEL"	S	280
3039	IMPERIAL GERMAN MAIL STEAMER "TRAVE"	S	280
3040	IMPERIAL GERMAN MAIL STEAMER "WERRA"	S	280
3041	IMPORTED MESSENGER/ 1879	S	290
3042	IMPORTED MESSENGER/ (Vig.) 1880	S	290
3043	IMPOSING THE CARDINAL'S BERETTA	S	20
3044	IN A TIGHT PLACE - GETTING SQUEEZED/ (19.12x15.10) 1860	M	385
3045	IN AND OUT OF CONDITION	S	245
3046	IN AND OUT OF CONDITION	L	540

3047	IN AND OUT OF CONDITION/ (Fat man & thin man) 1880	TC	80
3048	IN FULL BLOOM/ (Vig.) 1870	S	70
3049	IN FULL DRESS	S	70
3050	IN GOD IS OUR TRUST/ (Vig.) 1874	S	75
3051	IN MEMORIAM/ N. Currier	S	25
3052	IN MEMORY OF/ (Couple and Child) (13x8.3) N. Currier	S	45
3053	IN MEMORY OF/ #280/ 1845, N. Currier	S	25
3054	IN MEMORY OF/ #318/ (12.12x8.12) N. Currier	M	60
3055	IN MEMORY OF/ #370/ 1845, N. Currier	S	45
3056	IN MEMORY OF/ (Warship in background)	S	45
3057	IN MEMORY OF/ #184/ 1846, N. Currier	S	45
3058	IN MEMORY OF/ #191/ 1846, N. Currier	S	45
3059	IN MEMORY OF/ #280/ N. Currier	S	45
3060	IN MEMORY OF/ #153/ 1846, N. Currier	S	45
3061	IN MEMORY OF/ 1845, N. Currier	S	45
3062	IN MEMORY OF/ N. Currier	M	60
3063	IN MEMORY OF/ 1872	S	45
3064	IN MEMORY OF/ (13.2x9.3) N. Currier	S	50
3065	IN MEMORY OF/ (St. Paul's) 1847, N. Currier	S	50
3066	IN MEMORY OF/ (St. Paul's) 1849	S	50
3067	IN MEMORY OF/ (St. Paul's) Und.	S	50
3068	IN MEMORY OF/ (12.2x10.13) (St. Paul's) N. Currier	S	50
3069	IN THE HARBOR/ (8.9x12.12)	S	395
3070	IN THE INDIAN PASS	S	315
3071	IN THE MOUNTAINS/ (7.15x12.7)	S	265
3072	IN THE MOUNTAINS/ (Deer)	M	420
3073	IN THE NORTHERN WILDS - TRAPPING BEAVER/ (7.15x12.8)	S	485
3074	IN THE SPRINGTIME	S	150
3075	IN THE WOODS	S	160
3076	IN THE WOODS/ (No children wading) (12.7x7.15)	S	160
3077	INAUGURATION OF WASHINGTON	S	240
3078	INCREASE OF FAMILY, AN/ (15.14x12.14) 1863	M	270
3079	INDEPENDENCE HALL, PHILADELPHIA 1776/ (8.3x12.8)	S	295
3080	INDEPENDENT GOLD HUNTER ON WAY TO CALIFORNIA/ (12.8x8.7) N. Currier	S	1200
3081	INDIAN BALL PLAYERS (12.8x18.7)	M	1375
3082	INDIAN BEAR DANCE, THE (12.2x17.14)	M	1375
3083	INDIAN BEAUTY, THE/ (Vig.)	S	90
3084	INDIAN BUFFALO HUNT/ (12.2x17.14)	M	1400

All prints are published by Currier & Ives unless otherwise stated.

3085	INDIAN BUFFALO HUNT - ON THE PRAIRIE BLUFFS	M	1400
3086	INDIAN FALLS	S	215
3087	INDIAN FAMILY/ (12.4x8.8) N. Currier	S	230
3088	INDIAN FAMILY, THE/ (12x9) N. Currier	S	230
3089	INDIAN HUNTER/ (12.1x8.8) 1845, N. Currier	S	345
3090	INDIAN HUNTER, THE	S	230
3091	INDIAN LAKE - SUNSET/ (14.12x22.13) 1860	L	1200
3092	INDIAN PASS, THE - ROCKY MOUNTAINS/ (9.13x16.14)	M	850
3093	INDIAN SUMMER, SQUAM LAKE, NH/ (9.9x16.14) 1868	M	880
3094	INDIAN TOWN/ (8.8x12.8)	S	315
3095	INDIAN WARRIOR, THE/ (12.1x8.9) 1845, N. Currier	S	255
3096	INDIANS ATTACKING THE GRIZZLY BEAR (12.2x17.14)	M	1400
3097	INFANCY OF JESUS/ (12.2x8.9) 1849, N. Currier	S	20
3098	INFANCY OF THE VIRGIN/ (12.11x8.11) 1849, N. Currier	S	20
3099	INFANT BROOD, THE/ (8.12x12.6) (Companion to #815)	S	485
3100	INFANT BROOD, THE/ (Oval) (Companion to #816)	S	700
3101	INFANT JESUS PREACHING IN THE TEMPLE	S	20
3102	INFANT ST. JOHN, THE	S	20
3103	INFANT ST. JOHN, THE/ #84	S	20
3104	INFANT ST. JOHN, THE / EL CHIQUITO SN. JUAN	S	20
3105	INFANT SAVIOUR, THE	S	20
3106	INFANT SAVIOUR, THE / EL SALVATOR DEL MUNDO	S	20
3107	INFANT SAVIOUR & ST. JOHN/ #67	S	20
3108	INFANT SAVIOUR & ST. JOHN	S	20
3109	INFANT SAVIOUR WITH MARY AND JOSEPH	S	20
3110	INFANT TOILET	S	105
3111	INFANTRY MANEUVERS - BY THE DARKTOWN VOLUNTEERS/ (Vig.) (Companion to #868) 1887	S	230
3112	INGLESIDE WINTER, THE/ (8x12.9)	S	585
3113	INITIATION CEREMONIES OF THE DARKTOWN LODGE/ (Vig.)	S	255
3114	INITIATION CEREMONIES OF THE DARKTOWN LODGE/ "Grand Boss Charging the Candidate"/ (Vig.) 1887	S	255
3115	INNISFALLEN	M	110
3116	INNOCENCE/ 1848, N. Currier	S	75
3117	INNOCENCE/ 1848, N. Currier	L	120
3118	INTERIOR OF FORT SUMTER DURING THE BOMBARDMENT/ (8.7x11.15)	S	305
3119	INTO MISCHIEF/ 1857	S	145
3120	INTO MISCHIEF/ 1857	M	240
3121	INTO MISCHIEF/ (L. Maurer, del.) 1857	L	275

3122	INUNDATION, THE/ N. Currier	S	75
3123	INUNDATION, THE/ #635	S	105
3124	INVITING DISH, AN	S	135
3125	INVITING GIFT, AN/ 1870	S	115
3126	IRA D. SANKEY - THE EVANGELIST OF SONG/ (Vig.)	S	45
3127	IRISH BEAUTY, THE/ (Vig.)	S	65
3128	IRON R.M. STEAMSHIP "PERSIA" CUNARD LINE/ (8.4x12.13) N. Currier	S	300
3129	IRON STEAMSHIP "GREAT BRITAIN"/ N. Currier	S	300
3130	IRON STEAMSHIP "GREAT EASTERN"/ 1858	L	1350
3131	IROQUOIS/ (17.10x26.14) 1882	L	1500
3132	IROQUOIS - WINNER OF THE DERBY/ 1881	TC	85
3133	IROQUOIS/ 1881	S	275
3134	IRREPRESSIBLE CONFLICT, THE	M	300
3135	ISABELLA/ C. Currier	S	75
3136	ISABELLA/ (11.9x8.4) 1845, N. Currier	S	75
3137	ISABELLA/ (11.12x8.7) 1844, N. Currier	S	75
3138	ISABELLA/ (Vig.)	S	80
3139	ITALIAN LANDSCAPE/ (7.15x12.8)	S	75
3140	IVANHOE	S	65
3141	IVY BRIDGE, THE	S	115
3142	IVY CLAD RUINS, THE	S	150
3143	IVY CLAD RUINS, THE	M	225
3144	IVY CLAD RUINS, THE	M	225

J

Con#	Title	Folio	Value
3145	JACK ROSSITER/ (12.13x20.12) 1850, N. Currier	L	1575
3146	JACK ROSSITER/ (High-wheeled sulky) (12.12x20.15) 1850, N. Currier	L	1575
3147	JAMES/ (11.8x8.4) 1845, N. Currier	S	170
3148	JAMES A. GARFIELD	S	85
3149	JAMES BUCHANAN / Democratic Candidate/ (8.10x11.5) N. Currier	S	95
3150	JAMES BUCHANAN / Democratic Candidate for 15th President/ 1856, N. Currier	L	165
3151	JAMES BUCHANAN / 15th President/ #627/ (11.2x8.8) N. Currier	S	155
3152	JAMES BUCHANAN / 15th President/ #597/ N. Currier	S	155
3153	JAMES HAMMMILL AND WALTER BROWN IN THEIR / ...ROWING MATCH	L	2325

3154	JAMES G. BIRNEY/ 1844, N. Currier	S	85
3155	JAMES G. BIRNEY/ (12.1x8.11) 1844, N. Currier	S	90
3156	JAMES J. CORBETT/ (Heavyweight Champion)	M	405
3157	JAMES K. POLK / #29	S	95
3158	JAMES K. POLK / 11TH PRESIDENT/ (11.9x8.13) C. Currier	S	125
3159	JAMES K. POLK / 11TH PRESIDENT/ (11.11x8.10) N. Currier	S	125
3160	JAMES K. POLK / 11TH PRESIDENT/ (11.9x8.12) N. Currier	S	125
3161	JAMES K. POLK / 11TH PRESIDENT/ C. Currier	S	125
3162	JAMES K. POLK / 11TH PRESIDENT/ (11.10x8.14) N. Currier	S	125
3163	JAMES K. POLK / 11TH PRESIDENT/ (11.8x8.9) N. Currier	S	125
3164	JAMES K. POLK / NOMINATED FOR 11TH PRESIDENT	S	125
3165	JAMES K. POLK / PRESIDENT ELECT	S	125
3166	JAMES K. POLK / THE PEOPLE'S CANDIDATE	S	125
3167	JAMES K. POLK / THE PEOPLE'S CHOICE	S	125
3168	JAMES K. POLK / UNION COURSE, L.I./ 1850	M	520
3169	JAMES L. HEWITT & CO./ Stodart & Currier	S	160
3170	JAMES L. HEWITT & CO.	S	155
3171	JAMES MADISON - 4TH PRESIDENT/ (11.12x9.5) N. Currier	S	155
3172	JAMES MONROE - 5TH PRESIDENT/ (11.6x9.1) N. Currier	S	155
3173	JAMES MYERS, SAMUEL LEWIS - CHAS. C. MERCHANT/ (8.15x7.15) N. Currier	S	240
3174	JAMES STEPHENS	S	75
3175	JANE/ #19/ N. Currier	S	80
3176	JANE/ #47/ 1847, N. Currier	S	80
3177	JANE/ #47/ Und. N. Currier	S	80
3178	JANE/ #47/ 1845, N. Currier	S	80
3179	JANE/ #47/ 1845, N. Currier	S	80
3180	JANE/ #71/ 1848, N. Currier	S	80
3181	JANE/ Und.	S	80
3182	JAY EYE SEE / BY DICTATOR	S	290
3183	JAY EYE SEE / Record 2:01	L	1450
3184	JAY EYE SEE / Record 2:1	L	1475
3185	JAY EYE SEE / THE PHENOMENAL TROTTING GELDING/ 1884	L	1475
3186	JAY EYE SEE, 2:10/ 1886	TC	85
3187	JAY EYE SORE, DE GREAT WORLD BEATER/ (Vig.) 1885	S	220
3188	JEANETTE/ (11.12x8.10) 1846, N. Currier	S	75
3189	JEANETTE/ 1846, N. Currier	S	75
3190	JEANIE/ 1850, N. Currier	S	75
3191	JEFF D. HUNG ON A "SOUR APPLE TREE", or TREASON MADE ODIOUS/ (Vig.)	S	185

3192	JEFF DAVIS ON HIS OWN PLATFORM	S	185
3193	JEFFERSON DAVIS	S	185
3194	JEFF'S LAST SHIFT/ (Vig.)	S	180
3195	JEM MACE/ (14.14x12) 1870	M	305
3196	JENNIE/ (Vig.)	S	80
3197	JENNIE CRAMER/ (Vig.)	S	70
3198	JENNY LIND/ (Vig.) N. Currier	S	155
3199	JENNY LIND / ALS TOCHTER DES REGIMENTS	S	140
3200	JENNY LIND/ N. Currier	S	155
3201	JENNY LIND - THE SWEDISH NIGHTINGALE'S GREETING TO AMERICA/ N. Currier	M	300
3202	JEROME EDDY/ (Horse) 1882	S	290
3203	JERSEY CITY, HOBOKEN AND BROOKLYN/ 1858	S	390
3204	JERSEY LITCHFIELD BULL	S	120
3205	JERSEY PRIZE NIOBE .	S	120
3206	JERUSALEM/ 1846, N. Currier	S	35
3207	JERUSALEM FROM THE MOUNT OF OLIVES/ N. Currier	S	35
3208	JESUS AND THE CYRENIAN/ (12.15x9.3) 1848, N. Currier	S	20
3209	JESUS AND THE CYRENIAN/ (9.15x7.15) N. Currier	S	20
3210	JESUS AND THE TWELVE APOSTLES/ 1847, N. Currier	S	20
3211	JESUS ASCENDETH INTO HEAVEN	S	20
3212	JESUS ASCENDING INTO HEAVEN	S	20
3213	JESUS BEARING HIS CROSS/ #196/ (12.12x8.12) 1847, N. Currier	S	20
3214	JESUS BEARING HIS CROSS/ #48/ (12.15x9.3) 1848, N. Currier	S	20
3215	JESUS BEARING HIS CROSS/ (10.3x8) 1848, N. Currier	S	20
3216	JESUS BLESSING LITTLE CHILDREN/ 1867	S	20
3217	JESUS BLESSING LITTLE CHILDREN/ (12.11x8.2) 1867	S	20
3218	JESUS BLESSING LITTLE CHILDREN/ 1866	M	30
3219	JESUS CONDEMNED TO DEATH/ (13x9.2) 1848, N. Currier	S	20
3220	JESUS CONSOLES THE WOMEN OF JERUSALEM/ (9.15x7.15) N. Currier	S	20
3221	JESUS CONSOLES THE WOMEN OF JERUSALEM/ (12.9x8.11) 1848, N. Currier	S	20
3222	JESUS CRUCIFIED/ N. Currier	S	20
3223	JESUS CRUCIFIED/ (12.11x8.15) 1847, N. Currier	S	20
3224	JESUS DESPOILED OF HIS GARMENTS/ N. Currier	S	20
3225	JESUS DESPOILED OF HIS GARMENTS/ (9.15x7.15) N. Currier	S	20
3226	JESUS DESPOILED OF HIS VESTMENTS	S	20
3227	JESUS' FALL FOR THE FIRST TIME/ #49/ 1848, N. Currier	S	20
3228	JESUS' FALL FOR THE FIRST TIME/ (9.14x7.15) N. Currier	S	20
3229	JESUS' FALL FOR THE SECOND TIME/ #201/ N. Currier	S	20

3230	JESUS' FALL FOR THE SECOND TIME/ (9.13x7.14) N. Currier	S	20
3231	JESUS' FALL FOR THE THIRD TIME/ #55/ 1848, N. Currier	S	20
3232	JESUS' FALL FOR THE THIRD TIME/ (9.14x7.14) N. Currier	S	20
3233	JESUS IMPRINTS HIS FACE ON A CLOTH/ (12.13x9.12) N. Currier	S	20
3234	JESUS IS NAILED TO THE CROSS	S	20
3235	JESUS IS NAILED TO THE CROSS/ #205	S	20
3236	JESUS PLACED IN THE SEPULCHRE/ (12.11x8.15) 1847, N. Currier	S	20
3237	JESUS LAID IN THE SEPULCHRE/ (12.9x8.9) 1846	S	20
3238	JESUS MEETING HIS MOTHER/ N. Currier	S	20
3239	JESUS MEETS HIS MOTHER/ N. Currier	S	20
3240	JESUS MEETS ST. VERONICA/ N. Currier	S	20
3241	JESUS NAILED TO THE CROSS/ (13x9.3) 1848	S	20
3242	JESUS OF NAZARETH PASSES BY	S	20
3243	JESUS ON THE CROSS (15x11.4)	M	20
3244	JESUS ON THE CROSS (11.11x8.2)	S	20
3245	JESUS PUT INTO THE SEPULCHRE/ N. Currier	S	20
3246	JESUS TAKEN FROM THE CROSS/ (12.10x8.12) 1846	S	20
3247	JIB AND MAINSAIL RACE, A/ 1882	L	1075
3248	JOCKEY CLUB/ Cigar advertisement)	TC	70
3249	JOCKEY'S DREAM, THE/ (9.6x12.13) 1880	S	315
3250	JOHN/ (11.15x8.8) 1845, N. Currier	S	165
3251	JOHN ADAMS - 2ND PRESIDENT/ (11.9x9.4) N. Currier	S	170
3252	JO ANDERSON, MY JO	S	95
3253	JOHN BROWN/ (11.10x8.8) 1863	S	175
3254	JOHN BROWN - THE MARTYR/ (11.10x8.8) 1870	S	175
3255	JOHN BROWN - LEADER OF THE HARPER'S FERRY INSURRECTION/ (Vig.)	S	175
3256	JOHN BULL AND HIS FRIEND CLEVELAND/ (Vig.)	S	120
3257	JOHN BULL MAKES A DISCOVERY	S	120
3258	JOHN C. BRECKINRIDGE/ "Vice-Pres. of the U.S."/ (11.3x8.10)	S	125
3259	JOHN C. CALHOUN/ (Vig.) 1853, N. Currier	L	155
3260	JOHN C. FREMONT/ N. Currier	S	140
3261	JOHN C. HEENAN - CHAMPION OF THE WORLD/ (Vig.) 1860	S	285
3262	JOHN C. HEENAN - CHAMPION OF THE WORLD/ (Half length) (Vig.) 1860	S	285
3263	JOHN C. HEENAN - THE BENICIA BOY	M	410
3264	JOHN C. HEENAN - CHAMPION OF THE WORLD/ (Vig.)	S	285
3265	JOHN C. HEENAN - CHAMPION OF THE WORLD/ #631/ (Vig.) 1860	S	285
3266	JOHN ENNIS/ (12.14x9.3) 1879	S	125
3267	JOHN HANCOCK'S DEFIANCE/ (12.6x9) 1876	S	200

3268	JOHN J. DWYER - CHAMPION OF AMERICA	M	365
3269	JOHN JAY	VS	80
3270	JOHN L. SULLIVAN/ (15.15x12.7) 1883	M	350
3271	JOHN MILTON	M	105
3272	JOHN MITCHEL/ #589	S	55
3273	JOHN MITCHEL / THE FIRST MARTYR OF IRELAND/ 1848	S	55
3274	JOHN MITCHEL / THE FIRST MARTYR OF IRELAND/ Und.	S	55
3275	JOHN MORRISSEY/ 1860	M	120
3276	JOHN QUINCY ADAMS - 6TH PRESIDENT/ N. Currier	S	175
3277	JOHN QUINCY ADAMS - 6TH PRESIDENT/ N. Currier	S	175
3278	JOHN QUINCY ADAMS	S	175
3279	JOHN R. GENTRY - Record 2:00.50/ (Vig.)	S	290
3280	JOHN STRAUS! JOHN STRAUS!	S	100
3281	JOHN TYLER - 10TH PRESIDENT/ (11.8x9.1) N. Currier	S	175
3282	JOHN WESLEY/ N. Currier	S	65
3283	JOHN WESLEY PREACHING ON HIS FATHER'S GRAVE/ (8.4x12.3)	S	65
3284	JOHNNY AND LILY	S	70
3285	JOHNSON'S HOTEL/ (18.1x16.2) 1854, C. Currier	M	965
3286	JOHNSTON, PACER/ 1881	TC	85
3287	JOLLY DOG, A/ (12.10x8.15) 1878	S	125
3288	JOLLY HUNTERS, THE/ (7.15x12.7)	S	150
3289	JOLLY JUMPER/ (Vig.) (Companion to #5625) 1888	S	175
3290	JOLLY SMOKER, THE/ 1880	S	155
3291	JOLLY SMOKER, THE/ 1880	L	265
3292	JOLLY SMOKER, THE/ (2.15x4.12) 1880	TC	70
3293	JOLLY SMOKER, THE/ (3.7x4.8) (Oval) 1880	VS	100
3294	JOLLY SMOKER, THE/ (4.7x7.3) 1880	TC	70
3295	JOLLY YOUNG DUCKS/ 1866	M	285
3296	JOSEPH C. YATES	VS	65
3297	JOSEPH GRIMALDI	VS	55
3298	JOSEPHINE/ #81/ (11.15x8.6) 1848, N. Currier	S	70
3299	JOSEPHINE/ #251/ (11.6x8.7) 1847, N. Currier	S	70
3300	JOSEPHINE/ #251/ N. Currier	S	70
3301	JOSEPHINE/ (11.10x8.8) N. Currier	S	70
3302	JOSEPHINE/ (Vig.)	S	75
3303	JOSIE/ (Vig.)	S	75
3304	JUDGE FULLERTON/ (Vig.) 1873	S	290
3305	JULIA/ 1845, N. Currier	S	75
3306	JULIA/ N. Currier	S	75

3307	JULIA/ N. Currier	S	75
3308	JULIA/ #48/ (12.2x8.7) 1846, N. Currier	S	75
3309	JULIA/ #67/ 1848, N. Currier	S	75
3310	JULIA/ (12.1x8.10) N. Currier	S	75
3311	JULIA/ (Vig.)	S	80
3312	JULIA - I SHOULD LIKE TO BE TREATED LIKE A DOG/ (11.14x8.12) 1848, N. Currier	S	115
3313	JULIET	S	75
3314	JULIETTE	S	75
3315	June	S	75
3316	JUNO/ (Girls head)	VS	75
3317	JUNO - A CELEBRATED SETTER/ (8.9x7.2) N. Currier	S	295
3318	JUNO/ (Setter)	S	295
3319	JUNO/ (11.15x9.12)	S	295
3320	JUST CAUGHT - TROUT AND PICKEREL/ (12.8x9) 1872	S	220
3321	JUST MARRIED/ (Vig.)	S	100
3322	JUST MY STYLE/ (Vig.) 1871	S	100

K

Con#	Title	Folio	Value
3323	KAISER WILHELM DER GROSSE OF THE NORTH GERMAN LLOYD LINE	S	245
3324	KATE/ (Vig.)	M	120
3325	KATE/ (Vig.)	S	80
3326	KATE/ (8.8x11.6) 1846, N. Currier	S	80
3327	KATZ-KILLS, IN WINTER, THE/ (8.7x12.8)	S	485
3328	KENILWORTH CASTLE	L	285
3329	KILKENNY CASTLE, IRELAND	S	90
3330	KILLERIES, THE - CONNEMARA/ (8x12.7)	S	100
3331	KILLENEY HILL, DUBLIN	S	90
3332	KIND, KIND AND GENTLE IS SHE	S	95
3333	KING OF THE FOREST, THE/ (Stag) (8.8x12.9)	S	200
3334	KING OF THE HOUSE/ (Baby in crib) (Companion to #5012)	S	80
3335	KING OF THE HOUSE, THE	S	80
3336	KING OF THE ROAD, THE/ 1869	L	1525
3337	KING OF THE TURF "DEXTER"	S	290
3338	KING OF THE ROAD, THE/ 1870	S	290

3339	KING OF THE TURF "St. JULIEN"/ 1880	L	1525
3340	KING WILLIAM III/ CROSSING THE BOYNE/ 1845, N. Currier	S	70
3341	KING WILLIAM III/ CROSSING THE BOYNE/ 1863	S	70
3342	KING WILLIAM III/ CROSSING THE BOYNE/ Und.	S	70
3343	KING WILLIAM III/ CROSSING THE BOYNE/ (J. Schutz, del.) Und.	S	70
3344	KING WILLIAM III/ PRINCE OF ORANGE/ Und.	S	75
3345	KING WILLIAM PRINCE OF ORANGE/ (Vig.) Und.	S	75
3346	KINGSTON / BY SPENDTHRIFT/ (Vig.) 1891	S	290
3347	KISS IN THE DARK, A/ 1881	S	485
3347A	KISS ME QUICK/ N. Currier	S	220
3348	KISS ME QUICK/ (8.14X11.9) N. Currier	S	220
3349	KISS ME QUICK/ #700/ (8.14X11.9) N. Currier [Old & New BEST 50]	S	500
3350	KITCH-EE-I-AA-BA OR THE BIG BUCK/ N. Currier	S	170
3351	KITTIES AMONG THE CLOVER/ 1873	S	140
3352	KITTIES AMONG THE ROSES/ (8.11x12.9) 1873	S	140
3353	KITTIES BREAKFAST/ 1857	L	255
3354	KITTIES LESSON/ (8.8x12.1) 1877	S	145
3355	KITTIES ON A FROLIC	S	145
3356	KITTIES ON A FROLIC/ (8.2x12.6) 1877	S	145
3357	KITTY/ (Girl's head)	VS	100
3358	KITTY/ (Gray kitten) N. Currier	S	150
3359	KITTY AND POLLY/ (Companion to #4829)	M	225
3360	KITTY AND ROVER	S	140
3361	KITTY IN CLOVER/ 1872	S	140
3362	KITTY'S DINNER/ (8.8x11.9)	S	145
3363	KNITTING LESSON, THE	M	380
3364	KNOCKED INTO A COCKED HAT/ 1848	M	195
3365	KONIG WILHELM VON PREUSSEN IN DER SCHLACT VON SEDAN IN FRANKREICH/ (8.14x12.7)	S	50
3366	KOSSUTH/ (8.10x11.3) N. Currier	S	70
3367	KREMLIN/ Record 2:07.75/ (Vig.) 1893	S	290

L

Con#	Title	Folio	Value
3368	LA ALEMADA DE MEXICO / THE PUBLIC PARK OF MEXICO	S	90
3369	LA CIGARITA/ (Women smoking cigar)	TC	70
3370	LA GITANA	S	60
3371	LA MUZURKA	S	80
3372	LA REINE DES ANGES	S	60
3373	LADDER OF FORTUNE/ (11.10x8.13) 1875	S	185
3374	LADIES' BOUQUET	S	130
3375	LADIES' BOUQUET/ (Vig.) 1870	S	130
3376	LADIES' BOUQUET	S	130
3377	LADIES LOYAL UNION LEAGUE, THE/ (9x12.8) 1863	S	185
3378	LADY & MOOR/ (7.14x9.12) N. Currier	S	105
3379	LADY EMMA, GEORGE WILKES AND GENERAL BUTLER/ (16.14x26.8) 1865	L	1550
3380	LADY FULTON/ (Vig.) 1857	S	290
3381	LADY MAUD/ (Vig.) 1876	S	290
3382	LADY MOSCOW/ (12.15x21.1) 1850, N. Currier	L	1575
3383	LADY MOSCOW, ROCKET AND BROWN DICK/ 1857, N. Currier	L	1650
3384	LADY OF THE LAKE/ (11.9x8.9) N. Currier	S	85
3385	LADY OF THE LAKE	S	85
3386	LADY OF THE LAKE/ (11.10x8.3) 1870	S	85
3387	LADY SUFFOLK/ (12.13x20.11) 1850, N. Currier	M	1175
3388	LADY SUFFOLK/ (17.10x26.12) 1852, N. Currier	L	2125
3389	LADY SUFFOLK/ Record 2:26	L	1775
3390	LADY SUFFOLK AND LADY MOSCOW/ (17.12x26.7) 1850, N. Currier	L	1800
3391	LADY SUTTON/ (13x21.1) 1849, N. Currier	L	1600
3392	LADY SUTTON/ 1850, N. Currier	S	290
3393	LADY THORN/ 1871	S	290
3394	LADY THORN AND MOUNTAIN BOY/ IN THEIR GREAT MATCH/ 1867	L	1550
3395	LADY THORN AND MOUNTAIN BOY/ TROTTING FOR A PURSE/ 1867	L	1550
3396	LADY WASHINGTON/ (Vig.) N. Currier	L	195
3397	LADY WASHINGTON	S	90
3398	LADY WASHINGTON/ (J. Cameron, del.)	M	145
3399	LADY WOODRUFF, MILLER'S DAMSEL, GENERAL DARCY AND STELLA/ (17x27.10) 1857	L	1625
3400	LADY'S BOUQUET, THE/ (Vig.) 1862	S	115
3401	LADY'S BOUQUET, THE/ (Vig.)	S	115
3402	LAFAYETTE	S	145
3403	LAFAYETTE AT THE TOMB OF WASHINGTON/ (11.14x8.8) 1845, N. Currier	S	105

3404	LAFAYETTE LAKE NEAR TALLAHASSEE, FLORIDA/ (8.7x12.7)	S	370
3405	LAKE AND FOREST SCENERY/ (10x15.6)	M	495
3406	LAKE GEORGE, BLACK MOUNTAIN/ (8.2x12.10)	S	260
3407	LAKE GEORGE, NY/ (8x12.8)	S	250
3408	LAKE GEORGE, WHITE MOUNTAINS/ (8.2x12.10)	S	255
3409	LAKE IN THE WOODS, THE/ (8.7x12.6)	S	215
3410	LAKE LUGANO, ITALY	S	90
3411	LAKE LUGANO, ITALY	L	145
3412	LAKE MEMPHREMAGOG / Owl's Head/ (8x12.8)	S	280
3413	LAKE MOHONK/ (8.8x12.6)	S	240
3414	LAKE OF THE DISMAL SWAMP, THE / Virginia	L	320
3415	LAKE OF THE DISMAL SWAMP, THE/ (8x12.8)	S	175
3416	LAKE THUN - NEAR THE ALPS/ (Oval)	VS	120
3417	LAKE THUN - NEAR THE ALPS	S	95
3418	LAKE WINNEPOSOGIS, MANITOBA, CANADA	S	275
3419	LAKE WINNIPISEOGEE, NEW HAMPSHIRE/ (14.6x20.6)	L	2750
3420	LAKE WINNIPISEOGEE, NEW HAMPSHIRE	VS	300
3421	LAKES OF KILLARNEY, THE/ 1868	S	90
3422	LAKES OF KILLARNEY, THE/ 1867	L	280
3423	LAKESIDE HOME/ (9.11x16.15) 1869	M	345
3424	LAMB AND THE LINNET, THE/ (8.8x12.5)	S	95
3425	LANCASHIRE BELL RINGERS, THE	S	110
3426	LANDING A TROUT/ (Vig.) (Companion to #864) 1879	S	275
3427	LANDING IN THE WOODS, A/ (8.8x12.8)	S	145
3428	LANDING OF COLUMBUS/ #427	S	145
3429	LANDING OF COLUMBUS AT SAN SALVADOR/ (9x12.15) 1876	S	145
3430	LANDING OF COLUMBUS, OCTOBER 11, 1492/ 1846, N. Currier	S	145
3431	LANDING OF COLUMBUS, OCTOBER 11, 1492/ 1847, N. Currier	S	145
3432	LANDING OF THE AMERICAN FORCES UNDER GENERAL SCOTT AT VERA CRUZ/ (8.6x13.1) 1847, N. Currier	S	155
3433	LANDING OF THE PILGRIMS AT PLYMOUTH/ (8.4x12.11) N. Currier	S	300
3434	LANDING OF THE PILGRIMS AT PLYMOUTH/ (Group coming up hill) N. Currier	S	300
3435	LANDING OF THE PILGRIMS AT PLYMOUTH MASS, DEC. 22/ (Group standing at top of hill) 1876 [Old BEST 50]	S	355
3436	LANDSCAPE AND CATTLE	M	350
3437	LANDSCAPE AND RUINS	M	245
3438	LANDSCAPE CARDS / MOONLIGHT AND WINTER EFFECTS../ (9 Cards)	S	785
3439	LANDSCAPE CARDS / SYLVAN LAKE.../ (9 Cards)	S	785
3440	LANDSCAPE FRUIT AND FLOWERS/ (F. Palmer, del.) (19.12x27.8) 1862 [Old & New BEST 50]	L	5500

All prints are published by Currier & Ives unless otherwise stated.

3441	LANDSCAPE - MORNING/ (About 36x9)	L	585
3442	LANERCOST PRIORY, ENGLAND	M	180
3443	LAPPED ON THE LAST QUARTER/ (Vig.) 1880	S	300
3444	LAST DITCH OF THE CHIVALRY, THE/ (Vig.)	M	190
3445	LAST DITCH OF THE DEMOCRATIC PARTY, THE	M	185
3446	LAST GUN OF THE "ARCTIC"/ (13.13x10.7) 1855, N. Currier	M	430
3447	LAST HIT IN THE GAME/ (Vig.) 1886	S	265
3448	LAST LEADERS OF HUNGARY/ N. Currier	S	60
3449	LAST SHAKE, THE/ 1885	S	75
3450	LAST SHOT, THE/ (17.9x25.8) 1858	L	2875
3451	LAST SUPPER, THE / Verily I Say, etc./ (11.7x16.12)	M	25
3452	LAST SUPPER, THE / Apostles keyed in English and Spanish/ N. Currier	S	20
3453	LAST SUPPER, THE / Apostles keyed/ N. Currier	S	20
3454	LAST SUPPER, THE / La Ultima Sena	S	20
3455	LAST SUPPER, THE / Verily I Say Unto You.../ (8x12.8)	S	20
3456	LAST SUPPER, THE / Verily I Say Unto You.../ (8x11.8)	S	20
3457	LAST WAR-WHOOP, THE/ (First state) (18.3x25.9) 1856, N. Currier	L	3200
3458	LAST WAR-WHOOP, THE/ (Second state) (18.3x25.9) 1856, Currier & Ives	L	3200
3459	LAUGH No. 1/ (Vig.) 1879	S	290
3460	LAUGH No. 2/ (Vig.) 1879	S	290
3461	LAURA / #390/ (8.12x12.4) 1846, N. Currier	S	85
3462	LAURA	S	85
3463	LAWN TENNIS AT DARKTOWN - A SCIENTIFIC PLAYER/ (Vig.) 1885	S	265
3464	LAWN TENNIS AT DARKTOWN - A SCIENTIFIC STROKE/ (Vig.) 1885	S	265
3465	LAYING BACK" / Stiff for a Brush/ (Vig.) 1878	S	265
3466	LAYING BACK" / Stiff for a Brush/ 1878	TC	75
3467	LE MARECHAL MacMAHON/ (12x9.8) (Vig.)	S	60
3468	LE PETIT ST. JEAN / The Infant St. John/ (13x10) N. Currier	S	20
3469	LE PETIT ST. JEAN / El Chiquito St. Juan/ N. Currier	S	20
3470	LE SAUVEUR DU MONDE/ N. Currier	S	20
3471	LEADERS, THE / Jay Eye See, 2:10/ Maud S, 2:08.75/ St. Julien, 2:11.25/ (17.15x27.8) 1888	L	960
3472	LEARN SOMETHING / (Motto) (Vig.)	S	275
3473	LEARNING TO RIDE	S	125
3474	LEE AT THE GRAVE OF STONEWALL JACKSON	S	125
3475	LEND ME YOUR WATCH!/ N. Currier	S	265
3476	LEONORA	S	70
3477	LES MEMBRES DE GOVERNMENT PROVISOIRE/ 1848, N. Currier	S	75
3478	LET NOT MERCY AND TRUTH FORSAKE THEE	S	120

3479	LETTING THE CAT OUT OF THE BAG	M	260
3480	LEVEE NEW ORLEANS, THE/ (19.15x29.14) 1884 [New BEST 50]	L	11900
3481	LEWIS CASS/ N. Currier	S	70
3482	LEWIS CASS/ (2 oval portraits in rectangle) N. Currier	S	90
3483	LEXINGTON/ (Horse) (Vig.)	S	290
3484	LEXINGTON OF 1861, THE/ (8x12.5)	S	260
3485	LIBERTY/ (Vig.)	S	195
3486	LIBERTY/ (Vig.) 1876	S	195
3487	LIBERTY FRIGHTENING THE WORLD	TC	95
3488	LIEUT. GENL. N.B. FORREST	S	100
3489	LIEUT. GENL. ULYSSES S. GRANT AT THE SIEGE OF VICKSBURG JULY 4TH, 1863	S	105
3490	LIEUT. GENL. ULYSSES S. GRANT / #740 General-in-Chief/ (11.13x8.15)	S	90
3491	LIEUT. GENL. ULYSSES S. GRANT / General-in-Chief/ (11.11x9.1)	S	90
3492	LIEUT. GENL. ULYSSES S. GRANT / #754 Genreal-in-Chief/ (Vig.)	S	90
3493	LIEUT. GENL. WILLIAM T. SHERMAN/ (Vig.)	S	100
3494	LIEUT. GENL. WINFIELD SCOTT/ (Vig.) 1861	L	100
3495	LIEUT. GENL. WINFIELD SCOTT / #477/ (Vig.)	S	85
3496	LIEUT. GENL. WINFIELD SCOTT/ (Vig.)	S	85
3497	LIEUT. GENL. WINFIELD SCOTT/ (Vig.) 1861	M	95
3498	LIFE AND AGE OF MAN, THE	S	245
3499	LIFE AND AGE OF MAN, THE /#87/ N. Currier	S	245
3500	LIFE AND AGE OF MAN, THE/ N. Currier	S	245
3501	LIFE AND AGE OF WOMAN, THE /#262/ (8.14x12.10) 1850, N. Currier	S	245
3502	LIFE AND AGE OF WOMAN, THE /#262/ (8.12x12.13) 1850, N. Currier	S	245
3503	LIFE AND DEATH/ (11.14x9.14)	S	95
3504	LIFE IN NEW YORK / Cuffy dancing for eels	S	295
3505	LIFE IN NEW YORK / The Breadth of Fashion-5th Avenue/ (Vig.)	S	350
3506	LIFE IN NEW YORK / That's so!/ (Vig.)	S	365
3507	LIFE IN THE CAMP / Preparing for Supper/ (15.9x21.2) 1863	L	1175
3508	LIFE IN THE COUNTRY / Evening/ (11.5x15.8)	M	835
3509	LIFE IN THE COUNTRY / Morning/ (11.3x15.7) 1862	M	835
3510	LIFE IN THE COUNTRY / Morning	S	240
3511	LIFE IN THE COUNTRY / Out For A Day's Shooting/ 1859	L	3925
3512	LIFE IN THE COUNTRY / The Morning Ride/ (17.12x25.15) 1859	L	3400
3513	LIFE IN THE WOODS / Returning to Camp/ (18.13x27.10) 1860	L	3400
3514	LIFE IN THE WOODS / Starting out/ (19.4x27.8) 1860	L	3450
3515	LIFE OF A FIREMAN / The Fire/ (17.2x25.14) 1854, N. Currier	L	2475
3516	LIFE OF A FIREMAN / The Metropolitan System/ (17x26.4) 1866 [Old & New BEST 50]	L	3700

All prints are published by Currier & Ives unless otherwise stated.

3517	LIFE OF A FIREMAN / The New Era/ (17.1x25.14) 1861 [New BEST 50]	L	3000
3518	LIFE OF A FIREMAN / The Night Alarm/ (16.14x25.14) 1854, N. Currier [Old BEST 50]	L	2625
3519	LIFE OF A FIREMAN / The Race/ (16.15x25.13) 1854, N. Currier	L	2650
3520	LIFE OF A FIREMAN / The Ruins/ (16.15x26) 1854, N. Currier	L	2525
3521	LIFE OF A HUNTER, THE / Catching a Tartar/ (18.10x27.4) 1861	L	5000
3522	LIFE OF A HUNTER, THE / A Tight Fix/ (18.12x27.1) 1861 [Old & New BEST 50]	L	52000
3523	LIFE OF A SPORTSMAN, THE / Camping in the Woods/ (8.7x12.7) 1872	S	440
3524	LIFE OF A SPORTSMAN, THE / Coming Into Camp/ (8.8x12.9) 1872	S	440
3525	LIFE OF A SPORTSMAN, THE / Going Out/ (8.7x12.8) 1872	S	440
3526	LIFE OF A TRAPPER / A Sudden Halt/ (17.3x26.4) 1866	L	5500
3527	LIFE ON THE PRAIRIE / The Buffalo Hunt/ (18.7x27.1) 1862 [Old & New BEST 50]	L	5650
3528	LIFE ON THE PRAIRIE / The Trapper's Defence/ (18.7x27.2) 1862 [Old & New BEST 50]	L	5650
3529	LIGHT AND SHADOW	M	295
3530	LIGHT ARTILLERY	M	315
3531	LIGHT OF THE DWELLING, THE	S	90
3532	LIGHTHOUSE POINT	VS	135
3533	LIGHTNING EXPRESS, THE	S	1700
3534	LIGHTNING EXPRESS/ (Vig.)	S	1950
3535	LIGHTNING EXPRESS" TRAINS, THE / Leaving the Junction/ (17.14x27.14) [Old & New BEST 50]	L	13800
3536	LIGHTNING EXPRESS TRAINS LEAVING THE JUNCTION/ 1871	S	2375
3537	LILLIPUTIAN KING	S	90
3538	LILLY	VS	75
3539	LILLY AND HER KITTY	S	130
3540	LILY LAKE, NEAR ST. JOHN, NB/ (8.8x12.8)	S	240
3541	LIME KILN CLUB, DE / A Temperance Racket/ (Vig.) 1883	S	230
3542	LIMITED EXPRESS", A/ (Vig.) 1884	S	390
3543	LINCOLN/ (Vig.)	M	165
3544	LINCOLN AT HOME/ 1867	S	110
3545	LINCOLN AT HOME/ (16.14x23.13)	L	260
3546	LINCOLN FAMILY, THE/ (8.2x12.8) 1867	S	80
3547	LINCOLN FAMILY, THE/ (8.1x12.7) 1867	S	80
3548	LINCOLN STATUE, THE/ (Vig.)	S	110
3549	LINCOLN "THREE IN ONE PICTURE"	S	430
3550	LINCOLN "THREE IN ONE PICTURE"	S	430
3551	LINE SHOT - THE AIM/ (Vig.) 1881	S	260
3552	LINE SHOT - THE RECOIL/ (Vig.) 1881	S	260

3553	LION AND THE LAMB/ N. Currier	S	120
3554	LION HUNTER, THE/ (8.2x13) N. Currier	S	165
3555	LIONS OF THE DERBY, THE/ (Comic) (Vig.)	S	220
3556	LIONS OF THE DERBY, THE/ IROQUOIS AND ARCHER	S	240
3557	LISMORE CASTLE / COUNTY WATERFORD/ (8x12.6)	S	90
3558	LITERARY DEBATE IN THE DARKTOWN CLUB / QUESTION SETTLED/ (Vig.)	S	255
3659	LITERARY DEBATE IN THE DARKTOWN CLUB / SETTLING THE QUESTION/ (Vig.)	S	255
3560	LITTLE ALMS-GIVER, THE/ (8.9x12.)	S	100
3561	LITTLE ANNA	S	80
3562	LITTLE ANNIE/ (Vig.)	S	80
3563	LITTLE ANNIE AND HER KITTIE/ (11.6x8.6)	S	125
3564	LITTLE ANNIE AND HER KITTIES	S	125
3565	LITTLE ARTHUR/ (Horse) N. Currier	L	1290
3566	LITTLE ASTRONOMER, THE	S	120
3567	LITTLE BAREFOOT/ (8.8x11.7) 1872	S	110
3568	LITTLE BASHFUL	S	90
3569	LITTLE BEAR, THE	S	90
3570	LITTLE BEAU, THE/ (11.8x8.10)	S	85
3571	LITTLE BEAUTY, THE/ (11.9x8.9)	S	100
3572	LITTLE BEAUTY/ (Vig.)	M	120
3573	LITTLE BEGGAR	S	105
3574	LITTLE BELLE, THE/ (Vig.)	S	85
3575	LITTLE BLOSSOM/ (11.2x8.2)	S	90
3576	LITTLE BLUEBELL/ (Vig.)	S	90
3577	LITTLE BO-PEEP	S	110
3578	LITTLE BOUNTIFUL/ (11.14x8.10)	S	90
3579	LITTLE BOUQUET/ 1872	S	90
3580	LITTLE BOUQUETS / (Group of Four) (Vig.)	S	180
3581	LITTLE BOY BLUE	S	110
3582	LITTLE BROTHER/ (11.6x8.2) 1865	S	90
3583	LITTLE BROTHER/ (Vig.)	S	90
3584	LITTLE BROTHER / #586/ (Companion to #3708)	S	95
3585	LITTLE BROTHER AND I	S	90
3586	LITTLE BROTHER AND SISTER / #702/ 1863	S	95
3587	LITTLE BROTHER AND SISTER/ 1875	S	95
3588	LITTLE BROTHER AND SISTER/ (Vig.)	S	95
3589	LITTLE BROTHERS/ (11.7x8.6) (Companion to #3710) 1875	S	95
3590	LITTLE BROTHERS, THE/ (11.9x8.5) 1863	S	95

3591	LITTLE BRUNETTE/ (15.7x12)	M	120
3592	LITTLE BUSY BEE/ (11.9x8.7) 1872	S	110
3593	LITTLE BUTTERFLY/ (11.4x8.5)	S	90
3594	LITTLE CAROLINE/ N. Currier	S	90
3595	LITTLE CARRIE/ (Vig.)	S	90
3596	LITTLE CAVALIER, THE	S	90
3597	LITTLE CHARLIE	S	85
3598	LITTLE CHARLIE AND HIS HORSE/ 1874	S	95
3599	LITTLE CHARLIE / THE PRIZE BOY/ (Vig.) 1855	S	90
3600	LITTLE CHERUBS, THE/ (11.1x8)	S	60
3601	LITTLE CHIEFTAIN, THE	S	90
3602	LITTLE CHILDREN / LOVE ONE ANOTHER	S	100
3603	LITTLE COLORED PET/ 1881	S	85
3604	LITTLE DAISY/ (11.12x10.8) (Vig.)	S	85
3605	LITTLE DOLLY/ (Vig.) 1872	S	85
3606	LITTLE DOT/ (Vig.) 1872	S	85
3607	LITTLE DRESSMAKER, THE/ (11.12x8.12)	S	130
3608	LITTLE DRUMMER BOY/ (Vig.)	S	100
3609	LITTLE EMMA	S	85
3610	LITTLE EMMIE	S	85
3611	LITTLE EMMIE/ (11.15x8.1) 1872	S	85
3612	LITTLE EMPEROR, THE	S	65
3613	LITTLE ELLA	S	100
3614	LITTLE ELLEN	S	85
3615	LITTLE EVA	S	85
3616	LITTLE FAIRY/ (12x8.7)	S	85
3617	LITTLE FANNIE	S	85
3618	LITTLE FANNY/ N. Currier	S	85
3619	LITTLE FAVORITE, THE / (10x7.12) (Oval) N. Currier	S	95
3620	LITTLE FAVORITE, THE / (10x7.10) (Oval) N. Currier	S	95
3621	LITTLE FAVORITE, THE /#103/ N. Currier	S	85
3622	LITTLE FIREMAN, THE/ (25x18.4) 1857	L	320
3623	LITTLE FLORA/ (Vig.) 1874	S	85
3624	LITTLE FLORA/ 1879	S	90
3625	LITTLE FLOWER GATHERER	S	95
3626	LITTLE FLOWER GIRL, THE / #589/ (Companion to #3632) 1853	S	95
3627	LITTLE FLOWER GIRL, THE/ (Vig.) 1863	S	95
3628	LITTLE FLOWER GIRL/ (Vig.)	S	95
3629	LITTLE FOLKS IN THE COUNTRY (12x8.8)	S	105

3630	LITTLE FREDDIE	S	85
3631	LITTLE FRUIT BEARER/ (Vig.) 1873	S	105
3632	LITTLE FRUIT GIRL, THE / #590/ (12x8.12) (Companion to #3626) 1863	S	105
3633	LITTLE FRUIT GIRL, THE/ (Vig.)	S	105
3634	LITTLE GAME OF BAGATELLE BETWEEN OLD ABE, THE RAIL SPLITTER, AND LITTLE MAC, THE GUNBOAT GENERAL	S	260
3635	LITTLE GEORGIE/ (Vig.)	S	85
3636	LITTLE GROGGY, A/ (Companion to #1224) 1884	S	125
3637	LITTLE HARRY / #617/ N. Currier	S	90
3638	LITTLE HARRY/ (Vig.)	S	90
3639	LITTLE HERO/ (Vig.)	S	85
3640	LITTLE HIGH STRUNG/ (Comic) 1879	S	155
3641	LITTLE HIGHLANDER, THE/ (11.13x8.12)	S	85
3642	LITTLE JAMIE	S	85
3643	LITTLE JANE	S	85
3644	LITTLE JANE / #615/ N. Currier	S	85
3645	LITTLE JANICE	S	85
3646	LITTLE JENNIE/ (Vig.)	S	90
3647	LITTLE JOHNNIE AND BESSIE	S	85
3648	LITTLE JOHNNY	S	95
3649	LITTLE JULIA/ (Vig.)	S	85
3650	LITTLE KATE / #321/ (Vig.) 1851, N. Currier	S	85
3651	LITTLE KATE	S	85
3652	LITTLE KATIE	S	85
3653	LITTLE KITTIE AND HER KITS	S	130
3654	LITTLE KITTIES AMONG THE ROSES	S	135
3655	LITTLE KITTY/ (Vig.)	S	125
3656	LITTLE LILY	S	85
3657	LITTLE LIZZIE/ (Vig.)	S	85
3658	LITTLE LIZZY / #324/ (Vig.)	S	85
3659	LITTLE LULU	S	85
3660	LITTLE MAGGIE/ (Vig.)	S	85
3661	LITTLE MAMIE	S	85
3662	LITTLE MAMMA, THE/ (10.2x7.12) N. Currier	S	85
3663	LITTLE MANLY/ (Vig.) 1874	S	85
3664	LITTLE MARTHA / #320/ (Vig.)	S	85
3665	LITTLE MARTHA / #320	S	90
3666	LITTLE MARTHA/ (Vig.) 1873	S	85
3667	LITTLE MARY/ (Vig.) N. Currier	S	90

3668	LITTLE MARY	S	90
3669	LITTLE MARY AND HER LAMB	S	130
3670	LITTLE MARY AND THE LAMB/ (11.8x8.8) 1877	S	130
3671	LITTLE MAY BLOSSOM/ (Vig.) 1874	S	85
3672	LITTLE MAY BLOSSOM	S	85
3673	LITTLE MAY QUEEN/ (11.10x8.4)	S	85
3674	LITTLE MAY QUEEN	S	85
3675	LITTLE MECHANIC, THE/ (12x8.6)	S	115
3676	LITTLE MERRY BOY	S	85
3677	LITTLE MINNIE	S	85
3678	LITTLE MINNIE / TAKING A TEA	S	120
3679	LITTLE MORE GRAPE CAPT. BRAGG," A/ (8.4x12.11) N. Currier	S	140
3680	LITTLE MORE GRAPE CAPT. BRAGG, A/ (8x12.8) N. Currier	S	140
3681	LITTLE MOTHER, THE	S	90
3682	LITTLE MOURNER/ (8.8x11.6) 1872	S	35
3683	LITTLE NELLIE/ (10.8x8.13)	S	90
3684	LITTLE NELLY/	S	90
3685	LITTLE ORPHAN GIRL, THE	S	85
3686	LITTLE PETS, THE/ (11.14x9)	S	95
3687	LITTLE PILGRIMS/ (11.12x8.12) 1873	S	85
3688	LITTLE PLAYFELLOW, THE/ N. Currier	S	85
3689	LITTLE PLAYMATES, THE/ (11.13x8.8) N. Currier	S	85
3690	LITTLE POTATO BUGS/ N. Currier	S	85
3691	LITTLE PROTECTOR, THE	S	95
3692	LITTLE PROTECTOR, THE/ 1867	S	95
3693	LITTLE PRUDY/ (Vig.)	S	85
3694	LITTLE RECRUIT, THE/ 1863	M	120
3695	LITTLE RED RIDING HOOD	L	360
3696	LITTLE RED RIDING HOOD/ (12x8.11)	S	160
3697	LITTLE ROSEBUD/ (Vig.) 1870	S	85
3698	LITTLE ST. JOHN, THE BAPTIST/ (11.9x8.8)	S	20
3699	LITTLE SARAH/ (Vig.) N. Currier	S	90
3700	LITTLE SARAH/ (Vig.)	S	90
3701	LITTLE SARAH/ 1874	S	90
3702	LITTLE SARAH/ (Vig.) 1876	S	90
3703	LITTLE SCHOLAR, THE	S	105
3704	LITTLE '76	S	180
3705	LITTLE SHORE BIRD	S	90
3706	LITTLE SISTER/ 1865	S	85

3707	LITTLE SISTER/ 1878	S	85
3708	LITTLE SISTER / #587/ (Vig.) (Companion to #3584)	S	95
3709	LITTLE SISTER/ (Vig.)	S	85
3710	LITTLE SISTERS/ (Companion to #3589)	S	95
3711	LITTLE SISTERS / #610	S	85
3712	LITTLE SISTER'S FIRST STEP/ 1872	S	95
3713	LITTLE SISTER'S FIRST STEP	S	95
3714	LITTLE SISTER'S RIDE	S	95
3715	LITTLE SISTERS, THE	S	95
3716	LITTLE SISTERS, THE/ 1865	M	135
3717	LITTLE SISTERS, THE/ 1862	M	130
3718	LITTLE SLEEPY/ (Companion to #6657)	S	85
3719	LITTLE SNOWBIRD	S	225
3720	LITTLE STUDENTS, THE / (11.4x8.9) (Oval)	S	145
3721	LITTLE SUNBEAM/ (11.2x8.2)	S	85
3722	LITTLE SUNSHINE/ 1868	S	85
3723	LITTLE SWEETHEART/ (Vig.) 1875	S	85
3724	LITTLE TEA PARTY, THE/ (12x8.8)	S	155
3725	LITTLE TEACHER, THE/ (11.11x8.2)	S	155
3726	LITTLE THOUGHTFUL	S	85
3727	LITTLE VIOLET/ 1874	S	85
3728	LITTLE VOLUNTEER, THE/ 1861	S	90
3729	LITTLE VOLUNTEERS, THE	S	90
3730	LITTLE WANDERER/ (13.14x9.15)	S	145
3731	LITTLE WHITE DOGGIES/ (8.2x12.8) 1877	S	135
3732	LITTLE WHITE KITTIES / EATING CAKE	S	135
3733	LITTLE WHITE KITTIES / FISHING/ (8.5x12.4) 1871	S	145
3734	LITTLE WHITE KITTIES / INTO MISCHIEF	S	135
3735	LITTLE WHITE KITTIES / PLAYING BALL	S	145
3736	LITTLE WILD FLOWER/ (11.1x8.4)	S	90
3737	LITTLE WILLIAM AND MARY/ (Vig.)	S	90
3738	LITTLE WILLIE/ (Vig.)	S	90
3739	LITTLE YACHTSMAN/ (12.2x8.15) 1875	S	125
3740	LITTLE ZOUAVE, THE/ (Vig.) 1861	S	85
3741	LIVING CHINESE FAMILY, THE/ (8.5x12.5) N. Currier	S	140
3742	LIVINGSTON GUARDS QUICK STEP/ N. Currier	S	110
3743	LIZZIE	S	85
3744	LIEWELLYN - THE GREAT/ (11.8x8.8) N. Currier	S	65
3745	LOADING COTTON/ 1870	S	1200

All prints are published by Currier & Ives unless otherwise stated.

3746	LOBSTER SAUCE/ N. Currier	S	260
3747	LOBSTER SAUCE/ N. Currier	M	330
3748	LOG CABIN OR TIPPECANOE WALTZ/ N. Currier	S	95
3749	LOLA MONTEZ/ N. Currier	S	80
3750	LOLA MONTEZ AS MARIQUITA/ (11.12x8.7) N. Currier	S	85
3751	LOLA MONTEZ, BELLE OF THE WEST/ N. Currier	S	85
3752	LONDON FROM KEW GARDENS/ (8.7x12.8)	S	130
3753	LONDONDERRY, IRELAND/ (7.15x12.7)	S	95
3754	LONDONDERRY / IRELAND (7.15x12.7)	L	270
3755	LONDONDERRY, ON THE RIVER FOYLE, IRELAND/ (8.7x12.6)	S	95
3756	LONG ISLAND SOUND/ (9.14x17) 1869	M	770
3757	LONG LIVE THE REPUBLIC/ N. Currier	M	195
3758	LONGFELLOW/ (Poet) (Vig.) 1881	S	160
3759	LONGFELLOW/ (Horse) 1871	S	290
3759A	LONGFELLOW/ (Horse) 1881	TC	85
3760	LOOK AT MAMA / #229/ (11.4x8.10) N. Currier	S	85
3761	LOOK AT MAMA/ (11.10x8.9)	S	85
3762	LOOK AT MAMA/ N. Currier	S	85
3763	LOOK AT PAPA/ (12.1x8.11) N. Currier	S	85
3764	LOOK AT PAPA/ (11.11x8.8)	S	85
3765	LOOK AT PAPA/ 1872	S	85
3766	LOOK AT PAPA/ (11.12x8.10) N. Currier	S	85
3767	LOOKING DOWN THE YO-SEMITE/ (8.8x12.8)	S	365
3768	LOOKING IN/ (8.7x12.2) (Shows man reading ad for N. Currier) N. Currier	S	210
3769	LOOKING OUT/ N. Currier	S	100
3770	LOOKING UNTO JESUS/ (8.10x10.9) 1870	S	20
3771	LOOKOUT MOUNTAIN, TENNESSEE AND THE CHATTANOOGA RAIL-ROAD/ (15x20.7) 1866	L	6700
3771A	LORD BE WITH YOU, THE/ (Motto) (Vig.)	S	70
3772	LORD BE WITH YOU, THE/ (Motto) (Vig.) 1872	S	70
3773	LORD BE WITH YOU, THE/ (Vig.) 1878	S	20
3774	LORD'S PRAYER, THE/ (Vig.) N. Currier	S	25
3775	LORD'S PRAYER, THE	S	20
3776	LORD'S PRAYER, THE & THE ANGELICAL SALUTATION/ N. Currier	S	25
3777	LORD BYRON/ N. Currier	S	45
3778	LORD'S SUPPER, THE/ N. Currier	S	25
3779	LOSS OF THE STEAMBOAT "SWALLOW"/ (8.2x12.7) 1845, N. Currier	S	440
3780	LOSS OF THE STEAMER "CIMBRIA"/ (8.5x13.11) 1883	S	375
3781	LOSS OF THE U.S.M. STEAMSHIP "ARCTIC"/ (8.6x12.13) 1854	S	370

3782	LOST/ (8.10x12.10) (Companion to #6756) N. Currier	S	120
3783	LOST CAUSE/ (8.7x12.8) 1872	S	125
3784	LOST IN THE SNOW - DOGS OF ST. BERNARD/ (8.8x12.8)	S	195
3785	LOTTIE	S	75
3786	LOUE SOIT A JAMAIS J.C. DANS LE TRES SAINT SACREMENT DE L'AUTEL/ N. Currier	S	20
3787	LOUIS KOSSUTH/ (8.12x11.15) 1849, N. Currier	S	65
3788	LOUIS KOSSUTH AND HIS STAFF/ N. Currier	S	65
3789	LOUIS NAPOLEON BONAPARTE/ (8.11x11.12) 1849, N. Currier	S	80
3790	LOUISA/ 1850, N. Currier	S	75
3791	LOUISA/ 1849, N. Currier	S	75
3792	LOUISA/ (Half length) N. Currier	S	75
3793	LOUISA/ #135/ N. Currier	S	75
3794	LOUISA/ (Full length) N. Currier	S	80
3795	LOUISA V. PARKER AS EVA IN "UNCLE TOM'S CABIN"/ C. Currier	S	95
3796	LOVE IS THE LIGHTEST/ (8.9x11.14) 1847, N. Currier	S	135
3797	LOVE IS THE LIGHTEST/ (Vig.)	S	135
3798	LOVE LETTER / #210/ N. Currier	S	100
3799	LOVE LETTER/ N. Currier	S	95
3800	LOVE LIFE AT WINDSOR CASTLE	S	80
3801	LOVE'S LIGHT MAKES HOME BRIGHT/ (Motto) (Vig.)	S	130
3802	LOVE ONE ANOTHER/ (Motto) (Vig.)	S	130
3803	LOVE THE OLD DOG, TOO	S	125
3804	LOVELY CALM, A/ (Vig.) (Companion to #559) 1878	S	235
3805	LOVERS, THE/ (11.11x8.8) 1846, N. Currier	S	100
3806	LOVERS, THE/ (11.10x8.8)	S	100
3807	LOVER'S ADIEU, THE/ (11.9x8.8) 1852, N. Currier	S	100
3808	LOVER'S ADIEU, THE/ (11.15x9.14) N. Currier	S	100
3809	LOVER'S LEAP/ 1886	S	90
3810	LOVER'S QUARREL / #167/ 1846, N. Currier	S	100
3811	LOVER'S QUARREL / #443/ (11.12x9.8) 1846, N. Currier	S	100
3812	LOVER'S QUARREL / #167 (11.14x8.9)	S	90
3813	LOVER'S RECONCILIATION / #168/ (Feathers in hair) 1846, N. Currier	S	100
3814	LOVER'S RECONCILIATION / #442/ (11.12x8.8) 1846, N. Currier	S	100
3815	LOVER'S RECONCILIATION / #168/ (11.12x8.9)	S	100
3816	LOVER'S RECONCILIATION / #442/ 1846, N. Currier	S	100
3817	LOVER'S RETURN, THE/ 1852, N. Currier	S	100
3818	LOVER'S RETURN, THE/ 1846, N. Currier	S	100
3819	LOVER'S WALK, THE/ 1849, N. Currier	S	100

All prints are published by Currier & Ives unless otherwise stated.

3820	LOVER'S WALK, THE/ (11.14x8.9)	S	100
3821	LOVE'S LIGHT / Makes Home Bright/ (Motto) (Vig.) 1874	S	130
3822	LOVE'S MESSENGER/ N. Currier	S	90
3823	LOW PRESSURE STEAMBOAT "ISAAC NEWTON"/ (16.4x28.4) 1855, N. Currier	L	2975
3824	LOW WATER IN THE MISSISSIPPI/ (17.15x27.15) (Companion to #2819) 1868	L	4650
3825	LOWER LAKE OF KILLARNEY/ (7.15x12.7)	S	95
3826	LOYAL UNION LEAGUE CERTIFICATE/ (9x12.8) 1863	S	75
3827	LUCILLE/ Record 2:21/ (Vig.) 1878	S	290
3828	LUCILLE GOLDDUST	S	290
3829	LUCKY ESCAPE, THE/ N. Currier	M	370
3830	LUCRETIA/ N. Currier	S	75
3831	LUCRETIA / #268/ N. Currier	S	80
3832	LUCRETIA R. GARFIELD	S	80
3833	LUCY/ (Vig.) N. Currier	S	85
3834	LUCY/ N. Currier	S	85
3835	LUCY / #117/ N. Currier	S	85
3836	LUCY / BY GEO. M. PATCHEN	S	300
3837	LUCY RECORD 2:15 DRIVEN BY SAM KEYES	S	300
3838	LUDVIG KOSSUTH, THE HUNGARIAN LEADER/ (11.15x9) 1849, N. Currier	S	70
3839	LUGGELAW / COUNTY WICKLAW/ (8.6x12.7)	S	85
3840	LUKE BLACKBURN/ (Horse) (Vig.) 1880	S	290
3841	LUKE BLACKBURN/ (Horse) 1881	TC	85
3842	LULA / BAY MARE/ (16.9x24.13) 1876	L	1425
3843	LULA / RECORD 2:15 DRIVEN BY CHAS. S. GREEN	S	300
3844	LUSCIOUS PEACHES	S	155
3845	LUXURY OF TOBACCO, THE	S	240
3846	LYDIA/ N. Currier	S	85

M

Con#	Title	Folio	Value
3847	MAC" / (Race Horse) (17.5x26.4) 1853	L	1675
3848	MAC AND ZACHERY TAYLOR/ (12.10x20.13) 1851, N. Currier [Old BEST 50]	L	2025
3849	MAC-CUT-MISH-E-CA-CU-CAC/ (Indian Chief) (Vig.)	S	260
3850	MACHINERY HALL/ (7.15x12.15)	S	195
3851	MADAME CELESTE AS "MIAMI"/ (8.14x12.2) 1848, N. Currier	S	125
3852	MADE. VESTRIS/ N. Currier	S	60
3853	MADISON, THE CAPITOL OF WISCONSIN/ C. Currier	S	390
3854	MADLE TAGLIONI AS LA BAYADERE/ N. Currier	S	85
3855	MADLLE AUGUSTA IN LA BAYADERE/ 1873, N. Currier	S	85
3856	MADLLE AUGUSTA IN LA BAYADERE/ N. Currier	S	85
3857	MADLLE CELESTE AS THE WILD ARAB BOY/ N. Currier	S	85
3858	MADLLE FANNY ELSSLER IN LA TARANTULE/ N. Currier	S	90
3859	MADLLE FANNY ELSSLER IN THE CARCOVIENNE/ N. Currier	S	95
3860	MADLLE TAGLIONI AS LA BAYADERE/ N. Currier	S	85
3861	MADONNA DI SAN SISTO	S	20
3862	MADONNA OF THE SHAWL	S	20
3863	MAGADINO, LAKE MAGGIORE/ (Switzerland)	L	345
3864	MAGGIE/ (Vig.)	S	80
3865	MAGIC CURE/ (2 views on one sheet) (Vig.) 1890	S	235
3866	MAGIC GROTTOES	VS	95
3867	MAGIC GROTTOES	S	75
3868	MAGIC GROTTOES, THE	M	110
3869	MAGIC LAKE/ (On #3438)	VS	100
3870	MAGIC LAKE/ (10.8x14.8)	M	175
3871	MAGIC LAKE, THE	M	175
3872	MAGNIFICENT BUILDING FOR THE WORLD'S FAIR OF 1851/ N. Currier	S	200
3873	MAGNIFICENT NEW STEAMER "PRISCILLA", THE	S	305
3874	MAGNIFICENT NEW STEAMER "PURITAN", THE	M	465
3875	MAGNIFICENT NEW STEAMER "PURITAN", THE	S	305
3876	MAGNIFICENT NEW STEAMSHIP "CITY OF ROME"	S	305
3877	MAGNIFICENT O'CONNELL FUNERAL CAR/ (7.15x12.12) 1847, N. Currier	S	55
3878	MAGNIFICENT STEAMSHIP "BRITANNIC" OF THE WHITE STAR LINE	S	305
3879	MAGNIFICENT STEAMSHIP "CITY OF NEW YORK: OF THE INMAN LINE	S	305
3880	MAGNIFICENT STEAMSHIP "CITY OF PARIS" OF THE INMAN LINE	S	305
3881	MAGNIFICENT STEAMSHIP "CITY OF ROME"	S	310
3882	MAGNIFICENT STEAMSHIP "GERMANIC"/ (7.8x14.4)	S	310

All prints are published by Currier & Ives unless otherwise stated.

3883	MAGNIFICENT STEAMSHIP "MAJESTIC" WHITE STAR LINE	S	310
3884	MAGNIFICENT STEAMSHIP "NEW YORK" OF THE AMERICAN LINE	S	310
3885	MAGNIFICENT STEAMSHIP "PARIS" OF THE AMERICAN LINE	S	310
3886	MAGNIFICENT STEAMSHIP "ST. LOUIS" OF THE AMERICAN LINE	S	310
3887	MAGNIFICENT STEAMSHIPS, THE	L	1675
3888	MAIDEN ROCK, MISSISSIPPI RIVER/ (Daylight scene) (7.15x12.8)	S	485
3889	MAIDEN ROCK, MISSISSIPPI RIVER/ (Moonlight scene)	S	525
3890	MAIDEN'S PRAYER, THE	S	45
3891	MAIDEN ROCK, MISSISSIPPI RIVER/ (7.15x12.8)	S	470
3892	MAIN BUILDING/ (7.14x12.14) 1876	S	190
3893	MAIN OF COCKS, A / "The First Battle"/ (Vig.)	M	195
3894	MAINE GIANTESS, THE	S	85
3895	MAJ. GENL. FRANZ SIGEL / HERO OF THE WEST	S	85
3896	MAJ. GENL. JOHN C. FREMONT	S	90
3897	MAJ. GENL. PHILIP SHERIDAN / U.S. ARMY/ (Vig.)	S	95
3898	MAJ. GENL. PHILIP SHERIDAN / RALLYING HIS TROOPS	S	95
3899	MAJOLICA / OWNED BY NATHAN STRAUS	L	1425
3900	MAJOLICA / Record 2:15/ 1885	TC	85
3901	MAJ. GENL. AMBROSE E. BURNSIDE / COMMANDER-IN-CHIEF OF THE ARMY OF THE POTOMAC/ 1862	S	95
3902	MAJ. GENL. AMBROSE E. BURNSIDE / AT THE BATTLE OF FREDERICKSBURG, VA	S	100
3903	MAJ. GENL. BENJ. F. BUTLER / OF MASS./ (Vig.)	S	85
3904	MAJ. GENL. FRANZ SIGEL / HERO OF THE WEST	S	85
3905	MAJ. GENL. GEORGE B. McCLELLAN / AT THE BATTLE OF ANTIETAM, MD/ (11.15x8.10) 1862	S	120
3906	MAJ. GENL. GEORGE B. McCLELLAN / GENERAL-IN-CHEIF	S	100
3907	MAJ. GENL. GEORGE B. McCLELLAN / THE PEOPLE'S CHOICE	S	105
3908	MAJ. GENL. GEORGE B. McCLELLAN / U.S. ARMY/ (Vig.)	S	100
3909	MAJ. GENL. GEORGE B. McCLELLAN / U.S. ARMY/ (Signature over title) (Vig.)	S	105
3910	MAJ. GENL. GEORGE B. McCLELLAN / U.S. ARMY (3/4 length portrait)	S	100
3911	MAJ. GENL. GEORGE G. MEADE / AT THE BATTLE OF GETTYSBURG/ (11.11x9.2) 1863	S	105
3912	MAJ. GENL. GEORGE G. MEADE / COMMANDER-IN-CHIEF, ETC.	S	100
3913	MAJ. GENL. HENRY W. HALLECK	M	120
3914	MAJ. GENL. HENRY W. HALLECK/ (Vig.)	S	90
3915	MAJ. GENL. HENRY W. HALLECK/ U.S.A	S	85
3916	MAJ. GENL. JOHN C. FREMONT/ (Vig.)	S	90
3917	MAJ. GENL. JOHN E. WOOL	M	120
3918	MAJ. GENL. JOHN E. WOOL/ (Vig.)	S	85

3919	MAJ. GENL. JOHN POPE/ (Vig.)	S	95
3920	MAJ. GENL. JOHN POPE	S	95
3921	MAJ. GENL. JOSEPH HOOKER/ (On Horseback)	S	95
3922	MAJ. GENL. JOSEPH HOOKER, COMMANDER-IN-CHIEF OF THE "ARMY OF THE POTOMAC"/ 1862	S	95
3923	MAJ. GENL. JOSEPH HOOKER / FIGHTING JOE	S	95
3924	MAJ. GENL. NATHL. P. BANKS	S	95
3925	MAJ. GENL. PHILIP SHERIDAN / RALLYING HIS TROOPS AT THE BATTLE OF CEDAR CREEK, VA	S	105
3926	MAJ. GENL. PHILIP SHERIDAN / U.S. ARMY/ (Vig.)	S	105
3927	MAJ. GENL. Q. A. GILMORE / U.S. ARMY/ (Vig.)	S	90
3928	MAJ. GENL. U.S. GRANT / AT THE SIEGE OF VICKSBURG	S	105
3929	MAJ. GENL. WILLIAM S. ROSECRANS / AT THE BATTLE OF MURFREESBORO	S	95
3930	MAJ. GENL. WILLIAM S. ROSECRANS / U.S. ARMY	S	90
3931	MAJ. GEN. WILLIAM T. SHERMAN / VICTORIOUS MARCH	S	115
3932	MAJ. GENL. WILLIAM T. SHERMAN / U.S. ARMY/ (Vig.)	S	115
3933	MAJ. GENL. WINFIELD SCOTT / AT VERA CRUZ/ 1847, N. Currier	S	95
3934	MAJ. GENL. WINFIELD SCOTT/ (Vig.) N. Currier	L	155
3935	MAJ. GENL. WINFIELD SCOTT / GENERAL-IN-CHIEF OF U.S. ARMY / #99/ (12.4x8.10) 1846, N. Currier	S	95
3936	MAJ. GENL. WINFIELD SCOTT / GENERAL-IN-CHIEF OF U.S. ARMY/ N. Currier	S	95
3937	MAJ. GENL. WINFIELD SCOTT HANCOCK / AT THE BATTLE OF SPOTTSYLVANIA COURT HOUSE, VA/ (11.6x8.12)	S	95
3938	MAJ. GENL. Z. TAYLOR / BEFORE MONTEREY/ (12.12x8.5) (Vig.) 1846, N. Currier	S	90
3939	MAJ. GENL. ZACHARY TAYLOR / "ROUGH AND READY"/ (Vig.) N. Currier	S	95
3940	MAJOR ROBERT ANDERSON/ (Vig.)	S	80
3941	MAJOR SAMUEL RINGGOLD/ (Vig.) 1846, N. Currier	S	75
3942	MA-KO-ME-TA / BEAR'S OIL / Indian Chief/ C. Currier	S	190
3943	MAMA'S DARLING	L	165
3944	MAMA'S DARLINGS	S	80
3945	MAMA'S JEWEL	S	80
3946	MAMA'S PET/ 1878, N. Currier	S	85
3947	MAMA'S PET/ N. Currier	S	85
3948	MAMA'S PETS/ N. Currier	S	85
3949	MAMA'S ROSEBUD/ (14.8x10.9) 1858	M	145
3950	MAMBRINO/ 1879	S	290
3951	MAMBRINO / THE SIRE OF IMPORTED MESSENGER	S	290
3952	MAMBRINO PILOT, DAISY BURNS, AND ROSAMOND	L	1375

3953	MAMA'S DARLINGS/ (Vig.)	S	80
3954	MAMA'S PET / #544	S	85
3955	MAMA'S PETS/ N. Currier	S	85
3956	MAMMA'S TREASURE	M	135
3957	MAMMOTH IRON STEAMSHIP "GREAT EASTERN", THE / 22,500 Tons, 300 Horse-Power/ #466/ (Vig.)	S	310
3958	MAMMOTH IRON STEAMSHIP "GREAT EASTERN", THE/ (Vig.)	S	310
3959	MAMMOTH IRON STEAMSHIP "GREAT EASTERN", THE / 22,500 Tons, 2,600 Horse-Power/ (Vig.)	S	310
3960	MAMMOTH IRON STEAMSHIP "LEVIATHAN"	S	310
3961	MAN OF WORDS / MAN OF DEEDS, WHICH DO YOU THINK THE COUNTRY NEEDS?/ (Vig.) 1868	S	270
3962	MAN OF WORDS, THE / THE MAN OF DEEDS	S	270
3963	MAN THAT GAVE BARNUM HIS TURN, THE	S	210
3964	MAN THAT KEPT THE BRIDGE, THE/ (Vig.) 1881	S	195
3965	MAN THAT KNOWS A HORSE, THE/ (Comic) (10.1x13.9) 1877	M	605
3966	MAN WHO DRIVES TO WIN, THE/ 1876	S	290
3967	MANAGING A CANDIDATE	M	185
3968	MANIFESTATION OF THE SACRED HEART	S	20
3969	MANSION OF THE OLDEN TIME, A/ (8.8x12.7)	S	195
3970	MAP OF CENTERVILLE, MICHIGAN/ (19.6x25.12) N. Currier	L	735
3971	MAP OF MT. VERNON/ C. Currier	S	285
3972	MAP OF PROPERTY AT / JAMAICA, L.I./ N. Currier	L	925
3973	MAP OF THE PROPERTY / CHELSEA NEW YORK/ N. Currier	M	280
3974	MAP OF THE / WESTERN LAND DISTRICT WISCONSIN/ N. Currier	L	755
3975	MAPLE SUGARING / EARLY SPRING IN THE NORTHERN WOODS/ (8.7x12.8) 1872 [Old & New BEST 50]	S	1375
3976	MARCH AWAY! MARCH AWAY! BUCKLER AND BONNET BLUE!/ N. Currier	S	85
3977	MARCUS MORTON / GOV. OF MASS/ N. Currier	S	70
3978	MARGARET / #128/ (11.11x8.10) 1846, N. Currier	S	85
3979	MARGARET / #85/ (11.15x8.6) 1848, N. Currier	S	85
3980	MARGARET / #128/ (12x8.9) 1849, N. Currier	S	85
3981	MARGARET / #128/ N. Currier	S	85
3982	MARGARET/ (Vig.)	S	85
3983	MARGUERITE/ N. Currier	S	85
3984	MARIA / (Half-length, bridal veil and roses in hair) N. Currier	S	80
3985	MARIA / W. K. Hewitt on stone/ (Vig.)	S	85
3986	MARIA / #48/ 1846, N. Currier	S	85
3987	MARIA / (12.3x8.10) 1845, N. Currier	S	85
3988	MARIA / #48/ (Oval) 1846, N. Currier	S	85

3989	MARIA / #79/ 1848, N. Currier	S	85
3990	MARIA / (12.2x8.8) N. Currier	S	85
3991	MARIA / (Vig.)	S	80
3992	MARIA / #48	S	85
3993	MARINE BARK "CATALPA"/ N. Currier	S	400
3994	MARINE BARK "THE AMAZON"/ N. Currier	S	400
3995	MARION'S BRIGADE CROSSING THE PEDEE RIVER, SC/ (12.7x8.14)	S	595
3996	MARRIAGE, THE / #140/ (11.12x8.12) N. Currier	S	100
3997	MARRIAGE, THE/ N. Currier	S	95
3998	MARRIAGE, THE	S	90
3999	MARRIAGE CERTIFICATE / #634 WHOM GOD HATH JOINED/ 1848, N. Currier	S	75
4000	MARRIAGE CERTIFICATE / #570 WHOM GOD HATH JOINED/ 1848, N. Currier	S	75
4001	MARRIAGE CERTIFICATE/ 1857	S	75
4002	MARRIAGE CERTIFICATE #634/ (Vig.) 1865	S	75
4003	MARRIAGE CERTIFICATE/ (Vig.) 1875	S	75
4004	MARRIAGE CERTIFICATE/ 1877	S	75
4005	MARRIAGE CERTIFICATE/ 1869	S	75
4006	MARRIAGE CERTIFICATE	S	75
4007	MARRIAGE CERTIFICATE / For Colored People	S	75
4008	MARRIAGE EVENING, THE/ #317/ (11.5x8.8) N. Currier	S	95
4009	MARRIAGE EVENING	S	90
4010	MARRIAGE MORNING, THE / #316/ N. Currier	S	90
4011	MARRIAGE MORNING/ #316	S	90
4012	MARRIAGE OF QUEEN VICTORIA TO PRINCE ALBERT	S	75
4013	MARRIAGE OF THE FREE SOIL AND LIBERTY PARTIES/ (Political Cartoon)	S	185
4014	MARRIAGE VOW, THE/ N. Currier	S	90
4015	MARRIAGE VOW, THE/ 1846, N. Currier	S	95
4016	MARRIED/ 1845, N. Currier	S	85
4017	MARTHA/ #134/ (3/4 length) N. Currier	S	85
4018	MARTHA/ #134/ (Half-length) N. Currier	S	80
4019	MARTHA/ #134/ (Sarony on stone) N. Currier	S	85
4020	MARTHA/ (3/4 length) N. Currier	S	85
4021	MARTHA/ (Vig.)	S	80
4022	MARTHA WASHINGTON/ (12.8x9.12)	S	80
4023	MARTHA WASHINGTON	M	90
4024	MARTHA WASHINGTON/ #832	S	80
4025	MARTHA WASHINGTON/ (Vig.)	VS	75

All prints are published by Currier & Ives unless otherwise stated.

4026	MARTHA WASHINGTON	S	80
4027	MARTHA WASHINGTON/ (Vig.)	M	90
4028	MARTIN VAN BUREN/ C. Currier	VS	75
4029	MARTIN VAN BUREN, CHAMPION OF DEMOCRACY/ (Vig.) N. Currier	S	115
4030	MARTIN VAN BUREN, CHAMPION OF DEMOCRACY/ N. Currier	S	120
4031	MARTIN VAN BUREN / 8TH PRESIDENT/ (11.7x9.2) N. Currier	S	125
4032	MARTIN VAN BUREN / 8TH PRESIDENT/ N. Currier	S	125
4033	MARTIN VAN BUREN / 8TH PRESIDENT/ (17x12.8) N. Currier	M	160
4034	MARTIN VAN BUREN / 8TH PRESIDENT/ (12.1x10) N. Currier	S	125
4035	MARTIN VAN BUREN / FREE SOIL CANDIDATE/ N. Currier	S	125
4036	MARY / #41/ (12.2x8.11) 1845, N. Currier	S	90
4037	MARY / #41/ (12.1x8.11) 1845, N. Currier	S	90
4038	MARY/ 1845, N. Currier	S	90
4039	MARY/ (11.14x8.7) N. Currier	S	90
4040	MARY / (3/4 length, dressed for the street) N. Currier	S	90
4041	MARY / #65/ (11.15x8.7) 1848, N. Currier	S	90
4042	MARY / (Half-length) (Rural background) (Vig.) N. Currier	S	90
4043	MARY / (Half-length) (Rural background, different from preceding) (Vig.) N. Currier	S	90
4044	MARY / #97/ (Vig.) N. Currier	S	90
4045	MARY / #41	S	90
4046	MARY / (Vig.)	S	90
4047	MARY	M	105
4048	MARY / #41/ (12.1x8.11) N. Currier	S	90
4049	MARY AND HER LITTLE LAMB	M	190
4050	MARY ANN / #339/ N. Currier	S	80
4051	MARY ANN/ C. Currier	S	80
4052	MARY ANN/ N. Currier	S	80
4053	MARY ELIZABETH / #64/ (12x8.8) 1846, N. Currier	S	80
4054	MARY ELIZABETH/ 1846, N. Currier	S	80
4055	MARY JANE / #95/ 1846, N. Currier	S	80
4056	MARY JANE / #95/ 1850, N. Currier	S	80
4057	MARY JANE/ 1850, N. Currier	S	80
4058	MARY, QUEEN OF SCOTS/ (Vig.) 1870	S	50
4059	MARY, QUEEN OF SCOTS/ 1845, N. Currier	S	50
4060	MARY, QUEEN OF SCOTS/ #111/ N. Currier	S	50
4061	MARY, QUEEN OF SCOTS LEAVING FRANCE	S	60
4062	MARY'S LITTLE LAMB	S	135
4063	MASHERS, THE/ (Vig.) 1884	S	225

4064	MASONIC CHART/ (13.7x9.12) 1876	S	65
4065	MASSACHUSETTS/ (Ship)	M	435
4066	MASTER R. W. OSBORN/ (Midget) (11x8.6) N. Currier	S	95
4067	MATCH AGAINST TIME, A/ (Vig.) 1878	S	565
4068	MATER DOLOROSA/ N. Currier	S	50
4069	MATER DOLOROSA	S	50
4070	MATERNAL AFFECTION/ 1845, N. Currier	S	65
4071	MATERNAL AFFECTION/ 1846, N. Currier	S	65
4072	MATERNAL AFFECTION/ N. Currier	S	65
4073	MATERNAL HAPPINESS/ (11.10x8.9) 1849, N. Currier	S	65
4074	MATERNAL PIETY/ (12.1x8.10) N. Currier	S	65
4075	MATILDA/ (3/4 length, rounded corners) N. Currier	S	80
4076	MATILDA/ (3/4 length, urn on left) N. Currier	S	80
4077	MATILDA/ #154/ 1847, N. Currier	S	80
4078	MATILDA/ #154/ N. Currier	S	80
4079	MATING IN THE WOODS, "RUFFED GROUSE"/ (8.8x12.8) 1871	S	560
4080	MATTIE	S	80
4081	MATTIE HUNTER/ RECORD 2:12/ 1881	S	305
4082	MATTIE HUNTER/ Record 2:15/ 1881	TC	85
4083	MATTIE HUNTER/ 1879	S	290
4084	MAUD MULLER/ (Vig.)	L	290
4085	MAUD S. RECORD 2:09.75/ (Vig.) 1881	S	290
4086	MAUD S. AND ST. JULIEN/ 1884	S	290
4087	MAXY COBB/ 1882	TC	85
4088	MAY QUEEN, THE/ (Horse) 1876	S	290
4089	MAY QUEEN, THE/ (Girl) N. Currier	S	75
4090	MAY QUEEN, THE/ (Girl)	S	75
4091	MAYFLOWER SALUTED BY THE FLEET/ (19.5x28) 1886	L	1525
4092	MAZEPPA PLATE 1/ (8.2x12.6) 1846, N. Currier	S	70
4093	MAZEPPA PLATE 2/ (8.2x12.7) 1846, N. Currier	S	70
4094	MAZEPPA PLATE 3/ (8.2x12.7) 1846, N. Currier	S	70
4095	MAZEPPA PLATE 4/ (8.3x12.6) 1846, N. Currier	S	70
4096	M'DONOUGH'S VICTORY ON LAKE CHAMPLAIN/ (7.15x13.2) 1846	S	515
4097	MEADOW IN SPRINGTIME - THE TWIN LAMBS/ (16.12x24.13) 1867	L	620
4098	MEADOW IN SPRINGTIME, THE	L	475
4099	MEADOWSIDE COTTAGE	M	345
4100	MEDALLA MILAGROSA - MIRACULOUS MEDAL/ N. Currier	S	65
4101	MEETING OF THE WATERS, THE/ (8x12.8) 1868	S	85
4102	MEETING OF THE WATERS IN THE VALE OF AVOCA	L	295

4103	MELROSE ABBEY/ (Vig.)	S	95
4104	MELROSE ABBEY/ (7.14x12.6)	S	95
4105	MELROSE ABBEY	M	140
4106	MERCHANTS EXCHANGE, NEW YORK, WALL STREET/ (8.6x12.8) N. Currier	S	680
4107	MERRY CHRISTMAS, A/ (Motto) (Vig.) 1876	S	995
4108	MERRY CHRISTMAS, A/ (Motto) (Vig.)	S	995
4109	MERRY CHRISTMAS, A/ #123/ (Companion to #2721) N. Currier	S	350
4110	MERRY, MERRY MAIDEN AND THE TAR/ (Vig.) 1879	S	125
4111	MEXICAN FANDANGO/ 1848, N. Currier	S	120
4112	MEXICAN GUERILLEROS/ (8.7x12.12) 1848, N. Currier	S	115
4113	MEXICANS EVACUATING VERA CRUZ/ (8.7x12) 1847, N. Currier	S	120
4114	MIDDLESEX PAUPER LUNATIC ASYLUM LONDON ENGLAND/ (Vig.) N. Currier	M	120
4115	MIDNIGHT/ Record 2:18.25/ 1879	S	290
4116	MIDNIGHT RACE ON THE MISSISSIPPI, A/ (Natchez and Eclipse) (18.7x28.2) 1860 [Old & New BEST 50]	L	5800
4117	MIDNIGHT RACE ON THE MISSISSIPPI, A/ (Memphis and James Howard) (9x13.3) 1875 [New BEST 50]	S	770
4118	MIDSUMMER NIGHT'S DREAM, A	L	320
4119	MILIGROSA IMAGEN	S	60
4120	MILITARY COLLEGE OF CHAPULTEPEC/ (8.6x12.6) 1847, N. Currier	S	100
4121	MILITARY RING, THE/ (Political Cartoon) (Vig.) 1872	S	180
4122	MILL BOY AND BLONDINE/ 1881	S	290
4123	MILL-COVE LAKE/ (8.8x12.8)	S	370
4124	MILL DAM AT "SLEEPY HOLLOW", THE/ (17x22.8)	L	1525
4125	MILL IN THE HIGHLANDS	M	405
4126	MILL RIVER SCENERY	L	1225
4127	MILL-STREAM, THE/ (11.1x15.10)	M	415
4128	MILLARD FILLMORE - 13TH PRESIDENT/ (Very Rare) 1856, N. Currier	S	335
4129	MILLARD FILLMORE - 13TH PRESIDENT/ (Vig.) 1857, N. Currier	L	345
4130	MILLARD FILLMORE - 13TH PRESIDENT - NATIONAL AMERICAN CANDIDATE.../ 1856, N. Currier	S	S 295
4131	MILLARD FILLMORE - WHIG CANDIDATE FOR VICE PRESIDENT/ (Rare) (11.14x8.14) 1848, N. Currier	S	325
4132	MILLER'S HOME	M	380
4133	MIND YOUR LESSON, FIDO	S	125
4134	MINER, STEVENS & CO.	L	2175
4135	MINIATURE LANDSCAPES/ (10 views)	M	745
4136	MINIATURE LANDSCAPES No. 1	S	379
4137	MINIATURE SHIP "RED, WHITE, AND BLUE"	S	285

4138	MINIATURE SHIP "RED, WHITE, AND BLUE"/ (Vig.)	S	285
4139	MINK TRAPPING/ "PRIME"/ (19.1x27.12) 1862 [Old & New BEST 50]	L	10300
4140	MINNEHAHA - "Laughing Water"/ (Vig.)	S	145
4141	MINNEHAHA FALLS, MINNESOTA	M	390
4142	MINNIE	VS	85
4143	MINNE/ (Vig.)	S	75
4144	MINUTE-MEN OF THE REVOLUTION, THE/ (8.14x12.12) 1876	S	230
4145	MIRACULOUS MEDAL/ N. Currier	S	45
4146	MIRACULOUS IMAGE OF ST. FRANCIS XAVIER	S	20
4147	MISCHIEF AND MUSIC/ (12.6x8.1)	S	135
4148	MISCHIEVOUS LITTLE DOGGIE/ (9.4x7.13)	S	135
4149	MISCHIEVOUS LITTLE KITTIE	S	135
4150	MISCHIEVOUS LITTLE KITTIES/ (12.6x8.1) 1877	S	135
4151	MISERIES OF A BACHELOR, THE/ (12x9) (Companion to #568)	S	180
4152	MISS ELIZABETH REED - THE LILLIPUTIAN QUEEN	S	135
4153	MISS ELIZABETH REED - MISS HANNAH CROUSE/ (Midget and Giantess) (11.12x8.14) N. Currier	S	140
4154	MISS JANE CAMPBELL/ (Giantess) (11.3x8.11)	S	140
4155	MISS MARTHA JONES - THE LILLIPUTIAN QUEEN/ (11.11x8.5) N. Currier	S	140
4156	MISS S. PHILLIPS/ N. Currier	S	135
4157	MISS SUSAN BARTON/ (Mammoth Lady) (12.1x8.12) 1849, N. Currier	S	165
4158	MISS WOODFORD/ (Horse) 1885	S	270
4159	MISSIONARY CHAPEL AT WHEELOCK/ C. Currier	S	120
4160	MISSISSIPPI IN TIME OF PEACE/ (18.4x27.12) 1865 [New BEST 50]	L	5300
4161	MISSISSIPPI IN TIME OF WAR/ (18.4x27.12) 1865	L	5300
4162	MIXED AT THE FINISH/ (Vig.) 1880	S	295
4163	MODEL ARTISTS AS THE THREE GRACES/ N. Currier	S	125
4164	MODERN COLLEGE SCULL GRADUATING WITH ALL HONORS/ 1876/ (Comic)	M	310
4165	MODERN COLOSSUS, THE/ (10.10x16.12) N. Currier	M	275
4166	MOLLIE McCARTHY/ 1881	TC	85
4167	MOLLIE McCARTHY, THE RACING QUEEN/ (Vig.) 1878	S	290
4168	MOMENTOUS QUESTION, THE - "Ah, Billy, My Beauty, Can't You Give Us An Eye Opener? Yes, Sir-ee"/ (Companion to #1223) 1853, N. Currier	S	330
4169	MOMENTOUS QUESTION, THE - IS MY FACE GOOD FOR A DRINK?/ N. Currier	S	330
4170	MOMENTOUS QUESTION, THE	S	280
4171	MONROE CHIEF/ 1881	TC	90
4172	MONUMENT/ (Virginia) (8.4x12.7)	S	200
4173	MOONLIGHT/ (Companion to #5887)	VS	145

4174	MOONLIGHT/ (10x15)	S	105
4175	MOONLIGHT IN FAIRYLAND	S	85
4176	MOONLIGHT IN THE TROPICS/ (8.7x12.9)	S	105
4177	MOONLIGHT ON LAKE CATALPA, VIRGINIA	M	230
4178	MOONLIGHT ON LONG ISLAND SOUND	S	520
4179	MOONLIGHT ON THE LAKE	M	260
4180	MOONLIGHT ON THE MISSISSIPPI/ (8.7x12.6)	S	400
4181	MOONLIGHT PROMENADE, THE	S	95
4182	MOONLIGHT PROMENADE, THE/ (7.15x12.6)	S	95
4183	MOONLIGHT / THE CASTLE/ (8.2x12.9)	S	100
4184	MOONLIGHT / THE RUINS	S	95
4185	MOOSE AND WOLVES / A NARROW ESCAPE/ (8.6x12.7)	S	300
4186	MOOSEHEAD LAKE/ (7.15x12.8)	S	250
4187	MORE FREE THAN WELCOME/ (8x12.8)	S	190
4188	MORE FRIGHTENED THAN HURT	S	200
4189	MORE FRIGHTENED THAN HURT/ (8.2x12.8) N. Currier	S	200
4190	MORE PLUCKY THAN PRUDENT/ (Comic R.R. Scene) (8.15x12.4) 1885	S	280
4191	MORE THAN WELCOME	S	125
4192	MORGAN LEWIS/ C. Currier	S	70
4193	MORGAN LEWIS	VS	65
4194	MORNING/ (11x8.4)	S	95
4195	MORNING GLORIES	S	120
4196	MORNING IN THE WOODS/ (14.13x20.2) 1852, N. Currier	L	2725
4197	MORNING IN THE WOODS/ (14.12x20.8) 1865	L	2625
4198	MORNING OF LIFE, THE/ (8.9x12.8)	S	120
4199	MORNING OF LIFE, THE/ (8.7x12.8) 1874	S	120
4200	MORNING OF LOVE, THE/ (11.7x8.5)	S	95
4201	MORNING PRAYER, THE/ (9.14x8) (Oval) N. Currier	S	20
4202	MORNING PRAYER, THE / #7/ (11.12x8.5) N. Currier	S	20
4203	MORNING PRAYER, THE/ (Vig.) 1857, N. Currier	L	40
4204	MORNING PRAYER, THE/ (Vig.) 1862, N. Currier	M	30
4205	MORNING PRAYER, THE / #7	S	20
4206	MORNING PRAYER, THE/ "DEFEND US FROM ALL EVIL"/ (Companion to #1773) C. Currier	S	20
4207	MORNING RECREATION, THE/ (11.14x8.9) N. Currier	S	125
4208	MORNING RIDE, THE / #681/ (2 children) 1849, N. Currier	S	130
4209	MORNING RIDE, THE / #861/ 1849, N. Currier	S	120
4210	MORNING ROSE, THE/ (11.13x8.10) 1849, N. Currier	S	115
4211	MORNING ROSE, THE/ (12x8.10)	S	90

4212	MORNING ROSES/ (Vig.)	S	90
4213	MORNING STAR, THE/ (Vig.)	S	75
4214	MORNING STAR, THE/ 1846, N. Currier	S	75
4215	MORNING STAR / #499	S	75
4216	MOSES AND THE DECALOGUE/ N. Currier	S	20
4217	MOSS ROSE, THE	S	100
4218	MOSS ROSE, THE/ (Vig.) 1847, N. Currier	S	100
4219	MOSS ROSE, THE/ (Tinted background, round corners) (Vig.) 1847, N. Currier	S	100
4220	MOSS ROSES AND BUDS/ (Vig.) 1870	S	100
4221	MOSS ROSES AND BUDS	S	90
4222	MOST HOLY CATHOLIC FAITH/ (11.15x8.8) 1872	S	20
4223	MOST HOLY SACRIFICE/ (12.7x8.5) 1872	S	20
4224	MOST REV. JOHN HUGHES, DD., THE/ (Vig.) 1864	M	20
4225	MOST REV. JOHN HUGHES, DD., THE	S	20
4226	MOST REV. JOHN McCLOSKEY, D.D., THE	S	20
4227	MOST REV. M. J. SPALDING, D.D., THE/ (11.9x8.6)	S	20
4228	MOTHER AND CHILD/ (11.10x8.10) 1846, N. Currier	S	95
4229	MOTHERLESS, THE/ N. Currier	S	75
4230	MOTHERLESS, THE	S	75
4231	MOTHER'S BLESSING, THE/ (14.15x11.4)	M	135
4232	MOTHER'S DREAM, THE	S	90
4233	MOTHER'S DREAM, THE	M	135
4234	MOTHER'S JOY/ (11.11x8.11) 1846, N. Currier	S	95
4235	MOTHER'S JOY/ (Vig.) 1859, N. Currier	S	95
4236	MOTHER'S JOY/ (10.3x8.3) (Oval)	S	105
4237	MOTHER'S PET/ (11.14x8.10) N. Currier	S	110
4238	MOTHER'S TREASURE, A/ (Vig.) N. Currier	S	90
4239	MOTHER'S WING/ (Hen & chickens) 1866	M	230
4240	MT. HOLYOKE FEMALE SEMINARY, SOUTH HADLEY, MASS/ N. Currier	S	355
4241	MT. VESUVIUS, ITALY	S	75
4242	MOUNT WASHINGTON AND THE WHITE MOUNTAINS/ (14.15x20.6) 1860	L	3225
4243	MOUNTAIN PASS, SIERRA NEVADA/ (17.8x25.14) 1867	L	3850
4244	MOUNTAIN RAMBLE, A/ (8.7x12.6)	S	170
4245	MOUNTAIN SPRING, WEST POINT, NEAR COZZEN'S DOCK, THE/ (11.1x15.10) 1862	M	795
4246	MOUNTAIN STREAM, THE/ (9.11x16.12)	M	500
4247	MOUNTAINEER'S HOME, THE/ (9.10x16.15)	M	620
4248	MOUNTAINEER'S RETURN, THE/ N. Currier	S	140

4249	MR. AUGUST BELMONT'S POTOMAC AND MASHER/ (19.14x27.15) 1891	L	1525
4250	MR. BONNER'S HORSE "JOE ELLIOTT"/ (17x26.10) 1873	L	1500
4251	MR. FRANK WORK'S CELEBRATED TEAM/ (Vig.)	S	290
4252	MR. J. PROCTOR	S	95
4253	MR. JAS. R. KEENE'S BAY COLT, 3 YRS., FOXHALL/ (Vig.)	S	290
4254	MR. PLACIDE/ N. Currier	S	80
4255	MR. PIERRE LORILLARD'S BR. COLT "IROQUOIS"/ (Vig.) 1881	S	290
4256	MR. WM. H. VANDERBILT DRIVING HIS MAGNIFICENT TEAM "MAUD S." AND "ALDINE"/ (Vig.) 1883	S	290
4257	MR. WM. H. VANDERBILT'S CELEBRATED ROAD TEAM / Lysander and Leander/ (Vig.)	S	290
4258	MR. WILLIAM H. VANDERBILT'S CELEBRATED ROAD TEAM	L	1550
4259	MR. WM. H. VANDERBILT'S CELEBRATED ROAD TEAM / Small Hopes and Lady Mac/ (Vig.)	S	290
4260	MRS. FISH AND THE MISSES FOX/ (8.10x11.10) 1852, N. Currier	S	195
4261	MRS. GEORGE JONES - THE TRAGIC ACTRESS/ 1838, N. Currier	S	95
4262	MRS. JAMES K. POLK/ (11.12x8.9) 1846, N. Currier	S	85
4263	MRS. LUCRETIA R. GARFIELD/ (Vig.)	M	95
4264	MRS. LUCY I. BLISS/ (Vig.)	S	65
4265	MUCKROSS ABBEY, KILLARNEY	S	75
4266	MUD S. - DE GREAT RECORD BUSTER/ (Vig.) 1885	S	255
4267	MULE TEAM ON A DOWN GRADE, A/ (Vig.) 1881	S	260
4268	MULE TEAM ON AN UP GRADE/ (Vig.) 1881	S	260
4269	MURDER OF MISS JANE McCREA/ (11.9x8.6) 1846, N. Currier	S	200
4270	MUSIC/ (Horse) 1875	S	290
4271	MUSIC / Chestnut Mare/ (16.12x25) 1875	L	1450
4272	MUSIC HATH CHARMS/ (12.5x8.6) 1875	S	150
4273	MUSTANG TEAM, THE	M	445
4274	MY ABSENT LOVE/ (11.11x9.4) (Oval)	S	75
4275	MY BOYHOOD HOME	S	185
4276	MY BOYHOOD'S HOME	S	185
4277	MY BROTHER/ 1846, N. Currier	S	80
4278	MY CHARMING GIRL/ (Vig.)	S	80
4279	MY CHILD/ (12.2x8.10) 1849, N. Currier	S	95
4280	MY CHILD! MY CHILD!/ (12.4x8.2) (Companion to #6007)	S	85
4281	MY CHOICE (Vig.)	S	80
4282	MY CHOICE/ N. Currier	M	90
4283	MY COTTAGE HOME/ (16.1x23.7) 1866	L	1150
4284	MY COTTAGE HOME	VS	200
4285	MY DARLING BOY/ N. Currier	S	90

4286	MY DARLING GIRL/ (Full Length) N. Currier	S	85
4287	MY DARLING GIRL/ N. Currier	S	90
4288	MY DARLING GIRL/ KISS ME QUICK	S	95
4289	MY DEAR LITTLE PET/ (Vig.) 1877	S	100
4290	MY FAVORITE HORSE	S	170
4291	MY FAVORITE PONY/ (11.14x8.8)	S	160
4292	MY FATHER LAND/ N. Currier	S	75
4293	MY FAVORITE/ (Female Head) (Vig.)	S	75
4294	MY FAVORITE	S	75
4295	MY FIRST FRIEND/ N. Currier	S	95
4296	MY FIRST LOVE/ N. Currier	S	90
4297	MY FIRST PLAYMATE / #620	S	90
4298	MY FIRST PLAYMATE	S	90
4299	MY FRIEND AND I/ (11.15x8.5) 1846, N. Currier	S	75
4300	MY GENTLE DOVE/ (Vig.) 1871	S	75
4301	MY GENTLE LOVE/ (Vig.) 1872	S	75
4302	MY HEARTS DESIRE	S	75
4303	MY HEARTS TREASURE	S	75
4304	MY HERO/ (12x9.8)	S	80
4305	MY HIGHLAND BOY/ (Vig.) N. Currier	S	80
4306	MY HIGHLAND BOY/ (Vig.)	S	80
4307	MY HIGHLAND GIRL/ (Vig.)	S	80
4308	MY HIGHLAND GIRL/ (Vig.) N. Currier	S	80
4309	MY HIGHLAND GIRL/ N. Currier	S	80
4310	MY INTENDED/ (11.15x8.7) 1847, N. Currier	S	80
4311	MY KITTY AND CANARY/ (12.6x8.2) 1871	S	130
4312	MY LIPS SHALL PRAISE THEE*/ (Vig.)	S	20
4313	MY LITTLE DRUMMER BOY	S	105
4314	MY LITTLE FAVORITE	S	85
4315	MY LITTLE FAVORITE/ (Child holding dog)	M	125
4316	MY LITTLE FAVORITE	M	125
4317	MY LITTLE FRIEND/ (11.11x8.5) 1845, N. Currier	S	85
4318	MY LITTLE PET/ 1845, N. Currier	S	85
4319	MY LITTLE PLAYFELLOW / #104/ (11.15x8.10) 1847, N. Currier	S	95
4320	MY LITTLE PLAYFELLOW/ (11.14x8.6) N. Currier	S	95
4321	MY LITTLE PLAYFELLOW/ (9.6x7.7) N. Currier	S	95
4322	MY LITTLE PLAYFELLOW / #104/ (Vig.)	S	95
4323	MY LITTLE PLAYFELLOW/ (9.8x7.8) N. Currier	S	95
4324	MY LITTLE PLAYFELLOW	S	85

4325	MY LITTLE PLAYMATE	S	85
4326	MY LITTLE WHITE BUNNIES	S	145
4327	MY LITTLE WHITE BUNNIES / Receiving a Visitor	S	145
4328	MY LITTLE WHITE KITTENS	S	140
4329	MY LITTLE WHITE KITTIE / AFTER THE GOLDFISH (12.11x7.15)	S	145
4330	MY LITTLE WHITE KITTIE / FISHING	S	145
4331	MY LITTLE WHITE KITTIE / ITS FIRST MOUSE	S	140
4332	MY LITTLE WHITE KITTIES / INTO MISCHIEF	S	140
4333	MY LITTLE WHITE KITTIES / LEARNING THEIR ABC'S	S	140
4334	MY LITTLE WHITE KITTIES / PLAYING BALL/ (8x12.9) 1870	S	140
4335	MY LITTLE WHITE KITTIES / PLAYING BALL	S	140
4336	MY LITTLE WHITE KITTIES / PLAYING DOMINOES	S	140
4337	MY LITTLE WHITE KITTIES / #520	S	140
4338	MY LITTLE WHITE KITTIES / TAKING THE CAKE / #344	S	140
4339	MY LITTLE WHITE KITTIES / TAKING THE CAKE/ 1877	S	140
4340	MY LITTLE WHITE KITTIES / THEIR FIRST MOUSE/ (8x12.4)	S	140
4341	MY LITTLE WHITE KITTIES / THEIR FIRST MOUSE/ 1871	S	140
4342	MY LONG TAIL BLUE/ N. Currier	S	140
4343	MY LOVE AND I/ (8.6x12.8) 1872	S	115
4344	MY OWN MAMA	S	95
4345	MY OWN SWEET PET	S	95
4346	MY OWN TRUE LOVE	S	80
4347	MY PET BIRD	S	120
4348	MY PET BIRD/ (Vig.)	M	170
4349	MY PICTURE/ 1856, N. Currier	L	165
4350	MY PONY AND DOG/ (8.4x12.4)	S	140
4351	MY PONY AND DOG/ (8.12x11.8)	S	140
4352	MY PRETTY IRISH GIRL	S	75
4353	MY SISTER/ 1846, N. Currier	S	80
4354	MY SWEETHEART/ (Vig.)	S	75
4355	MY SWEETHEART	L	125
4356	MY THREE WHITE KITTENS	S	140
4357	MY THREE WHITE KITTIES / LEARNING THEIR ABC'S/ (8.2x12.8)	S	140

N

Con#	Title	Folio	Value
4358	NANCY/ N. Currier	S	90
4359	NANCY / #255/ N. Currier	S	90
4360	NANCY HANKS/ 1892	S	290
4361	NAPOLEON/ (Vig.)	M	95
4362	NAPOLEON / #174/ (Vig.)	S	80
4363	NAPOLEON AT ST. HELENA/ (12.4x8.4) N. Currier	S	85
4364	NAPOLEON AT ST. HELENA/ C. Currier	S	85
4365	NAPOLEON AT WATERLOO/ N. Currier	S	80
4366	NAPOLEON BONAPARTE / EMPEROR OF FRANCE	M	90
4367	NAPOLEON CROSSING THE ALPS/ (Vig.) N. Currier	S	95
4368	NAPOLEON CROSSING THE ALPS/ C. Currier	S	95
4369	NAPOLEON EMPEROR OF FRANCE/ (11.15x8.11) 1847, N. Currier	S	85
4370	NAPOLEON / IN THE HIGHEST DEGREE OF HIS PROSPERITY/ N. Currier	S	85
4370A	NAPOLEON / THE HERO OF 100 BATTLES/ (Vig.) N. Currier	S	85
4371	NAPOLEON / THE HERO OF 100 BATTLES/ N. Currier	S	85
4372	NAPOLEON'S STRATEGY/ (Vig.) 1870	S	90
4373	NAPOLEON EUGENE LOUIS / PRINCE IMPERIAL OF FRANCE/ (11x9)	S	75
4374	NAPOLEON II - DUKE OF REICHSTADT/ N. Currier	S	75
4375	NAPOLEON III	S	75
4376	NARRAGANSETT S. COMPANY'S STEAMER "BRISTOL"	S	345
4377	NARRAGANSET S. COMPANY'S STEAMER "PROVIDENCE" OF THE FALL RIVER LINE/ (Vig.)	S	345
4378	NARROW WAY, THE/ N. Currier	S	120
4379	NARROWS FROM FORT HAMILTON/ (8.3x11.10) N. Currier	S	360
4380	NARROWS FROM STATEN ISLAND, THE/ (8.2x11.11) N. Currier	S	360
4381	NARROWS, NEW YORK BAY TO STATEN ISLAND/ (7.15x12.7)	S	360
4382	NARROWS, NEW YORK BAY TO STATEN ISLAND	S	360
4383	NAT LANGHAM / CHAMPION OF THE MIDDLE WEIGHTS/ (14.12x12.4)	M	430
4384	NATIONAL CADETS 9th REGT. NEW YORK STATE ARTILLERY/ N. Currier	S	160
4385	NATIONAL DEMOCRATIC BANNER OF 1860 / Hon. John C. Breckinridge	S	225
4386	NATIONAL DEMOCRATIC BANNER OF 1860 / Hon. Stephen A. Douglas/ (12x8.10)	S	225
4387	NATIONAL DEMOCRATIC BANNER OF VICTORY/ (12.11x8.10) 1868	S	215
4388	NATIONAL GAME, THE - THREE "OUTS" AND ONE "RUN"(Political Cartoon) (Vig.)	M	290
4389	NATIONAL UNION REPUBLICAN BANNER,1860/ (Lincoln and Hamlin) 1860	S	400
4390	NATIONAL UNION REPUBLICAN BANNER,1868/ (Grant and Colfax) 1868	S	225

All prints are published by Currier & Ives unless otherwise stated.

4391	NATIONAL WASHINGTON MONUMENT IN THE CITY OF WASHINGTON, D.C./ (12.2x8.8) N. Currier	S	265
4392	NATIONAL WASHINGTON MONUMENT, WASH. D.C.	L	660
4393	NATURAL AND THE SPIRITUAL, THE/ (11x8.3) N. Currier	S	20
4394	NATURAL BRIDGE, VA (8.8x12.8)	S	275
4395	NAUGHTY CAT*/ 1874	S	140
4396	NAVAL BOMBARDMENT OF VERA CRUZ/ (8.3x13.1) 1847, N. Currier	S	210
4397	NAVAL HEROES OF THE U.S., PLATE 1/ 1846, N. Currier	S	555
4398	NAVAL HEROES OF THE U.S., PLATE 2/ 1846, N. Currier	S	555
4399	NAVAL HEROES OF THE U.S., PLATE 3/ 1846, N. Currier	S	555
4400	NAVAL HEROES OF THE U.S., PLATE 4/ 1846, N. Currier	S	810
4401	NAZARETH OF GALILEE/ (8.8x12.8)	S	20
4402	NEARER MY GOD TO THEE / (Motto) (Vig.)	S	85
4403	NEAREST WAY IN SUMMER TIME, THE/ (11.5x15.14)	M	550
4404	NEARING THE FINISH LINE/ (19.10x28) 1888	L	1125
4405	NECK AND NECK TO THE WIRE/ N. Currier	L	1400
4406	NECKER/ N. Currier	S	75
4407	NELLIE/ (Vig.)	S	75
4408	NELSON	S	290
4408A	NEPTUNE HOUSE, NEW ROCHELLE, WESTCHESTER CTY. N.Y./ N. Currier	L	2325
4409	NETTIE/ 1874	S	290
4410	NETTIE/ (Vig.)	S	290
4411	NEW BROOD, THE / (Chickens) (8.2x12.8)	S	145
4412	NEW CACHUCHA, THE/ N. Currier	S	20
4413	NEW *CONFEDERATE CRUISER*, THE/ 1872	S	230
4414	NEW ENGLAND BEAUTY, A	S	75
4415	NEW ENGLAND COAST SCENE, OFF BOSTON LIGHT	S	390
4416	NEW ENGLAND COAST SCENE/ (8.7x12.8)	S	375
4417	NEW ENGLAND HOME, A/ (8x12.8)	S	195
4418	NEW ENGLAND HOMESTEAD, A/ (7.9x12.8) 1852, N. Currier	S	205
4419	NEW ENGLAND SCENERY/ (23.7x16.6) 1866	L	2250
4420	NEW ENGLAND WINTER SCENE/ (16.7x23.10) 1861 [Old & New BEST 50]	L	7500
4421	NEW EXCURSION STEAMER *COLUMBIA*/ (19.5x34.8) 1877	L	1550
4422	NEW FASHIONED GIRL, THE/ (Vig.)	S	235
4423	NEW FOUNTAIN OF DEMOCRACY, THE/ (Political Cartoon) (Vig.) 1872	S	185
4424	NEW HAT MAN, THE	S	185
4425	NEW JERSEY FOX HUNT/ *Taking breath*/ (Vig.) 1876	S	225
4426	NEW JERSEY FOX HUNT/ *A Smoking Run*/ (Vig.) 1876	S	225
4427	NEW PALACE STEAMER *PILGRIM* OF THE FALL RIVER LINE/ (8.10x14.8) 1883	M	800

4428	NEW ST. PATRICK'S CATHEDRAL, THE/ (12.8x9.1)	S	115
4429	NEW STEAMSHIP "ETRURIA" THE	S	350
4430	NEW STEAMSHIP "PAVONIA" THE	S	350
4431	NEW STEAMSHIP "UMBRIA" OF THE CUNARD LINE, THE	S	350
4432	NEW SUSPENSION BRIDGE, NIAGARA FALLS/ (8.6x12.8)	S	300
4433	NEW YORK AND BROOKLYN/ (20.10x32.12) 1875	L	2375
4434	NEW YORK AND BROOKLYN/ (Jersey City and Hoboken Water Front) (20.14x32.14) 1877	L	2125
4435	NEW YORK BAY FROM BAY RIDGE, L.I./ 1860	L	1425
4436	NEW YORK BAY FROM BAY RIDGE, L.I./ (8.7x12.7)	S	405
4437	NEW YORK BAY FROM THE TELEGRAPH STATION/ (8.3x11.9) N. Currier	S	405
4438	NEW YORK BEAUTY, THE/ (Vig.)	S	75
4439	NEW YORK CLIPPER SHIP "CHALLENGE"/ (8.12x12.12) N. Currier	S	680
4440	NEW YORK CRYSTAL PALACE FOR THE EXHIBITION/ N. Currier	L	2550
4441	NEW YORK CRYSTAL PALACE/ (7.14 x12.6) N. Currier	S	390
4442	NEW YORK CRYSTAL PALACE/ (7.14x12.6) N. Currier	S	390
4443	NEW YORK FERRY BOAT/ (8.8x12.8)	S	775
4444	NEW YORK FERRY BOAT/ (8x12.8)	S	775
4445	NEW YORK FIREMAN'S MONUMENT, GREENWOOD CEMETERY, L.I./ (10.7x14.6) 1855, N. Currier	M	300
4446	NEW YORK FROM WEEHAWKEN/ 1835, C. Currier	S	655
4447	NEW YORK LIGHT GUARD'S QUICK STEP/ (Vig.) 1839, N. Currier	S	115
4448	NEW YORK, LOOKING NORTH FROM THE BATTERY/ 1860	S	425
4449	NEW YORK PILOT'S MONUMENT/ (10.4x14.15) 1855, N. Currier	M	250
4450	NEW YORK YACHT CLUB REGATTA/ (17.5x27.13)	L	3625
4451	NEWFOUNDLAND DOG	S	145
4452	NEWFOUNDLAND DOG/ (8.3x11.3)	S	145
4453	NEWPORT BEACH/ (8.8x12)	S	320
4454	NIAGARA BY MOONLIGHT	M	370
4455	NIAGARA FALLS/ (8x10.2) N. Currier	S	220
4456	NIAGARA FALLS/ (14.12x20.1) N. Currier	L	580
4457	NIAGARA FALLS FROM GOAT ISLAND / (Daylight) (9.5x15.12)	M	360
4458	NIAGARA FALLS FROM GOAT ISLAND / (Night scene) (9.5x15.12)	M	360
4459	NIAGARA FALLS FROM GOAT ISLAND	S	220
4460	NIAGARA FALLS FROM TABLE ROCK/ (8.4x11.11) N. Currier	S	275
4461	NIAGARA FALLS FROM THE CANADA SIDE/ (7.15x12.7)	S	220
4462	NICE AND TEMPTING OYSTERS	S	240
4463	NICE FAMILY PARTY, A/ (Political Cartoon)	M	185
4464	NIGGER" IN THE WOODPILE, THE/ (Political Cartoon)	M	240

4465	NIGH TO BETHANY/ N. Currier	S	25
4466	NIGH TO BETHANY	S	25
4467	NIGHT/ (8.4x11.2)	S	75
4468	NIGHT AFTER THE BATTLE / BURYING THE DEAD/ 1846, N. Currier	S	110
4469	NIGHT AFTER THE BATTLE / BURYING THE DEAD/ 1847, N. Currier	S	110
4470	NIGHT AFTER THE BATTLE/ 1862	S	145
4471	NIGHT BEFORE THE BATTLE / THE PATRIOT'S DREAM	M	225
4472	NIGHT BY THE CAMP-FIRE/ (10.6x14.15) 1861	M	575
4473	NIGHT EXPRESS, THE/ "The Start"/ (8.8x12.12) [New BEST 50]	S	1950
4474	NIGHT ON THE HUDSON, A/ "Through at Daylight"/ (18x27.12) 1864 [New BEST 50]	L	3100
4475	NIGHT SCENE AT A JUNCTION/ 1881	L	10300
4476	NIGHT SCENE AT AN AMERICAN RAILWAY JUNCTION/ (18x27.11) 1876	L	10700
4477	NIGHT SCENE AT AN AMERICAN RAILWAY JUNCTION/ 1876	L	10700
4478	NIGHTMARE IN THE SLEEPING CAR, A/ (Vig.) 1875	S	375
4479	NILLS TOWER, NAWORTH	S	65
4480	NINETY AND NINE/ (8.11x12.8) 1875	S	20
4481	NIP AND TUCK!/ (Comic) (Vig.) 1878	S	290
4482	NIP AND TUCK" RACE, A	M	450
4483	NIPPED IN THE ICE	S	670
4484	NO MA'AM, I DIDN'T COME TO SHOOT BIRDS/ (2.14x4.12) 1880	TC	70
4485	NO MA'AM, I DON'T CARE TO SHOOT BIRDS/ 1880	S	195
4486	NO, NO FIDO	VS	95
4486A	NO, NO FIDO	TC	70
4487	NO ONE TO LOVE ME"/ (Comic) (Vig.) 1880	S	240
4488	NO ROSE WITHOUT A THORN/ (12.7x8.15) N. Currier	S	135
4489	NO SLATE HERE/ (Cartoon) (Vig.)	S	175
4490	NO TICK HERE	S	245
4491	NO TIME HERE - PLAYED OUT	S	260
4492	NO YOU DON'T / #264	S	95
4493	NO YOU DON'T/ (Companion to #3348)	S	80
4494	NOAH'S ARK / #20/ (Sarony del.) N. Currier [Old BEST 50]	S	290
4495	NOAH'S ARK/ N. Currier	S	210
4496	NOAH'S ARK/ (8.5x12.8) N. Currier	S	210
4497	NOAH'S ARK/ (8x12.8)	S	210
4498	NOAH'S ARK/ (8.7x12.8)	S	210
4499	NOBBY TANDEM, A	VS	110
4499A	NOBBY TANDEM, A/ 1879	TC	60
4500	NOISY PETS	S	115

4501	NOONTIDE / A SHADY SPOT	S	180
4502	NORTH AMERICAN INDIANS/ (17.9x13)	M	1300
4503	NORTH RIVER FERRY BOAT/ (Vig.)	S	395
4504	NORTH SEA WHALE FISHERY/ (8.12x12.12) N. Currier	S	1175
4505	NORTH SIDE VIEW ON THE NORTH CHINCHA ISLAND	S	195
4506	NORTHERN BEAUTY, THE/ (Vig.)	S	75
4507	NORTHERN SCENERY	VS	120
4508	NOSE OUT OF JOINT, THE/ N. Currier	S	95
4509	NOSE OUT OF JOINT, THE/ #310/ N. Currier	S	85
4510	NOSEGAY, THE/ #603/ (Vig.)	S	105
4511	NOSEGAY, THE/ #603/ N. Currier	S	105
4512	NOSEGAY, THE/ (Vig.) 1870	S	105
4513	NOT CAUGHT/ (13x20.12) N. Currier	M	270
4514	NOT CAUGHT YET/ (Fox Trap) (8x12.8) N. Currier	S	205
4515	NOTCH HOUSE, WHITE MOUNTAINS, N.H., THE	S	415
4516	NOTHING VENTURED / NOTHING HAVE	S	115
4517	NOTICE TO SMOKERS AND CHEWERS/ (Advertising card)	S	400
4518	NOTICE TO SMOKERS AND CHEWERS/ (Rebus) N. Currier	S	655
4519	NOVA SCOTIA SCENERY/ (9.11x16.12) 1868	M	520
4520	NOW AND THEN/ (2 views on one sheet) N. Currier	M	270
4521	NUESTRA SENORA DE GUADALUPE - OUR LADY OF GUADALUPE/ N. Currier	S	20

O

Con#	Title	Folio	Value
4522	O DAT WATERMILLION*/ (Vig.) 1882	S	255
4523	O! THERE'S A MOUSIE!	S	125
4524	OBDURATE MULE - GOING BACK ON THE PARSON/ (Vig.) 1890	S	215
4525	OBSERVATIONS ON THE CURE OF STRABISMUS/ N. Currier	VS	100
4526	OCCIDENT/ (16.6x25) 1876	L	1525
4527	OCCIDENT/ Record 2:16.75	S	290
4528	OCEAN STEAMER IN A HEAVY GALE, AN	S	395
4529	OCTOBER LANDSCAPE	M	545
4530	ODD FELLOW / Friendship, Love and Truth/ #572/ N. Currier	S	75
4531	ODD FELLOWS/ (Man, full length) N. Currier	S	75
4532	ODD FELLOWS/ #572/ N. Currier	S	75
4533	ODD FELLOWS CHART/ 1877	S	75

4534	ODD FELLOWS CHART/ (For Colored people)	S	75
4535	ODD TRICK, THE*/ (Companion to #4613) (Vig.) 1884	S	105
4536	OFF A LEE SHORE/ (8.8x13.8)	S	800
4537	OFF FOR THE WAR / #198/ 1861	S	125
4538	OFF FOR THE WAR/ 1861	S	125
4539	OFF FOR THE WAR - THE SOLDIER'S ADIEU/ (Companion to #2858) 1861	S	130
4540	OFF HIS NUT/ (Companion to #4597) (Vig.) 1886	S	290
4541	OFF ON FIRST SCORE/ (12.2x19) 1891	M	1025
4542	OFF ON FIRST SCORE/ (12.2x18.15) 1893	M	1025
4543	OFF THE COAST IN A SNOWSTORM / TAKING A PILOT/ (8.14x12.14)	S	830
4544	OFF THE PORT	S	855
4545	OH HOW FINE/ (8.9x12.10) N. Currier	S	100
4546	OH HOW NICE/ (8.9x12.9) N. Currier	S	100
4547	OH SWEETLY WE WILL SING LOVE/ N. Currier	S	85
4548	OLD BARN FLOOR, THE/ (15.14x23.14) 1868	L	2925
4549	OLD BLANFORD CHURCH, PETERSBURG, VA/ (F.F.P. on grave, for F.F. Palmer)	S	205
4550	OLD BRIDGE, THE	S	185
4551	OLD BULL DOG ON THE RIGHT TRACK, THE/ (Political Cartoon) (Vig.)	M	265
4552	OLD CASTLE, THE	S	100
4553	OLD CREDIT PLAYED OUT/ (Vig.) 1871	S	250
4554	OLD DARBY AND JOAN	S	125
4555	OLD FARM GATE, THE/ 1864	L	1450
4556	OLD FARM HOUSE / Williamsburg, L.I./ (Crayon Studies) N. Currier	S	305
4557	OLD FARM HOUSE, THE/ (Winter scene) 1872	S	1025
4558	OLD FEUDAL CASTLE	S	100
4559	OLD FORD BRIDGE, THE/ (8.8x12.9)	S	225
4560	OLD GENERAL READY FOR A MOVEMENT, THE/ (Vig.)	M	160
4561	OLD HOMESTEAD, THE/ (9.12x14.12) 1855, N. Currier	M	495
4562	OLD HOMESTEAD, THE/ (10.13x15.7)	M	495
4563	OLD HOMESTEAD IN WINTER, THE/ (18.10x26.8) 1864	L	6800
4564	OLD IRONSIDES	S	255
4565	OLD KENTUCKY HOME, DE/ 1883	S	220
4566	OLD LADY WHO LIVED IN A SHOE, THE	S	195
4567	OLD MANSE, THE/ (8.8x12.8)	S	190
4568	OLD MANSION HOUSE, GOWANUS ROAD/ (8.2x14.5) N. Currier	S	255
4569	OLD MARE THE BEST HORSE, THE/ (15.13x23.13) 1881	L	1100
4570	OLD MASSA'S GRAVE	S	85
4571	OLD MILL IN SUMMER, THE/ (8.7x12.8)	S	300

4572	OLD MILL-DAM AT SLEEPY HOLLOW/ (8.8x12.6)	S	370
4573	OLD NEPTUNE, THE GREAT BLACK SEA LION	S	180
4574	OLD NORMAN CASTLE, THE/ N. Currier	S	100
4575	OLD NORMAN CASTLE, THE/ N. Currier	L	175
4576	OLD OAKEN BUCKET/ (15.4x22.8) 1864	L	1575
4577	OLD OAKEN BUCKET/ (8.8x12.8) 1872	S	215
4578	OLD PLANTATION HOME, THE/ (8.7x12.8) 1872	S	600
4579	OLD RUINED CASTLE	S	95
4580	OLD RUINS, THE/ (8x12.8)	S	95
4581	OLD RUINS, THE/ (Vig.)	S	95
4582	OLD SAW-MILL, L.I./ (Vig.) N. Currier	S	335
4583	OLD SLEDGE/ (11.12x9)	S	275
4584	OLD STONE HOUSE, L.I./ (Vig.) N. Currier	S	295
4585	OLD SUIT AND THE NEW, THE/ 1879	S	190
4586	OLD SUIT AND THE NEW, THE/ 1880	TC	80
4587	OLD TENNANT PARSONAGE ON MONMOUTH BATTLEFIELD, THE/ (11.14x16.4) 1859, C. Currier	M	575
4588	OLD WAY, THE - THE NEW WAY/ "I Gave Credit - I Sell For Cash"/ (8.9x12.14) 1870	S	580
4589	OLD VIRGINNY	S	120
4590	OLD WEIR BRIDGE , THE LAKES OF KILLARNEY	M	205
4591	OLD WINDMILL, THE/ (10.8x14.15)	M	510
4592	ON A POINT/ (9.14x14.14) 1855, N. Currier	M	610
4593	ON A STRONG SCENT/ (Vig.) 1880	S	220
4594	ON BOARD THE GREAT WESTERN STEAMSHIP/ (Vig.) N. Currier	S	90
4595	ON DE HAF SHELL/ (Vig.) 1886	S	225
4596	1876 - ON GUARD/ 1876	S	145
4597	ON HIS STYLE/ (Companion to #4540) (Vig.) 1886	S	265
4598	ON THE COAST OF CALIFORNIA	S	365
4599	ON THE DOWNS, AT EPSOM	S	115
4600	ON THE HOME STRETCH/ (Companion to #2363) (Vig.) 1882	S	270
4601	ON THE HUDSON / (Shows steamer "St. John") 1869	S	290
4602	ON THE HUDSON/ 1869	S	295
4603	ON THE JUNIATA/ (9.11x16.15) 1869	M	395
4604	ON THE LAKE/ (8.6x12.7)	S	180
4605	ON THE MISSISSIPPI / (Broadside of steamer "Mayflower") (8x12.8) 1869	S	435
4606	ON THE MISSISSIPPI/ (8x12.8) 1869	S	435
4607	ON THE MISSISSIPPI LOADING COTTON/ (7.15x12.7) 1870 [Old & New BEST 50]	S	1200
4608	ON THE OWAGO	S	200

All prints are published by Currier & Ives unless otherwise stated.

4609	ON THE ST. LAWRENCE - INDIAN ENCAMPMENT	S	325
4610	ON THE SEINE	VS	85
4611	ONCONVANIENCE OF SINGLE LIFE, THE	S	185
4612	ONE FLAG - ONE COUNTRY - ZWEILAGER	S	205
4613	ONE FOR HIS NOB*/ (Companion to #4535) (Vig.) 1884	S	120
4614	ONE FOR HIS PET/ 1884	S	95
4615	ONE OF THE HEAVYWEIGHTS	S	95
4616	ONLY DAUGHTER, THE/ (10.1x7.12) N. Currier	S	85
4617	ONLY DAUGHTER, THE	S	85
4618	ONLY DAUGHTER, THE / PET OF THE FAMILY/ N. Currier	S	85
4619	ONLY LIVING GIRAFFES IN AMERICA/ N. Currier	S	95
4620	ONLY SON, THE/ N. Currier	S	85
4621	ONLY SON, THE	S	85
4622	OPERATIC QUADRILLES/ N. Currier	S	90
4623	ORANGEMENS CHART, O.B.L./ (10x13.11)	S	20
4624	OREGON/ (Steamship) (7.12x13.2) N. Currier	S	360
4625	ORIENTAL LANDSCAPE	L	495
4626	ORIGIN OF THE SPECIES/ (8x12.11) 1874	S	145
4627	ORIGINAL "GENERAL TOM THUMB", THE	S	130
4628	ORMONDE/ 1889	S	290
4629	ORNAMENTAL CARDS/ (16 on sheet)	S	315
4630	OSAGE WARRIOR	M	955
4631	OSCAR J. DUNN, LIEUT. GOV. OF LOUISIANA/ (11.13x8.7)	S	65
4632	OSTEND DOCTRINE, THE/ N. Currier	S	155
4633	O'SULLIVAN'S CASCADE, LAKE OF KILLARNEY/ (7.15x12.7)	S	105
4634	OTHELLO	M	495
4635	OULD TIMES" AT THE DONNYBROOK FAIR/ (Dance) (8.1x12.9)	S	110
4636	OUR BOAT SETS LIGHTLY ON THE WAVE/ N. Currier	S	120
4637	OUR CABINET/ 1885	L	250
4638	OUR FATHER WHO ART IN HEAVEN/ (Vig.)	S	20
4639	OUR FATHER WHO ART IN HEAVEN/ (Vig.) 1876	M	25
4640	OUR LADY OF GUADALUPE/ N. Currier	S	20
4641	OUR LADY OF KNOCK	S	20
4642	OUR LADY OF LOURDES	S	20
4643	OUR LADY OF MERCY/ (8.2x11.5)	S	20
4644	OUR LADY OF MT. CARMEL/ 1859, N. Currier	S	20
4645	OUR LADY OF MT. CARMEL	S	20
4646	OUR LADY OF REFUGE	S	20
4647	OUR LADY OF THE LIGHT	S	20

4648	OUR LADY OF THE ROSARY/ (11.15x8.15)	S	20
4649	OUR LADY OF THE SEVEN SORROWS	S	20
4650	OUR PASTURE/ (Sheep) N. Currier	S	170
4651	OUR PASTURE/ (Cows) (8.3x13.2) N. Currier	S	170
4652	OUR PETS / FAST ASLEEP/ (11.2x9.1)	S	85
4653	OUR PETS / WIDE AWAKE	S	85
4654	OUR REDEEMER/ (8.8x12.1)	S	20
4655	OUR SAVIOUR/ (8.4x11.12)	S	20
4656	OUR SAVIOUR AT PRAYER	S	20
4657	OUR SAVIOUR / EL SENOR/ N. Currier	S	20
4658	OUR VICTORIOUS FLEETS IN CUBAN WATERS/ (18x30.15) 1898	L	1150
4659	OUR VILLAGE HOME	VS	185
4660	OUT FOR A DAY'S SHOOTING / OFF FOR THE WOODS/ (17.14x26) 1869	L	3650
4661	OUTLET OF THE NIAGARA RIVER, THE/ (7.15x12.8)	S	280
4662	OUTLET OF THE NIAGARA RIVER, THE / LAKE ONTARIO	S	280
4663	OUTWARD BOUND/ #377/ (8x12.9) 1845, N. Currier	S	715
4664	OUTWARD BOUND/ #377/ (Similar to No. 2228) (Only one copy known) N. Currier	S	1525
4665	OUTWARD BOUND/ 1846, N. Currier	S	655
4666	OUTWARD BOUND	S	715
4667	OUTWARD BOUND / (Religious scene, boat)	S	20
4668	OVER THE GARDEN WALL	M	140
4669	OYSTER PADDY/ (Vig.) 1875	S	295
4670	OYSTER SUPPER, AN/ (8.2x12.12) N. Currier	S	280
4671	OYSTERS IN THE LATEST STYLE	S	335

P

Con#	Title	Folio	Value
4672	PACIFIC COAST STEAMSHIP CO.'S "STATE OF CALIFORNIA"/ 1878	L	2100
4673	PACIFIC MAIL STEAMSHIP COMPANY'S STEAMER "GREAT REPUBLIC" (7x13.12) (Vig.)	S	345
4674	PACING A FAST HEAT/ 1892	M	565
4675	PACING A FAST HEAT/ 1893	M	565
4676	PACING CHAMPIONS ON THEIR METTLE	S	290
4677	PACING FOR A GRAND PURSE/ (20x28.5) 1890	L	1500
4678	PACING FOR A GRAND PURSE	L	1500
4679	PACING HORSE "BILLY BOYCE" OF ST. LOUIS/ (16.14x26.8) 1868	L	1500

4680	PACING IN THE LATEST STYLE/ 1893	L	1475
4681	PACING KING "HAL POINTER" / Record 2:04.50/ (Vig.)	S	285
4682	PACING KING "ROBERT J." / Record 2:01.50/ (Vig.) 1894	S	285
4683	PACING KING "ROBERT J." / Record 2:01.50/ (18.5x27) 1894	L	1400
4684	PACING KING "ROBERT J." IN HIS RACE WITH "JOE PATCHEN"/ (Vig.) 1894	S	285
4685	PACING WONDER "LITTLE BROWN JUG"/ Record 2:11.75/ (Vig.) 1882	S	375
4686	PACING WONDER "SLEEPY TOM" THE BLIND HORSE /Record 2:12 1/4/ (Vig.)	S	295
4687	PACING WONDER "SLEEPY TOM" THE BLIND HORSE/ (Vig.)	S	295
4688	PADDLE WHEEL STEAMSHIP "MASSACHUSETTS", THE	L	1425
4689	PADDY AND THE PIGS	M	245
4690	PADDY MURPHY'S "JANTIN CAR"/ (7.14x12.10)	S	195
4691	PADDY RYAN / "The Trojan Giant"/ (15.14x12.3)	M	295
4692	PAGE, THE/ 1846, N. Currier	S	75
4693	PAIR OF NUTCRACKERS/ (Squirrels) (12x8.8)	S	205
4694	PAP, SOUP, AND CHOWDER/ (Political Cartoon) N. Currier	S	185
4695	PAPAL BENEDICTION, THE	S	20
4696	PAPA'S COMING/ (8.8x12) 1872	S	75
4697	PAPA'S DARLINGS/ (Vig.) 1877	S	70
4698	PAPA'S DARLINGS / #356/ (Vig.)	S	80
4699	PAPA'S NEW HAT/ (Vig.)	S	75
4700	PAPA'S PET/ (Vig.)	S	85
4701	PARLEY, A / Prepared For An Emergency/ (17.4x26.6)	L	4950
4702	PAROLE / BROWN GELDING BY IMP. LEAMINGTON/ (3 Adtl. lines) (Vig.) 1877	S	290
4703	PAROLE / BROWN GELDING BY IMP. LEAMINGTON/ (2 Adtl. lines) (Vig.) 1877	S	290
4704	PAROLE / BROWN GELDING BY IMP. LEAMINGTON/ 1879	L	1450
4705	PAROLE/ 1881	TC	85
4706	PARSON'S COLT, THE/ (Vig.) 1879	S	240
4707	PARSON'S COLT, THE/ 1880	L	1000
4708	PARSON'S COLT, THE/ 1880	TC	85
4709	PART OF THE BATTLE OF SHILOH	S	145
4710	PARTHENON OF ATHENS/ N. Currier	M	180
4711	PARTING, THE / OR THE SAILORS WIFE/ N. Currier	S	110
4712	PARTING HOUR, THE/ #673/ N. Currier	S	95
4713	PARTING HOUR, THE/ (Companion to #6653)	S	95
4714	PARTRIDGE SHOOTING/ (12.10x20.3) 1852, N. Currier	L	2250
4715	PARTRIDGE SHOOTING/ 1855, N. Currier	S	410
4716	PARTRIDGE SHOOTING/ N. Currier	S	395

4717	PARTRIDGE SHOOTING/ 1865, N. Currier	L	2050
4718	PARTRIDGE SHOOTING/ 1870	S	400
4719	PARTRIDGE SHOOTING/ (8.7x12.7)	S	400
4720	PAST AND THE FUTURE, THE/ (Oval)	L	320
4721	PASTURE IN SUMMER, THE / THE DRINKING TROUGH/ (16.11x24.15) 1867	L	1100
4722	PASTURE / NOONTIDE	M	325
4723	PATH THROUGH THE FIELDS, THE/ (8.8x12.8)	S	170
4724	PATH THROUGH THE WOODS, THE	S	170
4725	PATRIOT OF 1776, A/ "Defending His Homestead"/ (8.14x12.7) 1876	S	205
4726	PATTERN IN CONNEMARA, A/ (Dance)	S	85
4727	PAUL AND VIRGINIA/ "Lost in the Woods"	S	125
4728	PAUL AND VIRGINIA'S DEPARTURE FOR FRANCE/ (11.13x8.6) N. Currier	S	95
4729	PAULINE/ N. Currier	S	80
4730	PAULINE / Forget Me Not/ N. Currier	S	80
4731	PAWLE/ 1881	S	80
4732	PEACE/ (8.10x12.13)	S	140
4733	PEACE AND PLENTY/ (9.15x16.13) 1871	M	400
4734	PEACE BE TO THIS HOUSE/ (Motto) (Vig.) 1872	S	210
4735	PEACEFUL LAKE, THE	S	160
4736	PEACEFUL RIVER, THE	S	160
4737	PEACHES AND GRAPES / FIRST PRIZE/ (Vig.) 1870	S	155
4738	PEEK-A-BOO/ (11.12x8.8)	S	110
4739	PEERLESS BEAUTY, THE	S	70
4740	PEERLESS GOLDSMITH MAID DRIVEN BY BUDD DOBLE, THE/ "Queen of the Turf"	S	290
4741	PEERLESS GOLDSMITH MAID DRIVEN BY BUDD DOBLE, THE/ "Queen of the Trotters"	S	290
4742	PELHAM/ 1850, N. Currier	L	1550
4743	PENITENT MULE, A / "The Parson On Deck"/ (Vig.) 1890	S	225
4744	PENNSYLVANIA HALL, BRISTOL COLLEGE/ N. Currier	M	290
4745	PENSYLVANIA (Sic.) RAILROAD SCENERY/ (8.8x12.7)	S	760
4746	PEOPLE IN THE TUILERIES, THE/ (8.1x12.9) N. Currier	S	85
4747	PEOPLE'S EVENING LINE/ 1881	TC	95
4748	PEOPLES LINE, HUDSON RIVER	L	1275
4749	PERCHERON STALLION DUE DE CHARTRES IMPORTED BY A. ROGY	L	1250
4750	PERFECT BLISS/ (Vig.) 1879	M	200
4751	PERFECT BLISS/ 1880	S	135
4752	PERFECT BLISS/ (4.7x7.3) 1880	TC	80
4753	PERMANENT FAIR GROUNDS OF THE QUEENS COUNTY AGRICULTURAL SOCIETY, MINEOLA, L.I./ 1867, C. Currier	L	1275

All prints are published by Currier & Ives unless otherwise stated.

4754	PERRY'S VICTORY ON LAKE ERIE/ N. Currier [Old BEST 50]	S	625
4755	PERSIAN BEAUTY	S	75
4756	PET OF THE FAMILY, THE	S	75
4757	PET OF THE FAMILY, THE / ON CHRISTMAS MORNING/ (Vig.)	S	155
4758	PET OF THE FANCY, THE/ (Comic) 1879	S	195
4759	PET OF THE FANCY, THE	S	125
4760	PET OF THE FANCY, THE/ 1880	TC	75
4761	PET OF THE LADIES, THE	S	120
4762	PETS IN SPRINGTIME/ (8x12.7)	S	120
4763	PEYTONA" AND "FASHION"/ (17.13x28.10) N. Currier [Old BEST 50]	L	12600
4764	PHALLAS / RECORD 2:13.5	S	290
4765	PHALLAS / DRIVEN BY E.D. BLITHERS - RECORD 2:15.5	L	1150
4766	PHALLAS / Record 2:13.75/ 1882	TC	85
4767	PHEBE/ (11.13x8.3) 1846, N. Currier	S	85
4768	PHEBE / #393/ 1846, N. Currier	S	85
4769	PHENOMENAL TROTTING GELDING JAY EYE SEE BY DICTATOR	L	1175
4770	PHILOSOPHER IN ECSTASY, A/ (Vig.) 1872	S	150
4771	PHILOSOPHY OF TOBACCO, THE	S	190
4772	PHOEBE/ (11.14x8.4) 1846, N. Currier	S	80
4773	PHOTOGRAPH MARRIAGE CERTIFICATE	S	80
4774	PIC-NIC PARTY, THE	M	260
4775	PIC-NIC PARTY, THE/ 1858	L	620
4776	PICADOR/ 1883	M	315
4777	PICKEREL/ (8.7x12.8) 1872	S	205
4778	PICTURESQUE LANDSCAPES/ (6 small views)	S	370
4779	PIEDMONT/ 1882	S	290
4780	PIGEON SHOOTING - PLAYING THE DECOY/ (19x27.10) 1862	L	2975
4781	PILGRIM'S PROGRESS, THE/ N. Currier	S	55
4782	PILOT BOAT IN A STORM	S	460
4783	PILOT BOAT IN A STORM/ (7.14x12.6)	S	460
4784	PINCH TAKEN, THE/ (Companion to #5945) N. Currier	S	105
4785	PIONEER CABIN OF THE YO-SE-MITE VALLEY/ (8.8x12.8)	S	500
4786	PIONEER'S HOME, THE / ON THE WESTERN FRONTIER/ (18.12x26.14) 1867	L	2375
4787	PLACID LAKE, ADIRONDACKS/ (Cottage & carriage in foreground)	S	260
4788	PLACID LAKE, ADIRONDACKS	S	260
4789	PLAN OF GILBERT'S BALANCE FLOATING DRY DOCK/ (20x30.11) N. Currier	L	840
4790	PLAN OF NEW HAVEN CONNECTICUT/ C. Currier	L	920
4791	PLAN OF THE SCHOOL HOUSE/ (Vig.) N. Currier	S	190

4792	PLAN OF THE CITY OF NEW YORK/ (Bradford Map) 1849, N. Currier	L	980
4793	PLATNER & SMITH/ N. Currier	S	145
4794	PLAYED OUT/ (Horse) (Vig.) 1871	S	305
4795	PLAYFUL	M	185
4796	PLAYFUL FAMILY, THE/ N. Currier	S	130
4797	PLAYFUL FAMILY, THE	S	130
4798	PLAYFUL PETS, THE/ N. Currier	S	130
4799	PLAYFUL PETS, THE	S	130
4800	PLAYING DOMINOS	S	135
4801	PLAYMATES, THE/ N. Currier	S	130
4802	PLAYMATES, THE	S	130
4803	PLAYMATES, THE/ (12x8.10)	S	130
4804	PLEASE GIVE ME A LIGHT, SIR/ 1879	S	200
4805	PLEASE GIVE ME A LIGHT, SIR/ 1880	TC	70
4806	PLEASURE	S	185
4807	PLEASURE /A FREEMONTER BEFORE THE ELECTION/ N. Currier	S	185
4808	PLEASURES OF THE COUNTRY / SWEET HOME	M	330
4809	PLEASURES OF THE COUNTRY / WINTER	S	1150
4810	PLUCK-ONE OF THE RIGHT SORT/ (10.13x15) N. Currier	M	200
4811	PO-CAN-TECO FROM IRVING PARK, THE/ (5.7x7.7) (Oval)	VS	185
4812	POCAHONTAS BOY/ Record 2:31	L	1400
4813	POCAHONTAS SAVING THE LIFE OF CAPTAIN JOHN SMITH/ N. Currier	S	250
4814	POINT OF THE JOKE, THE/ (Companion to #758) 1879	S	195
4815	POINTER, THE/ (12.13x9) 1848, N. Currier	S	225
4816	POINTERS/ (8.7x12.14) 1846, N. Currier	S	255
4817	POINTING A BEVY/ (24.13x19.10) 1866	L	1500
4818	POLISHED OFF/ (Companion to #2399) (Vig.) 1888	S	235
4819	POLITICAL ARENA, THE	S	200
4820	POLITICAL "BLONDINS" CROSSING SALT RIVER/ 1860	M	320
4821	POLITICAL DEBATE IN THE DARKTOWN CLUB / Settling the Question/ (Vig.) 1884	S	225
4822	POLITICAL DEBATE IN THE DARKTOWN CLUB / The Question Settled/ (Vig.) 1884	S	225
4823	POLITICAL GYMNASIUM, THE	M	300
4824	POLITICAL SIAMESE TWINS, THE	M	210
4825	POLKA, THE, No. 1/ N. Currier	S	85
4826	POLKA, THE, No. 2/ N. Currier	S	85
4827	POLKA, THE, No. 3/ N. Currier	S	85
4828	POLKA, THE, No. 4/ N. Currier	S	85

4829	POLLY AND KITTY / ROSES HAVE THORNS/ (Companion to #3359)	M	225
4830	POMONA'S TREASURES	S	75
4831	POMPON ROSE, THE/ N. Currier	VS	110
4832	POND IN THE WOODS, THE	M	340
4833	PONTO/ (Boy and Dog)	S	105
4834	PONY TEAM, THE/ (7.15x12.10)	S	140
4835	PONY WAGON, THE	S	135
4836	POOL, THE/ (4 Scenes) (Vig.)	S	320
4837	POOL OF SILOAM, THE/ (8.6x12.5) N. Currier	S	20
4838	POOR DOLLY	S	75
4839	POOR TRUST IS DEAD / Bad Pay Killed Him/ (12.14x9) 1868	S	275
4840	POPE LEO XIII/ (11.15x8.6) (Vig.) 1878	S	20
4841	POPE PIUS IX, A.D./ N. Currier	S	20
4842	POPE PIUS IX, A.D./ (Vig.) N. Currier	S	20
4843	POPE PIUS IX / #243/ (Vig.) N. Currier	S	20
4844	POPE PIUS IX / BESTOWING THE PAPAL BENEDICTION	S	20
4845	POPE PIUS IXth / LYING IN STATE	S	20
4846	POPPING THE QUESTION/ 1847, N. Currier	S	95
4847	PORT OF NEW YORK, THE/ (20.6x32.15) 1872	L	3000
4848	PORT OF NEW YORK, THE/ (20.10x33.4) 1878	L	3000
4849	PORT OF NEW YORK, THE/ 1892	L	2875
4850	PORTRAIT OF A GIRL/ 1846, N. Currier	S	75
4851	PORTUGUESE MARINER'S SONG, THE/ N. Currier	S	85
4852	POSITIVE PROCESS, FROM A NEGATIVE RESULT/ (Companion to #1369) (Vig.) 1890	S	240
4853	POST OFFICE, NEW YORK, THE/ (8.4x12.8) N. Currier	S	480
4854	POT LUCK/ (11.12x8.13) N. Currier	S	85
4855	POULTRY SHOW ON THE BUST/ (Vig.) 1883	S	225
4856	POULTRY SHOW ON THE ROAD/ (Vig.) 1883	S	225
4857	POULTRY YARD, THE/ 1870	M	275
4858	POWER OF MUSIC, THE/ (Companion to #1030) N. Currier	S	165
4859	PRAIRIE FIRES OF THE GREAT WEST/ (8.7x12.8) 1871 [New BEST 50]	S	1150
4860	PRAIRIE HENS/ (8.9x12.7)	S	365
4861	PRAIRIE HUNTER, THE/ 1852, N. Currier	L	2875
4862	PRAIRIE ON FIRE/ (8x11.4) N. Currier	S	365
4863	PRAIRIE WOLVES ATTACKING A BUFFALO BULL	M	1350
4864	PRAISE THE LORD / O MY SOUL/ (Vig.)	S	40
4865	PRAY "GOD BLESS PAPA AND MAMA"/ N. Currier	S	50
4866	PRAY "GOD BLESS PAPA AND MAMA"	S	50

4867	PREMIUM FRUIT/ (Vig.) 1875	S	160
4868	PREMIUM POULTRY	S	155
4869	PREPARING FOR CONGRESS/ 1863	S	155
4870	PREPARING FOR MARKET/ (Child in doorway, no toy.) (18.16x27.4) 1856, N. Currier [Old & New BEST 50]	L	3425
4871	PREPARING FOR MARKET/ (18.16x27.4) 1856, N. Currier	L	3425
4872	PREPARING FOR MARKET/ (18.16x27.4) 1856, N. Currier	L	3425
4873	PRESIDENT CLEVELAND AND HIS CABINET/ (Vig.) 1884	S	215
4874	PRESIDENT CLEVELAND AND HIS CABINET/ (Vig.) 1884	L	285
4875	PRESIDENT CLEVELAND AND HIS CABINET/ (Vig.) 1893	L	285
4876	PRESIDENT HARRISON AND HIS CABINET/ (Vig.) 1889	S	210
4877	PRESIDENT HARRISON AND HIS CABINET/ (Vig.) 1889	L	270
4878	PRESIDENT HAYES AND CABINET/ (9x12.11) 1877	S	210
4879	PRESIDENT LINCOLN AND HIS CABINET/ (Vig.) 1876	S	260
4880	PRESIDENT LINCOLN AND SECRETARY SEWARD/ (12.2x9.12) (Oval) 1865	S	265
4881	PRESIDENT LINCOLN AT GENERAL GRANT'S HEADQUARTERS/ 1865	M	350
4882	PRESIDENT LINCOLN AT HOME/ (Reading Scriptures to Wife and Son) (Oval)	S	120
4883	PRESIDENT LINCOLN AT HOME/ (Reading Scriptures to Wife and Son)	S	120
4884	PRESIDENTIAL FISHING PARTY OF 1848, THE/ N. Currier	S	180
4885	PRESIDENTIAL RECEPTION IN 1789 BY GEN. WASHINGTON AND MRS. WASHINGTON/ (18.13x12.4) 1876	S	235
4886	PRESIDENTS OF THE UNITED STATES, THE / (Washington to Harrison) 1842, N. Currier	S	155
4887	PRESIDENTS OF THE UNITED STATES, THE / (Group of Presidents from Washington to Tyler) 1842, N. Currier	S	155
4888	PRESIDENTS OF THE UNITED STATES, THE / (Washington to Tyler) 1842, N. Currier	S	155
4889	PRESIDENTS OF THE UNITED STATES, THE / (Washington to Polk) 1844, N. Currier	S	155
4890	PRESIDENTS OF THE UNITED STATES, THE / (Washington in center, Q.J. Adams on right) 1844, N. Currier	S	155
4891	PRESIDENTS OF THE UNITED STATES, THE / (Washington in center, Monroe on left) 1844, N. Currier	S	155
4892	PRESIDENTS OF THE UNITED STATES, THE / (Similar to preceding, but reversed) 1844, N. Currier	S	155
4893	PRESIDENTS OF THE UNITED STATES, THE / (Slight change in composition) 1844, N. Currier	S	155
4894	PRESIDENTS OF THE UNITED STATES, THE / (Upright) 1845, N. Currier	S	155
4895	PRESIDENTS OF THE UNITED STATES, THE / (Upright) 1846, N. Currier	S	155
4896	PRESIDENTS OF THE UNITED STATES, THE / (11 Portraits) 1847, N. Currier	S	155
4897	PRESIDENTS OF THE UNITED STATES, THE / #854/ 1848, N. Currier	S	155

4898	PRESIDENTS OF THE UNITED STATES, THE / 1789 TO 1850/ 1848, N. Currier	S	155
4899	PRESIDENTS OF THE UNITED STATES, THE / Zachary Taylor/ 1848, N. Currier	S	155
4900	PRESIDENTS OF THE UNITED STATES, THE / 1789 TO 1850/ 1850, N. Currier	S	155
4901	PRESIDENTS OF THE UNITED STATES, THE/ (Washington to Polk) N. Currier	S	155
4902	PRESIDENTS OF THE UNITED STATES, THE/ (Washington to Tyler/ N. Currier	S	155
4903	PRESIDENTS, THE/ OF THE UNITED STATES 1789 TO 1861	S	155
4904	PRESIDENTS, THE/ OF THE UNITED STATES 1789 TO 1869	S	155
4905	PRESS GANG, THE/ (Vig.) N. Currier	S	75
4906	PRETTY AMERICAN, THE/ (Vig.)	S	75
4907	PRETTY DOLLY/ (Vig.) 1873	S	85
4908	PRETTY POLL/ N. Currier	S	95
4909	PRETTY STORY, THE/ (7x5.1)	S	80
4910	PRIDE OF AMERICA, THE/ N. Currier	S	200
4911	PRIDE OF AMERICA, THE/ (11.14x8.10)	S	185
4912	PRIDE OF KENTUCKY/ (Vig.)	S	80
4913	PRIDE OF KILDARE, THE/ (Vig.)	S	70
4914	PRIDE OF THE GARDEN/ (Vig.) 1873	S	130
4915	PRIDE OF THE SOUTH, THE/ (Vig.) 1870	S	75
4916	PRIDE OF THE WEST, THE/ (Girl on horse) N. Currier	S	75
4917	PRIDE OF THE WEST, THE/ (Girl on horse) (11.10x8.8) 1847	S	75
4918	PRIDE OF THE WEST, THE/ (Vig.) 1870	S	75
4919	PRIMARY DRAWING STUDIES/ (8 Views)	S	310
4920	PRIME TOBACCO/ (Vig.) 1875	S	205
4921	PRINCE ALBERT/ 1848, N. Currier	S	65
4922	PRINCE ALBERT/ N. Currier	S	65
4923	PRINCE ALBERT /#11/ N. Currier	S	65
4924	PRINCE ALBERT/ (10.1x7.15) N. Currier	S	65
4925	PRINCE" AND "LANTERN"/ (16.10x25.14) 1857, N. Currier	L	1550
4926	PRINCE AND PRINCESS OF WALES (11.13x8.10)	S	70
4927	PRINCE OF THE BLOOD/ (Head of Horse) 1893	L	400
4928	PRINCE OF WALES AND FAMILY/ (8.3x12.4)	S	70
4929	PRINCE OF WALES, THE	S	65
4930	PRINCE OF WALES AND FAMILY/ (10.14x8.8)	S	70
4931	PRINCE OF WALES AT THE TOMB OF WASHINGTON	S	70
4932	PRINCE WILKES RECORD 2:14 3/4/ (Horse)	S	290
4933	PRINCESS ROYAL OF ENGLAND	S	65

4934	PRIZE BLACK HAMBURG GRAPES/ (17.13x14.12)	M	225
4935	PRIZE BOY, THE	L	235
4936	PRIZE BOY, THE/ (25.8x18.11)	L	265
4937	PRIZE FAT CATTLE/ (Vig.)	S	195
4938	PRIZE FIGHTER, THE/ (Oval)	M	270
4939	PRIZE GRAPES / A FOUR POUND BUNCH/ 1865	M	270
4940	PRIZE HERD, A	L	570
4941	PRIZE JERSEY LITCHFIELD BULL	S	185
4942	PRIZE JERSEY "NIOBE"/ (Cattle)	S	185
4943	PRIZE SETTER, A	S	250
4944	PRIZE TROTTER, A/ (Vig.) 1873	S	290
4945	PRIZE TROTTER, A / CLEAR THE TRACK!	S	290
4946	PROCTOR KNOTT/ (Vig.) 1888	S	290
4947	PRODIGAL SON IN MISERY, THE/ (11.13x8.8) N. Currier	S	140
4948	PRODIGAL SON RECEIVING HIS PATRIMONY/ N. Currier	S	140
4949	PRODIGAL SON RETURNS TO HIS FATHER/ N. Currier	S	140
4950	PRODIGAL SON WASTING HIS SUBSTANCE/ (11.11x8.7) N. Currier	S	140
4951	PROFIT AND LOSS/ (Vig.) 1880	S	285
4952	PROGRESS OF INTEMPERANCE	S	245
4953	PROGRESS OF INTEMPERANCE/ PLATE 1/ "The Invitation to Drink"/ (12.11x9.13) 1841, N. Currier	S	105
4954	PROGRESS OF INTEMPERANCE/ PLATE 2/ "Sick and Repentant"/ (12.12x9.13) 1841, N. Currier	S	105
4955	PROGRESS OF INTEMPERANCE/ PLATE 3/ "The Relapse"/ (12.12x9.15) 1841, N. Currier	S	105
4956	PROGRESS OF INTEMPERANCE/ PLATE 4/ "The Ruined Family"/ (12.12x9.13) 1841, N. Currier	S	105
4957	PROGRESS OF INTEMPERANCE/ PLATE 5/ "The Expectant Wife"/ (12.12x9.14) 1841, N. Currier	S	105
4958	PROGRESS OF INTEMPERANCE/ PLATE 6/ "The Robber"/ (12.12x9.13) 1841, N. Currier	S	105
4959	PROGRESS OF THE CENTURY, THE/ (8.14x12.6) 1876	S	685
4960	PROGRESSIVE DEMOCRACY - PROSPECT OF A SMASH UP/ (Political Cartoon) (Vig.)	M	280
4961	PROMISING FAMILY, A/ "Black and Tan"/ (8.4x12.5) 1868	S	150
4962	PROPAGATION SOCIETY / MORE FREEDOM THAN WELCOME/ 1853, N. Currier	VS	170
4963	PROPOSAL, THE/ N. Currier	S	90
4964	PROTECTED STEEL CRUISER PHILADELPHIA U.S. NAVY	M	365
4965	PROTEINE/ Record 2:18/ (Vig.) 1878	S	290
4966	PROVIDENCE AND STONINGTON STEAMER CO.'s STEAMER "RHODE ISLAND"	S	380

4967	PROVIDENCE AND STONINGTON STEAMER CO.'s STEAMER "RHODE ISLAND"	L	1400
4968	PROVIDENCE AND STONINGTON STEAMER "MASSACHUSETS"	L	1400
4969	PROVIDENCE AND STONINGTON STEAMSHIP CO.'S STEAMERS	L	1400
4970	PROVISIONS DOWN/ (11.7x8.6) N. Currier	S	630
4971	PUPPIES NURSERY, THE (12.8x8.7)	S	150
4972	PUPPY/ N. Currier	S	120
4973	PURITAN" AND "GENESTA" ON THE HOME STRETCH/ (16.13x24.2)	L	1650
4974	PURSUIT, THE/ (18x25.10) 1856, N. Currier	L	2800
4975	PURSUIT, THE/ (Elopement) (Companion to #1716) (8.5x12.11) N. Currier	S	105
4976	PURSUIT OF THE MEXICANS BY THE U.S. DRAGOONS/ 1847, N. Currier	S	115
4977	PUSS IN BOOTS (12.10x10)	S	150
4978	PUSSY'S RETURN	S	125
4979	PUT UP JOB, A/ (Vig.) (Companion to #1820) 1883	S	285
4980	PUTTING ON HIS AIRS/ (Companion to #5960)	S	155
4981	PUZZLE FOR A WINTER'S EVENING, A/ (10.3x13.15)	S	325
4982	PUZZLE FOR A WINTER'S EVENING, A/ N. Currier	S	325
4983	PUZZLE PICTURE - OLD SWISS MILL/ (8.7x12.8) 1872	S	325
4984	PUZZLED FOX, THE/ 1872	S	325
4985	PUZZLED FOX, THE / FIND THE HORSE LAMB	S	325

Q

Con#	Title	Folio	Value
4986	QUADRILLES / FROM AUBER'S CELEBRATED OPERA/ (Vig.)	S	75
4987	QUADRILLES / FROM AUBER'S CELEBRATED OPERA	S	75
4988	QUAIL OR VIRGINIA PARTRIDGE/ (8.8x12.7) 1871	S	320
4989	QUAIL SHOOTING/ (13x20.6) 1852, N. Currier	L	2825
4990	QUAIL SHOOTING/ (8.7x12.7)	S	445
4991	QUAILS / (No trees) N. Currier	S	320
4992	QUAILS/ N. Currier	S	320
4993	QUARREL, THE/ N. Currier	S	85
4994	QUEEN OF ANGELS/ N. Currier	S	20
4995	QUEEN OF ANGELS, THE	S	25
4996	QUEEN OF BEAUTY / #108/ N. Currier	S	75
4997	QUEEN OF BEAUTY, THE/ (Vig.)	S	75
4998	QUEEN OF BEAUTY, THE / #108	S	75

4999	QUEEN OF CATTLE/ 1876	M	280
5000	QUEEN OF CATTLE, THE / THE CHAMPION STEER	L	510
5001	QUEEN OF HEARTS/ (Vig.) 1857	L	225
5002	QUEEN OF LOVE, THE/ (Vig.)	S	75
5003	QUEEN OF LOVE AND BEAUTY/ (Vig.) 1870	S	75
5004	QUEEN OF LOVE AND BEAUTY/ (Vig.)	S	75
5005	QUEEN OF THE AMAZONS ATTACKED BY A LION/ N. Currier	S	65
5006	QUEEN OF THE ANGELS, THE/ N. Currier	S	60
5007	QUEEN OF THE BALL, THE/ (Vig.) 1870	S	70
5008	QUEEN OF THE BLONDES	S	75
5009	QUEEN OF THE BRUNETTES/ 1873	S	75
5010	QUEEN OF THE FLOWERS	S	80
5011	QUEEN OF THE GARDEN/ 1873	S	130
5012	QUEEN OF THE HOUSE/ (9.6x11.10) (Companion to #3335) 1875	S	75
5013	QUEEN OF THE SOUTH/ (Portrait) (Vig.)	S	75
5014	QUEEN OF THE SOUTH/ (Vig.)	S	75
5015	QUEEN OF THE TURF "LADY THORN"	S	290
5016	QUEEN OF THE TURF, "MAUD S."/ Record 2:10/ (18.4x28) 1880	L	1475
5017	QUEEN OF THE WEST, THE/ (Girl)	S	75
5018	QUEEN OF THE WOODS/ N. Currier	M	90
5019	QUEEN OF THE WOODS, THE/ (Vig.)	M	90
5020	QUEEN VICTORIA/ (10x7.12) C. Currier	S	70
5021	QUEEN VICTORIA / #12/ N. Currier	S	70
5022	QUEEN VICTORIA / #12/ 1848, N. Currier	S	70
5023	QUEEN VICTORIA / #12/ (Vig.) N. Currier	S	70
5024	QUEEN VICTORIA/ (8.8x12) N. Currier	S	70
5025	QUEEN VICTORIA	S	70
5026	QUEEN VICTORIA/ (Vig.)	S	70
5027	QUEEN VICTORIA'S COURT QUADRILLES/ N. Currier	S	70
5028	QUEEN'S OWN, THE/ (11x15.13) 1875	M	235
5029	QUEEN'S OWN, THE/ 1880	TC	75
5030	QUEENSTOWN HARBOR	M	150
5031	QUEENSTOWN HARBOR, COVE OF CORK, IRELAND	S	95
5032	QUESTION SETTLED, THE	S	160

R

Con#	Title	Folio	Value
5033	RAAL CONVANIENCE, A/ (Companion to #4151)	S	185
5034	RABBIT CATCHING / THE TRAP SPRING/ (7.15x12.8)	S	645
5035	RABBIT HUNT, THE / ALL BUT CAUGHT/ (8.6x12.6) 1849, N. Currier	S	325
5036	RABBITS IN THE WOODS/ (8.8x12.8)	S	260
5037	RACE FOR THE AMERICAN DERBY/ (Vig.) 1878	S	290
5038	RACE FOR BLOOD, A/ (19.14x28.6) 1890	L	1600
5039	RACE FOR BLOOD, A/ (19.14x28.6) 1894	L	1550
5040	RACE FOR THE QUEEN'S CUP, THE/ (8.8x12.8)	S	455
5041	RACE FROM THE WORD "GO"/ 1891	L	1575
5042	RACE ON THE MISSISSIPPI, A/ (The "Eagle" and "Diana") (7.14x12.8) 1870	S	680
5043	RACE TO THE WIRE/ 1891	L	1200
5044	RACHEL/ (11.12x8.5) N. Currier	S	80
5045	RACING CHAMPIONS ON THEIR METTLE/ 1889	L	1450
5046	RACING CRACKS AT THE STARTING POST/ 1886	L	1450
5047	RACING KING SALVATOR, MILE RECORD 1:35 1/2	S	290
5048	RACING KING SALVATOR, MILE RECORD 1:35 1/2	L	1175
5049	RACQUET RIVER / "ADIRONDACKS"	S	310
5050	RADICAL PARTY ON A HEAVY GRADE, THE/ (Vig.)	M	185
5051	RAFTING ON THE ST. LAWRENCE/ (9.15x15.7)	M	470
5052	RAIL CANDIDATE, THE	M	215
5053	RAIL SHOOTING/ (8.5x12.12)	S	745
5054	RAIL SHOOTING ON THE DELAWARE/ (12.14x20.2) 1852, N. Currier [Old BEST 50]	L	4850
5055	RAIL SPLITTER AT WORK REPAIRING THE UNION	S	190
5056	RAILROAD SUSPENSION BRIDGE NEAR NIAGARA FALLS, THE/ (10.4x15.7) 1856, N. Currier	M	480
5057	RALLY ROUND THE FLAG	S	205
5058	RAPIDS OF DUNASS ON THE SHANNON (8.8x12.10)	S	95
5059	RARUS/ BY CONKLIN'S ABDALLAH/ (Vig.) 1876	S	290
5060	RARUS/ BY CONKLIN'S ABDALLAH/ (Vig.) 1877	S	290
5061	RARUS/ BY CONKLIN'S ABDALLAH/ 1877	S	290
5062	RARUS/ Record 2:13.25/ 1881	TC	85
5063	RARUS" AND "GREAT EASTERN"/ (Vig.) 1877	S	290
5064	RASPBERRIES/ 1863	S	155
5065	RASPBERRIES/ 1870	S	155
5066	RASPBERRIES	S	155
5067	RATHGALLAN HEAD (12.14x8.9)	S	80
5068	RATTLING HEAT, A/ 1891	M	645
5069	RATTLING HEAT, A/ 1893	M	545

5070	RAVENSWOOD, L.I./ (11.4x50) N. Currier	L	1575
5071	R.B. CONKLIN'S BAY GELDING "RARUS", THE "KING OF THE TROTTERS"/ (16.11x26.1) 1878	L	1450
5072	R. CORNELL WHITE'S NEW PALATIAL EXCURSION STEAMER "COLUMBIA"/ 1877	L	1725
5073	READING THE BIBLE/ 1848, N. Currier	S	20
5074	READING THE BIBLE/ N. Currier	S	20
5075	READING THE SCRIPTURES/ N. Currier	S	20
5076	READING THE SCRIPTURES / "Search the scriptures,"/ N. Currier	S	20
5077	READING THE SCRIPTURES/ 1871	S	20
5078	READY FOR BATTLE/ (Deer) (8.6x12.6)	S	190
5079	READY FOR A FROLIC/ (11.10x8.12) 1874	S	140
5080	READY FOR AN OFFER/ (11.12x9.6)	S	85
5081	READY FOR THE RACE/ 1891	L	1475
5082	READY FOR THE SIGNAL / THE CELEBRATED RUNNING HORSE HARRY BASSETT/ (17x25.13) 1872	L	1500
5083	READY FOR THE START	S	290
5084	READY FOR THE TROT / BRING UP YOUR HORSES/ (18x27) 1877	L	1575
5085	READY FOR THE TROT / BRING UP YOUR HORSES/ (17.14x26.14) 1877	L	1575
5086	REBECCA/ (3/4 length) 1846, N. Currier	S	80
5087	REBECCA/ (Full length) 1846, N. Currier	S	80
5088	REBECCA/ (11.11x8.4) 1846, N. Currier	S	80
5089	RECHABITE/ (12.6x8.14) 1849, N. Currier	S	80
5090	RECONCILIATION, THE/ (Vig.) N. Currier	S	85
5091	RE-CONSTRUCTION/ (Vig.) N. Currier	S	180
5092	RECORD OF BIRTH AND BAPTISM	S	50
5093	RED CLOUD / BY LEGAL TENDER	L	1350
5094	RED CLOUD / BY LEGAL TENDER/ (Vig.)	S	290
5095	RED HOT REPUBLICANS ON THE DEMOCRATIC GRIDIRON/ (Political Cartoon) (Vig.)	S	185
5096	REDEEMER/ N. Currier	S	20
5097	REDEEMER, THE	S	20
5098	REDEMPTION / REPUDIATION/ (2 views) 1875	S	200
5099	REDPATH/ 1882	S	290
5100	REDPATH/ (Vig.) 1875	S	290
5101	REDPATH/ 1885	S	290
5102	REFRESHING FOUNTAIN, A/ 1879	S	145
5103	REGATTA OF THE NEW YORK YACHT CLUB / "Coming In"/ 1854, N. Currier	L	2650
5104	REGATTA OF THE NEW YORK YACHT CLUB / "Rounding the S.W. Spit"/ (17.13x28) 1854, N. Currier	L	2650

5105	REGATTA OF THE NEW YORK YACHT CLUB / "The Start"/ (17.13x28) 1854, N. Currier	L	2650
5106	REGISTER FOR COLORED PEOPLE, A	S	135
5107	REGULAR HUMMER/ (Vig.) 1879	S	285
5108	REGULAR HUMMER/ 1880	TC	80
5109	REINDEER POLKA/ C. Currier	S	95
5110	REJECTED, THE	S	75
5111	REMEMBER THE SABBATH DAY TO KEEP IT HOLY/ N. Currier	S	30
5112	REMEMBER THE SABBATH DAY TO KEEP IT HOLY	M	60
5113	RENOWNED TROTTER "PRINCE WILKES," RECORD 2:14 3/4	L	1400
5113A	REPUBLICAN BANNER FOR 1860/ (12x8.10)	S	335
5114	REPUBLICAN PARTY GOING TO THE RIGHT HOUSE, THE	M	310
5115	RESCUE, THE/ (8.14x12.7) 1876	S	305
5116	RESCUED/ (Dog and Children)	S	100
5117	RESCUED/ (Dog and Boy)	S	95
5118	RESIDENCE OF LORD BYRON, THE/ N. Currier	S	90
5119	RESIGNATION/ (11.11x8.13) 1847, N. Currier	S	65
5120	RESULT IN DOUBT, THE/ (Vig.) (Companion to #1808) 1884	S	225
5121	RESULT IN DOUBT, THE/ (Vig.) 1884	M	280
5122	RESURRECTION, THE/ N. Currier	M	25
5123	RESURRECTION, THE	S	20
5124	RESURRECTION OF CHRIST, THE/ (12.1x8.11) N. Currier	S	20
5125	RETURN, THE/ (10.13x8.10) (Oval) (Companion to #1875)	S	85
5126	RETURN FROM EGYPT, THE/ N. Currier	S	25
5127	RETURN FROM ELBA/ (Napoleon) N. Currier	L	165
5128	RETURN FROM THE PASTURE, THE	L	860
5129	RETURN FROM THE PASTURE, THE / (Cottage has thatched roof)	L	860
5130	RETURN FROM THE PASTURE, THE / (Woman and child outside)	L	860
5131	RETURN FROM THE WOODS, THE/ (11.2x15.6)	M	710
5132	REUNION ON THE SECESH-DEMOCRATIC PLAN/ (Vig.) 1862	S	180
5133	REVENGE/ (Dogs) (Companion to #1971) N. Currier	S	130
5134	REV. JOHN WESLEY/ (8.8x8) N. Currier	S	65
5135	REV. RICHARD ALLEN	S	65
5136	REV. WILLIAM McALLISTER/ (16.2x12.8) (Oval) C. Currier	M	85
5137	REVD. CHARLES WESLEY, A.M./ (Vig.) N. Currier	S	65
5138	REVD. CHRISTOPHER RUSH, THE/ N. Currier	S	65
5139	RHODE ISLAND/ (Ship)	M	420
5140	RIDE TO SCHOOL, A/ (7.14x4.14) Companion to # 1081	VS	375
5141	RIGHT MAN FOR THE RIGHT PLACE, THE/ (Vig.) N. Currier	S	180

5142	RIGHT MAN FOR THE RIGHT PLACE, THE	S	180
5143	RIGHT REVEREND T. HOLLY, D.D./ (Vig.) 1875	S	65
5144	RIP VAN WINKLE'S COTTAGE IN THE CATSKILLS	S	290
5145	RIPE CHERRIES/ (7.15x12.7) 1870	S	155
5146	RIPE FRUIT/ (Vig.) 1875	S	155
5147	RIPE FRUIT/ (Vig.)	S	155
5148	RIPE FRUITS	VS	180
5149	RIPE STRAWBERRIES	S	155
5150	RIPTON/ 1850, N. Currier	L	1475
5151	RISING FAMILY, A/ (18.4x23.12) 1857	L	4350
5152	RIVAL CHARMS	S	75
5153	RIVAL QUEENS, THE/ (12.1x8.6)	S	70
5154	RIVAL ROSES/ (Vig.) 1873	S	95
5155	RIVER BOAT PASSING THE PALISADES/ 1869	S	480
5156	RIVER SONG/ C. Currier	S	75
5157	RIVER ROAD, THE	S	185
5158	RIVER ROAD, THE	M	705
5159	RIVER SHANNON, THE	S	95
5160	RIVER SIDE, THE/ N. Currier	S	190
5161	RIVER SIDE, THE / #142	S	190
5162	RIVER SIDE, THE/ (7.15x12.6)	S	190
5163	RIVER SIDE, THE/ (8.7x12.8)	S	190
5164	RIVER SIDE, THE	M	445
5165	ROAD - SUMMER, THE/ (17.12x26.3) 1853, N. Currier	L	5000
5166	ROAD TEAM AT A "TWENTY GAIT", A	S	290
5167	ROAD TEAM AT A "TWENTY GAIT", A/ 1883	TC	80
5168	ROAD TO THE HOLY CROSS, THE/ (8.10x11.13) N. Currier	S	20
5169	ROAD TO THE HOLY CROSS, THE	S	20
5170	ROAD TO THE VILLAGE, THE	M	265
5171	ROAD - WINTER, THE/ (17.11x26.8) 1853, N. Currier [Old & New BEST 50]	L	21900
5172	ROAD-SIDE, THE/ N. Currier	M	500
5173	ROADSIDE, THE	S	200
5174	ROADSIDE COTTAGE	M	385
5175	ROADSIDE MILL, THE/ (7.15x12.8) 1870	S	330
5176	ROBERT BLUM/ (9x11.12) 1849, N. Currier	S	70
5177	ROBERT BROWN ELLIOTT	S	65
5178	ROBERT BURNS	M	95
5179	ROBERT BURNS AND HIS HIGHLAND MARY/ (11.11x8.10) 1846, N. Currier	S	75

All prints are published by Currier & Ives unless otherwise stated.

5180	ROBERT BURNS AND HIS HIGHLAND MARY	S	75
5181	ROBERT BURNS AND HIS HIGHLAND MARY/ N. Currier	S	75
5182	ROBERT BURNS AND HIS HIGHLAND MARY/ C. Currier	S	75
5183	ROBERT EMMET/ N. Currier	S	65
5184	ROBERT EMMET, DUBLIN/ (11.11x8.5) 1803	S	70
5185	ROBERT EMMET / IRELAND'S "MARTYR OF FREEDOM" (11.11x8.8)	S	65
5186	ROBERT EMMET / IRELAND'S "MARTYR OF FREEDOM"	S	65
5187	ROBERT EMMET'S BETROTHED	S	65
5188	ROBERT McGREGOR/ Record 2:18/ (Vig.) 1882	S	290
5189	ROBINSON CRUSOE AND HIS MAN FRIDAY/ (12.11x8.12) 1874	S	180
5190	ROBINSON CRUSOE AND HIS PETS/ (12.7x8.8) 1874	S	180
5191	ROBINSON CRUSOE AND HIS PETS/ 1874	S	180
5192	ROBINSON CRUSOE AND HIS PETS	L	445
5193	ROCHESTER UNION GRAY'S QUICK STEP, THE/ N. Currier	S	90
5194	ROCK OF AGES/ (11.12x8.13) 1873	S	65
5195	ROCKY MOUNTAINS, THE/ (Buffalo in foreground) (8.8x12.8)	S	820
5196	ROCKY MOUNTAINS, THE - EMIGRANTS CROSSING THE PLAINS/ (17.7x25.13) 1886 [Old & New BEST 50]	L	16650
5197	ROLL OF HONOR/ (13x9) 1874	S	120
5198	ROMEO AND JULIET/ N. Currier	S	80
5199	ROSANNA/ 1849, N. Currier	S	75
5200	ROSANNA/ N. Currier	S	80
5201	ROSANNA / #285/ N. Currier	S	80
5202	ROSE, THE/ (Vig.)	S	105
5203	ROSE, THE/ (1 Rose, 5 Buds & Butterfly) N. Currier	S	125
5204	ROSE, THE/ (2 Roses, 3 Buds)	S	105
5205	ROSE/ (Girl) N. Currier	S	90
5206	ROSE, THE/ (1 Roses, 5 Buds)	S	105
5207	ROSE AND LILY	S	85
5208	ROSE AND LILY/ (Heads) (Vig.)	S	75
5209	ROSE OF BEAUTY/ N. Currier	S	75
5210	ROSE OF BEAUTY, THE/ (Vig.)	S	75
5211	ROSE OF KILLARNEY	S	75
5212	ROSE OF KILLARNEY, THE/ N. Currier	S	80
5213	ROSE OF MAY, THE/ 1847, N. Currier	S	80
5214	ROSE OF MAY, THE/ N. Currier	S	85
5215	ROSE OF MAY/ 1870	S	95
5216	ROSE / OF MAY, THE	S	95
5217	ROSEBUD AND EGLANTINE/ (Heads) (Vig.)	S	80

5218	ROSERK ABBEY	M	95
5219	ROSES, AND ROSEBUDS/ 1862	M	185
5220	ROSIE	S	75
5221	ROSS CASTLE, LAKE OF KILLARNEY	M	105
5222	ROSS TREVOR/ (8.8x12.8)	S	90
5223	ROUNDING A BEND" ON THE MISSISSIPPI - THE PARTING SALUTE/ (18.4x27.14) 1866	L	6800
5224	ROUNDING THE LIGHT SHIP/ (18.3x27.15) 1870	L	2450
5225	ROUTE TO CALIFORNIA, THE/ (8.7x12.8) 1871 [New BEST 50]	S	1700
5226	ROWDY BOY/ Record 2:13.75/ (Vig.) 1879	S	290
5227	ROWING HIM UP A SALT RIVER/ N. Currier	M	430
5228	ROY WILKES/ Record 2:14.5/ 1889	S	290
5229	ROY WILKES/ Record 2:08.5/ (Vig.)	M	370
5230	ROY WILKES/ Record 2:12.75/ 1890	S	290
5231	ROYAL BEAUTY, THE	S	75
5232	ROYAL FAMILY OF ENGLAND, THE	S	70
5233	ROYAL FAMILY OF PRUSSIA, THE	S	60
5234	ROYAL MAIL STEAMSHIP "AMSTERDAM" OF THE NETHERLANDS LINE	S	375
5235	ROYAL MAIL STEAMSHIP "ARABIA"/ 1853, N. Currier	L	1100
5236	ROYAL MAIL STEAMSHIP "ASIA"/ 1851, N. Currier	L	1100
5237	ROYAL MAIL STEAMSHIP "AUSTRALASIAN"/ 1861	L	1100
5238	ROYAL MAIL STEAMSHIP "BOTHNIA"	S	375
5239	ROYAL MAIL STEAMSHIP "EUROPA"/ N. Currier	L	1100
5240	ROYAL MAIL STEAMSHIP "PERSIA"/ (15.8x23.8) 1856, N. Currier	L	1100
5241	ROYAL MAIL STEAMSHIP "SCOTIA"	L	1100
5242	ROYAL MAIL STEAMSHIP "SCOTIA"/ (8x12.12)	S	375
5243	ROYAL MAIL STEAMSHIP "VEENDAM"	S	375
5244	ROYAL MAIL STEAMSHIP ZAANDAM OF THE NETHERLANDS LINE	S	375
5245	R.T.Y.C. SCHR. CAMBRIA 199 TONS	L	1300
5246	RUBBER, THE/ (11.11x8.14)	S	285
5247	RUBBER, THE/ " Put To His Trumps"/ (19.12x15.13) N. Currier	M	1150
5248	RUFFED GROUSE / PHEASANT OR PARTRIDGE/ (8.8x12.8) 1871	S	335
5249	RUINS, THE / THE CASTLE	VS	100
5250	RUINS OF CHEPSTOW CASTLE/ (2.11x4.3) (Oval)	VS	100
5251	RUINS OF THE ABBEY, THE/ N. Currier	M	120
5252	RUINS OF THE ABBEY	S	80
5253	RUINS OF THE MERCHANT'S EXCHANGE, N.Y./ (9.7x12.5) 1835, N. Currier	S	1600
5254	RUINS OF THE PLANTER'S HOTEL / NEW ORLEANS/ N. Currier	S	1600

All prints are published by Currier & Ives unless otherwise stated.

5255	RUN DOWN/ 1877	S	225
5256	RUN DOWN/ (Companion to #6783) 1884	S	225
5257	RUN OF LUCK, A/ (10.7x15) 1871	S	225
5258	RUNNING THE "MACHINE"/ (Political Cartoon)	M	300
5259	RURAL ARCHITECTURE No. 1/ 1856, N. Currier	M	315
5260	RURAL ARCHITECTURE No. 2/ 1856, N. Currier	M	315
5261	RURAL LAKE, THE	M	345
5262	RURAL SCENERY	S	165
5263	RUSH FOR THE HEAT/ 1884	L	1350
5264	RUSH FOR THE POLE/ 1877	L	1425
5265	RUSTIC BASKET/ (Vig.)	S	115
5266	RUSTIC BRIDGE, CENTRAL PARK, N.Y. (8.8x12.5)	S	335
5267	RUSTIC STAND OF FLOWERS/ (Vig.) 1875	S	120
5268	RUTHERFORD B. HAYES/ 19TH PRESIDENT	S	155
5269	RYSDYK'S HAMBLETONIAN/ 1871	S	325
5270	RYSDYK'S HAMBLETONIAN"/ (Vig.) 1871	S	325
5271	RYSDYK'S HAMBLETONIAN / SIRED BY OLD ABDALLAH	S	325
5272	RYSDYK'S HAMBLETONIAN / THE GREAT SIRE OF TROTTERS	S	325
5273	RYSDYK'S HAMBLETONIAN/ 1876	L	2025
5274	RYE AND ROCK/ (Vig.) 1884	S	245

S

Con#	Title	Folio	Value
5275	SCANDAGA CREEK/ (Companion to #1933)	VS	200
5276	SACRAMENT OF ST. JAMES/ N. Currier	S	20
5277	SACRED HEART/ N. Currier	S	25
5278	SACRED HEART OF JESUS / #18/ N. Currier	S	25
5279	SACRED HEART OF JESUS / #34/ N. Currier	S	25
5280	SACRED HEART OF JESUS / #34	S	25
5281	SACRED HEART OF JESUS	M	25
5282	SACRED HEART OF MARY / #19/ (12.13x8.10) 1848, N. Currier	S	25
5283	SACRED HEART OF MARY / #35/ (12.4x8.13)	S	25
5284	SACRED MOTTO TOKENS/ (12.9x8.15) 1874	S	25
5285	SACRED TO THE MEMORY OF / 1847, N. Currier	S	40
5286	SACRED TO THE MEMORY OF / #191/ 1846, N. Currier	S	40
5287	SACRED TO THE MEMORY OF / #185/ 1846, N. Currier	S	40

5288	SACRED TO THE MEMORY OF / #193/ 1849, N. Currier	S	40
5289	SACRED TO THE MEMORY OF / 1872	S	40
5290	SACRED TOMB OF THE BLESSED REDEEMER/ (8.6x12.9)	S	20
5291	SACRED TOMB OF THE BLESSED VIRGIN/ (8.4x12.8)	S	20
5292	SAFE SAILING	S	180
5293	SAGE OLD SMOKE, A/ (Vig.) 1888	S	220
5294	SAILOR BOY, THE/ N. Currier	S	190
5295	SAILOR FAR-FAR-AT-SEA, THE/ (11.14x8.9) N. Currier	S	185
5296	SAILOR'S ADIEU/ (11.15x8.6) N. Currier	S	150
5297	SAILOR'S ADIEU/ (12x9) N. Currier	S	150
5298	SAILOR'S ADIEU / #15/ N. Currier	S	150
5299	SAILOR'S ADIEU/ (11.15x8.8) N. Currier	S	150
5300	SAILOR'S ADIEU / #16/ 1847, N. Currier	S	150
5301	SAILOR'S ADIEU/ (12.6x8.5)	S	150
5302	SAILOR'S BRIDE, THE/ (11.12x8.9) 1849, N. Currier	S	130
5303	SAILOR'S RETURN, THE/ #15/ (12x8.5) 1847, N. Currier	S	150
5304	SAILOR'S RETURN, THE/ (12x8.8) N. Currier	S	150
5305	SAILOR'S RETURN, THE / #16/ N. Currier	S	150
5305A	SAILOR'S RETURN, THE/ (Ship on right) Currier & Ives	S	150
5306	SAILOR'S RETURN, THE/ (12.2x8.7) N. Currier	S	150
5307	SAINT ANNE	S	20
5308	SN. ANTHONY OF PADUA/ (12.1x8.11) 1849, N. Currier	S	20
5309	SN. BENEDICT THE MOOR	S	20
5310	ST. BRIDGET, ABBESS OF KILDARE/ 1848, N. Currier	S	20
5311	SAINT BRIDGET	S	20
5312	ST. CATHERINE	S	20
5313	ST. CATHERINE OF SIENNA	S	20
5314	ST. CECELIA	S	20
5315	ST. CHARLES BORROMEO	S	20
5316	ST. CLOTILDE	S	20
5317	ST. ELIZABETH	S	20
5318	SAA EMELLIA - STE EMELIE/ 1846, N. Currier	S	20
5319	ST. EMELIE/ N. Currier	S	20
5320	ST. EMILY/ 1846, N. Currier	S	20
5321	ST. FERDINAND, THE KING/ N. Currier	S	20
5322	ST. FINEEN'S WELL, IRELAND	S	80
5323	ST. FRANCIS OF ASSISI	S	20
5324	ST. FRANCIS OF PAUL	S	20
5325	ST. FRANCIS XAVERIO/ (12x8.11) 1849, N. Currier	S	20

5326	ST. IGNATIUS OF LOYOLA	S	20
5327	ST. JAMES	S	20
5328	ST. JEAN BAPTISTE INSPIRATA/ N. Currier	S	20
5329	ST. JOHN, N.B. RIVER / INDIAN TOWN	S	255
5330	ST. JOHN THE BAPTIST	S	20
5331	ST. JOSEPH/ N. Currier	S	20
5332	ST. JOSEPH - SN. JOSE	S	20
5333	ST. JUAN BATTISTA	S	20
5334	ST. JULIEN / BY VOLUNTEER, DAM BY SAYRE'S HENERY CLAY	L	1350
5335	ST. JULIEN / BY VOLUNTEER	S	290
5336	ST. JULIEN/ 1880	S	290
5337	ST. JULIEN - "King of the Turf"/ 1880	L	1350
5338	ST. LAWRENCE/ Horse	S	290
5339	ST. LAWRENCE/ 1852, N. Currier	L	1625
5340	ST. LOUIS, THE KING/ N. Currier	S	50
5341	ST. LOUIS, THE KING	S	50
5342	ST. LOUIS ROI/ 1849, N. Currier	S	40
5343	ST. A. MADALENA/ (11.10x8.4) N. Currier	S	20
5344	ST. MARGARET	S	20
5345	ST. MARY - STA. MARY/ N. Currier	S	20
5346	ST. MARY'S ABBEY - HIGHLAND FALLS/ (Oval)	VS	95
5347	ST. MICHAEL	S	20
5348	ST. MICHAEL - SAN MIGOEL / #326/ N. Currier	S	20
5349	ST. MICHAEL - SAN MIGOEL/ N. Currier	S	20
5350	ST. NICHOLAS/ (12.1x8.10) N. Currier	S	20
5351	ST. PATRICK/ (Vig.) N. Currier	S	20
5352	ST. PATRICK - SAN PATRICO	S	20
5353	ST. PATRICK, THE APOSTLE OF IRELAND	S	20
5354	ST. PAUL	S	20
5355	SAINT PETER/ N. Currier	S	20
5356	ST. PETER - SAN PEDRO/ N. Currier	S	20
5357	ST. PETER RECEIVING THE KEYS/ (11.15x8.8)	S	20
5358	ST. PHILOMENA/ 1845, N. Currier	S	20
5359	ST. PHILOMENA	S	20
5360	ST. RAMON NO NACIDO/ (12x8.8) 1849, N. Currier	S	20
5361	ST. RAPHAEL. SAN RAFAEL	S	20
5362	ST. RITA DE CASIA - STE. RITTE DE CASIA/ N. Currier	S	20
5363	ST. RITA DE CASIA - STE. RITTE DE CASIA	S	20
5364	ST. ROSE OF LIMA	S	20

5365	ST. THERESA	S	20
5366	ST. VINCENT DE PAUL	S	20
5367	SALE OF BLOODED STOCK, A/ (Vig.) 1880	S	340
5368	SALE OF THE PET LAMB, THE/ N. Currier	M	520
5369	SALE OF THE PET LAMB, THE	S	220
5370	SALMON FISHING/ (8.8x12.8) 1872	S	1175
5371	SALMON LEAP, NEAR BALLYSHANNON / IRELAND	S	100
5372	SALMON LEAP / RIVER SHANNON	M	185
5373	SAM PURDY/ (Stallion)	S	290
5374	SAMUEL J. TILDEN/ (Vig.)	S	65
5375	SAN ANTONIO DE PADUA	S	20
5376	SAN ANTONIO - SAINT ANTHONY	S	20
5377	SAN LUIS REY/ 1849, N. Currier	S	20
5378	SANCHO/ A CELEBRATED POINTER/ (Head of dog.) N. Currier	S	275
5379	SANCHO/ A CELEBRATED POINTER/ (9.13x11.13) N. Currier	S	275
5380	SANCHO/ A CELEBRATED POINTER/ (11.13x8.7) N. Currier	S	275
5381	SANCTUARY OF OUR LADY OF GUADALUPE	S	20
5382	SANTA ANNA'S MESSENGERS REQUESTING GENERAL TAYLOR/ N. Currier	S	135
5383	SANTA ANNA'S MESSENGERS REQUESTING GENERAL TAYLOR TO SURRENDER / (Changes in composition) N. Currier	S	135
5384	SANTA CLAUS/ (Stallion) 1882	S	290
5384A	SANTA CLAUS/ (Horse) 1882	TC	85
5385	SANTIAGO, CUBA	M	180
5386	SAPPHO/ (Girl)	VS	80
5387	SARAH BERNHARDT (Vig.)	S	160
5388	SARAH / #50/ C. Currier	S	80
5389	SARAH / #50/ N. Currier	S	80
5390	SARAH/ N. Currier	S	80
5391	SARAH / #77/ N. Currier	S	80
5392	SARAH/ 1876	S	80
5393	SARAH / #50	S	80
5394	SARAH ANN/ (12x8.7) 1846, N. Currier	S	80
5395	SARATOGA LAKE/ (2.13x3.15)	VS	165
5396	SARATOGA LAKE/ (8.8x12.8)	S	230
5397	SARATOGA SPRINGS	S	250
5398	SARATOGA SPRINGS N.Y.	S	260
5399	SATISFACTION!/ (7.6x12) N. Currier	S	120
5400	SAUCY KATE/ 1847	S	80
5401	SAUCY KAT/ (Vig.)	S	80

All prints are published by Currier & Ives unless otherwise stated.

5402	SAVED!/ (Companion to #6080)	M	145
5402A	SAVING IN RAILWAY FARES, A/ (Trains)	TC	105
5403	SAVIOUR OF THE WORLD/ (12.2x8.13) 1845, N. Currier	S	20
5404	SAVIOUR OF THE WORLD/ (12x8.5) N. Currier	S	20
5405	SAVIOUR OF THE WORLD/ C. Currier	S	20
5406	SAVIOUR'S INVITATION, THE/ 1866	M	20
5407	SCALES OF JUSTICE, THE/ N. Currier	S	175
5408	SCAPULAR, THE/ N. Currier	S	20
5409	SCARLET TANAGER	VS	255
5410	SCENE IN FAIRYLAND, A/ (8.8x12.80	S	90
5411	SCENE IN OLD ENGLAND, A	S	100
5412	SCENE IN OLD IRELAND, A	S	100
5413	SCENE OFF NEWPORT, A	S	380
5414	SCENE ON THE LOWER MISSISSIPPI, A	S	410
5415	SCENE ON THE SUSQUEHANNA, A	S	290
5416	SCENE OF CONNEMARA, IRELAND	S	95
5417	SCENERY OF IRELAND, THE/ "Upper Lake Killarney"/ (9.14x16.15) 1869	M	145
5418	SCENERY OF THE CATSKILL/ "Mountain House" (8x12.7)	S	295
5419	SCENERY OF THE CATSKILLS	S	295
5420	SCENERY OF THE CATSKILLS/ "The Catskill Falls of the Catskill Mountains"/ N. Currier	S	295
5421	SCENERY OF THE HUDSON NEAR "ANTHONY'S NOSE"/ (15x20.4)	L	2075
5422	SCENERY OF THE UPPER MISSISSIPPI / AN INDIAN VILLAGE	S	350
5423	SCENERY OF THE WISSAHICKON NEAR PHILADELPHIA	S	330
5424	SCENERY OF WICKLOW, IRELAND / THE DEVIL'S GLEN	S	95
5425	SCHOLAR'S REWARDS/ (12.11x9) 1874	S	190
5426	SCHOOL REWARDS/ (12.7x8.15) 1874	S	220
5427	SCHOOL REWARDS	M	340
5428	SCHOOL'S IN	VS	220
5429	SCHOOL'S OUT/ (5.8x7.8)	VS	255
5430	SCHOONER/ 1846, N. Currier	S	375
5431	SCHOONER YACHT "CAMBRIA"/ (8.12x12.12)	S	370
5432	SCHOONER YACHT "MADELINE"	S	370
5433	SCHOONER YACHT "MAGIC" OF THE N.Y. YACHT CLUB, THE	L	1675
5434	SCHOONER YACHT "MAGIC"	L	1675
5435	SCIENTIFIC SHAVING ON THE DARKTOWN PLAN/ (Vig.) 1890	S	225
5436	SCORING - COMING UP FOR THE WORD/ (17.2x26.8) 1869	L	1575
5437	SCORING FOR THE FIRST HEAT/ 1877	L	1450
5438	SCOTCH BEAUTY, THE	S	75

5439	SCOTCH CUTTER "MADGE"/ (8.14x12.12) 1881	S	325
5440	SCOTCH LADDIE, THE	S	70
5441	SCOTTISH BORDER, THE	M	155
5442	SEA OF TIBERIAS, THE	S	70
5443	SEAL OF AFFECTION/ (12.1x8.12) N. Currier	S	95
5444	SEAL OF AFFECTION/ 1846, N. Currier	S	95
5445	SEARCH THE SCRIPTURES/ N. Currier	S	20
5446	SEARCH THE SCRIPTURES/ (11.13x9.1) N. Currier	S	20
5447	SEARCH THE SCRIPTURES	S	20
5448	SEASON OF BLOSSOMS, THE/ (8.8x12.8)	S	210
5449	SEASON OF BLOSSOMS, THE/ (15.12x23.4) 1865	L	1250
5450	SEASON OF JOY, THE/ (8.8x12.8) 1872	S	195
5451	SECESSION MOVEMENT," THE/ (Vig.)	S	220
5452	SECOND BATTLE OF BULL RUN/ (8x12.9)	S	235
5453	SEE MY DOGGIE?/ N. Currier	S	115
5454	SEE MY NEW BOOTS!/ 1856, N. Currier	S	120
5455	SEE MY NEW BOOTS!	L	270
5456	SEE MY NEW BOOTS/ 1870	S	120
5457	SEE-SAW	M	355
5458	SEE-SAW	S	185
5459	SELLING OUT CHEAP/ (Political Cartoon) (Vig.)	S	185
5460	SELLING OUT CHEAP!	S	185
5461	SENSATION / Record 2:22.25/ (Vig.) 1876	S	290
5462	SERENADE/ 1866	S	75
5463	SERGEANT JASPER OF CHARLESTON/ 1876	S	335
5464	SERVICEABLE GARMENT, A/ N. Currier	M	200
5465	SET OF EIGHT, A	S	75
5466	SET OF FASHIONABLE QUADRILLES, THE/ N. Currier	S	125
5467	SET OF THE QUEENS COUNTRY DANCES/ N. Currier	S	105
5468	SETTER AND WOODCOCK/ (Vig.)	S	290
5469	SETTERS/ 1846, N. Currier	S	310
5470	SETTLING THE QUESTION/ 1885	S	250
5471	SEVEN CHURCHES OF CLONMACNOISE, ON THE RIVER SHANNON/ (8x12)	S	75
5472	SEVEN STAGES OF MATRIMONY/ N. Currier	S	145
5473	SHADE AND TOMB OF NAPOLEON, THE	S	90
5474	SHADE AND TOMB OF WASHINGTON, THE/ (8.8x12.7) 1876	S	90
5475	SHAKERS NEAR LEBANON/ (8x12.12) N. Currier [Old & New BEST 50]	S	2000
5476	SHAKESPEARE/ (Vig.)	M	90

5477	SHALL I?/ (Companion to #6052)	VS	740
5478	SHANTYING ON THE LAKE SHORE	L	2100
5479	SHARP BRUSH ON THE LAST QUARTER/ 1884	S	290
5480	SHARP BRUSH ON THE LAST QUARTER/ 1889	S	290
5481	SHARP PACE FROM START TO FINISH, A/ 1887	L	1425
5482	SHARP PACE FROM START TO FINISH, A/ 1884	L	1425
5483	SHARP RIFLE, A/ (Vig.) 1882	S	270
5484	SHARPSHOOTER, A/ (Vig.) 1882	S	270
5485	SHAUGHRAUN/ Act II, Scene I	M	125
5486	SHE HAD SO MANY CHILDREN SHE DIDN'T KNOW WHAT TO DO"	S	160
5487	SHEEP PASTURE, THE/ (8.7x12.7)	S	175
5488	SHEEP PASTURE, THE/ (10.14x14.14)	M	270
5489	SHERIDAN'S CAVALRY AT THE BATTLE OF FISHER'S HILL	S	250
5490	SHERMAN AND HIS GENERALS/ 1865	M	324
5491	SHING - GAA - BA - W'OSIN - OR THE FIGURED STONE / (Indian Chief) (Vig.) C. Currier	S	270
5492	SHIPS "ANTARCTIC" OF NEW YORK AND "THREE BELLS"/ N. Currier [Old BEST 50]	L	5100
5493	SHOEING THE HORSE/ (11.10x9) N. Currier	S	370
5494	SHOEMAKER, THE (11.14x8.7)	S	220
5495	SHOEMAKER'S CIRCUS, THE/ (Vig.) 1882	S	215
5496	SHOOTING ON THE BAY SHORE/ (9.12x13.8) 1883	S	1250
5497	SHOOTING ON THE BEACH/ (8.7x12.7)	S	1225
5498	SHOOTING ON THE PRAIRIE/ (8.8x12.9)	S	680
5499	SHORT HORNED BULL, GRAND DUKE/ N. Currier	M	200
5500	SHORT STOP AT A WAY STATION, A/ (Vig.) 1875	S	440
5501	SHRINE OF OUR LADY OF LOURDES	S	20
5502	SHUT THE DOOR/ (Companion to #608) 1880	S	125
5503	SIBYL'S TEMPLE	S	20
5504	SICKNESS AND HEALTH/ (10.7x14.13) N. Currier	M	280
5505	SIDE WHEELER, A / "BUSTIN" A TROTTER/ (Vig.)	S	290
5506	SIDE WHEELER "BUSTIN" A TROTTER, A/ (Horse comic) 1880	TC	75
5507	SIEGE AND CAPTURE OF VICKSBURG, MISS. (7.14x12.6)	S	235
5508	SIEGE OF CHARLESTON, THE	S	390
5509	SIEGE OF CONSTANTINE	S	70
5510	SIEGE OF LIMERICK, THE/ (8.2x12.11) 1848, N. Currier	S	70
5511	SIEGE OF LIMERICK, THE	S	70
5512	SIEGE OF VERA CRUZ / #458/ 1847, N. Currier	S	140
5513	SEIGE (Sic.) OF VERA CRUZ / #462/ (8.5x12.15) 1847, N. Currier	S	140
5514	SIGHTS AT THE FAIRGROUNDS / (2 oval portraits at top) 1888	L	1225

5515	SIGHTS AT THE FAIRGROUNDS/ 1888	L	1350
5516	SIGN OF THE CROSS, THE	S	20
5517	SIGNAL FIRES ON THE SLIEVENAMAN MOUNTAINS, IRELAND/ (8.3x12.5) 1848, N. Currier	S	95
5518	SILAS WRIGHT, JR./ C. Currier	VS	50
5519	SILVER CASCADE	VS	170
5520	SILVER CASCADE, NEAR ST. ANTHONY, MINN	S	285
5521	SILVER CASCADE, WHITE MOUNTAINS	S	280
5522	SILVER CREEK, CALIFORNIA/ (8.8x12.8)	S	385
5523	SIMPLY TO THE CROSS I CLING/ (Vig.) 1872	S	20
5524	SIMPLY TO THE CROSS I CLING/ (Vig.) 1874	S	20
5525	SIMPLY TO THE CROSS I CLING	L	35
5526	SINGLE/ (11.11x8.6) 1846, N. Currier	S	175
5527	SINGLE/ (12.1x8.9) 1845, N. Currier	S	175
5528	SINGLE / #341/ 1846, N. Currier	S	175
5529	SINKING OF THE BRITISH BATTLESHIP "VICTORIA"/ (8.14x12.9) 1893	S	280
5530	SINKING OF THE "CUMBERLAND" BY THE IRON CLAD "MERRIMAC"/ 1862	S	430
5531	SINKING OF THE STEAMSHIP "ELBE"	M	320
5532	SINKING OF THE STEAMSHIP "OREGON", OF THE CUNARD LINE/ 1888	S	270
5533	SINKING OF THE STEAMSHIP "OREGON", OF THE CUNARD LINE/ 1888	M	330
5534	SINKING OF THE STEAMSHIP "VILLE DU HAVRE"/ (8.8x12.11) 1873	S	260
5535	SIR MOSES MONTEFIORE	S	45
5536	SIR RICHARD SUTTON'S CELEBRATED CUTTER GENESTA	S	355
5537	SISTER JENNIE	S	75
5538	SISTERS, THE/ 1845, N. Currier	S	75
5539	SISTERS, THE/ 1847, N. Currier	S	75
5540	SISTERS, THE/ N. Currier	S	75
5541	SISTERS, THE/ 1852, N. Currier	S	75
5542	SISTERS, THE/ 1848, N. Currier	S	90
5543	SISTERS PRAYER, THE	S	50
5544	SIX MORAL SENTENCES/ (Rebus) (13.10x9.13) 1875	S	285
5545	SKATING CARNIVAL, THE	S	610
5546	SKATING SCENE / MOONLIGHT/ (8x12.9) 1868 [New BEST 50]	S	1450
5547	SKIN GAME, A/ (8.2x12.1) 1884	S	225
5548	SKINNER SKINNED, A/ (7.13x12) 1884	S	225
5549	SLEEPING BEAUTY, THE	S	85
5550	SLEEPY HOLLOW BRIDGE, TARRYTOWN, NY	S	245
5551	SLEEPY HOLLOW CHURCH / NEAR TARRYTOWN, NY (11.5x16.4)	M	635

5552	SLEEPY TOM, PACER RECORD 2:12.25	TC	85
5553	SLEEPY TOM, THE BLIND HORSE, THE PACING WONDER	S	290
5554	SLEIGH RACE, THE/ #90/ 1848, N. Currier [Old BEST 50]	S	1975
5555	SLEIGH RACE, THE/ (Title printed white) 1859	M	2875
5556	SLEIGH RACE, THE/ (L. Maurer, del.) 1859	L	12500
5557	SLEIGH RACE, THE	S	1900
5558	SLEIGH RACE, THE / #90 [New BEST 50]	S	2550
5559	SLOOP YACHT "MAYFLOWER"/ 1886	M	465
5560	SLOOP YACHT "POCAHONTAS" OF NEW YORK/ (19.5x28) 1881	L	1650
5561	SLOOP YACHT "VOLUNTEER"/ 1887	S	380
5562	SLOOP YACHTS "MISCHIEF" AND "ATLANTA"/ (19.4x28) 1882	L	1675
5563	SLUGGED OUT - BETTER LUCK NEXT TIME/ (Vig.) 1883	S	230
5564	SLUICE GATE, THE	VS	255
5565	SMALL HOPES" AND "LADY MAC"/ 1878	L	1475
5566	SMALL PROFITS AND QUICK SALES/ (Vig.) 1870	S	375
5567	SMELLING COMMITTEE, THE/ (Vig.) 1868	S	185
5568	SMOKER'S PROMENADE/ 1876	M	240
5569	SMOKING HIM OUT/ N. Currier	S	245
5570	SMOKING RUN, A/ 1880	TC	75
5571	SMUGGLER, TROTTING STALLION	S	290
5572	SMUGGLER, RECORD 2:15 1/2	S	290
5573	SMUGGLER	S	290
5573A	SMUGGLER	TC	85
5574	SMUGGLER" AND "JUDGE FULLERTON"/ (Vig.) 1876	S	290
5575	SNAKE IN THE GRASS/ (5.8x7.8)	VS	175
5576	SNAP APPLE NIGHT / ALL HALLOW EVE	M	650
5577	SNIPE SHOOTING/ (12.9x20.5) 1852, N. Currier	L	2950
5578	SNIPE SHOOTING/ (8.8x12.8)	S	615
5579	SNOWSHOE DANCE, THE/ (12.2x18.1)	M	1600
5580	SNOW STORM, THE/ [New BEST 50]	M	1975
5581	SNOWED UP - RUFFED GROUSE IN WINTER/ (15x20.6) 1867 [Old & New BEST 50]	L	5400
5582	SNOWY MORNING, A/ (11.9x16.6) 1864	M	2250
5583	SOCIABLE SMOKE, A/ 1880	S	225
5584	SOCIABLE SMOKE, A/ 1880	TC	75
5585	SOCIAL CUP/ 1883, N. Currier	M	340
5586	SOFIA/ 1846, N. Currier	S	75
5587	SOFT THING ON SNIPE!, A/ (Vig.) 1880	S	195
5588	SOLDIER BOY, THE/ "Off Duty"/ (11.13x8.3) 1864	S	135

5589	SOLDIER BOY, THE/ "On Duty"/ (11.12x8.5) 1864	S	135
5590	SOLDIER BOYS, THE/ (11.14x8.11)	S	135
5591	SOLDIER'S ADIEU, THE/ C. Currier	S	135
5592	SOLDIER'S ADIEU, THE/ N. Currier	S	135
5593	SOLDIER'S ADIEU, THE/ 1847, N. Currier	S	135
5594	SOLDIER'S BRIDE, THE (11.6x8.13)	S	130
5595	SOLDIER'S DREAM OF HOME, THE/ (7.13x12.5)	S	95
5596	SOLDIER'S DREAM OF HONOR	S	95
5597	SOLDIER'S GRAVE, THE/ (11.5x8.8) 1862	S	90
5598	SOLDIER'S GRAVE, THE/ (12.2x8.11) 1865	S	90
5599	SOLDIER'S HOME/ "The Vision"/ 1862	S	95
5600	SOLDIER'S MEMORIAL, THE/ 1863	M	195
5601	SOLDIER'S MEMORIAL, THE/ 1862	M	195
5602	SOLDIER'S MEMORIAL, THE	M	195
5603	SOLDIER'S RECORD, THE / 5th Regiment	M	195
5604	SOLDIER'S RECORD, THE / 150th Regiment	M	195
5605	SOLDIER'S RECORD, THE / 18th Regiment	M	195
5606	SOLDIER'S RETURN/ C. Currier	S	145
5607	SOLDIER'S RETURN/ 1840, N. Currier	S	145
5608	SOLDIER'S RETURN/ 1845, N. Currier	S	145
5609	SOLDIER'S RETURN/ 1846, N. Currier	S	145
5610	SOLDIER'S RETURN/ 1847, N. Currier	S	145
5611	SOLDIER'S RETURN/ 1849, N. Currier	S	145
5612	SOLOMON'S TEMPLE/ N. Currier	S	50
5613	SOME PUMPKINS/ N. Currier	M	350
5614	SON AND DAUGHTER OF TEMPERANCE/ (11.10x8.7) 1850, N. Currier	S	75
5615	SON OF TEMPERANCE / E.L. SNOW, SOCIAL UNION/ N. Currier	S	75
5616	SON OF TEMPERANCE / NO BROTHER SHALL MAKE BUY/ N. Currier	S	75
5617	SONGS OF MADAME ANNA BISHOP/ C. Currier	S	100
5618	SONS OF TEMPERANCE / LOVE, PURITY AND FIDELITY/ N. Currier	S	95
5619	SONS OF TEMPERANCE	S	95
5620	SONTAG" AND "FLORA TEMPLE"/ (17x26.7) 1855, N. Currier	L	1950
5621	SOPHIA/ (11.11x8.7) 1846, N. Currier	S	80
5622	SOPHIA	S	80
5623	SOPHIA	M	105
5624	SORREL DAN/ 1881	TC	85
5625	SORRY DOG, A/ (Companion to #3289) 1881	S	170
5626	SORRY HER LOT WHO LOVES TOO WELL/ (Vig.) 1879	S	85
5627	SOURCE OF THE HUDSON, THE (8.8x12.8)	S	315

5628	SOUTH CAROLINA'S "ULTIMATUM"/ (Political Cartoon)	M	190
5629	SOUTH SEA WHALE FISHERY/ (8.12x12.12) N. Currier	S	1200
5630	SOUTHERN BEAUTY, THE/ (Vig.)	S	75
5631	SOUTHERN BELLE, THE	S	75
5632	SOUTHERN CROSS/ (11.3x8.15) 1873	S	20
5633	SOUTHERN RIVER SCENERY/ (7.14x12.8) 1870	S	195
5634	SOUTHERN ROSE, THE	S	75
5635	SOUTHERN VOLUNTEERS, THE	S	200
5636	SPANIEL, THE/ (9x12.15) 1848, N. Currier	S	270
5637	SPANIEL, THE/ 1842, N. Currier	S	270
5638	SPANISH DANCE, THE/ N. Currier	S	125
5639	SPANISH DANCE, THE	S	125
5640	SPEAK MY DARLING!/ (11.10x9.4)	S	95
5641	SPEAK QUICK	S	85
5642	SPEAKING LIKENESS. A	S	85
5643	SPEEDING ON DARKTOWN TRACK/ 1892	S	260
5644	SPEEDING ON THE AVENUE/ (18.5x28.15) 1870	L	5450
5645	SPEEDING TO THE "BIKE"/ 1893	L	1325
5646	SPENDTHRIFT/ 1881	TC	95
5647	SPENDTHRIFT/ (Vig.) 1880	S	245
5648	SPERM WHALE "IN A FLURRY"/ 1852, N. Currier	S	1275
5649	SPICE OF THE TROTTING TRACK, THE/ 1876	M	530
5650	SPILLOUT ON THE SNOW, THE/ 1870	S	800
5651	SPILLOUT" ON THE SNOW, A/ (16.6x24.14)	L	4175
5652	SPIN ON THE ROAD, A/ 1880	TC	75
5653	SPIRIT OF '61, THE/ 1861	L	375
5654	SPIRIT OF '76 - STAND BY THE FLAG	S	290
5655	SPIRIT OF THE UNION/ (11.7x8.10) 1860	S	190
5656	SPIRIT OF THE UNION/ 1876	S	190
5657	SPIRITS FLIGHT	L	175
5658	SPIRITS FLIGHT, THE	S	90
5659	SPLENDID NAVAL TRIUMPH ON THE MISSISSIPPI/ 1862 [Old BEST 50]	L	2200
5660	SPLENDID NEW IRON STEAMER "ALBANY"	S	300
5661	SPLENDID TEA/ (Vig.) 1881	S	175
5662	SPLENDID STEAMSHIP AMERICA OF THE NATIONAL LINE	S	330
5663	SPLIT ROCK, ST. JOHNS, N.B.	S	270
5664	SPLITTING THE PARTY/ (Political Cartoon) (Vig.) 1852	S	185
5665	SPOILING A SENSATION/ (Vig.) (Companion to #1301) 1881	S	270
5666	SPONGING/ (Vig.) 1880	S	305

5667	SPORTS WHO CAME TO GRIEF, THE/ (Vig.) 1881	S	235
5668	SPORTS WHO LOST THEIR TIN/ 1878	S	240
5669	SPORTS WHO LOST THEIR TIN/ 1878	TC	70
5670	SPORTSMAN'S SOLACE, THE/ 1879	M	385
5671	SPRING/ 1849, N. Currier	S	230
5672	SPRING/ #453/ (Horses) N. Currier	S	225
5673	SPRING/ (Blond) 1870	S	75
5674	SPRING/ (Brunette)	S	75
5675	SPRING	M	90
5676	SPRING/ (Children) (8x12.10)	S	150
5677	SPRING FLOWERS/ 1861	M	290
5678	SPUNK VERSUS SCIENCE	TC	85
5679	SQUALL OFF CAPE HORN, A/ N. Currier	M	970
5680	SQUALL OFF CAPE HORN, A	S	700
5681	SQUIRREL SHOOTING/ (8.8x12.8)	S	500
5682	SQUIRREL SHOOTING	VS	315
5683	STABLE, THE / No. 1/ (15.5x15.8) N. Currier	M	980
5684	STABLE, THE / No. 2/ (15.4x15.6) N. Currier	M	980
5685	STABLE SCENE / No. 1/ (8.8x12.10) N. Currier	S	530
5686	STABLE SCENES / No. 2/ (8.8x12.10) N. Currier	S	530
5687	STAG AT BAY, THE/ (7.14x12.6)	S	150
5688	STAG AT BAY, THE	L	330
5689	STAG HOUNDS/ 1856, N. Currier	S	260
5690	STAG HUNT AT KILLARNEY	M	85
5691	STANCH POINTER, A/ 1870 & 1871	S	285
5692	STANCH POINTER, A	S	285
5693	STAR OF BEAUTY	S	75
5694	STAR OF LOVE	S	75
5695	STAR OF LOVE/ 1847, N. Currier	S	75
5696	STAR OF THE EAST, THE/ 1846, N. Currier	S	80
5697	STAR OF THE NIGHT, THE/ (Head) (Vig.)	S	75
5698	STAR OF THE NORTH/ N. Currier	S	75
5699	STAR OF THE NORTH, THE	S	75
5700	STAR OF THE OPERA, THE	S	75
5701	STAR OF THE ROAD, THE/ (8.5x12.11) 1849, N. Currier [Old BEST 50]	S	710
5702	STAR OF THE SOUTH	S	75
5703	STAR OF THE SOUTH, THE/ (Vig.)	S	75
5704	STAR OF THE WEST, THE/ (8.9x12.12) 1846, N. Currier	S	75
5705	STAR POINTER/ Record 1:59.25 (Vig.)	S	290

5706	STAR SPANGLED BANNER, THE/ (11.11x8.10)	S	235
5707	STAR SPANGLED BANNER, THE	S	235
5708	STARS OF THE TROTTING TRACK/ (21.14x28.8)	L	1550
5709	STARS OF THE TURF - No. 1/ 1885	L	1325
5710	STARS OF THE TURF - No. 2/ 1885	L	1325
5711	STARTING OUT ON HIS METTLE/ 1878	S	300
5712	STARTLING ANNOUNCEMENT, A/ (Vig.)	S	185
5713	STARUCCA VALE/ (10.7x15.4)	M	415
5714	STATE STREET, BOSTON, MASS./ (8.4x12.6) 1849, N. Currier	S	465
5715	STATEN ISLAND AND THE NARROWS FROM FORT HAMILTON/ (14.13x20.5) 1861	L	1700
5716	STATUE UNVEILED/ (Cartoon) (Vig.)	S	175
5717	STAUNCH POINTER, A/ 1871	S	305
5718	STAUNCH POINTER, A/ 1870	S	305
5719	STEADFAST IN THE FAITH	S	20
5720	STEAM CATAMARAN - H.W. LONGFELLOW/ (8.5x13.13)	S	335
5721	STEAM YACHT "ANTHRACITE", THE	S	295
5722	STEAM YACHT "CORSAIR/ 1881	L	1325
5723	STEAM YACHT "NAMOUNA"/ 1882	L	1300
5724	STEAM YACHT "POLYNIA"/ 1880	L	1375
5725	STEAMBOAT "EMPIRE"/ 1843, N. Currier	S	325
5726	STEAMBOAT "ISAAC NEWTON"/ (8.3x12.12) 1848, N. Currier	S	380
5727	STEAMBOAT "KNICKERBOCKER"/ (8.4x13) N. Currier [Old BEST 50]	S	560
5728	STEAMBOAT "PEERLESS" OF THE LAKE SUPERIOR LINE	L	1300
5729	STEAMBOAT "PRISCILLA"	S	325
5730	STEAMBOAT RACE ON THE MISSISSIPPI	S	710
5731	STEAMBOATS PASSING AT MIDNIGHT ON LONG ISLAND SOUND/ (8.8x12.8)	S	670
5732	STEAMER "DREW"/ (8.14x14.2) 1883	S	320
5733	STEAMER "DREW"	S	325
5734	STEAMER "MASSACHUSETTS"/ 1882	S	325
5735	STEAMER "MESSENGER" No. 2/ (8.4x13.1) N. Currier	S	325
5736	STEAMER "PENOBSCOT"/ (20x34.13) 1883	L	1625
5737	STEAMER PILGRIM	L	1625
5738	STEAMER PILGRIM - FLAGSHIP OF THE FALL RIVER LINE	S	325
5739	STEAMER "TEMPEST"/ 1882	S	325
5740	STEAMSHIP "ADRIATIC"/ (17x27.5) 1860	L	1250
5741	STEAMSHIP "ADRIATIC" / WHITE STAR LINE	S	325
5742	STEAMSHIP "ALASKA" OF THE GUION LINE	S	325
5743	STEAMSHIP "ALLER"	S	325

5744	STEAMSHIP "AMERICA"	S	325
5745	STEAMSHIP "ANTHRACITE"	S	325
5746	STEAMSHIP "ASSYRIAN MONARCH" OF THE MONARCH LINE	S	325
5747	STEAMSHIP "AUGUSTA VICTORIA"/ 1873	S	325
5748	STEAMSHIP "BELGENLAND" OF THE RED STAR LINE	S	325
5749	STEAMSHIP "BORUSSIA" REGULAR PACKET	S	325
5750	STEAMSHIP "BOTHNIA" OF THE CUNARD LINE	S	325
5751	STEAMSHIP "CALIFORNIA" OF THE ANCHOR LINE	S	325
5752	STEAMSHIP "CEPHALONIA"	S	325
5753	STEAMSHIP "CITY OF BALTIMORE" 2367 TONS	S	325
5754	STEAMSHIP "CITY OF BERLIN" OF THE INMAN LINE	S	325
5755	STEAMSHIP "CITY OF MONTREAL" OF THE INMAN LINE	S	325
5756	STEAMSHIP "CITY OF WASHINGTON"	S	325
5757	STEAMSHIP "DENMARK"	S	325
5758	STEAMSHIP "EGYPT" OF THE NATIONAL LINE/ (Vig.)	S	325
5759	STEAMSHIP "EGYPTIAN MONARCH" OF THE WILSON LINE	S	325
5760	STEAMSHIP "EIDER"	S	325
5761	STEAMSHIP "ETRURIA"	S	325
5762	STEAMSHIP "FLORIDA"	S	325
5763	STEAMSHIP "FRANKLIN"	S	325
5764	STEAMSHIP "FRIESLAND"	S	325
5765	STEAMSHIP "FRISIA"	S	325
5766	STEAMSHIP "GAANDAM"	S	325
5767	STEAMSHIP "GALILEO" OF WILSON LINE	S	325
5768	STEAMSHIP "GREAT NORTHERN"	S	325
5769	STEAMSHIP "HAMMONIA"/ (Vig.)	S	325
5770	STEAMSHIP "HERMANN"/ (8.4x12.10) N. Currier	S	325
5771	STEAMSHIP "HERMANN"	S	325
5772	STEAMSHIP IN A GALE	S	390
5773	STEAMSHIP "LAHN"	S	325
5774	STEAMSHIP "MAJESTIC" OF WHITE STAR LINE	S	325
5775	STEAMSHIP "MINNESOTA"	S	325
5776	STEAMSHIP "MISSISSIPPI"/ N. Currier	S	325
5777	STEAMSHIP "NOORDLAND"	S	325
5778	STEAMSHIP "OCEANIC" OF WHITE STAR LINE (8x12.6)	S	325
5779	STEAMSHIP "OREGON" OF THE CUNARD LINE	L	1275
5780	STEAMSHIP "OREGON" OF THE CUNARD LINE	S	325
5781	STEAMSHIP "PAVONIA"	S	325
5782	STEAMSHIP "PERIERE"	S	330

5783	STEAMSHIP "PERSIAN MONARCH"	S	325
5784	STEAMSHIP "PRESIDENT", THE/ (8.7x13) N. Currier	S	325
5785	STEAMSHIP "PRESIDENT", THE/ N. Currier	S	325
5786	STEAMSHIP "PRESIDENT" / The Largest in the World/ N. Currier	S	325
5787	STEAMSHIP "PURITAN" OF FALL RIVER LINE	S	325
5788	STEAMSHIP "RHODE ISLAND"/ (9x14) 1882	S	325
5789	STEAMSHIP "ROTTERDAM"	S	325
5789A	STEAMSHIP "ROYAL WILLIAM"/ 1838, N. Currier	L	1300
5790	STEAMSHIP "SAALE"	S	325
5791	STEAMSHIP "ST. PAUL"	S	325
5792	STEAMSHIP "SCYTHIA" OF CUNARD LINE	S	325
5793	STEAMSHIP "SERVIA"	S	325
5794	STEAMSHIP "SPAIN" OF THE NATIONAL LINE	S	325
5795	STEAMSHIP "SPREE"	S	325
5796	STEAMSHIP "TEUTONIC" OF THE WHITE STAR LINE	S	325
5797	STEAMSHIP "TRAAVE"	S	325
5798	STEAMSHIP "VANDERBILT"/ (16.14x26.12) 1857	L	1400
5799	STEAMSHIP "VILLE DE PARIS"	S	325
5800	STEAMSHIP "WASHINGTON"/ (8x12.13) 1847, N. Currier	S	325
5801	STEAMSHIP "WASHINGTON" FIRST AMERICAN OCEAN MAIL STEAMER/ (8.10x13.2) N. Currier	S	325
5802	STEAMSHIP "WASHINGTON" RESCUING THE PASSENGERS OF THE "WINCHESTER" OFF BOSTON/ (8.3x12.15) 1854	S	325
5803	STEAMSHIP "WESTERNLAND"	S	325
5804	STEAMSHIP "WILLIAM PENN"	S	325
5805	STEAMSHIP "ZEENDAM"	S	325
5806	STEAM YACHT "CORSAIR"	L	1250
5807	STEEL CRUISER "PHILADELPHIA"/ 1893	S	345
5808	STEEPLE CHASE CRACKS/ (Dogs and Monkeys)	S	245
5809	STEEPLE CHASER, A/ (Vig.) 1880	S	235
5810	STELLA/ (Vig.) 1872	S	75
5811	STELLA AND ALICE GREY - LANTERN AND WHALE-BONE/ (17.2x27.13) 1855, N. Currier	L	1825
5812	STEPHEN FINDING "HIS MOTHER" / (Political Cartoon) (Vig.)	M	200
5813	STEPHEN FINDING "HIS MOTHER" / (Political Cartoon)	M	200
5814	STEPPING STONES, THE/ (11.6x15.11)	M	235
5815	STILL HUNTING ON THE SUSQUEHANNA	M	630
5816	STOCK FARM, THE/ (9x12.5)	S	205
5817	STOCKS DOWN/ (8.9x12.10) 1849, N. Currier	S	520
5818	STOCKS UP/ (8.9x12.11) 1849, N. Currier	S	520

5819	STOLEN INTERVIEW/ (8.10x11.9) 1872	S	65
5820	STOLEN INTERVIEW/ (11.6x8.9) 1872	S	65
5821	STOPPING PLACE* ON THE ROAD - THE HORSE SHED/ (19.6x29.6) 1868	L	2800
5822	STORMING OF FORT DONELSON, THE/ (12.8x8.7) 1862	S	230
5823	STORMING OF FORT DONELSON, TENN.	S	230
5824	STORMING OF FORT DONELSON, TENN.	L	870
5825	STORMING OF THE BISHOP'S PALACE/ (12.12x8.5) 1847, N. Currier	S	115
5826	STORMING OF THE FORTRESS OF CHAPULTEPEC BY GENL. PILLOW/ (8.10x12.14) 1847, N. Currier	S	120
5827	STORMING THE CASTLE/ N. Currier	S	105
5828	STORMING THE CASTLE /"OLD ABE" ON GUARD	M	235
5829	STORMING THE HEIGHTS OF CERRO GORDO/ (8.4x12.10) 1847, N. Currier	S	115
5830	STORMING THE HEIGHTS OF CERRO GORDO/ 1847, N. Currier	S	115
5831	STORMING THE HEIGHTS OF MONTEREY/ (12.5x8.11) 1846, N. Currier	S	130
5832	STORY OF THE FIGHT, THE/ (17.3x13.9) (Vig.) 1863	M	295
5833	STORY OF THE FIGHT, THE/ 1863	S	95
5834	STORY OF THE GREAT KING	S	45
5835	STORY OF THE REVOLUTION/ (12.5x8.14) 1876	S	225
5836	STRATFORD ON AVON	S	95
5837	STRAW-YARD, WINTER, THE/ (11.2x15.7)	M	990
5838	STRAWBERRIES/ (8.3x12.12) 1863	S	155
5839	STRAWBERRIES/ 1870	S	155
5840	STRAWBERRY FEAST, A	S	175
5841	STRAWBERRY SEASON, THE/ (7.15x12.8) 1870	S	155
5842	STRICTLY CONFIDENTIAL/ (11.12x8.8)	S	95
5843	STRIDE OF A CENTURY/ 1876	M	370
5844	STRIPED BASS/ (8.7x12.6) 1872	S	360
5845	STYLE OB DE ROAD, DE/ (Vig.) 1884	S	225
5846	SUBURBAN GOTHIC VILLA, MURRAY HILL/ 1846, N. Currier	S	145
5847	SUBURBAN RETREAT, A (8.7x12.9)	S	180
5848	SUFFER LITTLE CHILDREN TO COME UNTO ME	S	20
5849	SUMMER / #454/ N. Currier	S	135
5849A	SUMMER/ (Girls head) (Vig.)	S	75
5850	SUMMER/ 1871	M	195
5851	SUMMER/ (Vig.) 1871	S	75
5852	SUMMER AFTERNOON	S	170
5853	SUMMER EVENING/ (8x12.8)	S	170
5854	SUMMER FLOWERS/ (Vig.) 1861	S	135
5855	SUMMER FLOWERS/ 1861	S	135

All prints are published by Currier & Ives unless otherwise stated.

5856	SUMMER FLOWERS/ 1861	M	270
5857	SUMMER FRUITS/ 1861	M	380
5858	SUMMER FRUITS	S	155
5859	SUMMER FRUITS AND FLOWERS/ (5.8x7.8)	VS	235
5860	SUMMER GIFT, THE/ (7.15x12.8) 1870	S	140
5861	SUMMER IN THE COUNTRY/ (7.15x12.7)	S	210
5862	SUMMER IN THE COUNTRY / #267	S	205
5863	SUMMER IN THE COUNTRY/ (8.7x7.12)	S	205
5864	SUMMER IN THE COUNTRY/ (16.2x23.7) 1866	L	1225
5865	SUMMER IN THE HIGHLANDS/ (15x20.7) 1867	L	930
5866	SUMMER IN THE WOODS	S	185
5867	SUMMER LANDSCAPE/ 1869	L	1200
5868	SUMMER LANDSCAPE / Haymaking	S	420
5869	SUMMER MORNING/ (7.14x12.7)	S	195
5870	SUMMER MORNING/ (10.6x14.12)	M	395
5871	SUMMER NIGHT, THE/ (8.8x12.8)	S	170
5872	SUMMER NOON/ N. Currier	S	170
5873	SUMMER NOON	S	170
5874	SUMMER RAMBLE, A	M	345
5875	SUMMER RETREAT, A/ (9.9x16.14) 1869	M	330
5876	SUMMER SCENES IN NEW YORK HARBOR/ 1863 [Old BEST 50]	L	4400
5877	SUMMER SHADES/ (15.2x22.12) 1859	L	980
5878	SUMMER TIME/ (17.11x14.7)	M	395
5879	SUMMER TIME	S	170
5880	SUMMER'S AFTERNOON, A	L	970
5881	SUMMIT OF HAPPINESS, THE/ (11.8x8.4) Companion to #1554	S	135
5882	SUNBEAM, THE	S	55
5883	SUNDAY IN THE OLDEN TIME	S	160
5884	SUNDAY MORNING - IN THE OLDEN TIME/ (15.2x19.10) N. Currier	M	560
5885	SUNDAY SCHOOL CERTIFICATE	S	50
5886	SUNDAY SCHOOL EMBLEMS/ (9 vignette views) (12.8x8.15) 1874	S	75
5887	SUNLIGHT/ (5.8x7.8) (Companion to #4173)	VS	120
5888	SUNNY HOUR, THE	S	100
5889	SUNNY MORNING	M	295
5890	SUNNY SOUTH, THE/ (7.14x12.7) 1870	S	220
5891	SUNNYSIDE	VS	155
5892	SUNNY SIDE / THE RESIDENCE OF THE LATE WASHINGTON IRVING, NEAR TARRYTOWN, N.Y. (14.13x20.8)	L	775
5893	SUNNYSIDE - ON THE HUDSON/ (8x12.8)	S	200

5894	SUNOL TO SULKY RECORD 2:08 1/4	TC	85
5895	SUNRISE ON LAKE SARANAC/ (18.11x27.4) 1860	L	2550
5896	SUNSET TREE, THE	M	295
5897	SURE HORSE FOR FIRST MONEY, THE/ 1886	L	1300
5898	SURE OF A BITE/ (Vig.) (Companion to #755) 1881	S	210
5899	SURE THING, A/ (Vig.) (Companion to #77) 1884	S	230
5900	SURPRISE, THE/ (17.14x25.11) 1858	L	3375
5901	SURPRISE PARTY, A/ (Vig.) (Companion to #997) 1883	S	220
5902	SURRENDER OF CORNWALLIS / AT YORKTOWN, VA./ 1846, N. Currier	S	255
5903	SURRENDER OF CORNWALLIS AT YORKTOWN, VA./ N. Currier	S	255
5904	SURRENDER OF CORNWALLIS AT YORKTOWN, VA./ 1845, N. Currier	S	255
5905	SURRENDER OF CORNWALLIS AT YORKTOWN, VA./ 1848, N. Currier	S	255
5906	SURRENDER OF CORNWALLIS AT YORKTOWN, VA./ 1852, N. Currier [Old BEST 50]	L	2450
5907	SURRENDER OF GENL. BURGOYNE AT SARATOGA, N.Y./ (15.12x24.13) 1852, N. Currier [Old BEST 50]	L	2450
5908	SURRENDER OF GENL. JOE JOHNSTON NEAR GREENSBORO, N.C./ (8.2x12.8) 1865	S	215
5909	SURRENDER OF GENL. LEE AT APPOMATTOX C.H., VA./ (11.15x8.14) 1865	S	220
5910	SURRENDER OF GENL. LEE AT APPOMATTOX C.H., VA./ 1868	S	220
5911	SURRENDER OF GENL. LEE AT APPOMATTOX C.H., VA./ 1873	S	220
5912	SURRENDER OF LORD CORNWALLIS/ (8.13x12.8) 1876	S	255
5913	SURRENDER OF LORD CORNWALLIS/ 1876	S	255
5914	SURRENDER OF NAPOLEON III	L	175
5915	SURRENDER OF PORT HUDSON, LA./ (7.15x12.8) 1863	S	225
5916	SUSAN/ 1844, N. Currier	S	80
5917	SUSAN/ 1846, N. Currier	S	80
5918	SUSAN/ 1847, N. Currier	S	80
5919	SUSAN/ 1848, N. Currier	S	80
5920	SUSAN/ N. Currier	S	80
5921	SUSAN/ (Vig.) N. Currier	S	80
5922	SUSAN / #46/ (Vig.) N. Currier	S	80
5923	SUSANNA/ (Shawl over head) 1849, N. Currier	S	80
5924	SUSANNA/ 1849, N. Currier	S	80
5925	SUSIE	VS	125
5926	SUSIE	S	75
5927	SUSSEX VALE - NEW BRUNSWICK/ (8.8x12.9)	S	185
5928	SWEET SIXTEEN	S	100
5929	SWEET SPRING TIME	M	330
5930	SWEETSER/ (Vig.) 1877	S	290

5931	SWEETSER / SLEEPY GEORGE AND LUCY SWEETSER/ (Vig.)	S	290
5932	SWELL SMOKER / GETTING THE SHORT END/ (Vig.) 1888	S	225
5933	SWELL SMOKER / GIVING LONG ODDS/ (Vig.) 1888	S	225
5934	SWELL SPORT ON A BUFFALO HUNT, A/ (Vig.) 1882	S	245
5935	SWELL SPORT STAMPEDED, A/ (Vig.) 1882	S	245
5936	SWIFT PACER "ARROW"/ Record 2:13.25/ (Vig.) 1888	S	290
5937	SWING OF THE FIRST HEAT, THE/ 1877	S	290
5938	SYLVAN LAKE / NEW YORK	S	180
5939	SYLVAN LAKE	S	180
5940	SYLVAN LAKE, THE/ #195	S	180

T

Con#	Title	Folio	Value
5941	TABLE D'HOTE, THE*/ N. Currier	S	95
5942	TACONY/ (17.14x26.6) 1853, N. Currier	L	1850
5943	TACONY AND MAC/ (17.5x26.8) 1853, N. Currier	L	1975
5944	TAKE A PEACH	S	130
5945	TAKE A PINCH/ (Companion to #4784) N. Currier	S	105
5946	TAKE BACK THE HEART THAT THOU GAVEST/ (Vig.) 1875	S	75
5947	TAKE CARE/ (Girl's Head) (Vig.)	S	75
5948	TAKE YOUR CHOICE/ (Girl's Heads)	S	75
5949	TAKE YOUR CHOICE/ (Three Girls) (Vig.)	S	75
5950	TAKING A BREATH	S	80
5951	TAKING A REST/ 1894	S	80
5952	TAKING A SMASH/ (Comic)	S	220
5953	TAKING A "SMILE"/ (8.2x12.6) 1854, N. Currier	S	245
5954	TAKING A BREATH/ 1880	TC	75
5955	TAKING COMFORT / (Oval)	VS	135
5956	TAKING COMFORT/ 1880	TC	75
5957	TAKING COMFORT/ 1879	S	195
5958	TAKING COMFORT	M	275
5959	TAKING IT EASY	TC	75
5960	TAKING OFF HIS AIRS/ (Companion to #4980)	S	195
5961	TAKING THE BACK TRACK - A DANGEROUS NEIGHBORHOOD/ (17.6x26.6) 1866 [Old BEST 50]	L	5900
5962	TAKING THE STUMP*, OR STEPHEN IN SEARCH OF HIS MOTHER/ (Political Cartoon) (Vig.) 1860	M	250

5963	TALKED TO DEATH/ 1873	S	70
5964	TALLYRAND /(Letter) N. Currier	VS	50
5965	TALLULAH FALLS, GEORGIA/ (8.8x12.7)	S	315
5966	TAMBOURINE DANCE, THE/ N. Currier	S	180
5967	TANTALLON CASTLE, COAST OF SCOTLAND/ (11.1x15.6)	M	190
5968	TASTE FOR THE FINE ARTS, A	S	340
5969	TEA PARTY, THE	S	130
5970	TEA WITH DOLLY	S	120
5971	TEAM FAST ON THE POLE, A/ (Vig.) 1883	S	300
5972	TEAM FAST ON THE SNOW, A/ (Vig.) 1853	S	300
5973	TEAM ON THE SNOW, A/ (13.8x7.8) 1883	M	1025
5974	TEAM THAT TAKES NO DUST, A/ (Vig.) 1875	S	320
5975	TEE-TO-TAL SOCIETY, THE/ N. Currier	S	210
5976	TELASCO AND AMARILLI/ (12.12x9.6) N. Currier	S	155
5977	TEMPLE OF JUPITER, THE	S	25
5978	TEMPLE OF SOLOMON	S	25
5979	TEMPLE OF SOLOMON, THE/ (8.9x12.14) 1846, N. Currier	S	25
5980	TEMPLE OF CHRIST, THE/ (12x8.9)	S	20
5981	TEMPTED/ (8.8x12.8) (Companion to #2928)	S	430
5982	TEMPTING FRUIT/ 1874	S	155
5983	TEMPTING LUNCH/ (7.15x12.8) 1870	S	155
5984	TEMPTING THE BABY	M	235
5985	TEN BROECK/ (Vig.) 1877	S	290
5986	TEN COMMANDMENTS, THE/ N. Currier	S	35
5987	TEN COMMANDMENTS, THE	S	35
5988	TEN VIRGINS, THE/ (12.7x7.15)	S	35
5989	TENNY"/ (Vig.) 1891	S	290
5990	TENNY"/ (Vig.) 1892	L	1325
5991	TENNY"/ (Vig.) 1892	S	290
5992	TERRA COTTA/ 1881	S	290
5993	TERRIBLE COLLISION BETWEEN THE STEAMBOATS "STONINGTON" AND "NARRAGANSETT"/ (8.7x13.8) 1880	S	400
5994	TERRIBLE COLLISION BETWEEN THE STEAMBOATS "DEAN RICHMOND" and "C. VANDERBILT"/ (7.13x12.5)	S	400
5995	TERRIFIC COMBAT BETWEEN "MONITOR" 2 GUNS, AND "MERRIMAC" 11 GUNS/ 1862	S	460
5996	TERRIFIC COMBAT BETWEEN "MONITOR" 2 GUNS, AND "MERRIMAC" 11 GUNS/ (Monitor on left, gunboats in rear firing) 1862	S	490
5997	TERRIFIC COMBAT BETWEEN THE "MONITOR" 2 GUNS, AND "MERRIMAC" 10 GUNS/ 1862 [Old BEST 50]	S	500
5998	TERRIFIC ENGAGEMENT BÈTWEEN THE "MONITOR" 2 GUNS, AND "MERRIMAC"...	L	1600

5999	TEXT WITH MODERN IMPROVEMENTS	S	90
6000	THAT BLESSED BABY	S	50
6001	THAT BLESSED BABY / #624	S	55
6002	THATCHED COTTAGE, THE/ (8.8x12.8)	S	185
6003	THATCHED ROOF, THE	S	125
6004	THAT'S WHAT'S THE MATTER/ (Vig.) 1882	S	205
6005	THEODORE FRELINGHUYSEN / HURRAH! HURRAH!/ N. Currier	S	120
6006	THEODORE FRELINGHUYSEN / NOMINATED FOR.../ N. Currier	S	120
6007	THEY'RE SAVED! THEY'RE SAVED!/ (8.4x12.6) (Companion to #4280)	S	85
6008	THIRD DAY OF THE SIEGE OF MONTEREY/ N. Currier	S	120
6009	THIRD HEAT IN TWO SIXTEEN, A/ (16.12x26.14) 1874	L	1475
6010	THIS CERTIFIES...HAS BEEN A MEMBER/ 1889	S	75
6011	THIS CERTIFIES THAT.../ FIRE DEPARTMENT/ (Rescued baby) 1889	L	295
6012	THIS CERTIFIES / THAT.../ FIRE DEPARTMENT/ 1877	L	420
6013	THIS CERTIFIES / THAT.../ FIRE DEPARTMENT/ 1889	L	420
6014	THIS CERTIFIES / THAT.../ LADIES LOYAL UNION LEAGUE/ (6 War scenes)	S	155
6015	THIS CERTIFIES / THAT.../ THE LOYAL UNION LEAGUE	S	220
6016	THIS CERTIFIES / THAT.../ SUNDAY SCHOOL	S	180
6017	THIS CERTIFIES / THAT.../ SUNDAY SCHOOL/ 1877	S	100
6018	THIS CERTIFIES / THAT.../ THE RITE OF / HOLY MATRIMONY	S	115
6019	THIS MAN FORGOT TO SHUT THE DOOR/ (Vig.) 1880	M	210
6020	THIS MAN WAS TALKED TO DEATH/ 1873	S	140
6021	THISTLE (YACHT) (20x28.1) 1887	L	1550
6022	THOMAS CORWIN/ (11.15x8.7) 1847, N. Currier	S	85
6023	THOMAS F. MEAGHER/ (11.2x8.5) 1852, N. Currier	S	90
6024	THOMAS FRANCIS MEAGHER / #621/ 1848, N. Currier	S	95
6025	THOMAS F. MEAGHER / (In Uniform) (Vig.)	S	105
6026	THOMAS JEFFERSON - 3RD PRESIDENT/ (11.13x9.5) N. Currier	S	210
6027	THOMAS JEFFERSON - THE BLACK WHIRLWIND OF THE EAST/ (16.11x25) 1875	L	1200
6028	THOMAS JEFFERSON - THE BLACK WHIRLWIND OF THE EAST/ (Vig.) 1880	S	290
6029	THOMAS WILDEY/ N. Currier	S	45
6030	THOU GAV'ST ME A BRIGHT SWORD, LADY/ N. Currier	S	45
6031	THOU HAST LEARNED TO LOVE ANOTHER/ (Vig.) 1875	S	235
6032	THOU SHALT NOT STEAL/ (Motto) (Vig.)	S	135
6033	THREE FAVORITES, THE/ (8.7x12.13) N. Currier	S	250
6034	THREE GRACES, THE/ (12.5x8.15) N. Currier	S	120
6035	THREE GREEDY KITTIES - AFTER THE FEAST	S	140

6036	THREE GREEDY KITTIES - AT THE FEAST	S	140
6037	THREE HOLY WOMEN, THE	S	20
6038	THREE JOLLY KITTENS / AFTER THE FEAST/ (8.3x12.6) 1871	S	140
6039	THREE JOLLY KITTENS / AT THE FEAST/ (8.3x12.7) 1871	S	140
6040	THREE LITTLE MAIDS FROM SCHOOL	L	280
6041	THREE LITTLE SISTERS, THE	M	230
6042	THREE LITTLE WHITE KITTENS / FISHING/ 1870	S	145
6043	THREE LITTLE WHITE KITTENS / FISHING/ 1871	S	145
6044	THREE LITTLE WHITE KITTENS / FIRST MOUSE	S	145
6045	THREE SISTERS, THE	S	90
6046	THREE SORRY KITTIES / AFTER THE FEAST	S	140
6047	THREE WHITE KITTENS, THE / PEACE	M	245
6048	THREE WHITE KITTENS, THE / WAR	M	245
6049	THROUGH EXPRESS, THE /(Vig.)	S	1725
6050	THROUGH THE BAYOU BY TORCHLIGHT [New BEST 50]	S	1750
6051	THROUGH TO THE PACIFIC/ (7.15x12.9) 1870 [New BEST 50]	S	1175
6052	THROW IF YOU DARE/ (Companion to #5477)	VS	665
6053	THY KINGDOM COME/ (Vig.) 1872	S	25
6054	THY WILL BE DONE/ (12.8x8.7) 1872	S	25
6055	THY WORD IS A LIGHT/ (8.7x12.8) 1872	S	20
6056	TICK, TICK, TICKLE/ (Vig.) 1873	S	115
6057	TICKLE! TICKLE!	S	115
6058	TIME IS MONEY/ 1873	S	205
6059	TIME IS PRECIOUS/ (Motto) (8.7x12.7) 1872	S	200
6060	TIME WORN ABBEY, THE	S	95
6061	TIP-TOP/ (Vig.) 1879	S	195
6062	TIP-TOP/ 1880	S	195
6063	TIP-TOP/ 1880	TC	75
6064	TIRED SOLDIER, THE	S	75
6065	T.J. JACKSON / LIEUT. GENL. STONEWALL JACKSON	S	155
6066	TO AVOID A SMASH, WE SELL FOR CASH/ 1875	M	425
6067	TO THE GOVERNOR'S GUARD 2ND REGT. N.Y. ARTILLERY/ N. Currier	S	145
6068	TO THE GRAND ARMY OF THE REPUBLIC	L	320
6069	TO THE / MEMORY OF / #370/ 1845, N. Currier	S	45
6070	TO THE / MEMORY OF/ (12.10x8.9) N. Currier	S	45
6071	TO THE MEMORY OF.../ (12.15x9.12) N. Currier	S	45
6072	TO THE MEMORY OF.../ 1845, N. Currier	S	45
6073	TO THE MEMORY OF.../ N. Currier	S	45

6074	TO THE MEMORY OF... / #78/ 1846, N. Currier	S	45
6075	TO THE MEMORY OF.../ 1846, N. Currier	S	45
6076	TO THE MEMORY OF...	S	45
6077	TO THE MEMORY OF WM. H. HARRISON/ N. Currier	S	95
6078	TO THE MEMORY OF WM. H. HARRISON / #135/ N. Currier	S	95
6079	TO THE RESCUE/ (7.13x12.7)	S	85
6080	TO THE RESCUE!/ (Companion to #5402)	M	115
6081	TO THY CROSS I CLING	S	20
6082	TOBOGGANING IN THE ALPS	S	590
6083	TOBOGGANING ON DARKTOWN HILL - GETTING A HIST/ (Vig.) 1890	S	260
6084	TOBOGGANING ON DARKTOWN HILL - AN UNTIMELY MOVE/ (Vig.) 1890	S	260
6085	TOCSIN OF LIBERTY, THE/ (9x12.6) 1876	S	220
6086	TOILETTE, THE/ (11.2x9) (Oval)	S	100
6087	TOLL-GATE, JAMAICA PLANK ROAD / Crayon Studies/ N. Currier	S	325
6088	TOLL-GATE, JAMAICA PLANK ROAD/ N. Currier	S	325
6089	TOLL-GATE, JAMAICA, L.I./ (Vig.) N. Currier	S	325
6090	TOM BOWLING/ 1881	TC	85
6091	TOM BOWLING / BY LEXINGTON, DAM LUCY FOWLER...	S	290
6092	TOM OCHILTREE/ (Vig.) 1877	S	290
6093	TOM PADDOCK/ (14.2x12.4)	S	155
6094	TOM SAYERS/ (Boxing Champion) (Vig.) 1860	S	235
6095	TOM SAYERS/ (Boxing Champion)	M	300
6096	TOM SAYERS/ (Boxing Champion) (1/2 Length, full face) (Vig.) 1860	S	240
6097	TOM SAYERS/ (Boxing Champion) (1/2 Length, profile to left) (Vig.) 1860	S	240
6098	TOMB AND SHADE OF NAPOLEON, THE/ N. Currier	S	95
6099	TOMB AND SHADE OF NAPOLEON, THE / #214/ N. Currier	S	95
6100	TOMB AND SHADE OF WASHINGTON, THE/ 1842	S	95
6101	TOMB OF GENL. W.H. HARRISON, THE/ (8.3x12.15) 1842, N. Currier	S	110
6102	TOMB OF GENL. W.H. HARRISON, THE/ (15x18.9) 1841, N. Currier	M	155
6103	TOMB OF KOSCIUSKO, THE / WEST POINT / #234/ N. Currier	S	120
6104	TOMB OF KOSCIUSKO, THE / WEST POINT / #234/ (8x12.7)	S	120
6105	TOMB OF LINCOLN, SPRINGFIELD, ILLINOIS	S	120
6106	TOMB OF NAPOLEON, ST. HELENA/ (10.4x8.3) N. Currier	S	85
6107	TOMB OF WASHINGTON, MOUNT VERNON, VA., THE/ (7.8x13.10) N. Currier	S	105
6108	TOMB OF WASHINGTON, THE / MOUNT VERNON, VA./ (8.4x12.12) N. Currier	S	105
6109	TOMB OF WASHINGTON, THE / MOUNT VERNON, VA.	S	105
6110	TOMB OF WASHINGTON, THE / MOUNT VERNON, VA.	M	165

6111	TOMB OF WASHINGTON, THE / MOUNT VERNON, VA.	L	205
6112	TOMB OF WASHINGTON, THE / MOUNT VERNON, VA./ (8.8x12.8)	S	110
6113	TOMMY TATEISH ONEJERO	S	65
6114	TONSORIAL ART IN THE DARKTOWN STYLE/ (Vig.) 1890	S	225
6115	TOO SWEET FOR ANYTHING	S	100
6116	TOP OF THE HEAP/ (Vig.) 1880	S	190
6117	TORONTO CHIEF, GENL. BUTLER AND DEXTER/ (17x27.4) 1866	L	1525
6118	TOWER OF SOLOMON, THE/ 1846, N. Currier	S	55
6119	TOY BRIDGE, THE	S	110
6120	TRAINING A TROTTER/ 1881	TC	80
6121	TRAINING DAY	M	225
6122	TRANSFIGURATION/ N. Currier	S	30
6123	TRAPPER'S CAMP-FIRE, THE/ 1866	L	1975
6124	TRAPPER'S CAMP-FIRE, THE/ 1866	L	1975
6125	TRAPPER'S LAST SHOT, THE/ (11x15.9)	M	1575
6126	TRAPPERS ON THE PRAIRIE - PEACE OR WAR?/ (17.3x26.5) 1866	L	5200
6127	TRAVELING ON HIS BEAUTY	S	75
6128	TREE OF DEATH, THE	S	85
6129	TREE OF DEATH, THE/ The Sinner/ (12.9x9) N. Currier	S	85
6130	TREE OF EVIL, THE/ N. Currier	S	75
6131	TREE OF GOOD, THE/ N. Currier	S	105
6132	TREE OF INTEMPERANCE/ (12.6x8.12) 1849, N. Currier	S	120
6133	TREE OF INTEMPERANCE	S	120
6134	TREE OF LIFE, THE / #21/ N. Currier	S	125
6135	TREE OF LIFE, THE/ C. Currier	S	120
6136	TREE OF LIFE, THE / ON EACH SIDE OF THE RIVER	S	125
6137	TREE OF LIFE, THE	L	245
6138	TREE OF LIFE - THE CHRISTIAN/ N. Currier	S	110
6139	TREE OF TEMPERANCE/ (12x8.14) 1849, N. Currier	S	125
6140	TREE OF TEMPERANCE/ 1872	S	125
6141	TRENTON FALLS, NEW YORK/ (8.8x12.7)	S	240
6142	TRENTON HIGH FALLS, NEW JERSEY/ (8.3x12.6)	S	235
6143	TRIAL BY JURY / THE JUDGE'S CHARGE	S	200
6144	TRIAL BY JURY / THE VERDICT	S	200
6145	TRIAL OF EFFIE DEANS, THE/ (14.6x23.13)	L	355
6146	TRIAL OF PATIENCE, THE	M	400
6147	TRIAL OF THE IRISH PATRIOTS AT CLONMEL/ (7.15x12.9) 1848, N. Currier	S	70
6148	TRIBUTE MONEY/ N. Currier	S	145

6149	TRIBUTE OF AUTUMN, THE/ (7.14x12.7) 1870	S	300
6150	TRINKET/ 1881	S	290
6151	TRINKET RECORD 2:10 3/4/ 1881	TC	85
6152	TRINKET / BY PRINCEPS, DAM QUIDA	S	290
6153	TRINKET", Record 2:14/ 1879	S	290
6154	TRINKET / BY PRINCEPS, DAM QUIDA	L	1425
6155	TRIUMPH OF FAITH/ 1874	M	55
6156	TRIUMPH OF THE CROSS/ (Vig.) 1874	S	20
6157	TROJAN QUICK STEP/ N. Currier	S	75
6158	TROLLING FOR BLUE FISH/ (18.8x27.14) 1866 [Old & New BEST 50]	L	9775
6159	TROPICAL AND SUMMER FRUITS/ 1867	L	1325
6160	TROPICAL AND SUMMER FRUITS/ 1867	S	170
6161	TROT "FOR THE GATE MONEY," A/ (16.6x24.14) 1869	L	1850
6162	TROT WITH MODERN IMPROVEMENTS, A/ (Vig.) 1881	S	290
6163	TROTTERS"/ (29x34.4)	L	1450
6164	TROTTER'S BURIAL, THE/ (9.1x12.12) 1878	S	295
6165	TROTTERS ON THE GRAND CIRCUIT / WARMING UP/ (17.8x27) 1877	L	1600
6166	TROTTERS ON THE SNOW	TC	105
6167	TROTTERS ON THE SNOW/ (Vig.)	S	1100
6168	TROTTING CRACKS" A MODEL STABLE/ 1868	L	4750
6169	TROTTING CRACKS" AT THE FORGE/ 1869 [Old & New BEST 50]	L	7800
6170	TROTTING CRACKS" ON THE SNOW/ (16.11x27.15) 1858	L	6400
6171	TROTTING FOR A GREAT STAKE/ (20x28.5) 1890	L	1575
6172	TROTTING GELDING "BILLY D." WITH "RUNNING MATE"/ (18.6x29.2) 1881	L	1425
6173	TROTTING GELDING "CLINGSTONE", RECORD 2:14/ (Vig.)	S	290
6174	TROTTING GELDING "FRANK"/ 1884	L	1250
6175	TROTTING GELDING "HARRY WILKES," - Record 2:14.75/ (Vig.) 1885	S	290
6176	TROTTING GELDING "PRINCE WILKES" - Record 2:14.75/ 1889	S	290
6177	TROTTING GELDING "ST. JULIEN" - Record 2:11.25/ 1881	S	290
6178	TROTTING GELDING "STEVE MAXWELL"/ 1881	S	290
6179	TROTTING HORSE "DARBY" - Record 2:16.50/ (Vig.) 1879	S	290
6180	TROTTING HORSE "GEORGE PALMER"	L	1250
6181	TROTTING HORSE "JUDGE FULLERTON"/ (11.8x20) 1874	M	565
6182	TROTTING KING "ST. JULIEN", Record 2:11.75/ 1881	TC	85
6183	TROTTING MARE "AMERICAN GIRL"/ 1870	L	1425
6184	TROTTING MARE "AMERICAN GIRL"/ (Vig.) 1871	S	290
6185	TROTTING MARE "AMERICAN GIRL"/ (16.13x26) 1870	L	1425
6186	TROTTING MARE "BELLE HAMLIN", Record 2:12.75 / (3/4 view) (Vig.) 1889	S	290

6187	TROTTING MARE "BELLE HAMLIN", Record 2:12.75 / (Vig.) 1889	S	290
6188	TROTTING MARE "BELLE HAMLIN" - Record 2:12.75 / (Changes in composition from preceding) (Vig.) 1889	S	290
6189	TROTTING MARE "GOLDSMITH MAID"/ (16.14x26.6) 1870	L	1500
6190	TROTTING MARE "LUCY"	S	290
6191	TROTTING MARE "MARTHA WILKES" - Record 2:08/ 1892	S	290
6192	TROTTING MARE "NANCY HANKS" BY HAPPY MEDIUM	S	290
6193	TROTTING MARE "NANCY HANKS" - Record 2:04/ (Vig.) 1892	S	290
6194	TROTTING MARE "SUNOL"/ (Vig.) 1889	S	290
6195	TROTTING ON THE ROAD/ (Vig.) 1873	S	290
6196	TROTTING QUEEN "ALIX", RECORD 2:03 3/4	L	1150
6197	TROTTING QUEEN "ALIX", BY PATRONAGE	S	290
6198	TROTTING QUEEN "MAUD S." - Record 2:08.75/ (Vig.) 1881	S	290
6199	TROTTING QUEEN "MAUD S." - Record 2:10 3/4/ 1881	TC	85
6200	TROTTING QUEEN "NANCY HANKS" - Record 2:04/ 1892	L	1325
6201	TROTTING STALLION "ALCRYON"/ (Vig.) 1889	S	290
6202	TROTTING STALLION "COMMODORE VANDERBILT"/ (12.15x21) 1871	L	1275
6203	TROTTING STALLION "DAN RICE"/ (16.10x26.3) 1866	L	1550
6204	TROTTING STALLION "DIRECTUM" / Record 2:05.25/ (18.8x27.14) 1894	L	1400
6205	TROTTING STALLION "GEORGE M. PATCHEN, JR." OF CALIFORNIA/ (16.10x25.8) 1866	L	1450
6206	TROTTING STALLION "GRAY EAGLE" OF KENTUCKY	L	1450
6207	TROTTING STALLION "HAMBLETONIAN MAMBRINO"/ 1879	S	290
6208	TROTTING STALLION "HANNIS"/ 1881	S	290
6209	TROTTING STALLION "HANNIS"/ (Vig.) 1877	S	290
6210	TROTTING STALLION "MAMBRINO CHAMPION"/ (18.10x25.4) 1867	L	1350
6211	TROTTING STALLION "MAMBRINO" GIFT/ 1874	S	290
6212	TROTTING STALLION "MAMBRINO" GIFT	S	290
6213	TROTTING STALLION "MONROE CHIEF" Record 2:18.25/ (Vig.) 1881	S	290
6214	TROTTING STALLION "NELSON", BY YOUNG ROLFE	M	545
6215	TROTTING STALLION "NELSON", Record 2:10/ (Vig.)	S	290
6216	TROTTING STALLION "NELSON", BY YOUNG ROLFE/ (Vig.)	M	545
6217	TROTTING STALLION "PALO ALTO"/ (Vig.) 1890	S	290
6218	TROTTING STALLION "PATRON" - Record 2:14.25/ (Vig.) 1887	S	290
6219	TROTTING STALLION "PHALLAS"/ (17.10x27) 1883	L	1375
6220	TROTTING STALLION "SANTA CLAUS" - Record 2:17.50/ (Vig.) 1881	S	290
6221	TROTTING STALLION "SMUGGLER"/ (Vig.) 1875	S	290
6222	TROTTING STALLION "SMUGGLER"/ 1874	S	290
6223	TROTTING STALLION "STAMBOUL" - Record 2:12.25/ (Vig.)	S	290
6224	TROTTING STALLION "STEAMBOAT"/ 1890	S	290

6225	TROTTING STALLION "TOM MOORE"/ (17.2x26.8) 1870	L	1400
6226	TROTTING STALLION WEDGEWOOD BY BELMONT	S	290
6227	TROUT BROOK, THE/ (11.3x15.8) 1862	M	1200
6228	TROUT FISHING/ (12.8x20.3) 1852, N. Currier	L	3225
6229	TROUT POOL, THE/ (8.8x12.7)	S	950
6230	TROUT STREAM, THE/ (14.11x20.2) 1852	L	3300
6231	TROUT VERSUS GOUT/ N. Currier	S	240
6232	TROY FIRE COMPANY/ N. Currier	S	310
6233	TRUE DAUGHTER OF THE NORTH/ 1870	S	65
6234	TRUE DAUGHTER OF THE SOUTH, THE/ (Vig.) 1870	S	65
6235	TRUE FRIENDS, THE	S	100
6236	TRUE ISSUE OR "THAT'S WHAT'S THE MATTER"/ (Political Cartoon) (Vig.) 1864	S	220
6237	TRUE PEACE COMMISSIONER, THE	S	140
6238	TRUE PORTRAIT OF OUR BLESSED SAVIOUR/ (11.15x8.8)	S	20
6239	TRUE PORTRAIT OF OUR VIRGIN MARY	S	20
6240	TRUE YANKEE SAILOR, THE/ N. Currier	S	190
6241	TRUST / IN THE LORD/ (Vig.) 1872	S	95
6242	TRUST ME TILL I SELL MY DOG/ 1873	S	385
6243	TRY OUR CLAMS/ (Vig.) 1875	S	285
6244	TRYING IT ON/ (Vig.) 1874	S	180
6245	TSHU-GUE-GA/ (Indian Chief) (Vig.) C. Currier	S	250
6246	TUG OB WAR, DE!/ (Vig.) (Companion to #1604) 1883	S	230
6247	TUMBLED TO IT/ (Vig.) (Companion to #2455) 1881	S	240
6248	TURN OF THE TUNE, THE/ (7.14x12.8) (Companion to #270) 1875	S	270
6249	'TWAS A CALM STILL NIGHT/ 1880	TC	80
6250	'TWAS A CALM STILL NIGHT/ (Vig.) 1875	S	185
6251	T.W. DORR / GOVERNOR OF RHODE ISLAND/ N. Currier	S	70
6252	'TWERE VAIN I TELL THEE ALL I FEEL/ (Vig.)	S	160
6253	TWILIGHT HOUR, THE	S	165
6254	TWIN BROTHERS, THE	S	95
6255	TWIN MONKEYS, THE	S	95
6256	TWIN MONKEYS, THE / "DARWIN'S THEORY"	S	115
6257	TWIN SCREW S. S. "KENSINGTON" OF THE RED STAR LINE	S	305
6258	TWIN SCREW STEAMER "CAMPANIA" OF THE CUNARD LINE	S	305
6259	TWIN SCREW STEAMER "DEUTSCHLAND" OF THE HAMBURG AMERICAN LINE	S	305
6260	TWIN SCREW STEAMER "LUCANIA" OF THE CUNARD LINE/ (8.9x14.15)	S	305
6261	TWO BEAUTIES, THE/ (Vig.)	S	75

6262	TWO LITTLE "FRAID CATS"	S	140
6263	TWO LITTLE FRAID CATS	S	140
6264	TWO MINUTE CLIP, A*/ 1893	M	550
6265	TWO PETS, THE / #31/ N. Currier	S	100
6266	TWO PETS, THE / #561/ N. Currier	S	105
6267	TWO PETS, THE	M	200
6268	TWO PETS, THE	S	95
6269	TWO SISTERS, THE/ (12.3x8.7) 1845, N. Currier	S	95
6270	TWO SISTERS, THE/ (10x8) 1845, N. Currier	S	95
6271	TWO SOULS WITH BUT A SINGLE THOUGHT"/ (9.12x13.8) (Vig.) 1889	S	220
6272	TWO TO GO/ 1882	S	225
6272A	TWO TO GO/ 1882	VS	95
6273	TWO TO GO/ 1892	L	1000
6274	TWO TO GO/ 1892	S	230
6275	TWO TWENTY" ON THE ROAD/ (Horse) (Vig.) 1875	S	330
6276	TWO WATCHERS, THE	S	105

U

Con#	Title	Folio	Value
6277	UNBERGABE DES KAISERS NAPOLEON III	S	45
6278	UNBOLTED/ (Companion to #587)	S	235
6279	UNCLE SAM" MAKING NEW ARRANGEMENTS/ (Political Cartoon) (Vig.) 1860	S	240
6280	UNCLE TOM AND LITTLE EVA/ N. Currier	S	145
6281	UNCONSCIOUS SLEEPER, THE	S	105
6282	UNDER CLIFF - ON THE HUDSON/ (8.8x12.8)	S	225
6283	UNDER THE ROSE/ (Vig.) 1872	S	80
6284	UNION IRON CLAD MONITOR "MONTAUK" DESTROYING THE REBEL STEAMSHIP "NASHVILLE"/ (8.1x12.9)	S	405
6285	UNION LEAGUE OF AMERICA CERTIFICATE/ (9x12.7) 1863	S	95
6286	UNION PLACE HOTEL, UNION SQUARE, N.Y./ (8.11x11.14) N. Currier	S	560
6287	UNION SOLDIER'S DISCHARGE CERTIFICATE/ (15x11.8) 1865	S	195
6288	UNION VOLUNTEER, THE/ 1861	S	130
6289	UNION VOLUNTEER, THE - HOME FROM THE WAR/ (13.9x17.12) 1863	L	335
6290	UNION VOLUNTEER, THE - OFF FOR THE WAR/ 1863	L	335
6291	UNITED AMERICAN / PATRIOTISM, CHARITY & HARMONY/ N. Currier	S	100

6292	U.S. ARMY LEAVING THE GULF SQUADRON/ (7.15x13) 1847, N. Currier	S	265
6293	UNITED STATES CAPITOL, THE	S	320
6294	UNITED STATES CAPITOL / WASHINGTON, D.C./ (7.15x12.7) N. Currier	S	320
6295	U.S. FRIGATE "ST. LAWRENCE" 50 GUNS, THE/ N. Currier	S	395
6296	UNITED STATES, LATE HOLT'S HOTEL/ N. Currier	M	500
6297	U.S.M. STEAMSHIP / "BALTIC"/ N. Currier	L	1000
6298	U.S. BRIG-OF-WAR SOMERS, THE/ N. Currier	S	440
6299	U.S. BRIG PORPOISE IN A SQUALL, THE/ N. Currier	S	380
6300	U.S. CRUISER "NEW YORK"	L	975
6300A	U.S. DRAGOONS/ (8.8x12.12) 1846, N. Currier	S	230
6301	U.S. DRAGOONS/ (8.6x12.10) 1847, N. Currier	S	230
6302	U.S. DRAGOONS/ (8.7x12.10) 1847, N. Currier	S	230
6303	U.S. FRIGATE "CONSTITUTION"/ N. Currier	S	535
6304	U.S. FRIGATE "CONSTITUTION" / #88/ N. Currier	S	535
6305	U.S. FRIGATE "CUMBERLAND" / #89/ 1848, N. Currier	S	465
6306	U.S. FRIGATE "CUMBERLAND" / #607/ 1848, N. Currier	S	465
6307	U.S. FRIGATE "INDEPENDENCE"/ 1841, N. Currier	S	465
6308	U.S. FRIGATE "ST. LAWRENCE"/ N. Currier	S	465
6309	U.S. FRIGATE "ST. LAWRENCE" /#295/ N. Currier	S	465
6310	U.S. FRIGATE "SAVANNAH"/ 1843, N. Currier	S	465
6311	U.S. FRIGATE "UNITED STATES" CAPTURING H. M. FRIGATE "MACEDONIAN"/ (8.2x12.15) N. Currier	S	480
6312	U.S. MAIL STEAMSHIP "ADRIATIC"/ N. Currier	S	340
6313	U.S. MAIL STEAMSHIP "ARCTIC"/ 1850, N. Currier	M	645
6314	U.S.M. STEAMSHIP / "ARCTIC"/ N. Currier	L	1150
6315	U.S.M. STEAMSHIP / "ATLANTIC"/ 1850, N. Currier	S	390
6316	U.S.M. STEAMSHIP "ATLANTIC" / #457/ 1852, N. Currier	S	390
6317	U.S.M. STEAMSHIP "ATLANTIC" / #458/ 1852, N. Currier	S	390
6318	U.S.M. STEAMSHIP "ATLANTIC"/ 1850, N. Currier	M	645
6319	U.S.M. STEAMSHIP "ATLANTIC"/ 1850, N. Currier	L	1150
6320	U.S.M. STEAMSHIP "BALTIC"/ 1852, N. Currier	S	390
6321	U.S. MAIL STEAMSHIP / "BALTIC"/ 1850	L	1150
6322	U.S. MAIL STEAMSHIP "CALIFORNIA"	S	355
6323	U.S. MAIL STEAMSHIP "PACIFIC"/ N. Currier	L	1150
6324	U.S. MAIL STEAMSHIP "PACIFIC"/ N. Currier	S	355
6325	U.S. MILITARY ACADEMY, WEST POINT/ (11.2x15.10) 1862	M	840
6326	U.S. POST OFFICE, NEW YORK/ (9.2x12.14)	S	470
6327	U.S. SHIP "NORTH CAROLINA"/ (9x12.14) 1843, N. Currier	S	485
6328	U.S. SHIP "NORTH CAROLINA"/ (9x12.13.2) 1843, N. Currier	S	485

6329	U.S. SHIP "NORTH CAROLINA"/ 1843, N. Currier	S	485
6330	U.S. SHIP "NORTH CAROLINA"/ 1844, N. Currier	S	485
6331	U.S. SHIP OF THE LINE "DELAWARE"/ (8.12x12.12) 1847, N. Currier	S	485
6332	U.S. SHIP OF THE LINE IN A GALE/ (8.5x12.13) N. Currier	S	200
6333	U.S. SHIP OF THE LINE "OHIO"/ (8.12x12.15) 1847, N. Currier	S	485
6334	U.S. SHIP OF THE LINE "PENNSYLVANIA"/ (8.12x13) N. Currier	S	485
6335	U.S. SHIP OF THE LINE "PENNSYLVANIA"/ N. Currier	S	485
6336	U.S. SLOOP OF WAR "ALBANY"/ (9.1x13.3) N. Currier	S	485
6337	U.S. SLOOP OF WAR IN A GALE/ (9.4x13.4) N. Currier	S	495
6338	U.S. SLOOP OF WAR "KEARSARGE"/ (8x12.8) 1864	S	500
6339	U.S. SLOOP OF WAR "KEARSARGE"/ 1864	S	500
6340	U.S. SLOOP OF WAR "VINCENNES"/ (8.15x12.15) 1845, N. Currier	S	495
6341	U.S. STEAM FRIGATE "MISSISSIPPI"/ (8.12x12.12) 1848, N. Currier	S	485
6342	U.S. STEAM FRIGATE "MISSISSIPPI" IN A TYPHOON/ (15.15x20.14)	L	1400
6343	U.S. STEAM FRIGATE "NIAGARA"/ (Vig.)	S	485
6344	U.S. STEAM FRIGATE "NIAGARA"	L	1275
6345	U.S. STEAM FRIGATE "PRINCETON"/ 1844, N. Currier	S	485
6346	U.S. STEAM FRIGATE "PRINCETON"/ 1845, N. Currier	S	485
6347	U.S. STEAM FRIGATE "WABASH"/ (8.8x12.14)	S	485
6348	UNSER KARL"/ (Vig.)	S	45
6349	UP IN A BALLOON/ 1876	S	195
6350	UP THE HUDSON	S	350
6351	UPPER AND LOWER BAY OF NEW YORK FROM THE BATTERY LOOKING SOUTHWEST (8.8x12.8)	S	515
6352	UPPER CANADA COLLEGE/ (11.14x17.14) N. Currier	M	695
6353	UPPER LAKE OF KILLARNEY, KERRY COUNTY, IRELAND	S	85

V

Con#	Title	Folio	Value
6354	VALKYRIE/ (10x13.9)	S	385
6355	VALLEY FALLS, VIRGINIA/ (8x12.8)	S	260
6356	VALLEY OF THE BLACK WATER, IRELAND	S	85
6357	VALLEY OF THE SHENANDOAH, THE/ (14.15x20.1) 1864	L	1300
6358	VALLEY OF THE SUSQUEHANNA/ (14.12x20.10)	L	1250
6359	VAN AMBURG & CO.'S TRIUMPHAL CAR PASSING THE ASTOR HOUSE/ (8x13) 1846, N. Currier	S	400
6360	VANTILE MACK, THE INFANT LAMBERT OR / GIANT BABY!	S	145

6361	VASE OF FLOWERS, THE/ (Vig.) 1847, N. Currier	S	115
6362	VASE OF FLOWERS, THE/ (Vig.) 1870	S	115
6363	VASE OF FLOWERS, THE	S	115
6364	VASE OF FRUIT/ 1864	M	275
6365	VELOCIPEDE, THE/ 1869	S	1350
6366	VENICE / FROM THE CANAL OF THE GUIDECCA / (Moonlight scene)	L	300
6367	VENICE / FROM THE CANAL OF THE GUIDECCA	L	300
6368	VERY REV. FATHER THOS. N. BURKE C.P./ (Vig.)	S	50
6369	VERY REVERED, THE / THEOBOLD MATHEW/ (8.15x11.3) 1848, N. Currier	S	45
6370	VERY REVERED, THE / FATHER THEOBOLD MATHEW	S	45
6371	VERY WARM CORNER, A/ (Vig.) 1883	S	225
6372	VICTORIOUS ATTACK ON FORT FISHER, N.C./ (15.11x22.13) 1865	L	1150
6373	VICTORIOUS BOMBARDMENT OF PORT ROYAL, S.C./ (8.4x11.15)	S	400
6374	VICTORY DOUBTFUL/ (8.2x12.8) (Companion to #579)	S	140
6375	VICTORY OF ROANOKE, THE	S	200
6376	VIEW DOWN THE RAVINE AT TRENTON FALLS, N.Y. (10.7x15.3)	M	550
6377	VIEW DOWN THE RIVER	VS	160
6378	VIEW FROM FORT PUTNAM / WEST POINT, HUDSON RIVER / #239/ N. Currier	S	235
6379	VIEW FROM FORT PUTNAM / WEST POINT, HUDSON RIVER/ (8x12.5)	S	230
6380	VIEW FROM FORT PUTNAM / WEST POINT, HUDSON RIVER/ (8x12.8)	S	235
6381	VIEW FROM PEEKSKILL, HUDSON RIVER, N.Y./ 1862	M	710
6382	VIEW FROM THE ROCK OF GIBRALTER...BURNING...MISSOURI/ N. Currier	S	400
6383	VIEW FROM WEST POINT/ C. Currier	S	290
6384	VIEW FROM WEST POINT / HUDSON RIVER/ N. Currier	S	290
6385	VIEW IN DUTCHESS COUNTY, N.Y.	L	1275
6386	VIEW IN SWITZERLAND/ (Vig.)	S	210
6387	VIEW NEAR HIGHBRIDGE, HARLEM RIVER, N.Y./ (10.14x15.8)	M	980
6388	VIEW OF ASTORIA, L.I.	M	1250
6389	VIEW OF BALTIMORE/ (8.1x12.11) 1848, N. Currier	S	610
6390	VIEW OF BOSTON/ 1848, N. Currier	S	610
6391	VIEW OF BUNKER HILL AND MONUMENT/ (8.7x12.1) N. Currier	S	255
6392	VIEW OF CHAPULTEPEC AND MOLINO DEL REY/ (8.6x12.8) N. Currier	S	105
6393	VIEW OF CHICAGO	S	660
6394	VIEW OF ESOPUS CREEK	S	265
6395	VIEW OF HARPERS FERRY, VA./ (14.11x20.5)	L	1150
6396	VIEW OF KING STREET, CITY OF TORONTO, N.C./ (11.14x17.14) N. Currier	S	320
6397	VIEW OF MAUCH CHUNK FROM THE NARROWS/ C. Currier	S	295

6398	VIEW OF MADISON THE CAPITAL OF WISCONSIN/ C. Currier	M	765
6399	VIEW OF NEW YORK/ 1860	S	505
6400	VIEW OF NEW YORK/ 1869	S	505
6401	VIEW OF NEW YORK/ [New BEST 50]	S	510
6402	VIEW OF NEW YORK FROM BROOKLYN HEIGHTS/ 1849, N. Currier	M	1400
6403	VIEW OF NEW YORK FROM BROOKLYN HEIGHTS/ 1849, N. Currier	M	1400
6404	VIEW OF NEW YORK FROM WEEHAWKEN/ (8.3x12.11) 1848, N. Currier	S	485
6405	VIEW OF NEW YORK FROM WEEHAWKEN/ 1849, N. Currier	L	1950
6406	VIEW OF NEW YORK, JERSEY CITY, HOBOKEN AND BROOKLYN/ (19.11x33.4) 1858	L	2050
6407	VIEW OF NEW YORK BAY FROM STATEN ISLAND	S	465
6408	VIEW OF PHILADELPHIA/ 1875	S	535
6409	VIEW OF SAN FRANCISCO, CALIFORNIA/ (14.14x29.14) 1851, N. Currier [Old BEST 50]	L	9075
6410	VIEW OF SANTIAGO / CUBA	S	130
6411	VIEW OF THE DISTRIBUTING RESERVOIR ON MURRAY'S HILL - CITY OF NEW YORK/ (8.1x12.12) 1842, N. Currier	S	460
6412	VIEW OF THE FEDERAL HALL OF THE CITY OF NEW YORK/ C. Currier	M	540
6413	VIEW OF THE GREAT CONFLAGRATION OF DEC. 16TH/ N. Currier	M	690
6414	VIEW OF THE GREAT CONFLAGRATION OF DEC. 16TH/ 1836, N. Currier	M	690
6415	VIEW OF THE GREAT CONFLAGRATION AT NEW YORK, JULY 19TH, 1845/ (8.3x12.12) 1845, N. Currier	S	515
6416	VIEW OF THE GREAT CONFLAGRATION AT NEW YORK, JULY 19TH, 1845/ (8.3x12.7) 1845, N. Currier	S	515
6417	VIEW OF THE GREAT RECEIVING RESERVOIR, YORKVILLE, CITY OF NEW YORK/ 1841, N. Currier	S	505
6418	VIEW OF THE GREAT RECEIVING RESERVOIR, YORKVILLE, CITY OF NEW YORK/ 1842, N. Currier	S	505
6419	VIEW OF HIGH FALLS AT TRENTON	S	235
6419A	VIEW OF HIGH FALLS OF TRENTON / West Canada Creek, N.Y.	L	1200
6420	VIEW OF THE HOUSES OF PARLIAMENT AND GOVERNMENT OFFICES, CITY OF TORONTO, N.C./ (11.14x17.14) N. Currier	S	355
6421	VIEW OF THE HUDSON RIVER FROM RUGGLES HOUSE/ (8.3x11.11) 1846, N. Currier	S	275
6422	VIEW OF THE PARK FOUNTAIN AND CITY HALL/ N. Currier	S	495
6423	VIEW OF THE PARK FOUNTAIN AND CITY HALL, N.Y./ (8x11.10) 1847, N. Currier	S	495
6424	VIEW OF THE PARK FOUNTAIN AND CITY HALL, N.Y. 1851	S	495
6425	VIEW OF THE TERRIFIC EXPLOSION/ (8.2x12.6) 1845, N. Currier	S	545
6426	VIEW OF WATERBURY, CONN./ (15.1x22.9) 1837, N. Currier	L	1325
6427	VIEW OF WEST END, ST CROIX / (West Indies) (8.6x16.4) N. Currier	S	420

All prints are published by Currier & Ives unless otherwise stated.

6428	VIEW OF WEST POINT/ C. Currier	S	350
6429	VIEW OF WEST ROCK, NEAR NEW HAVEN, CONN/ (15.11x23.7) 1864	L	1175
6430	VIEW ON BROADWAY, N.Y.	L	1575
6431	VIEW ON ESOPUS CREEK	S	270
6432	VIEW ON FULTON AVENUE, BROOKLYN/ (Vig.) N. Currier	S	300
6433	VIEW ON HUDSON RIVER / FROM RUGGLES HOUSE, NEWBURGH/ (8.8x12.7)	S	300
6434	VIEW ON HUDSON RIVER / FROM RUGGLES HOUSE, NEWBURGH/ (8.7x12.7)	S	305
6435	VIEW ON LAKE GEORGE, N.Y./ (15x20.6) 1866	L	1225
6436	VIEW ON LAKE GEORGE, N.Y.	S	335
6437	VIEW ON LONG ISLAND, N.Y./ (14.12x20.8) 1857	L	1350
6438	VIEW ON MONTGOMERY CREEK / NEAR THE HUDSON	S	300
6439	VIEW ON THE DELAWARE / NEAR EASTON, PENNA.	S	385
6440	VIEW ON THE DELAWARE / "WATER GAP" IN THE DISTANCE	L	1300
6441	VIEW ON THE HARLEM RIVER, N.Y. - THE HIGH BRIDGE/ 1852	L	1500
6442	VIEW ON THE HARLEM RIVER, N.Y. - THE HIGH BRIDGE	L	1425
6443	VIEW ON THE HOUSATONIC/ 1867	L	1350
6444	VIEW ON THE HUDSON	L	1650
6445	VIEW ON THE HUDSON / (More boats)	L	1700
6446	VIEW ON THE HUDSON	VS	230
6447	VIEW ON THE HUDSON - CROW'S NEST	S	285
6448	VIEW ON THE HUDSON - CROW'S NEST / (Changes in composition from preceding.)	S	275
6449	VIEW ON THE POTOMAC NEAR HARPERS FERRY/ (15x20.3) 1866	L	1200
6450	VIEW ON THE RHINE/ (8.8x12.8)	S	105
6451	VIEW ON THE RONDOUT	M	550
6451A	VIEW ON THE RONDOUT	S	310
6452	VIEW ON THE ST. LAWRENCE - INDIAN ENCAMPMENT/ (8x12.8)	S	290
6453	VIEW UP THE RIVER	VS	175
6454	VIGILANT AND VALKYRIE IN A "THRASH TO WINDWARD"/ (16x24.1) 1893	L	1850
6455	VIGILANT	S	385
6456	VILLA, DESIGNED FOR DAV. CODWISE, ESQ./ N. Currier	S	75
6457	VILLA ON THE HUDSON/ (9.14x17) 1869	M	520
6458	VILLA ON THE HUDSON	S	200
6459	VILLAGE BEAUTY, THE	S	75
6460	VILLAGE BLACKSMITH, THE/ (9.13x14.15)	M	720
6461	VILLAGE BLACKSMITH, THE/ (9.15x14.15)	M	720
6462	VILLAGE BLACKSMITH, THE/ (15.16x23.5) 1864	L	3000
6463	VILLAGE CHAPEL, NEAR PARIS	VS	90

6464	VILLAGE STREET, THE/ 1855	M	500
6465	VILLAGE STREET, THE	M	500
6466	VIOLA	L	135
6467	VIOLET AND DAISY	S	75
6468	VIRGIN AND CHILD	S	20
6469	VIRGIN AND CHILD, THE/ N. Currier	S	20
6470	VIRGIN MARY, THE/ (8.8x12.11) 1848, N. Currier	S	20
6471	VIRGIN MARY, THE/ 1849, N. Currier	S	20
6472	VIRGINIA/ N. Currier	S	75
6473	VIRGINIA/ (Vig.) N. Currier	S	80
6474	VIRGINIA HOME IN THE OLDEN TIME, A/ (8.7x12.8) 1872	S	270
6475	VIRGINIA WATER, WINDSOR PARK/ (8.8x12.8)	S	125
6476	VIRTUE, LOVE AND TEMPERANCE, LOVE, PURITY AND FIDELITY/ 1851, N. Currier	S	200
6477	VISION, THE/ N. Currier	S	20
6477A	VISTA DE LA CIUDAD DE NEW YORK	L	1050
6478	VOLTAIRE/ Record 2:21.25/ (Vig.) 1879	S	290
6479	VOLUNTARY MANNER IN WHICH SOME OF THE SOUTHERN VOLUNTEERS ENLIST, THE	S	185
6480	VOLUNTEER CROSSING THE FINISH LINE/ 1887	L	1500
6481	VOLUNTEER / MODELLED BY EDWARD BURGESS	L	1500
6482	VOLUNTEER / THE GREAT SIRE OF TROTTERS	S	295
6483	VOLUNTEER/ 1887	S	290

W

Con#	Title	Folio	Value
6484	WAA-NA-TAA OR THE FOREMOST IN BATTLE/ C. Currier	S	285
6485	WACHT AM DEM RHINE, DIE/ (12x8.8)	S	70
6486	WAIT FOR ME	S	100
6487	WAIT YOUR TURN/ (Vig.)	S	115
6488	WAITING FOR A BITE/ (8x11.14) N. Currier	S	220
6489	WAITING FOR A DRINK/ N. Currier	S	225
6490	WAKING UP THE OLD MARE/ (15.12x24) 1881	L	1100
6491	WAKING UP THE WRONG PASSENGER/ (Vig.) 1875	S	365
6492	WALKED HOME ON HIS EAR/ (11.15x9) 1878	S	135
6493	WALK IN!	S	95
6494	WAR	S	100

6495	WAR PRESIDENT, A/ (Political Cartoon) 1848, N. Currier	S	185
6496	WARMING UP	S	185
6497	WARMING UP/ (Vig.) 1884	S	240
6498	WARMING UP	L	1125
6499	WARREN MILLER/ (19x16.8)	M	115
6500	WARWICK CASTLE ON THE AVON/ (11.12x15.9)	M	145
6501	WASHINGTON/ (Half length, upright, slightly to right.) (23.4x13.7)	L	250
6502	WASHINGTON / #187/ N. Currier	S	160
6503	WASHINGTON/ (12x8.8) N. Currier	S	160
6504	WASHINGTON/ (12.2x8.12) N. Currier	S	160
6505	WASHINGTON/ 1880	S	160
6506	WASHINGTON/ (3/4 Length.)	M	205
6507	WASHINGTON	M	205
6508	WASHINGTON	VS	140
6509	WASHINGTON AND HIS CABINET/ 1876	S	215
6510	WASHINGTON AND LINCOLN/ (14.15x10.15) 1865	M	270
6511	WASHINGTON APPOINTED COMMANDER-IN-CHIEF/ (8.13x12.11) 1876	S	180
6512	WASHINGTON AS A MASON/ (12x8)	S	160
6513	WASHINGTON AS A MASON/ (11.13x8.6) 1868	S	160
6514	WASHINGTON AT HOME/ (16.12x23.15) 1867	L	380
6515	WASHINGTON AT MOUNT VERNON/ (12.7x8.3) 1852, N. Currier [Old BEST 50]	S	480
6516	WASHINGTON AT PRAYER	S	125
6517	WASHINGTON AT PRAYER/ N. Currier	S	125
6518	WASHINGTON AT PRINCETON/ (8.8x13) 1846, N. Currier	S	395
6519	WASHINGTON AT VALLEY FORGE/ (11.9x8.9) N. Currier	S	310
6520	WASHINGTON COLUMNS, THE - YOSEMITE VALLEY/ (8.7x12.8)	S	350
6521	WASHINGTON / CROSSING THE DELAWARE/ (Vig.) N. Currier	S	280
6522	WASHINGTON CROSSING THE DELAWARE / #224/ N. Currier	S	280
6523	WASHINGTON CROSSING THE DELAWARE / #69 [Old Best 50]	S	410
6524	WASHINGTON CROSSING THE DELAWARE	S	280
6525	WASHINGTON CROSSING THE DELAWARE/ 1876	S	280
6526	WASHINGTON" DRIVEN BY JOEL CONKLIN/ N. Currier	L	1100
6527	WASHINGTON FAMILY, THE	S	85
6528	WASHINGTON FAMILY/ (9x12.15) N. Currier	S	85
6529	WASHINGTON FAMILY/ N. Currier	S	85
6530	WASHINGTON FAMILY, THE/ 1867	S	85
6531	WASHINGTON FAMILY, THE	S	85
6532	WASHINGTON FAMILY / #70/ N. Currier	S	85

6533	WASHINGTON - FIRST IN VALOR, WISDOM, AND VIRTUE/ N. Currier	S	130
6534	WASHINGTON - FIRST IN VALOR, WISDOM, AND VIRTUE (11.14x8.12)	S	130
6535	WASHINGTON - FIRST IN WAR, FIRST IN PEACE, IN THE HEARTS OF HIS COUNTRYMEN / #34/ 1846, N. Currier	S	130
6536	WASHINGTON - FIRST IN WAR, FIRST IN PEACE, IN THE HEARTS OF HIS COUNTRYMEN / #265/ N. Currier	S	130
6537	WASHINGTON - FIRST IN WAR, FIRST IN PEACE, IN THE HEARTS OF HIS COUNTRYMEN/ (12x8.10) C. Currier	S	130
6538	WASHINGTON - FIRST IN WAR, FIRST IN PEACE, IN THE HEARTS OF HIS COUNTRYMEN / #71/ N. Currier	S	130
6539	WASHINGTON - FIRST IN WAR, FIRST IN PEACE, IN THE HEARTS OF HIS COUNTRYMEN/ N. Currier	S	130
6540	WASHINGTON - FIRST IN WAR, FIRST IN PEACE, IN THE HEARTS OF HIS COUNTRYMEN/ (11.13x8.5) C. Currier	S	130
6541	WASHINGTON - FROM THE PRESIDENT'S HOUSE/ 1848, N. Currier	S	235
6542	WASHINGTON IN THE FIELD/ N. Currier	S	175
6543	WASHINGTON, McCLELLAN AND SCOTT	M	355
6544	WASHINGTON, SHERMAN AND GRANT	M	355
6545	WASHINGTON TAKING COMMAND OF THE AMERICAN ARMY/ 1876	S	160
6546	WASHINGTON TAKING COMMAND OF THE AMERICAN ARMY/ 1848, N. Currier	S	160
6547	WASHINGTON TAKING LEAVE OF THE OFFICERS OF HIS ARMY AT FRANCE'S TAVERN/ N.Y./ (8.10x12.7) N. Currier [Old BEST 50]	S	400
6548	WASHINGTON'S DREAM	L	375
6549	WASHINGTON'S ENTRY INTO NEW YORK/ (10.8x15) 1857	M	775
6550	WASHINGTON'S FAREWELL TO THE OFFICERS OF HIS ARMY/ (8.12x12.1) 1876	S	335
6551	WASHINGTON'S HEADQUARTERS AT NEWBURGH, ON THE HUDSON/ (8.8x12.8)	S	175
6552	WASHINGTON'S RECEPTION ON THE BRIDGE AT TRENTON IN 1789/ (12.8x8.5) N. Currier	S	135
6553	WASHINGTON'S RECEPTION ON THE BRIDGE AT TRENTON IN 1789/ (8.4x12.6) N. Currier	S	135
6554	WASHINGTON'S RECEPTION BY THE LADIES/ (Upright, star and monogram at the top.) 1845, N. Currier	S	135
6555	WASHINGTON'S RECEPTION BY THE LADIES/ (Upright shield at top) 1845, N. Currier	S	135
6556	WASHINGTON'S RECEPTION BY THE LADIES/ (Shield and monogram at top) 1845, N. Currier	S	135
6557	WASHINGTON'S RECEPTION BY THE LADIES/ (Upright, small girl facing observer) 1845, N. Currier	S	135
6558	WASHINGTON'S RECEPTION BY THE LADIES/ (Upright) 1848, N. Currier	S	135
6559	WASHINGTON'S RECEPTION BY THE LADIES/ 1889	S	135
6560	WATCH ON THE RHINE, THE	S	75

6561	WATCHERS, THE	S	110
6562	WATER FOWL SHOOTING/ (8x12) N. Currier	S	660
6563	WATER JUMP, THE/ 1884	L	1475
6564	WATER JUMP AT JEROME PARK, THE	S	455
6565	WATER LILY, THE/ (10.5x14.12) N. Currier	M	275
6566	WATER NYMPH, THE	S	95
6567	WATER RAIL SHOOTING/ (8.2x12.11) 1855, N. Currier [Old BEST 50]	S	750
6568	WATER RAIL SHOOTING/ (8.2x12.8) 1870	S	690
6569	WATER RAIL SHOOTING/ (8.2x12.8)	S	690
6570	WATERFALL - MOON LIGHT	L	525
6571	WATERFALL, THE	VS	155
6572	WATERFALL - TIVOLI, ITALY/ (8.8x12.8)	S	95
6573	WATKIN'S GLEN, NEW YORK	S	300
6574	WAVERLY HOUSE/ (15x18.8) N. Currier	M	605
6575	WAY THEY CAME FROM CALIFORNIA, THE/ (10.15x17.6) 1849, N. Currier	M	1700
6576	WAY THEY CROSS THE ISTHMUS, THE/ (11x17.5) 1849, N. Currier	M	825
6577	WAY THEY GET MARRIED IN CALIFORNIA, THE/ N. Currier	M	1050
6578	WAY THEY GO TO CALIFORNIA/ N.Currier/ (10.15x17.7) 1849	M	2000
6579	WAY THEY RAISE A CALIFORNIA OUTFIT/ 1849, N. Currier	M	1000
6580	WAY THEY WAIT FOR THE "STEAMER" AT PANAMA/ (10.14x17.6) 1849, N. Currier	M	915
6581	WAY TO GROW POOR, THE - THE WAY TO GROW RICH	S	340
6582	WAY TO HAPPINESS, THE/ (9.13x2) N. Currier	S	50
6583	WAY TO HAPPINESS, THE/ (9.12x11.12) N. Currier	S	50
6584	WAY TO HAPPINESS, THE/ (11.13x8.12) N. Currier	S	50
6585	WAY TO HAPPINESS, THE/ #120/ N. Currier	S	50
6586	WAY TO HAPPINESS, THE/ (11.13x9.9) N. Currier	S	50
6587	WAYSIDE INN, THE/ (15.14x23.6) 1864	L	1825
6588	WE MET BY CHANCE/ (Vig.) 1875	S	220
6588A	WE MET BY CHANCE OR WAITED FOR THE SWELL	TC	80
6589	WE PARTED ON THE HILLSIDE	TC	75
6590	WE PARTED ON THE HILLSIDE / "AMID THE WINTER'S SNOW"	S	500
6591	WE PRAISE THEE, O LORD/ (Vig.)	S	20
6592	WE SELL FOR CASH/ 1875	S	390
6593	WE TRUST	S	260
6594	WEARING OF THE GREEN, THE	S	75
6595	WEDDING, THE/ (11.14x8.12) N. Currier	S	85
6596	WEDDING DAY, THE/ N. Currier	S	95
6597	WEDDING DAY, THE/ (7.2x8.14) N. Currier	S	90

6598	WEDDING DAY, THE/ C. Currier	S	95
6599	WEDDING DAY, THE/ #106/ N. Currier	S	90
6600	WEDDING DAY, THE/ (12.1x8.6) 1846, N. Currier	S	90
6601	WEDDING EVENING, THE	S	85
6602	WEDDING MORNING, THE/ N. Currier	S	90
6603	WEDGEWOOD," RECORD 2:19/ 1881	TC	85
6604	WELCOME/ (Motto) (Vig.) 1873	S	195
6605	WELCOME HOME/ (Motto)	S	185
6606	WELCOME / TAKE A DRINK/ N. Currier	S	175
6607	WELCOME TO OUR HOME/ (Motto) (Vig.) 1874	S	185
6608	WELL-BRED SETTER, A/ 1871	S	300
6609	WELL-BRED SETTER, A/ 1870	S	300
6610	WELL-BRED SETTER, A	S	300
6611	WELL BROKEN RETRIEVER, A/ 1870	S	300
6612	WELL BUNCHED AT THE LAST HURDLE/ (18.8x28.3) 1887	L	1125
6613	WELL - I'M BLOWED/ (Vig.) 1883	S	245
6614	WELL TOGETHER AT THE FIRST TURN"/ (17.1x26.6) 1886	L	1375
6615	WELL TOGETHER AT THE FIRST TURN"/ (17.1x26.7) 1886	L	1375
6616	WELL TOGETHER AT THE FIRST TURN"/ (16.14x25.15) 1873	L	1375
6617	WEST POINT FOUNDRY - COLD SPRING, HUDSON RIVER, N.Y.	M	1250
6617A	WEST POINT, FROM PHILLIPSTOWN/ (15.12x21.12)	L	1550
6618	WESTERN BEAUTY, THE/ (Vig.)	S	75
6619	WESTERN FARMER'S HOME, THE/ (8.8x12.8) 1871	S	405
6620	WESTERN RIVER SCENERY/ (11.8x16.9) 1866	M	850
6621	WE'VE HAD A HEALTHY TIME!/ (Vig.) 1880	S	275
6622	WHALE FISHERY / ATTACKING A RIGHT WHALE	S	1425
6623	WHALE FISHERY / ATTACKING A RIGHT WHALE/ [New BEST 50]	L	6800
6624	WHALE FISHERY, THE / CUTTING IN	S	1425
6625	WHALE FISHERY, THE / "IN A FLURRY"/ 1852, N. Currier	S	1425
6626	WHALE FISHERY, THE "LAYING ON"/ 1852, N. Currier [Old & New BEST 50]	S	1425
6627	WHALE FISHERY, THE - THE SPERM WHALE IN A FLURRY/ (16x24) [Old & New BEST 50]	L	6900
6628	WHALE FISHERY, THE. THE SPERM WHALE "IN A FLURRY"/ (9.8x12.11)	S	1425
6628A	WHAT IS IT? OR "MAN MONKEY" ON EXHIBITION	S	190
6629	WHAT SHALL THE HARVEST BE/ 1886	S	95
6630	WHAT'S SAUCE FOR THE GOOSE IS SAUCE FOR THE GANDER/ (11.9x17.6) 1851, N. Currier	M	385
6631	WHEAT FIELD, THE/ N. Currier	S	255
6632	WHEAT FIELD, THE	S	255

6633	WHEELMEN IN RED HOT FINISH*/ 1894	M	1400
6634	WHEN SHALL WE THREE MEET AGAIN?/ (8.12x12.7)	S	100
6635	WHEN THE FOLLOWING TIDE COMES IN/ (Vig.) 1879	S	120
6636	WHERE DO YOU BUY YOUR CIGARS?/ 1879	S	165
6637	WHERE DO YOU BUY YOUR CIGARS?/ 1880	VS	145
6637A	WHERE DO YOU BUY YOUR CIGARS?/ 1880	TC	75
6638	WHICH DONKEY WILL I TAKE?/ (Vig.) 1881	S	165
6638A	WHICH DONKEY WILL I TAKE?	TC	75
6639	WHICH OF US WILL YOU MARRY?/ (11.10x8.11) 1846, N. Currier	S	80
6640	WHITE DOGGIES INTO MISCHIEF	S	140
6641	WHITE DOG'S GOT HIM, DE!/ (Vig.) (Companion to #645) 1889	S	205
6642	WHITE FAWN, THE/ 1868	S	185
6643	WHITE HALL, BRISTOL COLLEGE, PA./ (10.2x13.10) 1835	S	265
6644	WHITE SQUADRON, U.S. NAVY/ 1893	L	1175
6645	WHO COMES HERE!/ (8.6x12.10) N. Currier	S	145
6646	WHO GOES THERE!/ N. Currier	S	150
6647	WHO SPEAKS FIRST/ (11.11x8.10)	S	135
6648	WHO'S AFRAID OF YOU?/ 1868	S	135
6649	WHO SAID RATS?	S	140
6650	WHO WILL LOVE ME?	S	100
6651	WHOSE CHICK ARE YOU?	S	125
6652	WHY DON'T HE COME? (11.12x8.15)	S	125
6653	WHY DON'T HE COME? / FIRST AT THE RENDEZVOUS/ (Companion to #4713)	S	125
6654	WHY DON'T YER COME ALONG?/ (Vig.) 1883	S	245
6655	WHY DON'T YOU TAKE IT?	S	250
6656	WICKLOW, IRELAND	M	125
6657	WIDE AWAKE/ (Companion to #3718)	S	80
6658	WIDE PATH, THE/ N. Currier	S	90
6659	WIDOW'S SON, THE	S	75
6660	WIDOW'S TREASURE, THE/ (12.2x8.14) N. Currier	S	75
6661	WIDOWER'S TREASURE, THE/ (12.2x8.14) N. Currier	S	75
6662	WI-JUN-JON - THE PIGEON'S EGG HEAD	M	265
6663	WILD CAT BANKER, A/ 1853, N. Currier	S	220
6664	WILD CAT TRAIN, A - NO STOP OVERS/ (Vig.) 1884	S	360
6665	WILD DUCK SHOOTING/ C. Currier	S	580
6666	WILD DUCK SHOOTING/ (8.14x12.14) N. Currier	S	540
6667	WILD DUCK SHOOTING/ (7.8x12.12) N. Currier	S	540
6668	WILD DUCK SHOOTING / #53/ N. Currier	S	525

6669	WILD DUCK SHOOTING/ N. Currier	L	4800
6670	WILD DUCK SHOOTING - A GOOD DAY'S SPORT/ (18.7x25.12) 1854, N. Currier [New BEST 50]	L	6150
6671	WILD DUCK SHOOTING - ON THE WING/ (8.3x12.7) 1870	S	580
6672	WILD DUCK SHOOTING - ON THE WING/ (7.15x12.7)	S	580
6673	WILD DUCK SHOOTING - ON THE WING/ (8x12.6)	S	580
6674	WILD FLOWERS	S	120
6675	WILD HORSES AT PLAY ON THE AMERICAN PRAIRIES (12.2x17.14)	M	1550
6676	WILD IRISHMAN*/ (Race Horse) (RARE) (19.5x26.5) N. Currier	L	1625
6677	WILD TURKEY SHOOTING/ (8.6x12.8) 1871 [Old BEST 50]	S	720
6678	WILD WEST IN DARKTOWN, THE - ATTACK ON THE DEADHEAD COACH/ (Vig.) 1893	S	250
6679	WILD WEST IN DARKTOWN, THE - THE BUFFALO CHASE/ (Vig.) 1893	S	250
6680	WILHELM I (Vig.)	S	55
6681	WILL HE BITE?/ 1868	M	200
6682	WILL YOU BE TRUE?/ (Oval)	S	95
6683	WILLIAM/ N. Currier	S	170
6684	WILLIAM A. GRAHAM/ WHIG CANDIDATE/ 1852, N. Currier	S	95
6685	WILLIAM AND SUSAN/ (Vig.) N. Currier	S	85
6686	WILLIAM BIGLER, GOVERNOR OF PENNSYLVANIA/ (11.7x8.11) N. Currier	S	65
6687	WILLIAM C, BOUCK/ C. Currier	VS	60
6688	WILLIAM F. JOHNSTON, GOVERNOR OF PENNA./ (11.12x8.12) 1848, N. Currier	S	80
6689	WM. H. SEWARD/ C. Currier	VS	65
6690	WILLIAM HENRY HARRISON/ N. Currier	S	135
6691	WILLIAM HENRY HARRISON / NINTH PRESIDENT OF THE U.S./ #27/ N. Currier	S	140
6692	WILLIAM HENRY HARRISON / NINTH PRESIDENT OF THE U.S./ (13x9) N. Currier	S	140
6693	WILLIAM HENRY HARRISON / NINTH PRESIDENT OF THE U.S./ (11.11x9.4) N. Currier	S	140
6694	WM. L. MARCY/ C. Currier	VS	65
6695	WILLIAM O. BUTLER/ (V. Pres. Candidate) (11.10x9) 1848, N. Currier	S	90
6696	WILLIAM P. DEWEES, M.D./ (Earliest known Currier print) (11.11x9.8) 1834, N. Currier	S	225
6697	WILLIAM PENN'S TREATY WITH THE INDIANS/ (8.4x12.9) N. Currier	S	240
6698	WILLIAM PENN'S TREATY WITH THE INDIANS/ N. Currier	S	240
6699	WILLIAM PENN'S TREATY WITH THE INDIANS/ (8.3x12.10) N. Currier	S	240
6700	WILLIAM, PRINCE OF ORANGE, LANDING AT TORBAY, ENGLAND/ (12.10x8.7)	S	115
6701	WILLIAM R. KING/ (Democratic Candidate for V. Pres. Candidate) (11.8x8.13) N. Currier	S	95

6702	WILLIAM R. KING/ (V. Pres. Candidate) (11.8x8.13) N. Currier	S	95
6703	WILLIAM SHAKESPEARE/ (Vig.)	M	125
6704	WILLIAM SMITH O'BRIEN, IRELAND'S PATRIOT/ (11.6x8.15) 1848, N. Currier	S	65
6705	WILLIAM STEDDING	S	70
6706	WILLIAM TELL - DEATH OF GESSLER/ (8.3x12.5)	S	95
6707	WILLIAM TELL - ESCAPING FROM THE TYRANT/ (8.5x12.8)	S	95
6708	WILLIAM TELL ESCAPING FROM THE TYRANT/ N. Currier	S	95
6709	WILLIAM TELL - REPLYING TO GESSLER/ (8x12.5)	S	95
6710	WILLIAM TELL - REPLYING TO THE GOVERNOR/ (9.2x12.1)	S	95
6711	WILLIAM TELL - SHOOTING THE APPLE ON HIS SON'S HEAD/ N. Currier	S	95
6712	WILLIAM TELL - SHOOTING THE APPLE ON HIS SON'S HEAD	S	95
6713	WILLIAM TELL'S CHAPEL/ (7.8x5.8)	VS	85
6714	WILLIAM TILLMAN, THE COLORED STEWARD	S	90
6715	WILLIAM W. BROWN/ (Colored Orator)	S	110
6716	WILLIE AND MARY	S	80
6717	WILLIE AND ROVER	S	120
6718	WILLIE'S LITTLE PETS/ (8.2x12.9)	S	130
6719	WINDMILL, THE/ (Vig.)	S	170
6720	WINDSOR CASTLE AND THE PARK	M	205
6721	WINE TASTERS, THE/ N. Currier	S	155
6722	WINFIELD SCOTT/ (Vig.)	M	130
6723	WINFIELD SCOTT - PEOPLE'S CHOICE FOR 13TH PRESIDENT/ (11.7x8.10) 1847, N. Currier	S	105
6724	WINFIELD SCOTT - WHIG CANDIDATE/ (11.8x8.8) 1852, N. Currier	S	105
6725	WINNING THE CARD, THE	L	1200
6726	WINNING "HANDS DOWN", WITH A GOOD SECOND/ (18.8x28.3) 1887	L	1400
6727	WINNING HORSES OF THE AMERICAN TURF	L	1350
6728	WINNING IN STYLE/ 1893	M	695
6729	WINTER/ N. Currier	S	670
6730	WINTER/ (Girl with mask)	S	115
6731	WINTER/ (Girl with mask)	L	225
6732	WINTER/ (Girl's head) 1870	S	90
6733	WINTER/ (Girl's head) (Vig.) 1870	S	90
6734	WINTER EVENING/ (10.6x15) 1854, N. Currier [New BEST 50]	M	1900
6735	WINTER EVENING/ 1856, N. Currier	M	1875
6736	WINTER IN THE COUNTRY - A COLD MORNING/ (18.5x27) 1864 [New BEST 50]	L	10300
6737	WINTER IN THE COUNTRY - GETTING ICE/ (18.8x27.1) 1864 [Old & New BEST 50]	L	11000

6738	WINTER IN THE COUNTRY - THE OLD GRIST MILL/ 1864 [Old & New BEST 50]	L	9500
6739	WINTER MOONLIGHT/ 1866	M	2350
6740	WINTER MORNING/ (11.5x15.5) 1861 [New BEST 50]	M	2100
6741	WINTER MORNING - FEEDING THE CHICKENS/ (14.4x20.10) 1863	L	5550
6742	WINTER MORNING IN THE COUNTRY/ (8.7x12.7) 1873 [New BEST 50]	S	1475
6743	WINTER PASTIME/ 1855, N. Currier	M	2500
6744	WINTER PASTIME/ 1870 [New BEST 50]	M	2500
6745	WINTER SCENE/ (5.8x7.8)	VS	1425
6746	WINTER SCENE IN THE COUNTRY	L	6000
6747	WINTER SPORTS - PICKEREL FISHING/ (8.7x12.8) 1872 [Old & New BEST 50]	S	1525
6748	WINTER TWILIGHT	VS	620
6749	WISE CHILD/ 1884	S	75
6750	WITH MALICE TOWARD NONE/ (Motto) 1875	S	130
6751	WIZARD'S GLEN, THE/ (14.12x14.12) 1868	M	195
6752	WOMAN TAKEN IN ADULTERY/ N. Currier	S	20
6753	WOMAN'S HOLY WAR/ (On Liquor) (11.3x8.10) 1874	S	350
6754	WOMEN OF '76, THE / MOLLY PITCHER/ N. Currier	S	340
6755	WOMEN OF '76, THE / MOLLY PITCHER	S	340
6756	WON!/ (12.11x8.11) (Companion to #3782) N. Currier	S	150
6757	WON BY A DASH/ 1892	M	545
6758	WON BY A FOOT/ (Vig.) 1883	S	225
6759	WON BY A NECK	L	1825
6760	WON BY A NECK	M	545
6761	WON BY A NECK / LADY THORN, GOLDSMITH MAID	L	1650
6762	WONDERFUL ALBINO FAMILY, THE / (1 additional line.)	S	95
6763	WONDERFUL ALBINO FAMILY, THE	S	95
6764	WONDERFUL ELIOPHOBUS FAMILY/ (8x12.8) 1870	S	95
6765	WONDERFUL MARE "MAUD S."/ Record 2:10.75/ 1880	S	290
6766	WONDERFUL MARE "MAUD S."/ Record 2:10.25	S	290
6767	WONDERFUL MARE "MAUD S." - PROPERTY OF WM. H. VANDERBILT,ESQ./ (Vig.) 1878	S	290
6768	WONDERFUL STORY, THE/ (12.12x8.4)	S	125
6769	WOOD-DUCKS/ (8.8x12.8)	S	450
6770	WOODCOCK/ (8.8x12.8) 1871	S	345
6771	WOODCOCK, SCOLOPAX MINOR/ (8.6x12.10) 1849, N. Currier	S	335
6772	WOODCOCK SHOOTING/ (8x12) N. Currier	S	565
6773	WOODCOCK SHOOTING / #175/ (8x12.10) 1855, N. Currier [Old BEST 50]	S	605
6774	WOODCOCK SHOOTING/ (13.1x20.5) 1852, N. Currier	L	3350

6775	WOODCOCK SHOOTING/ (8.2x12.7) 1870, N. Currier	S	565
6776	WOODING UP* ON THE MISSISSIPPI/ (18.4x27.13) 1863 [New BEST 50]	L	9675
6777	WOODLAND GATE, THE/ N. Currier	M	520
6778	WOODLANDS IN SUMMER	S	240
6779	WOODLANDS IN WINTER	S	455
6780	WOODS IN AUTUMN, THE/ (11.7x16.6)	M	500
6781	WORD AND THE SIGN, THE	S	20
6782	WORKING MEN'S BANNER/ (12.10x9) 1872	S	185
6783	WOUND UP*/ (Companion to #5256) 1884	S	230
6783A	WOUND UP/ 1877	S	230
6784	WOUNDED BITTERN, THE/ (8x12.8) N. Currier	S	100
6785	WREATH OF FLOWERS, A/ (Vig.)	S	95
6786	WRECK OF THE *ATLANTIC*/ (8.8x12.8) 1873	S	295
6787	WRECK OF THE *ATLANTIC*/ (8x12.8) 1873	S	295
6788	WRECK OF THE SHIP *JOHN MINTURN*/ (7.13x12.6) 1846, N. Currier	S	375
6789	WRECK OF THE STEAMSHIP *CAMBRIA*/ 1883	S	304
6790	WRECK OF THE STEAMSHIP *SCHILLER*/ (8.5x13) 1875	S	304
6791	WRECK OF THE U.S.M. STEAMSHIP *ARCTIC*/ (17.4x25.4) 1854, N. Currier	L	1325
6792	WRECKED BY A COW CATCHER/ (Vig.) 1885	S	380
6793	WRONG WAY - RIGHT WAY/ (8.8x12.14)	S	400
6794	W.W. BROWN/ (Colored author)	S	100

Y

Con#	Title	Folio	Value
6795	YACHT *COUNTESS OF DUFFERIN*, THE/ (9x13.2)	S	380
6796	YACHT *DAUNTLESS*, OF NEW YORK	S	380
6797	YACHT *DAUNTLESS*, OF NEW YORK/ (19.2x28)	L	1450
6798	YACHT *FLEETWING*, OF NEW YORK/ (8x12.7)	S	380
6799	YACHT *HAZE*, THE/ (16.12x27.8) 1861	L	1400
6800	YACHT *HENRIETTA*/ (17.12x27.13) 1867	L	1400
6801	YACHT *HENRIETTA*/ 1867	L	1400
6802	YACHT *HENRIETTA*	S	380
6803	YACHT *MADELEINE*/ (9.5x13.1)	S	380
6804	YACHT *MALLORY*/ 1861	L	1400
6805	YACHT *MARIA*/ 1861	L	1400
6806	YACHT *METEOR*/ (8.8x12.10)	S	585

6807	YACHT "METEOR"/ (19x27.10) 1869	L	1400
6808	YACHT "MOHAWK" OF NEW YORK/ 1877	L	1400
6809	YACHT "NORSEMAN"/ 1882	L	1400
6810	YACHT "PURITAN" OF BOSTON/ (15.3x21)	L	1400
6811	YACHT "PURITAN" / WINNER OF THE...AMERICAN CUP	M	700
6812	YACHT "REBECCA"/ 1861	L	1400
6813	YACHT "SAPPHO" OF NEW YORK/ (8.8x12.10)	S	380
6814	YACHT "SAPPHO" OF NEW YORK	S	380
6815	YACHT "SAPPHO" OF NEW YORK/ (18.8x28)	L	1450
6816	YACHT SQUADRON AT NEWPORT, THE/ (16.8x27.16) 1872	L	4375
6817	YACHT "VESTA"	S	380
6818	YACHT "VOLUNTEER"/ 1887	L	1450
6819	YACHTMAN'S SOLACE, THE	S	385
6820	YACHTMAN'S DELIGHT, THE	S	145
6821	YACHTS ON A SUMMER CRUISE/ (16.12x27.10) 1871	L	1650
6822	YANKEE DOODLE ON HIS MUSCLE (Vig.)	S	280
6823	YANKEE LOCKE/ (Comedian) C. Currier	L	335
6824	YANKEE TAR, THE/ C. Currier	S	195
6825	YEAR AFTER MARRIAGE, A/ (8.5x11.11) 1847, N. Currier	S	95
6826	YEAR AFTER MARRIAGE, A - THE MOTHER'S JEWEL/ (8.8x11.9) (Companion to #1461)	S	95
6827	YEAR BEFORE MARRIAGE, A - THE BRIDE'S JEWEL/ (8.5x11.9)	S	85
6828	YES OR NO?/ (8.11x12.2)	S	95
6829	YOSEMITE FALLS, CALIFORNIA/ (8.8x12.7)	S	380
6830	YOSEMITE VALLEY - CALIFORNIA, "THE BRIDAL VEIL" FALL/ (17.10x25.12) 1866	L	3800
6831	YOU DON'T MEAN IT/ (Vig.) 1872	S	75
6832	YOU WILL! WILL YOU?/ 1868	S	140
6833	YOUNG AFRICAN, THE/ N. Currier	S	90
6834	YOUNG AMERICA / #550/ (Vig.)	S	120
6835	YOUNG AMERICA/ (Vig.) 1873	S	120
6836	YOUNG AMERICA - CELEBRATING THE FOURTH/ (8x11.8) 1867	S	260
6837	YOUNG AMERICA - CELEBRATING THE FOURTH/ 1857	L	745
6838	YOUNG AMERICA / THE CHILD OF LIBERTY	S	150
6839	YOUNG BLOOD IN AN OLD BODY/ (8.7x12.7) 1874	S	325
6840	YOUNG BROOD, THE	S	265
6841	YOUNG BROOD, THE	L	535
6842	YOUNG CADETS, THE	TC	75
6843	YOUNG CAVALIER, THE/ (Vig.)	S	95
6844	YOUNG CHIEFTAIN/ N. Currier	S	85

6845	YOUNG CHIEFTAIN/ 1848, N. Currier	S	85
6846	YOUNG CIRCASSIAN/ N. Currier	S	65
6847	YOUNG CIRCASSIAN	S	65
6848	YOUNG COMPANIONS, THE/ N. Currier	S	95
6849	YOUNG COMPANIONS, THE	S	95
6850	YOUNG CONTINENTAL, THE/ (9x11.11) N. Currier	S	235
6851	YOUNG ENGLAND	S	50
6852	YOUNG FULLERTON/ (16x23) 1888	L	1250
6853	YOUNG GEORGIAN/ 1886	S	75
6854	YOUNG GEORGIAN, THE/ N. Currier	S	75
6855	YOUNG HOPEFUL/ (Vig.) 1874	S	80
6856	YOUNG HOUSEKEEPERS, THE/ (8.13x11.14) N. Currier	S	95
6857	YOUNG HOUSEKEEPERS, THE / Year After Marriage/ #608/ (8.12x11.14) N. Currier	S	95
6858	YOUNG HOUSEKEEPERS, THE / Year After Marriage/ #222/ N. Currier	S	95
6859	YOUNG LOVERS, THE/ N. Currier	S	100
6860	YOUNG MOTHER, THE/ N. Currier	S	85
6861	YOUNG MOTHER, THE/ (9x11) (Oval)	S	100
6862	YOUNG NAPOLEON/ (8.12x11.4) N. Currier	S	65
6863	YOUNG NAPOLEON/ CONTEMPLATING HIS FATHER'S SWORD/ (8.9x11.1) N. Currier	S	70
6864	YOUNG NAVIGATOR/ 1858	M	350
6865	YOUNG PROTECTOR/ N. Currier	S	90
6866	YOUNG RUFFED GROUSE/ (9.10x12.6) 1865	S	665
6867	YOUNG SAILOR, THE/ (8.12x12.2) 1849, N. Currier	S	185
6868	YOUNG SCOTLAND/ (Vig.)	S	80
6869	YOUNG SHEPHERDESS, THE	S	80
6870	YOUNG SOLDIER, THE/ (8.12x11.15) N. Currier	S	135
6871	YOUNG STUDENTS, THE/ (8.12x11.8)	S	135
6872	YOUNG VOLUNTEER, THE/ N. Currier	S	135
6873	YOUR PLAN AND MINE*/ (Vig.)	S	200

Z

Con#	Title	Folio	Value
6874	ZACHARY TAYLOR - NATIONAL CHOICE FOR 12TH PRESIDENT/ 1847, N. Currier	S	135
6875	ZACHARY TAYLOR - NATIONAL CHOICE FOR 12TH PRESIDENT / (Half length) 1847, N. Currier	S	135
6876	ZACHARY TAYLOR - PEOPLE'S CANDIDATE / #593/ N. Currier	S	130
6877	ZACHARY TAYLOR - PEOPLE'S CANDIDATE / #586/ N. Currier	S	130
6878	ZACHARY TAYLOR - THE PEOPLE'S CHOICE/ N. Currier	S	135
6879	ZACHARY TAYLOR - 12TH PRESIDENT OF THE UNITED STATES/ (11.4x8.14) 1849, N. Currier	S	145

Currier & Ives Trade Cards

Although Currier & Ives were primarily lithographers of decorative prints, they also did commercial work by introducing a line of trade cards for advertising. For the past several years these trade cards have increased in popularity and prices have risen. The valuations quoted below are for cards in very good condition. To be considered in very good condition, a card must be free of stains and discoloration, have good color, and have no holes, tears, or creases. The image should be centered on the card which should be uncut and measure about 3 1/4" x 5". Deduct a value of 10% or more for cards with poor or distracting imprints or stampings.

Most trade cards have the name of the Currier & Ives firm on them, those which do not are identified below by an asterisk " * " after the title.

Con#	Title	Size	Value
94	AMATEUR MUSCLE IN THE SHELL/ 1880	TC	70
346	BAD POINT ON A GOOD POINTER, A/ 1879	TC	65
366	BARE CHANCE, A/ 1879	TC	80
512	BETWEEN TWO FIRES/ 1879	TC	70
541	BITE ALL AROUND, A/ 1880	TC	70
548	BLACK DUCK SHOOTING/ 1879	TC	70
572	BLOOD WILL TELL/ 1879	TC	70
588	BOLTED!/	TC	65
605	BONESETTER RECORD 2:19/ 1881	TC	85
616	BOSS OF THE ROAD, THE/ 1880	TC	80
622A	BOSTON & BANGOR STEAMSHIP CO./ 1883	TC	95
629A	BOUND TO HEAR BEECHER	TC	75
632	BOUND TO SHINE/ 1880	TC	70
730	BULL DOZED!!/ 1877	TC	70

758A	BUTT OF THE JOKERS, THE/ 1879	TC	75
790	CAPITAL CIGAR, A	TC	70
863	CAUGHT NAPPING/ 1879	TC	80
865	CAUGHT ON THE FLY/ 1880	TC	75
1137	CLINGSTONE / Record 2:12/ 1882	TC	85
1209A	COLORING HIS MEERSCHAUM/ 1879	TC	75
1279	CRACK SHOT/ 1880	TC	70
1285	CRACK TROTTER BETWEEN THE HEATS/ 1880	TC	75
1287	CRACK TROTTER IN THE HARNESS OF THE PERIOD/ 1880	TC	75
1311	CROWD" THAT "SCOOPED" THE POOLS, THE/ 1878	TC	75
1313	CROWING MATCH	TC	70
1331	CUPID'S OWN/ (Cigar advertising card) 1880	TC	70
1388A	DARKTOWN FIRE BRIGADE, THE / Hook and Ladder Gymnastics/ 1888	TC	75
1397A	DARKTOWN FIRE BRIGADE / Under Full Steam, The/ 1888	TC	75
1456	DAWN OF LOVE	TC	70
1464	DEACON'S MARE, THE/ 1880	TC	75
1583	DIRECTOR/ (Horse) 1882	TC	85
1617A	DRAW POKER / Getting 'em Lively/ 1888	TC	70
1619A	DRAW POKER / Laying for 'em Sharp/ 1888	TC	70
1677A	EDWIN THORNE / Record 2:16 1/2/ 1882	TC	85
1804	FAIR MOON TO THEE I SING/ 1880	TC	75
1832A	FALSETTO/ 1881	TC	85
1960	FIRST BIRD OF THE SEASON, THE/ 1880	TC	75
2003A	$5 CUT RATE TO CHICAGO/ 1881	TC	100
2117	FOXHALL"/ 1882	TC	85
2150	FROLICKSOME KITS/ 1880	TC	75
2332	GENTEEL STEPPER, A	TC	65
2333	GENTEEL STEPPER, A/ (Used as an ad)	TC	65
2366	GETTING A HOIST/ 1879	TC	75
2382A	GIVING HIM TAFFY/ 1881	TC	70
2406	GOING TO THE FRONT/ 1880	TC	70
2418A	GOLDSMITH MAID/ Record 2:14/ 1881	TC	85
2436	GOOD LUCK TO YE/ (Women holding horseshoe)	TC	70

2453A	*GOT 'EM BOTH/ (Comic billiards) 1882*	*TC*	*75*
2467	*GRACES OF THE BICYCLE, THE/ 1880*	*TC*	*85*
2566	*GREAT BARTHOLDI STATUE, THE / (Daylight scene) (3x5.12) 1884*	*TC*	*100*
2567	*GREAT BARTHOLDI STATUE, THE / (Moonlight scene) (2.15x5.9) 1884*	*TC*	*100*
2568	*GREAT BARTHOLDI STATUE, THE / Liberty Enlightening the World*	*TC*	*100*
2586	*GREAT EAST RIVER BRIDGE, No. 1/ (Postcard) 1883*	*TC*	*90*
2587	*GREAT EAST RIVER BRIDGE, No. 2/ (Postcard) 1883*	*TC*	*90*
2588	*GREAT EAST RIVER BRIDGE, No. 3/ (Postcard) 1883*	*TC*	*90*
2656	*GREAT WALK- "Come In As You Can, The"/ 1879*	*TC*	*75*
2657	*GREAT WALK- "Go As You Please, The"/ 1879*	*TC*	*75*
2739	*HARRY WILKES/ Record 2:13 1/2/ (2.12x4.12) 1886*	*TC*	*85*
2753	*HAT THAT MAKES THE MAN, THE/ 1880*	*TC*	*75*
2755	*HATTIE WOODWARD/ 1881*	*TC*	*85*
2815	*HIGH TONED/ (2.15x4.12) 1880*	*TC*	*75*
2816	*HIGH TONED/ (3.7x4.9) 1880*	*TC*	*75*
2833	*HINDOO, WINNER OF THE KENTUCKY DERBY/ 1881*	*TC*	*85*
2934	*HOPEFUL/ RECORD 2:16 1/2 TO WAGON/ 1881*	*TC*	*85*
2943	*HORSE SHED STAKES/ 1880*	*TC*	*75*
2990	*HUNG UP - WITH THE STARCH OUT/ 1878*	*TC*	*70*
3020	*I WILL NOT ASK TO PRESS THAT CHEEK/ 1880*	*TC*	*70*
3047	*IN AND OUT OF CONDITION/ (Fat man & thin man) 1880*	*TC*	*80*
3132	*IROQUOIS - WINNER OF THE DERBY/ 1881*	*TC*	*85*
3186	*JAY EYE SEE, 2:10/ 1886*	*TC*	*85*
3248	*JOCKEY CLUB/ Cigar advertisement)*	*TC*	*70*
3286	*JOHNSTON, PACER/ 1881*	*TC*	*85*
3292	*JOLLY SMOKER, THE/ (2.15x4.12) 1880*	*TC*	*70*
3294	*JOLLY SMOKER, THE/ (4.7x7.3) 1880*	*TC*	*70*
3369	*LA CIGARITA/ (Women smoking cigar)*	*TC*	*70*
3466	*LAYING BACK" / Stiff for a Brush/ 1878*	*TC*	*75*
3487	*LIBERTY FRIGHTENING THE WORLD*	*TC*	*95*
3759A	*LONGFELLOW/ (Horse) 1881*	*TC*	*85*
3841	*LUKE BLACKBURN/ (Horse) 1881*	*TC*	*85*
3900	*MAJOLICA / Record 2:15/ 1885*	*TC*	*85*

4082	MATTIE HUNTER/ Record 2:15/ 1881	TC	85
4087	MAXY COBB/ 1882	TC	85
4166	MOLLIE McCARTHY/ 1881	TC	85
4171	MONROE CHIEF/ 1881	TC	90
4484	NO MA'AM, I DIDN'T COME TO SHOOT BIRDS/ (2.14x4.12) 1880	TC	70
4486A	NO, NO FIDO	TC	70
4499A	NOBBY TANDEM, A/ 1879	TC	60
4586	OLD SUIT AND THE NEW, THE/ 1880	TC	80
4705	PAROLE/ 1881	TC	85
4708	PARSON'S COLT, THE/ 1880	TC	85
4747	PEOPLE'S EVENING LINE/ 1881	TC	95
4752	PERFECT BLISS/ (4.7x7.3) 1880	TC	80
4760	PET OF THE FANCY, THE/ 1880	TC	75
4766	PHALLAS / Record 2:13.75/ 1882	TC	85
4805	PLEASE GIVE ME A LIGHT, SIR/ 1880	TC	70
5029	QUEEN'S OWN, THE/ 1880	TC	75
5062	RARUS/ Record 2:13.25/ 1881	TC	85
5108	REGULAR HUMMER/ 1880	TC	80
5167	ROAD TEAM AT A "TWENTY GAIT", A/ 1883	TC	80
5384A	SANTA CLAUS/ (Horse) 1882	TC	85
5402A	SAVING IN RAILWAY FARES, A/ (Trains)	TC	105
5506	SIDE WHEELER "BUSTIN" A TROTTER, A/ (Horse comic) 1880	TC	75
5552	SLEEPY TOM, PACER RECORD 2:12.25	TC	85
5570	SMOKING RUN, A/ 1880	TC	75
5573A	SMUGGLER	TC	85
5584	SOCIABLE SMOKE, A/ 1880	TC	75
5624	SORREL DAN/ 1881	TC	85
5646	SPENDTHRIFT/ 1881	TC	95
5652	SPIN ON THE ROAD, A/ 1880	TC	75
5669	SPORTS WHO LOST THEIR TIN/ 1878	TC	70
5678	SPUNK VERSUS SCIENCE	TC	85
5894	SUNOL TO SULKY RECORD 2:08 1/4	TC	85
5954	TAKING A BREATH/ 1880	TC	75

5956	TAKING COMFORT/ 1880	TC	75
5959	TAKING IT EASY	TC	75
6063	TIP-TOP/ 1880	TC	75
6090	TOM BOWLING/ 1881	TC	85
6120	TRAINING A TROTTER/ 1881	TC	80
6151	TRINKET RECORD 2:10 3/4/ 1881	TC	85
6166	TROTTERS ON THE SNOW	TC	105
6182	TROTTING KING "ST. JULIEN", Record 2:11.75/ 1881	TC	85
6199	TROTTING QUEEN "MAUD S." - Record 2:10 3/4/ 1881	TC	85
6249	'TWAS A CALM STILL NIGHT/ 1880	TC	80
6588A	WE MET BY CHANCE OR WAITED FOR THE SWELL	TC	80
6589	WE PARTED ON THE HILLSIDE	TC	75
6603	WEDGEWOOD," RECORD 2:19/ 1881	TC	85
6637A	WHERE DO YOU BUY YOUR CIGARS?/ 1880	TC	75
6638A	WHICH DONKEY WILL I TAKE?	TC	75
6842	YOUNG CADETS, THE	TC	75

BIBLIOGRAPHY

REFERENCE BOOKS ON CURRIER & IVES PRINTS

This selective bibliography may contain book titles which are no longer in print. In most cases, they can be found in the collections of larger public libraries and art museum libraries. Many may even be available from used and rare book dealers across the country.

William Abbatt. *SELECTION OF LITHOGRAPHS OF N. CURRIER AND CURRIER & IVES*, 1825-1866, edition of 200, published 1925.

Jane Cooper Bland. *CURRIER & IVES - A MANUAL FOR COLLECTORS*, Doubleday, Doran & Co., 1931.

Albert K. Baragwanath. *100 CURRIER & IVES FAVORITES*, Crown Pub.

Frederic A. Conningham. *THE AMERICAN ARTS LIBRARY - CURRIER & IVES*, World Pub. Co. 1950.

Frederic A. Conningham. *CURRIER & IVES PRINTS - AN ILLUSTRATED CHECK LIST*, Crown Pub. 1930-1983.

Russell Crouse. *MR. CURRIER & MR. IVES - A NOTE ON THEIR LIVES AND TIMES*, Garden City Pub., 1936.

John & Katherine Ebert. *OLD AMERICAN PRINTS FOR COLLECTORS*, Charles Scribner's Sons, 1974.

King & Davis. *THE WORLD OF CURRIER & IVES*, Random House, 1968.

Ewell L. Newman & Ladd MacMillan. *A GUIDE TO COLLECTING CURRIER & IVES*, Pyramid Communications Inc., 1975.

Harry Shaw Newman. The Old Print Shop: *BEST 50 CURRIER & IVES PRINTS - LARGE FOLIO SIZE*, National Process, 1930.

Harry Shaw Newman. The Old Print Shop: *BEST 50 CURRIER & IVES PRINTS - SMALL FOLIO SIZE*, National Process, 1930.

Harry T. Peters. *AMERICA ON STONE*, Doubleday, Doran & Co., 1931. Reprinted by Arno Press, 1976.

Harry T. Peters. *CALIFORNIA ON STONE*, Doubleday, Doran & Co., 1935. Reprint by Arno Press, 1976.

Harry T. Peters. *CURRIER & IVES*: Vol.#1 & Vol.#2, Doubleday Doran & Co., 1929-31. Reprinted by Arno Press, 1976.

Harry T. Peters. *CURRIER & IVES - PRINTMAKERS TO THE AMERICAN PEOPLE*, Doubleday & Co. 1942.

John Lowell Pratt. *CURRIER & IVES - CHRONICLES OF AMERICA*, Promontory Press, 1968.

Walton Rawls. *THE GREAT BOOK OF CURRIER & IVES' AMERICA*, Abbeville Press, 1979.

Bernard F. Reilly Jr.. *CURRIER & IVES: A CATALOGUE RAISONNE*, Gale Research Company, 1984.

Ron Schieber. *CURRIER & IVES TRADE CARD CHECK LIST*, published privately, 1988.

Jacques Schurre. *CURRIER & IVES PRINTS: a checklist of unrecorded C&I prints with values*, published privately, 1970-76.

Robert L. Searjeant. *CURRIER & IVES IN 20TH CENTURY AMERICA*, published privately, Rochester, N.Y., 1989.

Colin Simkin. *CURRIER & IVES' AMERICA*, Crown Publishers, 1952.

E.& L. Slobody and Philip A. Pines. *CURRIER & IVES - TROTTING: THE NATIONAL PASTIME OF EARLY AMERICA*, Benson Press, 1984.

U.S. Naval Academy Museum. *CURRIER & IVES NAVY: LITHOGRAPHS FROM THE BEVERLY R. ROBINSON COLLECTION*, 1983.

Warren A. Weaver. *LITHOGRAPHS OF N. CURRIER & CURRIER & IVES*, Holport Publishing, 1925.

PRINT DEALERS

The following is a list of print dealers and/or restorers who have elected to advertise in this third edition. If you are a print dealer and have an interest in placing an ad in the next edition, please call or write: Currier Publications, 241 Main Street, Stoneham, MA 02180, tel: (800) 344-0760.

FLORIDA

American Antique Prints
Robert Wieland
33 So.St. Andrews Drive
Ormond Beach, FL 32174
(904) 672-9972

(Please see Display Ad)

MARYLAND

Rudisill's Alt Print Haus
P.O.Box 199
Worton, MD 21678
(410) 778-9290

(Please see Display Ad)

MASSACHUSETTS

Robert P. Kipp
16 Wedgemere Road
Beverly, MA 01915
(508) 922-6852

(*Specializing in Restoration of Works on Paper*)

(Please see Display Ad)

PENNSYLVANIA

Currier & Ives Lithographs
George Cohenour
4301 Beaumont Road
Dover, PA 17315
(717) 292-5345

(Please see Display Ad)

VERMONT

Bob Bascom Prints
P.O.Box 4334
Burlington, VT 05406-4334

(802) 893-4082

(Please see Display Ad)

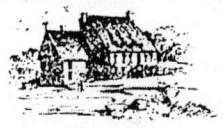

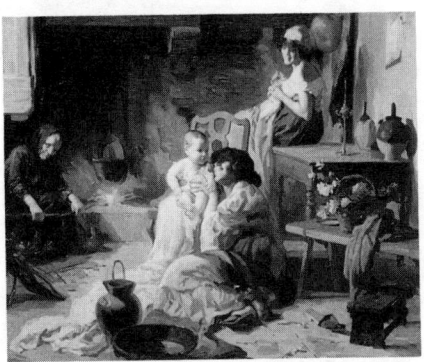

Important Notes

Important Notes

Important Notes

Important Notes

Important Notes

Important Notes

Important Notes

Important Notes

Important Notes

Important Notes

Important Notes

Important Notes

Important Notes